THE PRESIDENT'S MAN

Leo Crowley and Franklin Roosevelt

in Peace and War

Stuart L. Weiss

Southern Illinois University Press

Carbondale and Edwardsville

99   98   97   96   4   3   2

Library of Congress Cataloging-in-Publication Data

Weiss, Stuart L.
The president's man : Leo Crowley and Franklin Roosevelt in peace
and war / Stuart L. Weiss.
p.   cm.
Includes bibliographical references and index.
1. Roosevelt, Franklin D. (Franklin Delano), 1882–1945—Friends
and associates.   2. Crowley, Leo.   3. Politicians—United States—
Biography.   I. Title.
E807.W46   1996
973.917′092—dc20   95-14363
[b]   CIP
ISBN 0-8093-1996-9 (cloth)

Frontispiece: Leo Crowley. Courtesy of the
State Historical Society of Wisconsin

The paper used in this publication meets the minimum requirements
of American National Standard for Information Sciences—Permanence
of Paper for Printed Library Materials, ANSI Z39.48-1984. ∞

For Matthew, whose life enriched us all

Contents

Preface

Most books are planned. This book was not. It was at root accidental. I was not looking for a topic to exploit in an article, much less a book, and I did not search for a subject among the many well-known, obviously influential figures who served in the administrations of Presidents Franklin Roosevelt and Harry Truman. Otherwise, I should have chosen someone other than Leo T. Crowley, whose name always prompted friends and acquaintances to exclaim, "Leo, who!"

The exclamations were understandable. Only historians fascinated with the origins of the Cold War knew Crowley, and then only as the lend-lease administrator charged in Truman's *Memoirs* with abruptly and improperly cutting off aid to the Soviet Union just as the Second World War ended in Europe, embittering Joseph Stalin, impairing Soviet-American relations, perhaps fueling the Cold War. It was a sharp, major indictment, but far from clear-cut. Truman admitted signing the cut-off order without reading it; he also condemned Crowley for "policy-making," though at the same time admitting that Crowley executed the order "literally." Crowley responded with a lengthy (partially published) letter to the *New York Times* reciting the factors that prompted him to act in May 1945, but his public battle with Truman ended with that exchange in the fifties. There remained only his bitterness at the wrong he felt had been done to him.

Over the next ten years few historians mentioned the issue. By the mid-sixties, though, a symbiotic impulse generated by intervention in Vietnam and by the training of so-called radical historians awakened new interest in the origins of the Cold War and the responsibility—often the culpability—of American leaders. That meant a new focus on the first six months of Truman's presidency, the period when Crowley, as foreign economic administrator, twice cut off lend-lease. What had begun as a personal duel now emerged as a sharp, deeply researched debate among historians over the causes and significance of those events.

As an American historian specializing in the twentieth century and teaching in the divisive sixties and seventies, as well as being involved in the public argument over American policy in Vietnam, I was greatly interested in the debate over the origins of the Cold War, but I did not research it for publication. As for Crowley, he was just one name among many policy-makers whose work may have helped crack the Grand Alliance that fought World War II, and I had no reason to think his story worth an article, much less a book. But that was before a visit to Wisconsin some fifteen years ago.

I was finishing research on another topic in the manuscript room of the Wisconsin State Historical Society late on an afternoon in the seventies when an archivist, properly mindful of her researchers' fields, mentioned a new manuscript collection that might interest me. I had no time to review it that day, and we were leaving the next morning, so I asked my wife to scan it in the hour before the manuscript room closed.

Soon she was back, suggesting that I look at some possibly intriguing material. She was speaking of the papers of William T. Evjue, a noted Progressive editor of the Madison, Wisconsin, *Capital Times* before and during the New Deal and World War II. She said, and I soon saw, that the papers contained tax returns and letters suggesting that a Leo T. Crowley had embezzled from his Madison bank in the early thirties. A bell rang. Possibly this was the Crowley who had feuded with Truman over lend-lease in 1945. It was also possible that Crowley still lived in Madison. If so, I hoped to talk to him before leaving the city in the morning.

A few phone calls located the Crowley family, but not Leo. A sister said he had died in 1972, she had burned the papers he had left, and the family did not want to discuss his career. I should forget it.

Except for the sister's sharp, even hostile voice, I might have. But Evjue's collection had included a booklet—*Adviser to Presidents*, a ten-piece series based on interviews Crowley had given Laurence C. Eklund of the *Milwaukee Journal* in 1969. It had to be read with caution: Crowley was eighty years old, his health and memory were failing, and he acknowledged wanting to "set straight the record." Yet what he recalled, if half true, suggested a long, fascinating, and significant career in public service and business that greatly overshadowed his dispute with Truman. And this record compelled further research.

Lighting the shadows posed serious problems. The Franklin D. Roosevelt Library, containing not only the president's papers but also the diaries of Henry Morgenthau and J. F. T. O'Connor, was of the greatest importance. So were the James F. Byrnes Papers at Clemson University, the aforementioned Evjue Papers, and the innumerable documents of the Foreign Economic Administration in the National Archives. There were also important records in Crowley's hometown. Finally, three years after my first brief, unsuccessful contact with the Crowley family, the youngest sister, the only one then surviving, "recovered" some of his "burned" papers and placed them in my care. Much to my regret then and as my work on her brother's life continued, she and her husband could not or would not add anything major about his private or public affairs, and they warned me not to speak with a surviving Crowley brother. Regrettably, I did not. As for other family members who could have added greater dimension to Crowley and even bits from his wide-ranging discussions with his two eldest brothers, significant questions were rejected as violations of Crowley's and the family's privacy. Finally, men and women in Washington, DC, who had known Crowley well as both very close personal friends and associates or subordinates insisted that their idol had cherished his privacy and treated my inquiries regarding his government service accordingly.

Doors were opened slightly by men whose relationships with Crowley were largely professional. In Wisconsin this meant his broker, Harris Allen; in Oklahoma, it meant Morrison G. Tucker, whose discussions of his work under Crowley's leadership at the Federal Deposit Insurance Corporation and in the Alien Property Custodian's Office constantly fascinated and encouraged me; and in the nation's capital it meant Monroe Karasik, who had worked with Crowley in the Alien Property Custodian's Office and, like Tucker, admired him. Oddly, I received equal encouragement and much more significant insights from a group of men who disliked Crowley intensely. This fascinating, later very prominent set included Paul Nitze and George Ball, who worked with Crowley at the Foreign Economic Administration (the wartime agency charged most importantly with managing lend-lease). First the memoirs and letters and later the savage spoken criticism of Crowley by these and other pillars of the foreign policy establishment enriched my view of Crowley in ways documents could not. He had not been "one of them." He had not shared their bold vision of America's enlarged postwar role.

Ironically, doubtless inadvertently, surely significantly, the "junior wise men" described themselves better than Crowley. So, too, this book became, inadvertently, more than a sketch of an early to midcentury businessman, politician, and bureaucrat. It became the darker story of the businessman as speculator and embezzler, whose fraud was covered up in Wisconsin and Washington. It became, more importantly, the brighter story of a businessman as politician, fighting the Klan in Madison and building a successful, significant cross-party coalition in his home state's labyrinthine politics. And it became, more importantly even, the morally complex and compelling story of Crowley as a bureaucrat and politician in Washington, administering multiple major agencies, often simultaneously; handling some of Franklin Roosevelt's most critical personal and national political problems; and even negotiating with foreign powers; but also deeply involved in conflicts of interest a later generation would find unacceptable and even incomprehensible.

There is another story, however, and that more significant than Crowley's personal record. It is the story of the unknown or forgotten views, values, and purposes of Presidents Franklin Roosevelt and Harry Truman, of men who served them, and in some cases would serve their country and shape policy for many years after. It is the story of the embryonic Federal Deposit Insurance Corporation; of the Alien Property Custodian's Office; and of the Office of Economic Warfare. It is the story of the Foreign Economic Administration and the later, most controversial years of lend-lease. It is the story of the battles behind the scenes during the administrations of Roosevelt and Truman. It is, in sum, further of those little-known and little-understood but critical elements in that complex puzzle that was American policy and politics in the era that ranged from the New Deal to the Cold War. It was a story no historian could avoid writing. What began by accident a decade and a half ago became a compelling and enjoyable task.

I have mentioned some of the people who contributed to the writing of this story. However, it might not have been written but for the encouragement and aid in research and/or editing of many others. They include Professor Patrick Riddleberger and Librarian Donald Thompson at Southern Illinois University at Edwardsville; my son, Matthew; my daughter, Veronica; my wife, Rita; friend and critic Dr. Rachel Faries; and the staff of Southern Illinois University Press. I am, of course, ultimately responsible for the judgments made in this book.

The President's Man

1

The Plunger

In August 1969, Leo T. Crowley welcomed a reporter to his office in Chicago's Union Station. Almost eighty, Crowley still chaired the Chicago, Milwaukee, St. Paul, & Pacific Railroad, but discussing the "Milwaukee Road" was the least of reasons for the meeting. He had finally agreed to be interviewed for a *Milwaukee Journal* series embracing his many years in government and and business, but spotlighting his more than twelve years in key positions in the administrations of Presidents Franklin D. Roosevelt and Harry S. Truman. Previously, he had turned down similar requests and rejected at least two archival requests for his papers. He had refused, he wrote one friend, "because there are so many personal things that might damage men who are no longer available to defend themselves." Now (probably because of failing health), he would talk with the *Milwaukee Journal*'s Washington correspondent, Laurence Eklund. He would still be cautious, however. Though the *Journal* had agreed that it "would not print anything . . . detrimental to the character of other people," Crowley told Eklund that he would not give him the letters and documents he had brought from Washington; Eklund would get only what he could recall and chose to tell him.[1]

The interviews reflected it. Crowley's voice was strained, he was tired, and his memory required prodding. Even then, some events were conflated, some stories colored by old feuds, others lacked relevance. Crowley told Eklund he wanted to avoid "personalities"— "after twenty-five years [it] would be a mistake"—but when Eklund repeatedly asked about his feud with Truman over responsibility for the abrupt cut-off of lend-lease to Russia in May 1945, he finally responded. In so doing, he compared Roosevelt, who had depended on him and earned his respect, with Truman, who had betrayed him and

1

bought his contempt. And he spoke at length of other famous figures he had dealt with: Robert and Philip LaFollette in Wisconsin politics, Father Charles Coughlin on the national scene, and Charles de Gaulle in global politics. About them and other matters, he provided Eklund fascinating, if not confirmable, memory bites, but about his family and years in business, he said almost nothing. He expected his family "would give me hell" for the publicity even his limited responses would bring. Eklund could look elsewhere for more depth and breadth.[2]

Eklund did not. His talks with Crowley and his look at the the *Journal*'s files sufficed. When his ten-article series *Adviser to Presidents* appeared, it made fascinating reading; even Crowley's friends expressed amazement at the significance of his career. But their amazement would have been greater had Eklund poked more deeply into Crowley's career in business and politics and illuminated more fully his emergence from obscurity.[3]

Crowley had told Eklund little of his family's origins. He may not have known. As a matter of record, though, his paternal grandparents left Ireland with their first child and his father, Thomas Franklin, at midcentury and settled on a farm some twenty miles west of Madison, Wisconsin. There, while in his twenties, Thomas Franklin was married, favored with two sons, and widowed. After that, detesting farming, he left his sons with his parents and went to southern Wisconsin, where he found work as a section hand on the Chicago, Milwaukee, St. Paul & Pacific Railroad, the same Milwaukee Road his son Leo would chair some sixty years later. There, too, he met and shortly married Katherine Ryan, a schoolteacher from a prosperous Janesville family.[4]

By 1886 Tom Crowley was promoted to section foreman, Katie had borne one son, William; she was bearing another, Harry; and the family moved to Milton Junction, where a Milwaukee Road spur joined the Chicago and Northwestern. There they rented a small but respectable white frame house a few hundred yards from the railroad depot. And there, on August 15, 1889, Katie Crowley bore her third son, Thomas Leo.

There was nothing unusual about the child or his name until Katie decided, some two years later, to transpose his middle and first names and guide him toward the priesthood. Her first sons belonged to her husband and the Milwaukee Road, Leo would belong to her and the Church. Further, his new first name paid tribute to and linked him to

Pope Leo XIII, now famed for his impressive encyclical *Rerum No-varum*, with its strictures on the obligations of the capitalist toward the worker and society.

Designating young Leo as a candidate for the priesthood had a marked influence then and later. For ten years he enjoyed the quiet best of village and rural life but, more importantly, he absorbed the security and warmth of his mother's always lavish attention. She was nurturing with all her children, including her daughters and sons that followed, but with none so much as Leo. She found time to teach him to read, to instill the virtues of loyalty and service, and to protect him from the sometimes severe punishment her husband visited on Will and Harry, but she also taught him to protect himself. Her would-be priest learned to persuade and conciliate, even, though not consciously then, to dissemble and manipulate, also the arts of the salesman and politician. But for all Katie's influence young Leo was not destined for the priesthood. In 1899 his father was injured on the job, and the family, now eleven in number, found its circumstances sharply altered.

Having lost part of a foot, Tom Crowley could not work as a section foreman and was moved to Madison as a flagman. The work was less demanding, but it paid less; even with Will and Harry working, the family's standard of living declined. The Crowleys had to rent an apartment only ten feet from the railroad tracks, and Leo was soon clerking and delivering groceries to add a bit of sustenance. Katie did not complain, because Leo remained in school (and would graduate in time), but she might have had she foreseen the direction in which his clerking would lead.

By 1905 Crowley was delivering year-round for Dan Trainor's grocery, and his warm, winsome manners proved an immediate asset as housewives responded with tips that, unlike his wages, he was allowed to keep. Eventually—at age twenty-one—his savings and competence had grown so that he was ready to strike out for himself. Not surprisingly, he focused his eyes on one of Trainor's suppliers and a business he knew well, buying a twelfth share in the General Paper Company for a thousand dollars.

Recognizing that he must personally nurture his investment, Crowley went to work for the General Paper Company, pitching its wares in and near Madison. And he did well. He had that talent essential to the good salesman, the ability to sell himself, and the company's customers and earnings increased rapidly. By 1913 he was on his way.

And by 1919 his commissions, engorged by the wartime boom, enabled him to become the General Paper Company's sole owner. They also permitted him to move his family into a larger house some distance from the railroad whose often deadly rumble had been so much a part of their lives.

By then, unfortunately, the railroad had taken further toll on the family. Early in the decade Will lost most of a leg, and near its end Harry met the same fate. Tragedy took another, and even starker form, when Crowley's father died of tuberculosis in 1913. And, though a younger brother, Gene, returned safely from his military service in France, Crowley spent much of those years as in the earlier ones helping comfort his often sorrowing and worried mother. He was, by then, the patriarch of a family always close but more so because of the decade's tragedies, and he easily assumed his responsibility to provide for them. Soon after the war's end, he was preparing to risk everything he had created to buy a company larger and more diverse than his own. If successful, he could provide solid jobs for his four brothers and, perhaps, his sisters. He could also forge the base for the kind of wealth he had come to crave.

Crowley's purchase of the T. S. Morris Company, a wholesale building and contracting firm, again bares his talent at seizing an opportunity; likewise, it exhibits his skill at manipulation. Morris was terminally ill, in debt, and had little choice except to sell; even so, Crowley needed $19,000 for a down payment and had no cash. But he was hardly fazed. In March 1919 he secured a $6,000 loan on property he owned, but that left him far short of his goal. Fortunately, or perhaps predictably, given his personal charm, Crowley had forged a close bond with Milo Hagan, also of Irish descent and the first of a small group which would then and later boost his business and political fortunes. Hagan was prepared to help as a silent partner. So was W. D. Curtis, who believed Crowley's management would enable him to recover a loan to the T. S. Morris Company. On April 1 he loaned Crowley $15,000, though it was officially a lien against the Morris Company. And a day later the deed was transferred, Crowley signing it as president of the T. S. Morris Company. Soon, however, the T. S. Morris sign came down, and Crowley's new acquisition was swallowed in the now-renamed General Paper and Supply Company.[5]

During the early twenties, Crowley thrust himself into making his paper and supply company successful, to increase his own income, to give his brothers executive jobs, and to provide his mother and sisters with more comfort. Basically, he was still the super salesman, growing his customer base and persuading old friends to join his new ventures; but as his complex purchase of the T. S. Morris Company suggests, he could handle sophisticated methods of financing with considerable ease.

Crowley had borrowed heavily to enlarge his company, but he deplored its necessity; stronger capitalization equaled greater strength in his view. That meant incorporation in August 1919; the sale of $200,000 in stock, half of it common, half preferred the following spring; and the latter underwritten by a method he would use throughout his life, the guarantee of a life insurance policy. The proceeds easily eliminated the company's debt; they also made it possible to purchase a wholesale grocery in Beloit, which Harry was handed to run with Gene's assistance. But even that did not satisfy Crowley. In 1923 his board authorized him to double the corporation's preferred stock and to use the proceeds "for the investment which we have in mind." The secretive language was designed, apparently, to mask Crowley's purchase of stock in Madison's Bank of Wisconsin, his and his brothers' purchases of downtown real estate, and their purchases on the stock exchange. They were plunging now into areas beyond their experience and limited control, risking much to make much in a manner fashionable by the mid-twenties.[6]

Crowley was a gambler. He enjoyed the challenge as much as the money, betting on poker and bridge at home and horses at the track in Chicago, but he was obsessed with real estate. During the latter half of the twenties, he and his brothers, as well as Hagan and two other Irish friends, bought buildings and raw land in Madison, creating a pyramid of paper wealth, but also of debt and its service. Dane County's ledgers bulge with their trans actions from 1924 through the decade.[7]

How much Crowley, his brothers, and his friends cleared the sparse records do not reveal. Though he was paper rich by 1929, and took a $25,000 salary from his General Supply Company alone, the family's magnificent new "Tudor" home was heavily mortgaged: Crowley then felt that cash in the bank was practically sterile, credit the key to great wealth. Thus, late in 1929, he with his two elder brothers and a friend launched the Four Lakes Investment Company, placing $58,000 of borrowed money at his disposal, with the intention of doubling that sum within two years. There was no end to their plans;

there seemed little reason. Not only did population growth and prosperity appear endless, but Crowley had developed substantial political connections.[8]

Crowley's first known political venture occurred in 1926 as public debt and the Klu Klux Klan unsettled Madison. He worried that inadequate city management was impairing business generally and the real estate market in particular; he grew angry over the mayor's failure to deal with the Klan's attacks on fellow Catholics in "Little Italy"; and he felt great pressure to deal with both problems, but the Klan in particular. At thirty-six he was president of St. Mary's Hospital and Madison's leading Catholic layman; he was expected to lead.[9]

Crowley did so. He and his Irish friends found a candidate for mayor in Albert G. Schmedeman, a popular sixty-two-year-old main street merchant and retired politician and diplomat. Easygoing, Schmedeman was not a very successful businessman, but he had the advantage of being an Episcopalian in a Protestant town. And he had other solid qualifications. Once he had represented the "Irish" fourth ward on the Madison Common Council; in 1912 he had headed Woodrow Wilson's campaign for the presidency; and, more important, the city's largest ethnic group, Scandinavians, remembered that President Wilson had appointed him ambassador to Norway, while the city's large German element remembered that he had first requested Berlin. It helped, too, that Schmedeman was in tune with the rhetoric coming from President Coolidge's White House. "Madison is a large business concern," Schmedeman bubbled everywhere in town, signaling merchants, realtors, and bankers that he knew their well-being rested on fiscal soundness as well as law and order, and he would provide both.[10]

With Crowley working behind the scenes, Schmedeman defeated his opponent in the spring mayoralty race, then quickly mastered Madison's problems. The police dealt with the Klan's terrorism; City Hall was managed more efficiently, producing a better city bond rating; and real estate and small business improved. Soon, Schmedeman's popularity and reputation spread well beyond Madison, but insiders credited the city's achievements to Crowley's shrewd guidance, a point reinforced a few years later when Crowley openly aided Governor Schmedeman, and strengthened again in later years when Crowley spoke of "Schmedy" as a "close personal friend who trusted me."[11]

Theirs was a strange friendship. Crowley dominated a man twenty-five years his senior and steeped in experiences he could not begin to match. He managed Schmedeman as a parent might his children, and as he managed his family and most of the nurses at St. Mary's Hospital. And Schmedeman did not demur. Crowley had indulged his ambition and his pride in making him mayor of Madison. And Crowley was soon telling him that the State House was not beyond his grasp.

Crowley's plans for Schmedeman developed within the context of the 1928 presidential campaign. Like millions of "ethnics," he was captivated by the possibility that Al Smith, the Catholic governor of New York, might become the first member of his faith to govern the country. Beyond that he sensed an opportunity for Schmedeman to become the first Democratic governor in thirty-six years. Thus, in April, Crowley won election—the only time he would directly face the voters—as a Smith delegate to the Democratic National Convention. And in June, in Houston, he helped nominate the New Yorker.[12]

Winning in Texas in the summer was one thing; winning Wisconsin in the fall was another matter. Wilson had in 1912, but no Democratic presidential nominee had done so before or since. And the state had not elected a Democratic governor since 1892. The Panic of 1893, persistent religious and ethnic tensions, and World War I accounted for the Democrats' problems. After 1918, with most German ethnics having left the party, it struggled to survive. Its presidential candidates won only 14 percent of the vote in 1920 and 8 percent in 1924, and the party did not hold a single seat in the Wisconsin Senate after 1922. By 1928, it was a shell: a few Irish Catholic chiefs and their fiefdoms ranging Lake Michigan's urban areas, and a handful of "wet" Protestants scattered around the state. But the situation was critical, not hopeless. Among German Catholics resentment of Wilson's foreign policies was receding, while their distaste for prohibition was growing; and long-lost liberal Democrats, who for almost thirty years had supported the strong, reformist leadership of Senator Robert M. LaFollette and his Progressive Republicans in Republican primaries and general elections, were disgusted by the feuds that had recently erupted in Progressive Republican ranks.[13]

Upon "Fighting Bob's" death in 1925, Robert LaFollette, Jr. had inherited his seat and legislative acumen, but not his skill at party leadership. Feuding cost Progressive Republican gubernatorial candidates in the 1926 and 1928 primaries. They blamed the Stalwart (conservative) Republicans for exorbitant spending, however. Thus, the loss to Sheboygan Stalwart Republican Walter Kohler in the 1928 Republican primary suggested to many Progressive Republicans, as it did to Crowley, the potential for a Progressive-Democratic alliance. A Democratic triumph would punish the Stalwarts for their excesses.[14]

Senator LaFollette, almost certain of reelection to a term in his own right if he remained neutral, kept his peace. Others did not. In September 1928, William T. Evjue's Progressive Madison *Capital Times*, read statewide, condemned Kohler's Stalwart campaign for the "greatest debauchery and most flagrant expenditure of money" in Wisconsin history; then the publisher blessed Schmedeman, the Democratic primary winner, and Al Smith to boot. Evjue was anxious to punish the stalwarts and serve notice for the future. But he could only editorialize; others would have to act.[15]

The key Progressive Republican players were U.S. Senator John J. Blaine and Assistant Attorney General Frank Kuehl, once his secretary. Blaine was politically flexible. Also, he saw that the growth of Stalwart strength, coupled with the drain of "ethnics" and "wets" to Smith, could destroy the Progressives at all levels. The party's survival, then, required a liaison with the Democrats. Thus Blaine told Kuehl to broach an alliance and discuss tactics with Crowley.[16]

Blaine's choices were important then and later. Kuehl and Crowley knew one another: living in the same city and moving in intertwined political circles, it could not have been otherwise. But as Kuehl reminisced many years later, he and Crowley quickly became close friends and, significantly for both, enduring ones. Kuehl, who was more sophisticated and more restrained, had heard that Crowley, despite sometimes quaint diction, could "mesmerize a roomful"; now Crowley mesmerized him. Thinking of their many lunches that fall, Kuehl reflected, "Crowley always made me feel that I was on his side of the table." And always after, Crowley would greet him with, "Hello, my partner in crime."[17]

Crowley's easy charm penetrated Kuehl's reserve, and numerous lunches provided the two with several opportunities to learn more of each other's leaders and their politics. What Kuehl did not know about the Democrats, he soon gleaned from Crowley. His new friend warned him that many leading Democrats but most notably Milwaukee's John Callahan, most recently the party's chairman, strongly opposed campaign coalitions with the Progressives. They were afraid of losing their identity as a party. They preferred an independence that sometimes enabled them to play off Progressive and Stalwart Republicans and to bargain for small advantages. They cared little that their political strategy left them without hope for real power.[18]

But as Crowley's position suggests, there was another, more pragmatic faction in the Democratic party. The loudest voice in this group belonged to Charles E. Broughton. A Protestant and a "wet," Broughton, as the editor and part owner of the *Sheboygan Press*, insisted before the September primary that the Republican party could "decide who they want and we'll go in . . . and lick the whole bunch of them." After it, he sobered up. His paper would get the state's printing if Schmedeman won; and he would become a national committeeman if Smith won. He decided to sign off on an alliance with the Progressives.[19]

Crowley was also adapting. His religious and ethnic values were not noticeably different from those of other Irish-Catholic leaders, but his politics were. Perhaps it was Madison. It was ethnically diverse, like Milwaukee, but it was small enough that the successful businessman or politician could not withdraw into his religious or ethnic group. That Crowley clearly understood, as his choice of the Episcopalian Schmedeman for mayor two years before shows. He believed in winning and knew it required flexibility. It required a pragmatism of which a *Milwaukee Journal* staffer wrote, "In both politics and business, Crowley . . . does not hold fixedly to any specific formulas or methods."[20]

The description was apt. Crowley was conservative, but he wanted to win, for Smith, for Schmedeman, for himself: for the power it could bring, for the battle's excitement. Schmedeman's early speeches identified his campaign with the legendary elder LaFollette's quarter-century battle against "special interests." He needed the state wide organization Democrats lacked but Progressive Republicans could provide. The Progressives, in turn, wanted campaign funds and Democratic candidates to withdraw in districts where they would siphon votes. Crowley could get the money, perhaps he could arrange the withdrawals.

Crowley had recently developed a pipeline to the Democratic National Committee. A new connection with Wisconsin Bankshares, a burgeoning bank holding company, had led to contacts with the Schlitz brewery and its controling Uihlein family. The Uihleins hoped to elect in Al Smith a president who would seek the repeal or modification of prohibition, and they put Crowley through to Jouett Shouse and John Raskob, who ran Smith's campaign and the Democratic National Committee. It followed that on September 24 Shouse sent "Crowly" a letter and a check for $2,500.[21]

Four days later, Crowley received another check and letter. Shouse now thought he might have misspelled Crowley's name. He hoped his check had been received, was "delighted to know of the steps that are being taken," and noted "that other payments will be forwarded as *you* may direct." He hoped, however, that Crowley would "try to hold" expenditures to $20,000 if possible.[22]

Obviously Crowley had received Shouse's first letter: before the second one Kuehl had registered the "Progressive Republican Al Smith for President Club" with Wisconsin's secretary of state. Reporting it, the *Milwaukee Journal* quoted Kuehl's justification for "progressives and liberals" supporting Smith, but the Democratic newspaper noted that he named no other members of the new organization. In fact, it had none for a fortnight, not until Blaine endorsed Smith, and other prominent Progressives associated themselves with the "Club." Then came a parade of news stories celebrating the "Club's" purpose. Kuehl and Crowley had planned well and continued to coordinate their efforts, securing new, positive headlines almost daily.[23]

Between October 3 and November 26, Crowley turned over more than $25,000 in drafts from the DNC, almost the total amount the Smith "Club" reported getting. More significant, it was two and a half times the dollars Shouse sent the state Democratic Party. The totals marked his faith in Crowley's judgement. But Crowley had not been content with coordinating Kuehl's campaign. Moving between Progressive and Democratic camps, he worked hard to get LaFollette's support for Smith; and, on October 1, the *Milwaukee Journal* headlined that the Democratic senatorial candidate might "Quit for 'Bob,'" hoping that LaFollette would then endorse both Smith and Schmedeman. Six years later Crowley credited himself with the Democrat's withdrawal, explaining it as a gesture to an ailing LaFollette. Some decades later, however, he said that he had thought it might help elect a president and a governor.[24]

Though LaFollette did not endorse Smith or Schmedeman, and both lost in November, Kuehl's and Crowley's work brought a substantial improvement in both Democrats' percentages over those of earlier elections. Unfortunately, historians looking for the sources of Franklin Roosevelt's later triumphs have too greatly stressed Smith's call for repeal and his awakening of the urban ethnic; they have understated if not neglected such equal if not more critical models for Roosevelt's victories *and* the New Deal as the cooperation between Democratic regulars and Progressives that Kuehl and Crowley forged in 1928. Perhaps Crowley thought about the alliance's potential; perhaps, too, he thought about his meeting with Franklin Roosevelt in New York City during the campaign and his postmortem on Wisconsin to Governor-Elect Roosevelt soon after, but he could not have given much time to those matters. He had just been elected president of the Bank of Wisconsin.[25]

Crowley's assets were obvious. He had built several solid, prosperous businesses; and he was trading in real estate and the stock market with seemingly similar results. He had the symbols too: a magnificent home, a luxurious car, impeccable dress, and heavy contributions of time and money to St. Mary's hospital and various other Catholic and civil institutions. Altogether, such were the credentials that prompted Madison's Bank of Wisconsin to persuade Crowley to accept its presidency. Overextended in 1928, it desperately needed a miracle.

Crowley performed as hoped. Employing his favorite strategy, and one he would rely on later as a federal administrator, Crowley enlarged the bank's capital base. He sold $600,000 in new stock, buying a quarter of it for himself and his brothers, selling part of the remainder and an option to buy a controlling interest to Wisconsin Bankshares, a Milwaukee-based bank holding company. As Crowley expected, Bankshares investment and implied purchase, coupled with his reputation and his family's purchase, persuaded Madison businessmen that an investment in his bank was safe and would pay sizable dividends. And the Bank of Wisconsin did at first. Consequently, early in 1929 Bankshares exercised its option, which meant that almost overnight Crowley had scored another in his long list of triumphs during the golden twenties, this time as a banker.[26]

Though he continued in that role, Crowley assumed other responsibilities. Bankshares appointed him its personnel officer, placed him on its coordinating committee, and entrusted him with persuading more banks to join the holding company. And this he did. Before the year ended he talked the president of Madison's First National Bank

into selling out. Then he used the holding company's money to buy
the State Bank of Madison, merged it into his own bank, shifted the
combined operations to the new, larger facility, and renamed the whole
the State Bank of Wisconsin. In effect, Wisconsin Bankshares dominated the central square downtown, and Crowley was the most prominent banker in Madison.[27]

Crowley's career was soaring. Still the power behind Mayor
Schmedeman, he was also president of Madison's Board of Health, a
partner in the booming Goodall-Crowley Oil Company in Beloit, and a
member of the Wisconsin Bankshares executive committee. Also, he
grossed more than $64,000 in 1929. To be sure, taxes, interest charges,
and write-offs for bad debts took a deep bite; so did charitable contributions of almost $7,000; but that still left $37,000 in disposable income.
He had "made it." Everyone knew it. Just that spring Pope Pius X had
granted him the Order of St. Gregory the Great, honoring his presidency of St. Mary's Hospital as well as his generosity to Catholic
schools, and his investiture had been well covered. As the twenties
passed, all Madison was learning that Sir Leo Crowley was a star
whose light reached far beyond the city's confines, even as far as
Rome.[28]

Few Madisonians would ever think otherwise. But Crowley's fortunes soon began to disintegrate. In 1930 his many salaries—from his
paper company, his bank, and the Goodall-Crowley Oil Company—
rose, but his dividends shrank by two-thirds, and land sales and rents,
nearly half his previous year's income, disappeared altogether. Already the Great Depression was taking its toll. That year Crowley's net
income barely reached a thousand dollars. And his problems had just
begun.[29]

By 1931 Crowley, the once successful plunger, was thrashing
about, taking desperate and dangerous measures to remain afloat. Curiously at first glance, his gross income rose even as his income from
the family oil business and grocery company in Beloit disappeared. He
managed this miracle with a sizable increase in his salary from the
General Paper Company, though this was done only with the commission of several near and real improprieties. Crowley raised his salary
without a vote of his company's board. More significantly, the company borrowed the money for his raise and other purposes from the
First National Bank and some smaller banks, including his own. But
of greatest importance, he alone initialed individual loans of many

thousands, contrary to a Wisconsin law which stipulated that other bank officers must sign loans exceeding $1,000.[30]

It was not the first time Crowley exploited his presidency of the State Bank of Wisconsin and, previously, his Bank of Wisconsin. In 1931 and the two previous years, he had unilaterally signed loans of $210,000 for the Four Lakes Investment Company, with the funds being placed at his disposal. And that November he had deeded his surburban Edgewood home to his sister, who had quickly mortgaged it for $60,000 and placed the proceeds in his name. All told, he had borrowed well over a million dollars and was paying almost $27,000 annually in debt service.[31]

By the end of 1931 Crowley was floundering desperately, but few if any knew it. He not only covered his brothers' losses in the stock market and made his usual charitable donations, but he bought a luxurious automobile. He needed a continuing stream of credit; he needed other help; and appearances were crucial.[32]

Crowley fooled his good friend and ally Frank Kuehl, among others. That October Kuehl advised Crowley that Governor Philip LaFollette wanted him to serve as a special deputy banking commissioner, assisting the overloaded banking commission. Later, if and when the legislature established a banking review board, LaFollette wanted Crowley to represent Wisconsin Bankshares on the board. Kuehl argued that Crowley must accept in both cases. If the governor thought the banking crisis was so severe that he would abandon his campaign against chain banking, Crowley had no choice.[33]

Crowley agreed to both requests. He might not have refused in any case, but his dubious if not illegal banking methods made it imperative that he obtain as much cover as possible. Thus he served as a special deputy banking commissioner through the late fall. But his position assisting the banking commission was unofficial and his work not widely known or appreciated. This did not change until January 22, 1932, after statutory establishment of a Banking Review Board. Then Governor LaFollette was able to publicize his appointment as one of its five members, and he was in a position to gain much-needed recognition for his efforts.[34]

For Crowley the announcement could not have been more timely had he planned it. As Crowley's broker recalled, fifty auditors from Wisconsin Bankshares swarmed into the State Bank late that afternoon, a Friday, and they returned Saturday and Sunday to complete their audit. Thus Bankshares confirmed that Crowley had borrowed more than a million dollars and quickly kicked him out. After that Crowley was "sick" for several months.[35]

Such was Harris Allen's story almost fifty years after the event. But it was not the story that appeared in Madison's two major newspapers the week following. The *Capital Times* and the *Wisconsin State Journal* reported daily on discussions to merge the State Bank with the nearby First National Bank. Crowley was not mentioned as participating, but twice, the last time on January 29, it was reported that the directors had asked him to remain as president, but only until May 1.[36]

Crowley replied the next day in a letter addressed to State Bank's board of directors. But it appeared on the front page of the *Capital Times*, and it was obviously designed to reassure the public, as the earlier daily newspaper reports had been designed to do. Crowley wanted the bank's stockholders and depositors to know that the merger "has been no precipitate matter," and their deposits were safe. He wanted, also, to state his regrets that, "because of illness . . . I have been unable to act with you in arranging the details necessary to effect the merger." As for his leaving the bank immediately, there were more regrets, about ill health, about private business interests, and about his appointment to Wisconsin's Banking Review Board. And just to make certain that Madison understood that his departure was not dictated by problems at the bank, he ended on this emphatic note: "I am leaving the city temporarily upon the advice of my physician."[37]

Crowley was probably sick. His broker recalled it, unfortunately without stating that he had direct knowledge, but one of Crowley's creditors thought he did. Fifteen years later, Daniel H. Grady, a Portage lawyer, sued Crowley for nonfulfillment of a an agreement dating to 1931. In court he swore that after Crowley "was relieved from his duties . . . , I went up to his house [to dun him] and he was ill." Grady added that they had not talked business then because he did not feel like "irritating anyone in any way." It was not until two months later that he saw Crowley in a Madison hotel and asked for the $53,000 owed him. Then, he said, Crowley "told me of his financial condition" and asked for time: he owed Walter Kasten, who controlled Bankshares, a "large sum of money." Thus Grady affirmed that Bankshares had "terminated" Crowley in 1932, that Crowley had been "ill" or seemed to be then or "shortly after" his termination, and that Crowley had "financial difficulties" for some years after.[38]

Grady's account appears to have been confirmed when Crowley settled out of court in 1948; however, whether Crowley was physically seriously ill at the time of his termination is not verifiable. Without doubt, he was at the least severely depressed. His bank would have gone under had not the First National Bank, also a division of Bankshares, taken it over; and a state audit would have revealed his large overdrafts, illegally authorized loans, and flimsy collateral. He and his family would have been embarrassed; worse, he might well have been indicted for fraud.[39]

That Crowley did not suffer such dire consequences is probably attributable to the desire of the State Bank's directors to save their reputations and to the interest of Bankshares in saving its other banks at a time when failing public confidence was felling banks everywhere. Bankshares preferred quietly shearing Crowley of his presidency, stock, and $12,000 salary, then working out a long-term settlement of his and his brothers' indebtedness.

Other than a few bank directors with an obvious interest in silence, few people seriously thought or, more important, argued publicly that Crowley had abused his office and been terminated. Those who knew, such as Harris Allen, found it in their interest to keep silent. So did those, such as William Evjue, who merely suspected; too many important people would be hurt. And without an investigation, Crowley was virtually immune from speculation about his probity. His straitened finances were well cloaked: he was "one of Madison's successful and wealthy men," the *State Journal* noted. Also, he was Sir Leo, who had battled the Klan, fought for an addition to St. Mary's Hospital, given to Catholic charities, and been honored by the pope. Moreover, he had just been named not only to the state Banking Review Board but to the presidency of the Community Union, organizing relief in Madison. Crowley's legend lived on. He was still that rarity, a success and a saint.[40]

Crowley's friends thought no less. Some knew, some guessed that his bank would have failed had not First National and Bankshares absorbed it. In either case, if they knew about his personal "borrowing," most excused his methods as "shortcuts" other bankers had employed. In any event, his personal loans did not explain the State Bank's problems. Neither did the lightly collateralized loans Crowley had made from compassion for the small farmer and small businessman. When even "sound" property values and collateral had turned soft or worse, and banks were failing by the thousands, it was more reasonable to blame the state and nationwide economic collapse than Crowley for his bank's failure. In fact, when friends heard that he was ill, they sympathized with him as another of the depression's victims. Understandably, he needed the sun and warmth of Florida as his doctor advised, and they heartily approved when he took an apartment in Miami for a few weeks that winter.[41]

It is doubtful that Crowley rested quietly in Florida. He owed great sums, he had little or no income; and he had only one serious prospect: Governor LaFollette had named him chairman of the Banking Review Board in February. But what he might make of that role was difficult to imagine. Probably he did not know.

2

The Richelieu of Wisconsin

When Crowley returned to Madison in the spring of 1932 his future looked as gloomy as the economy whose ascent and collapse it had so closely paralleled. But only briefly. By the summer, he was an important force in Wisconsin, chairing its Banking Review Board and and salvaging its banks; a year after he was nominally the governor's aide but effectively running the state; in another two years he was managing a major federal agency and advising the president of the United States; and these were only the earlier signs of what would be a new and remarkable career in both government and business. Crowley was lucky: his good friend Albert Schmedeman was elected governor in a nationwide Democratic sweep in November 1932. But he also seized a meager opportunity months before when he might have remained in Florida paralyzed with despair.

Crowley had strong reasons to take the chairmanship of Wisconsin's Banking Review Board: the post offered some protection for Bankshares; it maintained his mask of community service, and it might open a future beyond the confines of his General Paper Company. The job would require visiting almost every hamlet in the state, talking nightly to depositors, bankers, and community leaders. But he could help save the economy of rural and small town Wisconsin, at the same making contacts that, coupled with a deeply depressed economy and a divided Republican party, might elect Schmedeman governor that November.

The problem facing the Banking Review Board was fairly simple. Banks depended on loan payments or foreclosures and sales to meet the demands of depositors. With the price of farm products and of farms having fallen sharply since the previous July farmers could not meet their loan payments, foreclosures did not provide liquidity, and

17

hundreds of farm-oriented banks could not pay off depositors and
went under. Rural Wisconsin—depositors, bankers, and bank stockholders, as well as farmers—was suffering when Crowley took over at
the Banking Review Board.

Technically, the board's power was only that of adviser to Wisconsin's Banking Commission, but Crowley's energy and answers to the
bank crisis, coupled with Kuehl's close relationship with Governor
LaFollette, ruled otherwise. Crowley's plan called for "stabilization
agreements" that could reopen many banks and, at least partially, save
all involved. It required segregating old and new deposits (those made
before a bank's collapse from those made after it reopened); liquidating the bank's collateral whatever the price received; giving "old" depositors prorated shares of the proceeds; and, most importantly as a
prerequisite, persuading "old" depositors to settle for less than they
originally deposited.[1]

Crowley proved equal to the task. Always the salesman, he spent
countless days driving across Wisconsin, speaking in small towns and
large, selling depositors on so-called stabilization agreements. Kuehl
usually went, too, as attorney-general carrying the state's imprimatur.
Many years later, remembering those evening meetings, Kuehl
laughed that the state's approval seemed less important than the impression Crowley made. Handsome, powerfully built, and wearing an
impeccably tailored blue suit, the prematurely white-maned Crowley
looked as much a banker as if he had been so made-up for a Holly-
wood movie. Indeed, he looked so "expensive" that Kuehl feared at
first that he might not connect with the dowdy and often ragged audi-
ences they met. Kuehl soon found, though, that Crowley had an easy
manner that made men and women even in rural and small-town Wisconsin believe he was "on their side of the table." But the majority of
depositors who voted for Crowley's stabilization agreements speak
more solidly to the effectiveness of his presentations. By January 1933
more than eighty banks were stabilized (or reorganized with new capital). And by midyear 1933 sixty more were stabilized. Much had been
done, and few would forget.[2]

Crowley's successful stabilization policy could only have enhanced his reputation for public service, but more significant for his
personal fortunes Mayor Schmedeman was elected governor and
asked him to serve at his right hand. Later, Crowley would in November 1932 recall Schmedeman's pleading with him the night of his

victory, "You got me elected, now you've got to help me." Unfortunately, neither Crowley nor Schmedeman ever recorded what form Crowley's help during the campaign had taken.[3]

The only paper trail was left by William T. Evjue of Madison's *Capital Times* in editorials early in 1933 and in a letter a decade later, and he was not Crowley's friend. He thought of Crowley as too conservative, an opportunist and, if the stories about his bank's collapse were true, worse. Accordingly, Evjue wrote in a 1933 column that Crowley "laid low during the whole campaign," emerging from his "cyclone cellar" only on "election night after early returns had indicated that Schmedeman would be elected." Then he rushed to the governor-elect's home, there to "take charge . . . as 'Al's best friend.' " And after the governor-elect named Crowley his personal secretary and main adviser, his "star began to rise again."[4]

Evjue's emphasis on Crowley's "nimbleness in taking advantage of an opening," though not untrue, distorts his part in the 1932 campaign. Crowley had helped Schmedeman get the Democratic nomination for governor that year; and, sensing a winner, he had backed New York's governor, Franklin Roosevelt, for president at an early date. Collaborating with Charles Broughton, the editor of the *Sheboygan Press*, he had helped overwhelm the Smith forces and secured Wisconsin's delegation for Roosevelt at July's Democratic National Convention.

During the summer and fall, Wisconsin Democrats had united behind their presidential nominee. But by mid-October, Schmedeman had come to Evjue's office at the *Capital Times* to spell out what the editor labeled a "tale of woe." He had complained that the Democratic National Committee was pouring huge sums of money into the national campaign, and that he was getting "practically none." Worse, Wisconsin's Democratic party leaders had secretly arranged with Stalwart Republicans to give him up for Walter Kohler, who was again their gubernatorial candidate. In return Stalwarts would abandon the Republican candidate for the Senate in favor of Democrat F. Ryan Duffy. As for Crowley, Schmedeman told Evjue, he could do nothing for him "openly" because of the "tremendous amount of money" Crowley owed Wisconsin Bankshares, in which Kohler was very influential. Neither could Broughton's *Sheboygan Press* help him, because Kohler's plumbing company was so powerful in the city. Thus he desperately needed the *Capital Times* endorsement. He was a "Progressive

Democrat," Schmedeman had insisted; he and Phil LaFollette were "fighting to achieve the same ends," and he would continue the fight with Evjue's help.[5]

As October ended, Evjue had endorsed Schmedeman, editorializing that the mayor's progressive speeches contrasted favorably with the conservative Democratic platform. Later, after Schmedeman's first three months as governor, the editor would write in his column that Schmedeman was as conservative as the Democratic platform. What had happened he partially explained then and in some degree implied years later, but with a slant that protected him against misjudgment during the campaign. Evjue argued that the Machiavellian Crowley "disappeared" during the campaign and reappeared the evening of Schmedeman's victory. But this story does not comport with his portrayal of Schmedeman or with Crowley's obvious political talents. Evjue described the mayor as a "timid" man who could not act without Crowley's direction behind the scenes; he could not admit the logical conclusion that Crowley orchestrated Schmedeman's visit to his office. Accordingly, he was not taken in during the campaign when Schmedeman insisted that he was a "Progressive Democrat"; it was Crowley's great influence over Schmedeman later, as governor, that explained how a "progressive" campaign was sadly transformed into a conservative administration.[6]

It seems likely that Evjue was blinded during the fall campaign by a burning desire to defeat the Stalwart Kohler, who had defeated Governor LaFollette in the Republican primary that September. He knew better than to believe Schmedeman or his mentor were converts to progressivism; certainly, Schmedeman's campaign displayed few signs of it. He and Crowley knew that Republican voters had denied Governor LaFollette renomination because of a work-relief act that increased taxes. Consequently, Schmedeman, like Franklin Roosevelt nationally, had promised to cut the budget and taxes; and Democratic legislative candidates, many handpicked by Crowley, had expediently promised the same. After the November election, then, budget-minded Republicans and Democrats controlled Wisconsin's legislature. Schmedeman and Crowley had to look elsewhere for answers to Wisconsin's critical relief and other fiscal problems.[7]

Even before Roosevelt and the New Deal arrived, Crowley saw answers to Wisconsin's fiscal problems in the nation's capital. During the first half of 1932, Congress had established the Reconstruction Finance Corporation, first to prop up major banks, industries, and railroads, later to lend money to the states for relief; and in December, shortly after Governor Schmedeman named him his chief aide, Crowley traveled to Washington to place Wisconsin's relief needs before the RFC's board. It was the first of several such trips, most of them highly successful, but this was not one of them. Crowley could not prove to the satisfaction of the RFC's board that Wisconsin had totally exhausted its own resources, a prerequisite for receiving relief funds.

Crowley returned to Wisconsin for Schmedeman's inauguration January 3 and was then named chairman of his executive council. Schmedeman needed him desperately. Democrats were thirsting for patronage after years of drought; the unemployed were crying for real or state-made jobs; and farmers were demanding mortgage relief and higher prices. Schmedeman was was not tough enough to deal with these demands. Crowley was. And Schmedeman was smart enough to know it: Crowley could provide the energy, judgment, and balance of warmth and steel that his administration needed.[8]

Much like Roosevelt a few months later, Schmedeman's budget message called for "drastic cuts" in spending. Unlike Roosevelt he had no choice. Wisconsin's constitution required a balanced budget, tax revenues were falling, and increasing tax rates was politically unfeasible. Thus the only solution for Wisconsin's problems (as for most states desiring to maintain services) was the federal government.

On January 28 Broughton wrote Democratic National Committee Chairman James Farley that he was "asked by Governor Schmedeman to arrange a conference with you for his personal representative Hon. Leo Crowley." Farley's reply was noncommittal, but wheels were turning. Roosevelt wrote Schmedeman, asking him to name a Progressive Republican, David Lilienthal, to Wisconsin's Public Service Commission. Schmedeman agreed, then wrote Farley that Broughton and Crowley would be arriving in Washington February 8. Could Farley recommend someone "familiar with the President [Elect's] policies" on unemployment relief to confer with them.[9]

When Farley recommended that the governor's emissaries talk to Jesse Jones, a Democratic member of the RFC's board, Crowley, at least, left for Washington. There he spoke with the millionaire from Houston and, though neither could know it, initiated a long, apparently close relationship. The two men shared values and temperaments. Crowley agreed with Jones's dictum that "the three most nec-

essary things to a satisfactory life were family, religion, and money."
That they came from different regions and that Jones was a Baptist,
Crowley a Catholic, mattered little. Both were self-made businessmen
and at root conservative, but they were also pragmatists open to novel
ideas and quick action as circumstances warranted. Otherwise, probably neither would have been in politics. Unfortunately for Crowley's
mission in Washington, Jones was a minority member of the RFC, and
he had to return home empty-handed.[10]

Crowley had hardly returned to Wisconsin when he found himself
returning to Washington with Schmedeman and Broughton. He hoped
to enjoy Roosevelt's inauguration, but on Thursday, March 2, he began
receiving phone messages from bankers in Racine and Milwaukee. As
he recalled years later, they "didn't think they could go through Saturday because of heavy withdrawals." They wanted the governor to
close the state's banks that night. So did the banking commissioner
and Banking Review Board. Crowley told them to make plans, but that
he did not want to advise the governor yet. First, he would try to get
the president-elect's views on the problem: Wisconsin's hopes for federal assistance depended on Roosevelt's goodwill.[11]

Shortly after midnight, Crowley, Schmedeman, and Broughton
met with Roosevelt in his Mayflower Hotel suite. Crowley spoke for
the group, outlining the crisis. Broughton thought he was "masterly,"
and that "the president-elect followed every utterance with keen interest," so much so that he later asked Crowley to "keep in contact with
him." Crowley more soberly remembered Roosevelt's telling them he
would close all the country's banks the next Monday, but they could
proceed with their plans in Wisconsin the next day. Crowley then
penned an order that Schmedeman signed just after 2:00 A.M. that
night; they immediately wired it to Madison; and Friday morning Wisconsin authorities declared a banking holiday.[12]

That morning's "extras" extolled Crowley's part in handling the
state's banking crisis. He was partly responsible; sometime Friday
morning, he had told reporters what was done, and knowing his dominance of Schmedeman, they had stressed his role. But he knew the crisis was not over; and on Monday he was in Milwaukee, exuding confidence, telling bankers that all solvent banks would reopen at the
same time.

In fact, they did not. Crowley, who was quickly appointed federal
deputy banking commissioner for Wisconsin, allowed only seven

banks to reopen when the federal banking holiday ended on March 13. Three were in Sheboygan, Broughton's bailiwick. Perhaps that was just coincidence, but both men believed political relationships were more firmly grounded on close personal loyalty, on favors given and received, than on issues. Thus, Broughton received the state's printing work, which the *Capital Times* had handled, and Crowley could count on strong support in dealing with the now Postmaster General Farley and Democratic Senator F. Ryan Duffy.[13]

Dispensing state contracts plagued Crowley, but not as much as distributing patronage. The limited number of contracts went to Democrats, but they often had to compete with Progressive Republicans for the positions not covered by civil service. Crowley recalled that "the number of applicants for any . . . position was so large that selection of any one . . . simply alienated hundreds of others and it was often better to reappoint the existing office holder." Perhaps needless to say, long-thirsty Democrats complained no matter what Crowley's decision, though they were most bitter when he replaced Stalwart Republicans with Progressive Republican leaders and their friends.[14]

Though Wisconsin Democrats received large chunks of federal patronage, they bitterly resented the loss of even one job to a Progressive Republican; the president was sacrificing the state party in his quest for Senator LaFollette's legislative support. By contrast, Crowley quietly applauded. Working with the president enabled him to repay old allies—such as ex-Senator Blaine, who was named a director of the RFC, and Kuehl, who went as his assistant—and gave him his own pipeline to Washington, boosting Wisconsin's prospects for federal assistance. This strategy, of course, meant problems. Schmedeman sympathized with loyal, disappointed office-seekers. Usually, he advised them to speak to Crowley; he, Duffy, and Broughton distributed patronage in collaboration with Farley and the president.[15]

Though Crowley "advised" while others approved the troublesome federal patronage, Duffy and Broughton were seldom in town, and Schmedeman was often ill and not to be seen. Sitting in his capitol office, Crowley took the heat from everyone—publishers, contractors, lawyers, and others—doing business with the state. According to his secretary, he saw an average two hundred people every working day and remained gracious and charming throughout. She did not know how many were "job seekers," she told a columnist, but "Leo has the knack of sending most of them away smiling . . . his own smile is infectious." She had noted what Kuehl and others had seen before, that Crowley could handle people because he truly liked them; he accepted them with all their flaws.[16]

To be sure, "Leo" was not always available. Still chairman of the Banking Review Board, he was supervising legislation that would coordinate Wisconsin's banking laws with those the federal government had established in the new Emergency Banking Act. In that capacity and as a deputy federal bank commissioner, Crowley was reading the reports of bank examiners, deciding which banks could safely reopen, which first needed more capital, and where it might be found, perhaps local businessmen, possibly the RFC. There was much to do. Crowley was a workaholic, many said. As it happened, except for three unmarried, working sisters living in his Edgewood home, he had no immediate family wondering when he would come home. He had never married. For company, he discussed business and politics with his older brothers, and played poker, bridge, or golf with friends as time allowed. He was too busy for much else. At times he would close his office door to phone Washington or to dash off letters. One visitor, unable to get through his door, said that Crowley was busier than the governor. A secretary had told him: "No, you can't see Mr. Crowley, but if you care to you can see Gov. Schmedeman."[17]

Though that tale may have been apocryphal, many others fed the growing impression that Crowley was not only busier than the governor but more powerful One pundit labeled him "the Richelieu of Wisconsin"—the power behind the throne—and that spring newspapers throughout Wisconsin reported the tribulations of the state's superintendent of public instruction when he encountered Crowley. Invited to the "Governor's office" to discuss his budget, the superintendent, none other than Crowley's nemesis, John Callahan, reported later that he had expected to see Schmedeman. "Imagine my surprise," he told newsmen. "I was ushered into the office of his prime minister. This gentleman proceeded to show me the various educational budgets. When he got to [one] cut . . . , I told the prime minister . . . that I didn't think he could get by with it. The prime minister thought he could. I lost."[18]

Callahan's charming anecdote covered his personal chagrin. It also illustrated Crowley's power and denigrated Schmedeman's. But it was on the mark. Years later Crowley might remember that " 'Schmedy' was a close personal friend who trusted me and [whom] I tried to serve."

In fact, as a letter Crowley sent Schmedeman reveals, he patronized the governor. It rang with instructions, such as "we would be in a position to . . . ," "you know that . . . ," you should also . . . ," and "I would be very certain to . . . ." Even more suggestive of their relationship was a newspaper report of Crowley's appearance during the "milk strike" that began that winter and lasted well into the spring. He was speaking when a farmer shouted, "Where is Schmedeman?" and another shouted back, "He is waiting for Crowley to finish his speech."[19]

Schmedeman was neither incompetent nor hiding; there can be little doubt, though, that he lacked Crowley's energy and stamina, his masterly way of managing people, and his problem-solving ability. These qualities were especially important when Wisconsin desperately needed Washington's assistance. Schmedeman knew it. So did Crowley. Told by the Unemployed Workers League that Dane County provided only 75 cents a week for food, Crowley sympathized: it "was a damn poor ration." He also acknowledged the need for federally funded public works. But the strongest pressure came from Wisconsin dairymen, whose prices for milk fell to new lows in 1933. By the spring, with milk at one cent a quart, some dairymen had formed a "milk pool," hoping through voluntary group action to reduce the milk supply and force prices up. But after other dairy farmers rejected this approach, pool leaders discussed strikes, blocking highways, and marches; and by April violence threatened Wisconsin, as it did some other nearby farm states. It appeared likely that the governor would have to call out the National Guard.[20]

Crowley recognized the danger and decided that the answer, if any, was in Washington. Measures emerging there might blunt the dairymen's fervor. And by mid-April he was traveling there almost weekly, seeking help. With the president he discussed the reduction of mortgage rates in an emerging farm bill. With Agriculture Secretary Henry Wallace, he stressed the regulation of milk production to raise prices. And at the RFC and the Justice Department, he discussed the financial and legal aspects of refinancing farm debts. However, talks with Henry Morgenthau, governor of the Farm Credit Administration and the president's close friend, were to be most productive. They involved action to reduce farmers' mortgages and monthly payments and tying that goal to another equally important if less immediate: liquifying farm mortgages, potentially a major asset of the nation's banks, including those within Crowley's purview as chairman of Wisconsin's

Banking Review Board. Crowley made an extremely favorable impression. Morgenthau promised that the FCA would shortly help Wisconsin's farmers, and soon he would be consulting Crowley and placing him in major federal posts.[21]

That spring, though, Crowley was focusing on impressing the dairymen back home and averting a strike by the milk pool. In early May, the *Wisconsin State Journal* reported that his proposals had inspired the launching of state committees to "cooperate with Secretary of Agriculture Wallace in administering production controls in the new farm bill," and that he was about to reveal Wisconsin's committee. Crowley had put out the story, hoping that even the suggestion of action would blunt the influence of the strike-prone milk pool leaders. Thus, he made it known a few days later that he was in Washington again, this time discussing the "dairy problem" with Wisconsin's senators and securing the president's assurances of federal help.[22]

Unhappily, the prospective action Crowley served up did not raise milk prices, and in mid-May strikers began dumping milk en route to cities near the lakeshore. That led Schmedeman to call out the National Guard. This act cost him the hostility of milk pool farmers, but Crowley, if he advised the governor's call for the Guard, which seems likely, would have done so privately, and thus was able to escape the farmer's wrath. Indeed, he won some favor with the farmers, as he received their petitions, spoke to them, and arranged a meeting with the governor. He could claim the role of peacemaker.[23]

Crowley's efforts were seldom so public as during the milk strike crisis, and while he could not prevent its explosion, he was devising a plan that would cope simultaneously with the larger farm problem and frozen bank assets. They revolved about the federal land banks and his influence with Morgenthau, who as Farm Credit Administration governor notably established the first local land bank office in Madison that June.

Crowley envisaged the federal land banks as having a double function. They would give Wisconsin banks federally guaranteed 4 percent bonds for their frozen farm mortgages. The farmer in turn would make his mortgage payments to the land bank, though the monthly amounts would be smaller than before the new policy, first because the land bank would take the mortgages at a price reflecting the drastic deflation that had occurred since the depression's onslaught and, second, because the payments would be spread over more years. The benefits to the farmer were clear. Crowley was impressed at least as much, however, by the concurrent liquification of the banks' otherwise frozen assets. As a result, they would be better able to meet the claims of depositors and the demands of new borrowers. Thus Madison's land bank office promised some help to Crowley in his efforts as chairman of Wisconsin's Banking Review Board to save more of the state's still-fragile banks.

Unfortunately, the wheels turned slowly. Wisconsin's land bank required approval of its mortgage appraisals by the seventh district headquarters in St. Paul, Minnesota, and officers there were extremely slow. Growing impatient, Crowley turned to his two old friends at the RFC. He pleaded with Kuehl to "use your influence and crowd ahead the program set forth in my letter on loans in closed banks," and he wrote Blaine a similar note.[24]

Both men responded favorably. Blaine promised to "expedite matters," and Kuehl seconded him with details, emphasizing that "Senator [actually Director] Blaine has arranged with the Board to give the closed banks all the attention they need in order to get money to the depositors." At the same time, Crowley found a continuing source of cooperation in his old partner, Milo Hagan, now Wisconsin's banking commissioner. That summer the two saved so many banks that even the ever-critical Evjue applauded. Much remained to be done, however a hundred and fifty banks closed during the banking holiday in March remained sealed. And there was no help yet from the RFC.[25]

Crowley was everywhere that summer of 1933. In July he was named Wisconsin's national recovery administrator, and in August he was trying to secure work for the state's unemployed in talks with Public Works Administrator (and Interior Secretary) Harold Ickes. When Crowley found Ickes slow to come up with the money, he turned to Kuehl at the RFC and, on September 1, his old ally informed him that Wisconsin would soon get "a million and three quarters, 'without strings.' "[26]

Crowley, not Kuehl, was credited with this boost to Wisconsin's relief and recovery program. As with the short-lived milk strike, reporters credited him with the state's accomplishments, saving their cold blasts for the governor. By the summer's end, most Wisconsin newspapers were striking the theme established by the superintendent of instruction that spring: Crowley was "the real governor" of the state, playing "Richelieu" to Schmedeman's Louis XIII. He was now "general overseer of all plans to bring Wisconsin through to prosperity." What would he do next?

Crowley denied political aspirations. Helping the governor bring relief and recovery to Wisconsin were his goals, cooperating with the federal government the means. The fiscal policy of the Schmedeman administration resembled that of the White House, deep cuts in the regular operating budget coupled with so-called emergency appropriations for relief. They were too small—the president's "minister for relief," Harry Hopkins, rightly stated that the state govermment "passed the buck" to Washington, which had funds, and to local and county units, which did not—but the charge by Hopkins's agent that Crowley was "the stumbling block" was unfair. The main "stumbling block" was the combination of Stalwart Republicans and conservative Democrats that dominated the state legislature.[27]

The president did not have this problem. Thus, feeding off Washington was Wisconsin's best hope, Crowley argued. Speaking at Sheboygan on October 3, he insisted that "we [in Wisconsin] must cooperate with the federal government"; given the depression's depth and reach, "no state could possibly get . . . out alone." Generally, Crowley said, he and Schmedeman believed the role of the states "must primarily be to assist" Washington, and that in "working with the federal government we are best serving the interests of the state."[28]

It is hardly surprising that in a speech stressing federal leadership Crowley should extol the president as its source, as "a man of action" who had entered the White House knowing "there was no hope in just letting things drift." Accordingly, Roosevelt quickly "presented concrete proposals," and "there has been a reversal of the tide." There was no denying problems with New Deal programs, but they were owing to lesser men who did not administer them in "the liberal spirit the President intended."

Crowley singled out the federal land banks as an example of conservatism and sloth in administration. "It is vitally necessary that [their] policies . . . in refinancing farm indebtedness be liberalized," he told Sheboygan's civic clubs. They were appraising land values too conservatively and, as a result, assuming farm mortgages too slowly. This was a local failure; it was not that of the governor of the Farm Credit Administration. It was "Mr. Morgenthau," Crowley stressed, who "came to this state . . . and ascertained that the appraisals were being made at such low figures that little real relief was being afforded the farmers." And "he gave instructions to liberalize" them. Unfortunately, Crowley advised his audience, "It has been very difficult to get the federal land banks to actually do this." And there was grave danger if the banks did not act quickly. Before long, snow would blanket the state's farms and make them difficult if not impossible to appraise.[29]

Crowley had kept Morgenthau informed about Wisconsin's farm mortgage problem since the spring. In essence, the president of the federal land bank at district headquarters in St. Paul, Minnesota, had instructed his appraisers to evaluate farms with the cold eyes of a banker. Consequently, the farmer who usually had creditors other than his mortgagor, did not receive much relief from refinancing even when, as was happening all too slowly, his application was approved. Crowley wanted a banker with a heart. He wanted a banker who would respond to the farmer's problems by restructuring all his obligations in one new first mortgage. He wanted a banker who, as the *State Journal* put it so aptly, would recognize that "farm mortgage loans . . . were not a banking but an assistance operation." In later years Crowley would insist that he generally disapproved of big government, but in 1933 he clearly approved using the Farm Credit Administration to aid desperate farmers and bankers. Given his own recent problems, he found it easy to empathize with them as victims of hard times.[30]

Prompted by Crowley, Morgenthau invited him, along with the president of the federal land bank in St. Paul and other federal officers, to Treasury Secretary William Woodin's office June 12. Morgenthau's anecdotal account of the meeting ignores Crowley's existence, despite the topic and Crowley's presence. Morgenthau suggests that the participants only discussed the rehabilitation of several hundred Wisconsin banks, not Wisconsin farmers. He also describes how he ran to the White House during the meeting, told the president of "*my* plan to open up the banks in Wisconsin through our buying the mortgages . . . they held," and learned that the president not only agreed with the plan but was preparing to announce it himself. However, Morgenthau admits knowing little about the plan, and more extensive evidence suggests that at the meeting in the Treasury secretary's office Crowley outlined *his* own plan to handle loans more liberally than St. Paul permitted, and that it was this outline that became the basis for action.[31]

There was no action, however, until September, when Morgenthau asked Crowley and the obstructive president of the seventh district land bank in St. Paul to meet him in Chicago. There he offered the St. Paul official one last chance to cooperate, then asked Crowley to take over in St. Paul. Crowley said he had too many jobs in Madison, but Morgenthau persuaded him to speak with the president before he refused. Later, Senator William Langer, North Dakota's governor in 1933, recalled that his farmers' distress had placed him in the Oval Office with Crowley, that Crowley agreed to go to St. Paul, and that the president said: "Now Leo, you know what the situation is up there . . . , and I am going to be guided by what you say." Obviously, Crowley had the "complete confidence of the President."[32]

Later that September Morgenthau's deputy informed the president of the seventh district land bank "of a reorganization of your regional unit during the week beginning October 9." He was out, as a meeting in St. Paul that week confirmed. Crowley was in. In the reorganized seventh district, he would be the FCA's general agent and Morgenthau's "personal representative" in St. Paul, charged with expediting farm mortgage applications. Newspaper reports indicated that Morgenthau had agreed that he might spend half his week in Madison advising Schmedeman, which caused one editor to question, tongue in cheek, how he could leave Wisconsin at all, when "he is actually the governor of the state." Another noted, no less playfully, "that he would receive $8500," not just another "thank you" or "no pay job." Most newspapers, however, marked his departure with encomiums that characterized his past efforts and their expectations. Typical of the rest, the *State Journal* first praised Crowley's "resourcefulness" and "tireless energy" when "guiding the governmental affairs of Wisconsin" that year, then forecast: "Under Mr. Crowley's direction the Federal Farm bank will move. Its employees will find that delays will not be countenanced. Decisions will be prompt and liberal."[33]

The *State Journal*'s forecast was right on the mark. When Crowley returned to St. Paul a week after his meeting with Morgenthau, he acted swiftly. He replaced the district headquarters's president, liberalized its appraisals, and simplified its loan processing. "Get results," Morgenthau had told his agents. And Crowley did. At the end of just one month he could tell the *Janesville Gazette* that the new model St. Paul bank had paid out $628,000 in just one day, a very significant amount because it was "the highest daily total paid by any of the land banks of the country." Then, for emphasis, "We loaned more money during the last week than in the entire 10 months' period prior to October 1."[34]

Crowley was not the only one blowing his horn that autumn. North Dakota's Republican governor, William Langer, labeled his handling of the bank "magnificent," and he, along with a number of other governors, senators, representatives, businessmen, and farmers in the FCA's seventh district were soon asking the president to appoint Crowley as the FCA's Washington head to replace Morgenthau, who was moving to the Treasury Department as acting secretary. Their number included Schmedeman, who advised the White House that appointing Crowley as FCA governor "would meet with the immediate approval of the Executive heads of middlewestern states . . . and do much to alleviate agricultural unrest in our midwest." And Senator Duffy agreed, stressing Crowley's "splendid work" at St. Paul, and suggesting that the president "ask Mr. Morgenthau about it."[35]

Altogether more than forty such recommendations reached the White House that November. Most, like Schmedeman's and Duffy's, referred to Crowley's accomplishments in St. Paul; some also asserted that Crowley was "a westerner who understands our farmers and can work with them . . . "; others from creamery owners, gave no reasons, but apparently recalled Crowley's handling of the milk strike; and finally, some Democratic leaders, including Iowa's governor, insisted that Crowley's appointment as governor of the Farm Credit Administration would strengthen their state parties. Only one writer sounded a discordant note. William B. Rubin, an aspiring Milwaukee Democrat and the milk pool's lawyer, called Crowley's association with "reactionary forces . . . , [an] unhappy record as a banker . . . , and service to the Big Interests" a "slap in the face to all progressives and liberals in Wisconsin." In part at least, Rubin was personally motivated—Crowley had outmaneuvered him more than once that year—but he had struck soft spots, and he would again when the occasion arose. [36]

As it happened, the president made his decision before most of the letters and telegrams arrived. William I. Myers, Morgenthau's deputy, was appointed to succeed him. As for Crowley, he claimed that he had been offered the job and turned it down. "I can remain away from my business only from three to six months," he told one reporter, then added: "I felt it my duty to stay at St. Paul until the organization is fully functioning." Further, "the work . . . is more to my liking."[37]

There can be little question that Crowley found his work in St.

Paul enjoyable. It brought great success, heady praise from bankers and other business leaders, and a political base that he would later find extremely helpful. Even so, it is difficult to believe that the president wanted to appoint him governor of the FCA, and he turned it down. There is no evidence to support his claim; and the appointment would have promoted him over Morgenthau's logical successor, Deputy Governor Myers, and others with higher rank, disrupting the FCA. Also, Crowley would display no reluctance two months later, when the president offered him a comparable post in Washington. He would go.

Crowley's dubious claim may have been prompted by a remark by Morgenthau that he deserved the governorship of the FCA (but Myers had priority), coupled with his own marked insecurity. In later years, when asked for information by publications such as *Who's Who*, he would pad nonexistent years to his education and honors. And he would, at times and especially when challenged, loudly remind subordinates of "who he was." Despite his significant achievements the past year—and they were many—he had not outgrown his search for a secure identity.[38]

Crowley would never again achieve the public prominence in Wisconsin he acquired after Schmedeman's election. Evjue wrote of his "star" ascending, which was true enough. More precisely, perhaps, Crowley had rebounded from the depths of his dismissal from the State Bank. He had poured his talents and energy into the Banking Review Board, and made the most of his opportunity. He had mentored Governor Schmedeman and become a force to reckon with: "the Richelieu of Wisconsin," the state's de facto governor. And he had gone on to notable achievements and respect in St. Paul and the surrounding region. What he had proposed and accomplished there reflected the essence of the early New Deal: a conservativism tempered with a compassionate pragmatism that emphasized the common interests of society's "have-lesses" and "have-mores." But those were evaluations for historians. Crowley spoke only of returning to his business in Madison.

It was not to be. That winter the president would call him to Washington. He wanted him to be the next, and to all intents and purposes, the first truly important chairman of the recently created Federal Deposit Insurance Corporation.

3

Cover-Up in the Capital, I

For more than half a century, the Federal Deposit Insurance Corporation has protected the bank deposits of millions of Americans. As an agency it was—and probably remains—popular, but much of what is thought to be known of its origins is myth. The FDIC was established early in the first term of President Franklin Roosevelt, and it carries the banner of the New Deal, but it was the product of neither. It was promoted by senior congressmen of both major parties and imposed on the White House. Until Congress forced his hand, President Roosevelt, the archetypal New Dealer, opposed deposit insurance as an experiment that was tried in several states and failed.[1]

The Great Banking Crisis of March 1933 reopened an earlier debate over federal deposit insurance, but significant action did not occur until May 10. Then the House Banking and Currency Committee brought in an insurance bill that would cover deposits in all banks 100 percent to $10,000, after that on a sliding scale, the program to be financed by assessments on the banks enrolled in the system. Soon after, the Senate Banking Committee reported its own bill, which differed chiefly in excluding banks that were not members of the Federal Reserve System and in postponing implementation of the bill until July 1, 1934. Neither plan appealed to Michigan's Republican and junior senator, Arthur Vandenberg. He argued, first, that neither contained a ceiling on the deposits guaranteed, and second, that the Senate's more limited bill would not restore confidence in the nation's smaller banks. Vandenberg then proposed an amendment providing coverage for deposits in *all* banks beginning July 1, 1933, but with a "temporary fund" managed by the Federal Reserve Board and a $2,500 ceiling.[2]

The Vandenberg amendment obviously influenced passage of the Glass-Steagall Deposit Insurance Act that June. Nonmember banks

were included, provided that they sought admission to the Federal Reserve System by July 1, 1936; coverage was restricted to $2,500 and a
"temporary fund" would begin operations on January 1, 1934. The
only major difference with the Vandenberg-amended Senate bill was
that it would be administered by a new Federal Deposit Insurance Corporation rather than the Federal Reserve Board. It is no wonder, then,
that Vandenberg saw himself as "father" of the FDIC and took a
strong, continuing interest in its three-member board of directors and,
before long, Crowley as its chairman.[3]

The Glass-Steagall Act made the comptroller of the currency,
J. F. T. O'Connor, a statutory member of the FDIC's board. A well-con-
nected and self-important lawyer from California soon to influence
Crowley's career for good and for ill, O'Connor played a part—surely
exaggerated in his diary—in shaping the embryonic FDIC. He asserts
that during the summer of 1933 the president instructed him to "consult Jim Farley and get two good names for directors" of the FDIC, and
more than a month later he, O'Connor, recommended Walter Cummings, a Chicago banker then assisting the Treasury secretary, as temporarily the second Democratic director and probably as chairman. As
for the Republican member required by statute, O'Connor jotted that
the president told him only that they must find "someone who would
not bear down too hard and insist on gilt-edge securities."[4]

By August 22, Cummings's appointment was approved; four days
later E. G. Bennett, an Ogden, Utah, banker, was named the Republican
member of the FDIC's board, though without O'Connor's help; and
three weeks later, both men, along with O'Connor, were sworn and
Cummings was chosen chairman. Then came months of hard work.
Working with Treasury and RFC officers, the FDIC board wrote by-
laws, fleshed out the FDIC's structure, appointed major officers, and
devised means of strengthening weaker banks. Insured banks would
be assessed half of one percent of their deposits as members of the
then-labeled temporary fund; but, while Federal Reserve members
would be insured automatically, nonmembers would be admitted to
the fund only after they were, as the Glass-Steagall Act required, found
solvent. In fact, solvency was defined so leniently all but a thousand of
the 7,800 nonmember banks qualified immediately. And with the
RFC's help, all but 140 nonmember banks qualified by the year's end.[5]

By then, Cummings had indicated that he would resign at the end
of January. Curiously, discussion of a successor began only in the

middle of that month. On January 14 the president finally asked O'Connor to speak with Morgenthau about "the question of a successor to Walter Cummings," and O'Connor may have done so, but Crowley's appointment originated with a different source.[6]

On January 16, Senator Duffy wrote the president, suggesting that he appoint Crowley to fill the vacancy Cummings's departure would create. Duffy pointed out that his "suggestion" had "the hearty endorsement of Governor Schmedeman, National Committeeman Charles Broughton, and Mr. Joseph Martin, chairman of the State Central Committee." These endorsements seemingly prompted the president to act, but not without seeking more objective counsel. He sent Duffy's recommendation to Morgenthau by way of his secretary, Marvin McIntyre, accompanied with a jotted note that seemed to ask McIntyre's opinion: "Do you think HM Jr. would want to consider this. Crowley is a good man as you know."[7]

Morgenthau did not record his answer then, but a month later he would write in his diary: "I felt largely responsible for his [Crowley's] nomination." Presumably in late January he told the president he approved Crowley's appointment. Everything he knew about him was extremely positive: his successes chairing Wisconsin's Banking Review Board; in "governing" Wisconsin for Governor Schmedeman; in liquifying farm mortgages; and as his own "can do" general agent at St. Paul's Federal District Land Bank. And most recently Crowley had crafted a bill for the Wisconsin legislature that could make all but a few of the state's banks admissible to the temporary fund. These were credits Morgenthau could not have ignored; nor could he his part in promoting Crowley's career that year. In that sense if no other, Morgenthau was chiefly responsible for the memo the president jotted at January's close: "Send in name of Leo Crowley of Wisconsin as Federal Bank Insurance boss. On Feb. 1. in place of Cummings."[8]

The president's prestige and the Democratic party's powerful majority in the Senate would have led to Crowley's automatic confirmation but for the intervention of the *Capital Times*'s William T. Evjue. Before Crowley's appointment even reached the Senate, the editor pulled his state tax records, then summarized what he believed his sins at the State Bank and in connected matters in a letter to Lowell Mellet, a politically friendly reporter with the *Washington News*. Evjue strongly implied Crowley's malfeasance as president of the State Bank of Wisconsin, then explicitly charged that he had used his political influence to head off a probe. He also estimated that Crowley owed $450,000, chiefly to Bankshares, and that, Evjue believed, accounted for the fact that the Banking Review Board was "unfair to small banks and made it difficult for them to exist." Evjue stated that he could raise other arguments against Crowley, but those made should be enough to stop his confirmation. Indeed, other people familiar with the points he had made "are wondering . . . that Crowley is to be placed in charge of a national agency insuring bank deposits."[9]

Writing Mellett did not relieve Evjue's anxieties. He would not publish undocumented charges regarding Crowley's affairs, and he must have doubted that the *Washington News* would. But Senator Vandenberg was another matter. He had helped shape the bill creating the FDIC, and he had displayed particular concern about the fate of smaller banks. Evjue decided to alert Vandenberg by telephone, and perhaps he did. In either case, he immediately wired him, advising: "Please get in touch with Lowell Mellett of Washington News. He has confidential information. . . . Show Mellett this telegram."[10]

Evjue's letter to Mellet and telegram to Vandenberg reached Washington February 1, while Crowley was enroute to a meeting in St. Paul. Only upon reaching Madison did he hear from Morgenthau that Senator Vandenberg had conveyed Evjue's charges to the Treasury Department and demanded an investigation. Morgenthau wanted him back in Washington immediately to deal with the threat. Such were the circumstances in which Crowley arrived in the Capital on Tuesday, February 6. There he may have read in the morning paper that the previous day Vandenberg had blocked unanimous consent to his confirmation, saying obscurely but insistently that he needed a few days to make inquiries into the matter. But Crowley would have heard the news quickly in any event; he had promised to call at Morgenthau's office upon his arrival.[11]

Crowley was fortunate that Morgenthau directed him to O'Connor. Himself a model of rectitude, Morgenthau could be squeamish if not priggish over most patronage; placing his nephew, Mortimer "Tim" Fox, in the FDIC was a notable exception. As for O'Connor, he had few known compunctions. Pretentious and openly ambitious, the comptroller had used his connections to obtain an office that was known as a political plum. And, though he was soon to seek double his salary in a top job at San Francisco's Federal Reserve Bank, he enjoyed his present power and status. In the autumn he had been thrilled at choosing Judge L. E. Birdzell, a friend from his native state of North Dakota, as the FDIC's general counsel. Now he looked forward to more such plums and apparently concluded that Crowley was like-minded. They could deal, the more so as he and Crowley belonged to a new breed in Washington—mutually protective, self-conscious Irish-Catholic politicians.[12]

In O'Connor's office, Crowley read Vandenberg's letter seeking "certain information about his connection with the State Bank of Wisconsin . . . and [his] loans." Then, after he and O'Connor evaluated the senator's concerns and how Crowley might deal with them, they discussed "certain policies of the FDIC," focusing on their division of its appointments; and, finally, the comptroller phoned Vandenberg. O'Connor's cryptic diary reveals no more particulars, but his actions over the next eight days leave no doubt that he decided to endorse Crowley's confirmation, even if at the expense of his obligations as supervisor of the nation's national banks.[13]

On Wednesday morning, O'Connor helped Crowley draft a letter for Vandenberg, accounting for his policies at the State Bank and his debts, and that afternoon Crowley carried it to the senator's office. What they discussed is not a matter of record, but there can be little doubt that Crowley employed both his charm and promises for the future: the next fall when Vandenberg was battling for his political life, Crowley sent him a note for his campaign, titling him the "Father of the F.D.I.C."; and thereafter they became, as Crowley accurately stressed later, "very close." Still, Vandenberg was not satisfied that day. He wanted the comptroller to have Crowley's banking methods examined.[14]

Vandenberg surely did not know O'Connor would permit Crowley to name the national bank examiner who would look into his record as a private banker, that Crowley would name a man who had worked in his State Bank, for whom he probably found his examiner's job, and whom he would later find a better post in the FDIC. Even so, the examiner's report did not fully satisfy the comptroller, and he sent it to Vandenberg on February 13, with a cautionary note: "My records do not show any criticism of Mr. Leo T. Crowley as a banker." And the next day, after the senator asked him for more information, O'Connor, who could have supplied it, again replied lamely, "I feel justified in standing on my letter to you of yesterday."[15]

Vandenberg could not have found O'Connor's comments reassuring, but he was even then reading letters and telegrams endorsing Crowley and asking that he do so. Some came from Wisconsin, but surely the most crucial came from people he knew and respected in his hometown of Grand Rapids. Twice he heard from Glenn Chamberlain, the vice-president of the Grand Rapids Gas Light Company, a friend who could address him as "Dear Arthur." Whether or not Chamberlain knew Crowley personally, he enclosed and strongly endorsed recommendations from business associates in Milwaukee whom Vandenberg might otherwise have discounted as business associates of Crowley and perhaps indebted to him. There were other significant endorsements, too. The Wisconsin Bankers Association sent the White House a resolution stating that Crowley, as chairman of the Banking Review Board, had "given his labors, his heart if you please, to the life blood of all banks in Wisconsin." The wording must have been impressive (especially as it neglected to note that Crowley remained a director in Wisconsin Bankshares and that Bankshares dominated Wisconsin banking). And against it and the many endorsements Crowley received there were only the broad, unproved charges of Evjue and a telegram from Rubin, briefly making similar indictments. Thus, Vandenberg withdrew his objections to Crowley's confirmation; and when, on February 14, Senator Duffy asked unanimous consent, his motion was quickly approved.[16]

On the surface at least, Crowley never appeared to doubt it. He had left Washington after his conversations with O'Connor and Vandenberg. On February 9, he was in Milwaukee, self-confidently informing the Wisconsin Bankers Association of new methods he and the Banking Review Board had devised to save Wisconsin banks, and of his lobbying for a bill in the legislature that would enable the RFC to rehabilitate Wisconsin's banks. Later that evening he listened as the FDIC's chief examiner reported his contributions. And after he left for Washington, he could read Schmedeman's tribute to talents "such that President Roosevelt has called him to Washington." Even so, Crowley had to be relieved when the Senate confirmed him. For two weeks his career, his reputation, and perhaps his liberty, had hung in the balance. Once more, though, he had not only covered his past, he had even found a way to win. But Crowley's clever manipulations notwithstanding, there is good reason to believe he had grown since losing his bank. In the two years since, he had worked hard and at some personal sacrifice as chairman of Wisconsin's Banking Review Board, as an "advisor" to Governor Schmedeman, and as a "can do" representative for Morgenthau at St. Paul's land bank. Finally, behind his confirmation lay more than two weeks of seducing O'Connor, securing endorsements, and charming Vandenberg. He had earned his way.[17]

Crowley was sworn in on February 21, and only ten days later found himself in a battle with O'Connor, which, if he lost, could render his job as chairman untenable. At issue was the minority party position on the FDIC's board, the key to controlling it. E. G. Bennett, who was leaving, had suggested that his assistant, Hubert Stronck, succeed him. Crowley was impressed with Stronck; he owned a bank management company, had published on bank management, and had worked for two comptrollers of the currency. With those endorsements, Crowley thought the president would send his name to the Senate, and he would have had not O'Connor and Farley intervened. O'Connor had phoned a Kansas City, Missouri, banker, who attacked Stronck's qualifications for the FDIC's board. Farley so advised the president, after which O'Connor phoned, saying that the "appt would be dynamite." Why, he did not say.[18]

That afternoon, March 8, Crowley wrote Marvin McIntyre, the president's assistant secretary. He felt that he had not fought strongly enough for Stronck at the White House the night before, and that for the president to appoint someone else because of a "political squabble . . . may embarrass the Corporation." He wrote Morgenthau, "I am more disturbed than ever as to who is going to be my associate as director and should have taken a more definite stand, but I have tried to act the part of a gentleman." Crowley reminded Morgenthau that he had to work with O'Connor; he did not want "an open break that perhaps would cause bitter enmities," but he was going to fight.[19]

Crowley wanted Morgenthau to intervene. Ten days before, he had told the secretary of his "terrible time with Jefty . . . ," had asked for his help, and been told he would have it. But Morgenthau did not want to tangle with O'Connor *and* Farley, Crowley did not have the clout to overcome Farley's objections, and Stronck's name was not sent to the Senate. Fortunately for Crowley, he was not publicly embarrassed; Bennett agreed to remain for a while. As for O'Connor, he began looking for opportunities to renew the battle.[20]

Crowley was, as he wrote the White House, truly pleased that Bennett was staying on. The Utah banker not only offered a "very happy solution" to his personal problem but also gave him "the benefit of Mr. Bennett's experience," which he truly needed. In mid-January, a White House meeting had decided that the permanent insurance system must not be allowed to become effective automatically on July 1, as the previous year's Glass-Steagall Act provided. The FDIC needed more time to strengthen a number of banks and examine them, to reexamine others, and to refine its methods. The answer, the administration decided, was a bill that would extend the temporary fund another year, until June 30, 1935.

Crowley had not been appointed when the decision to postpone was made, but he concurred with it; he wanted time to assess and, where he saw the need, seek refinement of the permanent insurance system. He was hardly confirmed as chairman, then, when he took a proprietary interest in the handling of the extension bill. He found the Senate agreeable to the administration's bill which, as drafted, insured deposits to $2,500, but not the House. According to his informant on the House Banking Committee, some "young radicals" there were bringing pressure to bear on their chairman, Alabama's Henry B. Steagall of Alabama. Ostensibly, they favored automatic application of the permanent plan, but with its deposit insurance ceiling set at $10,000; in fact, Crowley learned, they would accept a $5,000 limit.[21]

On April 18, Crowley sent his informant's report, along with his own assessment of the extension bill's problems, to the White House. Probably somewhat awed by his new office and uncertain of the proper protocol, he seemed reluctant to address the president directly and, when he did, embroidered his memos and reports with deferential, even obsequious language. This memo, like others he wrote during his first few months in Washington, he entrusted the president's secretary, Marvin McIntyre, to hand his boss when and as McIntyre thought best. Clearly, though, Crowley wanted the president to impress the House Banking Committee with his desire that it report out the administration's extension bill.[22]

Crowley wanted the president to be "emphatic" with Steagall. On April 19, he told Morgenthau that his informant on the banking committee said that "Steagall leaves the impression [there] that the president only jokes with him when he [Steagall] opposes the extension of our bill." If so, it was time the president took "a strong stand." And quickly. Otherwise, the temporary fund would lapse prematurely. Apparently, Crowley felt that Morgenthau, the president's close friend, could do far more than he, new in Washington, to persuade the president to prompt Steagall and his committee to defer to the Senate on the extension bill.[23]

Despite Crowley's direct and indirect efforts, it seems that the president made no effort to force Steagall's hand for another month. It was May 18, before, as the *New York Times* reported, he gave the committee chairman a "forceful piece of his mind," which apparently got his attention. On May 21, Crowley wrote the White House that the banking committee was considering extension of the temporary fund to June 30, 1935. It asked for several changes in the Senate bill, the most important being an increase in the coverage of deposits to $5,000 and elimination of a requirement that all insured banks join the Federal Reserve System. Excepting the latter condition, the Senate, the president, and Crowley found no problem with the House's demands; and that conflict was resolved by postponing the Federal Reserve requirement a year from July 1, 1936, to July 1, 1937. Consequently, June 16 found the temporary fund extended for another year, until June 30, 1935.[24]

While the Senate and House lurched toward compromise, Crowley worried about confidence in the FDIC and the nation's banks. Hoping to strengthen the public's faith in both, he told newsmen that the FDIC had operated for almost six months without a single bank failure. Technically he was correct; actually his statement skirted reality and exposed him to sharp public criticism for the first time since coming to the corporation. The *New York Herald-Tribune* satirized, "Now comes Leo T. Crowley with a panegyric on the guaranty of bank deposits that properly belongs with the rest of this [New Deal] humbuggery." The paper agreed with the *American Banker* that Crowley was "juggling definitions."[25]

Crowley did not respond, but Senator Vandenberg did. Speaking on the Senate floor, he defended Crowley as the FDIC's "very able chairman" and stressed the corporation's "amazing record" in restoring "public confidence" in "dependable banking operations." And with good reason. No longer did one or two or even more bank failures automatically threaten a run on other banks nearby; the public knew the FDIC would pay off depositors quickly and without question.[26]

If the FDIC was, as Professor John Kenneth Galbraith has put it, a "reliable lender of last resort," it also took the risks of a lender. No one understood that better than Crowley; he was determined that the banks the corporation insured would not become millstones, dragging it into insolvency. In mid-June, he approved a new form letter to be sent to state bank superintendents, seeking detailed information about banks that might apply for membership in the temporary fund. Unlike previous requests for certificates of solvency and balance sheets, Crowley's letter asked for specifics about the region's "economic situation" and a bank's "proposed management" and "Prospects for . . . Profitable Operation." He knew that such information did not guarantee a bank's survival or even sound loans, but a sound capital to deposits ratio, solid management, and profitable business prospects surely enhanced its chances. No less important to Crowley, it made acceptance of new banks less threatening.[27]

Just as the FDIC's new form letter suggests that Crowley had firmly grasped the institution's reins, a speech at the Wisconsin State Bankers Association convention provides compelling evidence of the strength he was bringing to the corporation. Parts of it were impromptu. On the first night Crowley heard the association president rehearse charges he had made throughout the state, that the FDIC, through the RFC, was forcing banks to accept money they did not want. The next day he blasted back. Capital investment in Wisconsin banks totaled less than 10 percent of total deposit liability, and that created an "unhealthy situation," especially as the banks had agreements with the FDIC to become solvent. The remedy was more capital, but local sources could not provide it. The bankers should understand, then, why the RFC must do so. The FDIC's "tremendous liability . . . here in Wisconsin gives it a distinct right to have some voice in the building of a sound capital structure and the efficient operation of your institutions." But "the bankers flattered themselves if they thought the government wanted to enter their banks." All the FDIC wanted was that they make the soundness of their banks their first duty.[28]

After Milwaukee, Crowley shifted his emphasis from strengthening capital structures to the classification of assets (loans), and he did so even more impressively. He wanted a uniform method of appraising loans and of ascertaining whether federal examiners might be forcing liquidations and freezing credit by undue harshness in classifying them. From the first, however, he recognized the subjective nature of asset classifications—loan values were related to geographically specific factors—and during the summer he persuaded Morgenthau to call a conference of federal examiners and managers from every agency—including the Federal Reserve and RFC—involved with the problem and from all parts of the country. He was grappling with a persistent problem in a country as large as the United States: he was attempting to combine a much-needed measure of uniformity with the distinctions required by a heterogeneous economy and a pluralistic political system.

When the conference met in mid-September, Crowley dominated the three daily sessions at which all the FDIC's senior officers, all its legal staff, and federal examiners of all ranks were present. First, he outlined the problem. Now that most bad assets were cleaned out, and many slower-paying ones could be reclassified because of federal guarantees, it was time to recognize that loans often could be prudently expanded to deal with the existing deflation. Second, it was essential to do more than find out the trouble a bank was in, by providing it "constructive supervision" that would help solve its problems. That was his speech, Crowley said. He was ready to listen; he wanted a "perfectly frank" discussion and as many "constructive suggestions as possible."[29]

Crowley turned the conference into a seminar. And he did so masterfully. He seemed to know offhand every examiner's name and state or district, including something of the praise or criticism directed against the banks or FDIC there. He wanted to know what his examiners had seen and heard. Beyond that, he was especially interested in reviewing asset classification. He asked examiners to avoid the "doubtful" column, which he labeled a "lazy and useless" category; and, also, to distinguish clearly between "slow" loans that were "safe" and those open to proper criticism. However, for all Crowley's leadership and attention to details, the problem of classifying assets in a manner that combined prudence with the depressed economy's urgent need for expanded credit was far from solved.

Whatever the conference's substantive achievements, most of those present must have left with a sense that it was worthwhile. Not so Jefty O'Connor. He was angry with everyone. Crowley had Bennett's support on the board; he now had Postmaster General and Democratic National Committee Chairman Farley's support in their patronage disputes; and he had cut short the comptroller's speech at the conference. Further, O'Connor knew it was well known that the Federal Reserve Board was balking at his request for a job at its San Francisco bank, and that Morgenthau wanted him out of his hair. Presumably, he did not hear the secretary ask Crowley "if he would be willing to go in as Governor of the Federal Reserve," adding that "bank examinations could be put there"; but he could not ignore the gossip in Washington or a *Chicago Tribune* headline reading, "Head of FDIC to be Made U.S. Banking Czar." And there was, finally, a tangible attack; on September 21 Morgenthau took his legal staff.[30]

Embittered, O'Connor used his position to send federal examiners from outside Wisconsin into the state, looking for evidence that would support a rumor he had heard at the recent conference. He jotted in his diary: "Complaint about Leo Crowley. Large indebtedness to Wisconsin banks." Then he added: "Crowley said he had arranged to take it out but his word has not been kept. Crowley *has never kept* a single promise. How unfortunate that a man in such a high position should have no sense of honor."[31]

O'Connor thought he had found a sword that would cut Crowley down to size. On October 5, he told Marvin McIntyre what he had learned, including "my saving Crowley in [the] Senate." And ten days later Crowley found himself in Morgenthau's office. During a morning session, the secretary told Crowley he wanted a record of his financial activities during the past few years. Crowley said he would supply it, and later that day he handed Morgenthau a letter he said included the required information. It advised Morgenthau that his older brothers had suffered heavy losses "in the market," and he had guaranted their notes to cover them. It added that his signature had not been required, and that he had not put up "any personal collateral." In any event, he had just spoken with his brothers, and they would arrange to take care of their debts without his endorsement. Then he would not have any financial obligations in any bank or similar institution. Also, he would not own any stock in banks, state or national. He would supply "additional confirmation" if the secretary wished.[32]

Morgenthau was not satisfied with Crowley's explanation; his annotations make that clear. Why, he questioned, had Crowley unnecessarily guaranteed his brothers' loans? And why did he refer to his "indirect obligation," when it was, as the secretary noted in the margin, "direct on his part"? Morgenthau saw enough problems to require that Crowley supply the "additional confirmation" he promised, in the form of an affidavit. Meanwhile, he intended to place some distance between himself and his protégé. He would say nothing more of the Federal Reserve appointment, and he would "sit" on Crowley when the occasion arose. Everyone would know he had cooled on him.[33]

If Crowley worried about falling from grace with Morgenthau, he did not show it. Somehow he was able to separate his personal and official affairs, and he was then very busy with the latter. The administration wanted to introduce an omnibus banking bill in January, and he did not like the idea. Title I contained uncontroversial revisions of the FDIC's permanent plan, and by itself was certain to meet with Congress's approval. Title II, however, was a different matter; it centralized the Federal Reserve System and was certain to meet with strong resistance from conservatives such as Virginia's Democratic Senator Carter Glass. Clearly, the administration had packaged the two titles in the belief that the first would protect the second, whereas Crowley feared the second would doom the first. But the decision to package the titles was made. His job was to secure the banking community's support.[34]

Crowley's address at the American Bankers Association annual convention that fall is significant for what it reveals about him and the FDIC at this juncture. He rehearsed the administration's contributions to the restoration of confidence since 1933, but he merely observed; he did not gloat. Neither did he claim the role of spokesman for the smaller bankers who forced the establishment of the FDIC the year before. He advocated conservative practices he believed essential to the success of the FDIC, but also likely to curry support with the nation's larger, more powerful bankers. ABA members could only approve, too, when Crowley told them what he had said earlier to Wisconsin bankers, that the FDIC's revised permanent plan would instruct banks to write off losses currently and acquire adequate capitalization as the price of admission to the corporation. They could only applaud, too, when he told them that the new permanent plan would retain the present $5,000 limit on deposit insurance. He told them that fixing the amount would aid the corporation (which it would), but the bankers knew an insurance ceiling meant fixed and lower premiums.[35]

Whereas Crowley spoke to the ABA as a partner, he lectured a meeting of state banking supervisors. In 1933, they had promised to "do anything" to save their banks, and most had. But some had not, and he found such situations "most discouraging." He warned them, as he had in his form letter in June, that they were admitting too many banks without considering capitalization, the services they would render, and their management, deposits, and profitability. Prudence, even self-preservation, again shaped Crowley's remarks. The corporation, he said, "did not wish to be in the business of supervising banks. This is your concern." But "we must protect not alone ourselves as the responsible supervising agency, but first and foremost . . . the depositors and the public in general."[36]

Crowley's speeches produced results, in conservative support for the FDIC's new permanent plan and in greater cooperation from state bank supervisors. But any sense of triumph was soon ripped from his mind. By mid-November, word of his debts and of the way he was confirmed was circulating through the administration.

O'Connor collected and followed up on both stories. Learning on November 17 that Senator LaFollette would attack Crowley's "banking record" from the Senate floor and insist that the information given the Senate in February was false, O'Connor jotted in his diary: "I checked up Hopkins Report and find it was not correct. Crowley suggested I appoint Hopkins to examine the banks which I did. I did not know Hopkins had been associated with Crowley in banks in Wisconsin. After Crowley became chairman FDIC he called Hopkins to Washington as supervising examiner in FDIC at increased salary."[37]

Three days later O'Connor spoke with Treasury Undersecretary Thomas Jefferson Coolidge and the newly confirmed chairman of the Federal Reserve Board, Marriner Eccles. He told them what he had learned excepting a few cosmetic touches to cover his part in the confirmation process. He said he felt compelled by "my moral and ethical duty" to "correct false information." However, he wanted them to act. Eccles replied that he knew about Crowley's debts—from Morgenthau—but he was not seriously concerned. Neither, it seemed, was Coolidge. He told O'Connor that if he was concerned, he should prepare a memorandum for Morgenthau, who was then resting in Florida.[38]

O'Connor does not say whether he did or not. He does remark that on November 23 he saw Crowley, who had heard that LaFollette was going to investigate him and was "greatly agitated," even, as O'Connor penned at another point, "broken up." With good reason. Crowley's problems had filtered through other cabinet offices and even the White House. Farley knew: Morgenthau had informed the postmaster general that he had an affidavit from Crowley indicating that his indebtedness was his brothers, not his, and that he found the explanation satisfactory. Farley told O'Connor he had argued the point with Morgenthau, saying, "That's pretty hard to explain to the public." And Emil Hurja, a key member of the Democratic National Committee, was aware of the factors surrounding Crowley's confirmation, and that he had repaid Vandenberg in the following fall with a letter the senator used to win reelection. So did key figures at the White House. Probably, then, the president did. Yet the heavens did not fall.[39]

On December 5, Crowley told O'Connor that he "called Senator La Follette and believed he would not press resolution of investigation." Why, Crowley did not say. Doubtless the senator saw that the price would be great. It would embarrass the president, whose policies he usually supported. Worse, it would cripple his brother's new term as governor, as people in Wisconsin would want to know why Philip had named Crowley to chair the state's Banking Review Board without checking into his sudden departure from the State Bank. On the other hand, Crowley may have promised Senator LaFollette, as he soon implied in a letter to Senator Glass, that he would be leaving Washington shortly.[40]

Probably there were moments that December when Crowley meant to resign. Ten months earlier, during his confirmation hearings, he had outwitted O'Connor and Vandenberg and successfully covered up his debts and banking methods. Since October, though, much of his cover had been ripped away. He had fended off Senator LaFollette, but O'Connor knew as much or more, and he was still bitter about lost patronage and fearful that his present post might disappear. If he handed his files to the Treasury, and it investigated, the last remnants of Crowley's cover would be blown. His superb work at the FDIC would not count. As 1934 ended, Crowley knew that his survival in Washington might be beyond his control; even his freedom might be at stake.

4

Cover-Up in the Capital, II

In 1934, Leo Crowley had little time or reason to enjoy the Christmas season. He had to massage Senator Glass's ego, as the senator's support or, at least, neutrality was essential to pass the administration's omnibus banking bill. But he had to be most concerned about his personal problems: O'Connor was retailing stories about his debts and banking methods in Wisconsin; Morgenthau was demanding an affidavit attesting that he had disposed of his debts; and his failure to deal with these threats would provoke the White House. His job, his reputation, even his liberty were at stake.

Of his many problems Crowley found Glass easiest to handle. The senator had phoned in mid-December, warning that an FDIC regulation setting maximum interest rates for banks, even those that were not part of the Federal Reserve System, exceeded the corporation's authority. Glass may have been correct: Crowley agreed that the FDIC was "skating on thin ice"; however, he added, somewhat undiplomatically, that the statute creating the FDIC was "a fool law," that fixing rates was "in the interest of recovery," and that the power to set them was somehow implied.[1]

Glass, a strict constructionist, was not amused, and a more tactful Crowley wrote him that, although the FDIC's board adopted its regulations on interest before he became chairman, it did so unanimously after its general counsel advised that the power was implied. However, he soothed, the board would review its policy "in light of your comments." Then he added other gentling words, and sent flowers. The result: On December 23, Glass responded: "There is no friend on earth from whom I would prefer to receive a floral tribute in token of personal affection than from you. I am distressed beyond expression that you are to leave Washington. . . . God only knows what will happen to the Deposit Insurance Corporation. Wherever you may be you will have my Devotion and best wishes for your success and happiness."[2]

Five days later, Crowley journeyed to the senator's home in Lynchburg. He brought a memorandum arguing the FDIC's authority to set interest rates for nonmember banks it insured, but he did not emphasize it. What he really wanted and obtained was Glass's agreement to write the questioned authority into the new omnibus banking bill, and when he returned to Washington he dashed off a deferential note to the senator, assuring him that he was willing to "adjust our differences in a satisfactory manner." Then he publicly closed the deal, telling reporters the senator had convinced him that the FDIC was not authorized to regulate interest rates but was drafting an amendment to the omnibus banking bill that would enable it to do so. Thus, Crowley turned a threat to FDIC policy into a commitment to legislation embracing it. His solution was hardly miraculous—Glass's objection had been legalistic not substantive—but it reflects some of his strengths: he courted Glass before he needed him; he remained solicitous after Glass's power and the FDIC's need waned.[3]

Making friends, whether political allies or merely constituents, marked Crowley as surely as his devotion to his family, his church, and his official responsibilities. Fortunately, too. As the new year began, he desperately needed their support. At noon on January 2 Morgenthau instructed him to come to his office, and Crowley knew the reason. The secretary wanted to discuss his affidavit of December 31, 1934, swearing that "he had no liability, direct or indirect, to any State or National Bank," or equity in any business "whose activities would be incompatible with his duties as a public servant." What Crowley did not know was that Morgenthau had seen O'Connor's "record" of his banking activities and debts; that O'Connor had informed the secretary that morning of a letter from a cousin of Crowley's, calling him a "liar and a crook"; and that Morgenthau had decided that O'Connor and Crowley should confront each other directly. But Crowley soon found out these particulars.[4]

That afternoon the two men met in Morgenthau's office, along with Undersecretary Thomas Coolidge, General Counsel Herman Oliphant, Federal Reserve Chairman Marriner Eccles, and Morgenthau's secretary (who took verbatim notes). O'Connor spoke first. He minimized his part in Crowley's confirmation the previous February, explaining that he only learned later that the examiner was Crowley's man and his report false. O'Connor stressed Crowley's promise to rid himself of his debts, then displayed an examiner's report showing that Crowley owed $800,000, primarily to national banks, where it was "carried as losses with delinquent interest." When Crowley replied that his obligation was "indirect," O'Connor disputed his definition and insisted that he be forced to resign. Others present agreed and, as Morgenthau's secretary noted, Crowley "broke down and cried. He became quite hysterical."

When Crowley recovered, Morgenthau sent him and O'Connor out of the room, then "expressed doubts about Crowley's honesty." He argued that Crowley's sizable obligations, however defined, contradicted his affidavit. The others, however, "felt that Crowley was telling the truth," though they admitted that he "merely generalized" when answering questions. In the end, liking Crowley, they advised caution.[5]

That afternoon, Morgenthau spoke to Senator Vandenberg who, O'Connor said, had agreed to confirm Crowley even though he knew the examiner's report was false. Vandenberg insisted that "Crowley was not confirmed until O'Connor cleared him," then he asked what the secretary intended. Morgenthau answered "that O'Connor will have to substantiate his statements or . . . withdraw them"; he did not tell Vandenberg that he had told Coolidge to investigate O'Connor's charges.[6]

Morgenthau was greatly disturbed by what he heard January 2. He had known about Crowley's debts for three months but assumed that Crowley would deal with them. He liked the man and did not want to believe his doubts. But on January 4 he received a note from Postmaster General Farley, enclosing an "unsolicited report" from a Madison resident who claimed that, in 1933, he had been an examiner of failed banks for Wisconsin's Public Funds Guaranty Department and recalled Crowley's problems. The writer's motives were surely questionable—he admitted that Crowley had fired him—but several charges caught Morgenthau's attention. According to the report, in 1931 Crowley had borrowed $60,000 against his house from his own bank, though the house was fairly appraised at $32,850. Also, he had borrowed half again the assessed valuation of his General Paper Company's building from his bank. And now, the writer concluded, he had heard "threats of a John Doe investigation of his State Bank."[7]

Suddenly, Morgenthau saw that Crowley's problems might range beyond his debts and conflicts of interest to malfeasance. Thus, he was dissatisfied with Coolidge's report and Crowley's memorandum of January 7. The undersecretary endorsed O'Connor's charge that Crowley or his family's businesses owed almost $900,000, but he thought the matter should be dropped, asserting that Crowley's "affairs" were "entirely known" and "settled" before his confirmation. As for Crowley, he now admitted his debts, but said they were collateralized by property or life insurance. He added that Wisconsin Bankshares, his major creditor, had never asked a favor of the FDIC, that he had never interceded for it, and that "nothing has ever developed which indicates that I cannot act fairly and impartially in my official contacts with them." Perhaps, but Crowley's assurances, like Coolidge's, did not answer troublesome questions now preying on Morgenthau's mind: were Crowley's debts adequately collateralized? Was he guilty of malfeasance, as Farley's report from Wisconsin suggested? Morgenthau told Coolidge and Crowley to send him more "complete reports."[8]

Eight days later both turned in lengthier statements. Crowley simply padded his earlier report, but Coolidge documented his debts and activities at his State Bank. Crowley, his companies, and a sister owed $1,166,055.02, more than was previously known, all to Wisconsin Bankshares or its branches. There was more. In 1928 and after, Crowley had written large overdrafts on his bank, and when auditors were about to examine the books, he had covered them with signed notes. As Wisconsin law forbade bank officers' borrowing over a thousand dollars from their bank without meeting exacting requirements, the loans were made by the Four Lakes Investment Company, a "dummy" organization. Also, Crowley's sister had mortgaged the family's house and credited the proceeds to his account. And a brother had borrowed for him against property he was deeded by the General Paper Company, also violating state law. The litany continued. One Crowley company with a net worth of $14,147 owed Madison's First Wisconsin National Bank $59,000, but records of the State Bank showed a liability of $75,000. To Coolidge, this was another example of shortages which had been a factor prompting the RFC to pump millions into Bankshares. Page after page, Coolidge drew a damning picture of fraud.[9]

Oliphant read Coolidge's report, and the next day he advised Morgenthau that the facts there suggested violations of Wisconsin penal statutes, among them embezzlement, false entries, and loans to bank officers. He believed Wisconsin authorities could indict Crowley on seven counts.[10]

Oliphant's memorandum and Coolidge's report were devastating and should have forced Crowley's resignation and the handing over of evidence of his transgressions to Wisconsin authorities. But neither action followed. Why not is explicable if not palatable. Crowley had not broken any federal statutes, and the federal government was not legally obligated to hand its findings to Wisconsin officials. As for Crowley's debts, conflict of interest, and flawed affidavit, ethics competed with political sense and lost. Exposing Crowley would hurt the administration, most importantly the president and Morgenthau. It would also hurt Senator Robert LaFollette and Governor Philip LaFollette, whose new Progressive party in Wisconsin supported the New Deal and whose support the the president wanted in his reelection campaign. Then, too, it would catch the cooperative Senator Duffy; Senator Glass, who was critical to passage of the banking bill; and, surely, Vandenberg, a moderate conservative who could become actively hostile. Moreover, moving against Crowley would almost certainly impair public confidence in the FDIC and endanger the millions of depositors it insured. At last, Morgenthau, Coolidge, and Oliphant could justify their silence in terms of the public interest.

Possibly the same factors weighed on the president, but that assumes knowledge he may have lacked. McIntyre asked O'Connor on January 4 "if Crowley had his indebtedness straightened up." And Morgenthau told the president at lunch on January 14 that Crowley and O'Connor were hurling charges at each other and might go public. O'Connor had just told him that Crowley was embezzling FDIC funds and ignoring corruption in the corporation's purchasing department. Morgenthau apparently did not specify Crowley's answer or countercharges. Later, though, he recorded the president's advising him, "If they do [go public], I will ask both of them to resign." Morgenthau does not record informing the president that day of Crowley's debts and how he incurred them. Indeed, Morgenthau does not record advising the president of Crowley's problems earlier that winter or even after the damning reports of Coolidge and Oliphant in the next two days.[11]

By mid-January some members of the administration wanted to see Crowley resign quietly, and O'Connor was looking for evidence that would force him out; but Crowley's future, though bleak, was hardly hopeless. He evoked sympathy. On January 7 Oliphant sent Morgenthau a note, warmly pointing out that Crowley had a brother and several sisters in his house, and had "fathered them all. . . . " And there were other keys to Crowley's true character, "in his devoutness, evidenced by his substantial gifts to hospitals, and other Catholic charities, and that he goes to church every day on his way to work." Of course, Oliphant wrote these words before he saw Coolidge's second report, but he knew enough. Crowley impressed him as a good man who had once used bad judgment.[12]

Whether Crowley had one or more character witnesses, or none after Coolidge reported on the fifteenth and Oliphant on the sixteenth, the comptroller remained his enemy. But Crowley had some leverage in the administration's omnibus banking bill. The president wanted it; what the president wanted O'Connor wanted; and, somehow, Crowley had acquired influence on the Hill, especially with Glass whose support was so essential for the bill's passage. Temporarily, this fact may have sufficed to terminate O'Connor's crusade against Crowley, but O'Connor insisted that Crowley twice told him that after the bill passed he was "willing to resign." Thus, when Morgenthau phoned him on March 12, asking that he substantiate the charges he made in January, he replied that a complete report was in his desk drawer. But there was no point to using it; Crowley told him he would resign when the banking bill passed.[13]

Ten days later Morgenthau phoned O'Connor again. Now the secretary seemed more anxious than the comptroller to secure evidence that would force Crowley out, though apparently he was most interested in that bearing on Crowley's alleged transgressions as chairman of the FDIC. O'Connor responded much as before. He did not feel right about using his report needlessly. "If [Crowley] should fade out, do you think it's necessary to injury anybody." When Morgenthau became insistent, O'Connor suggested a week's delay, asserting that "the only danger of holding it is if somebody up there, like our friend from Louisiana [Democratic Senator Huey Long] or somebody . . . should make it embarrassing here."[14]

In fact, O'Connor had come to terms with Crowley and did not want to release his report so long as Crowley upheld his side of the agreement. The evening after Morgenthau's second phone call, the two men went to dinner, then to the Broadway musical *Roberta*, and later to O'Connor's office. There they put final touches on an agreement drafted between Morgenthau's first and second phone calls. O'Connor would not give Morgenthau his reports; Crowley would resign May 15 or after the banking bill was passed; meanwhile, he would cut back the FDIC's statistical division, which was run by Mortimer Fox, Morgenthau's nephew; and he would vote with O'Connor on several issues before the FDIC's board. It was politics. O'Connor did not ask much, Crowley did not give much, and nothing of his own. In any event, he could now focus on the administration's banking bill.[15]

There was little opposition to the bill in the House, where the administration's package was approved on May 1. The Senate, however, proved a battleground. Glass fought Title II, charging that it centralized and politicized the Federal Reserve System. His strategy focused on separating Title I, which contained the FDIC's widely supported permanent plan, from Federal Reserve Board Chairman Eccles's controversial program, and in April he apparently persuaded Crowley to tell the Senate Banking Committee that the administration's "original thought" was to have two bills. Surely Glass was pleased, but Crowley's testimony consisted primarily of assuring the Senate that the FDIC was doing its job and could do it more effectively if Congress adopted the revisions in Title I. And there was little or no disagreement with that.[16]

Crowley's involvement increased as summer approached. If the banking bill did not pass by the end of June the temporary fund would expire, and the faulty permanent plan of 1933 would become effective. Lacking revisions the FDIC wrote into the new bill, the FDIC's future and its protection for depositors would be imperiled. According to John M. Blum, Morgenthau's biographer, in June "Crowley began to demand the separation of Title I from Title II, precisely Glass's objective," as Glass knew that Title II could not survive alone. Blum implies that Crowley was trying to save Title I and help the senator kill administration efforts to alter the Federal Reserve System, but the few clues available argue to the contrary. Crowley was obligated to Glass for sponsoring the section of Title I that clarified the FDIC's authority to regulate interest rates on nonmember, insured banks, but he knew that he was responsible first and last to the president's program and for the successful operation of the FDIC. In April, when he told the Senate Banking Committee that the administration at first thought about two bills, he had quickly added, "The President told us to keep them together."

There is stronger evidence, however, of Crowley's true rule than brief clips from his testimony. Crowley had not been satisfied with Title I as passed by the House. Large banks complained that the assessment of one-eighth of one percent of their deposits was unnecessarily high and might withdraw from the FDIC; and, more worrisome to Crowley, many smaller banks might have to leave the FDIC because they could not meet the House version's capital requirements for Federal Reserve membership by 1937, a crippling date the Senate had not yet voted to postpone. Thus, decoupling Title I to make certain of its enactment would not help the FDIC. A partial answer was a sixty-day extension of the temporary fund, which would provide time to secure the desired changes in Title I and salvage as much as possible of the administration's Title II. And as June ended, Crowley, Morgenthau, and Eccles achieved that goal.[17]

When, on August 19, both houses accepted the Conference Committee's report, the Federal Reserve Board obtained the authority sought by Eccles and the administration, while Crowley obtained a modified Title I that met his and the FDIC's specifications. The assessment on deposits was reduced to one-twelfth of one percent, assuaging banks with large deposits; and smaller banks would not be forced to enter the Federal Reserve System until 1942, when it was thought they would have stronger capital positions and easily qualify for membership. Crowley was pleased and thanked Senator Glass for his part in securing authority for the FDIC to control rates on time deposits. As for Glass, he had succeeded in modifying Title II and was credited with the bill's passage. Consequently, he gladly joined Crowley, Eccles, and others responsible for its success when the president signed it on August 23.[18]

With the FDIC firmly grounded, Crowley considered resigning. Perhaps it was the promise O'Connor had told Morgenthau about in March, but rumor had it that Crowley had received several corporate offers, one at four times his government salary. Queried by reporters on September 13, he carefully replied that he could not "afford" to stay in Washington indefinitely, but the report that he would soon head the Minneapolis-based Northwest Bancorporation was "unfair to the present management." Clearly, both statements were true, the latter by definition, the former because Crowley's $10,000 FDIC salary, even coupled with the $10,000 salary that he retained as president of his paper company in Madison and, possibly some dividends, amply covered his living expenses, but hardly touched his still-huge indebtedness. A larger salary would help, and Crowley thought seriously about private business offers; but he decided to speak with the Treasury secretary and the president before taking one. As Morgenthau was abroad, Crowley cabled that he would "try to defer any drastic move" until until he returned. Meanwhile, he would discuss the matter with the White House.[19]

The president prevailed on Crowley to reconsider. Losing an administrator was not the problem; losing Crowley's substantial political charms was. Crowley's connections were strongest where the president and New Deal were weakest, in the midwest with businessmen and bankers, on the Hill with conservatives such as Vandenberg and Glass. Many years later, Thomas Corcoran, New Dealer turned lobbyist, and the only New Dealer to attend Crowley's funeral, would speak glowingly of their friendship and of Crowley's influence. He recalled that early in 1934 the president told him to search out Crowley before testifying on securities regulation. Though he had been at the RFC for two years, and Crowley had just come to Washington, Roosevelt had suggested that Crowley could do much to smooth his trips to the Hill.[20]

Except for their Irish-Catholic heritage, Corcoran and Crowley could not have differed more sharply in background and in appeal. Corcoran was a product of the Ivy League and a Wall Street law firm, and he easily charmed Washington's elite; but his background and brashness tended to irritate if not frighten congressmen of earthier origins. By contrast, Crowley disdained Capital parties, he could not draft legislation, and he had just assumed his job, but he knew and liked the men on the Hill—and they him. He had already forged strong personal bonds with Senators Vandenberg, LaFollette, Duffy, and Glass; several midwestern congressmen he had worked with when FCA general agent in St. Paul; and Wisconsin congressman Michael Reilly, his informant on the House Banking Committee. But Crowley's influence ranged farther. Congressmen from the nation's heartland saw him as a solid businessman and banker, who spoke their language, who readily empathized with their problems, and who would do whatever he pledged. Crowley was a kindred spirit and, for that reason as well as his much-admired supervision of the FDIC, extremely influential on Capitol Hill.[21]

Roosevelt, the consummate politician, agreed, but he valued

Crowley's presence for other reasons. The summer of 1935 saw the passage of "radical" legislation that alienated many businessmen. Now, in September, their fears of the New Deal grew, as Joseph P. Kennedy, the maverick millionaire chairman of the Securities and Exchange Commission, resigned. If Crowley, who had secured their confidence by obtaining a reduction in bank deposit assessments that summer, also left, their fears would be confirmed. Bankers already chary with loans would lock their vaults, the struggling economy would suffer, and the New Deal and the president with it. This much the *Milwaukee Journal* stressed. It failed to mention another consideration, that Kennedy's departure, if followed by Crowley's, would leave the administration but one other prominent Catholic administrator: Postmaster General Farley. This Roosevelt could hardly afford with an election barely a year away, and he pressed Crowley to reconsider.[22]

Crowley dithered. In mid-October he reminded Morgenthau of his promise the previous March to "resign at his pleasure," then said he wanted to give Morgenthau "plenty of time to find a successor." Meanwhile, he hoped Morgenthau would not speak to the president about his promise the previous spring. Crowley seemed to be telling Morgenthau that he was reconsidering, and that the secretary would be wise to let the matter drop. Morgenthau did. He probably saw a battle to force Crowley out as futile. By the next spring, however, with the 1936 elections six months off, he would wish that he had tried.[23]

On May 1, Morgenthau received a note from Senator Burton K. Wheeler, enclosing carbons of letters he had written O'Connor and Jesse Jones. The Montana Democrat reported hearing "ugly rumors" about Crowley while in St. Paul: that he was "heavily involved" with some Wisconsin banks which the RFC was bailing out, and that this might account for their control over his appointments in the FDIC. Wheeler warned that the tales might spread during the campaign. In any event, he wanted to know if they were true, and he threatened a Senate investigation if the administration did not respond voluntarily and quickly.[24]

Worried, Morgenthau responded graciously but noncommittally, then he wrote O'Connor that he had not sent the report on Crowley they had discussed in March the year before. He advised him to either substantiate or withdraw the charges of corruption he then made against Crowley.[25]

Answering, O'Connor offered a letter as well as a memorandum affirming that Crowley's personal debt had been reduced to a bare $8,795, and that of the Crowley family's company to only $57,781. How this miracle was accomplished O'Connor made little effort to explain. He wrote that "Crowley and his interests" had owed Milwaukee's First National Bank $400,000, but that the bank "charged off" $157,000. As for the $600,000 owed Madison's First National Bank, Wisconsin Bankshares assumed it. O'Connor further reported that Wisconsin Bankshares had borrowed $4.5 million from the RFC, and he pointed out that the other banks involved with Crowley had sold preferred stock to the RFC, but he did not indicate the significance of these transactions, and their connection, if any, to the apparent disappearance of so much of Crowley's indebtedness. Finally, O'Connor did not include the "report" Morgenthau wanted. He reminded the secretary that the year before they had agreed to bury it because Crowley had promised to resign, but O'Connor left no doubt that, though Crowley had renigged, he wanted the report left unopened.[26]

Morgenthau could not believe he had said what O'Connor wrote in his letter. Boiling, he called the comptroller to his office. But to no purpose. O'Connor brought his diary, which he believed corroborated his version of Morgenthau's words on March 22, 1935. And effectively it did: he had told Morgenthau that the "report" was "bad," and the secretary had not made him produce it. By his silence, Morgenthau had agreed that it should not be opened, that Crowley should be permitted to resign quietly, without embarrassing him or, for that matter, others involved.[27]

Morgenthau was not pleased with O'Connor's explanation, and, as O'Connor saw, he remained extremely agitated. But it was only after the comptroller left that he thought through the situation. Crowley had renigged on his promise to resign; despite O'Connor's memorandum, Morgenthau believed Crowley still owed three-quarters of a million dollars, and he questioned the manner in which Crowley relieved himself of even a portion of his debts. What influence might he have employed at the RFC? What favors had he given bankers "in the know," as Wheeler had heard in St. Paul? Morgenthau decided to touch base with the White House.[28]

The secretary phoned McIntyre just as the president's secretary was about to call him. It was no coincidence. O'Connor had just warned the White House of Wheeler's threatened investigation and

blamed Morgenthau, saying that he had not acted against Crowley because his nephew was employed by the FDIC at a liberal salary. Possibly reflecting that warning, McIntyre told Morgenthau the president
wanted to see him, Jesse Jones, and the comptroller the next morning,
the last with his "report."[29]

Early the next morning, May 6, Crowley phoned Morgenthau to
say that he had heard about the meeting at the White House that day
and was upset because he had not been invited and could not rebut the
accusations O'Connor was certain to make. Crowley did not specify
them, but Morgenthau thought he knew what was worrying the FDIC
chairman—that morning he had received a Treasury memorandum
discussing Crowley's six appointees from Wisconsin and suggesting
that he review their salaries and prior associations with Crowley before
going to the White House. But Morgenthau did not reveal this to
Crowley; he only confirmed that the president did not want to see him
that morning, then hung up. Jesse Jones wanted to take the tunnel to
the White House with him.[30]

Morgenthau and Jones found that the president did not want a full
recital of the various reports that day. He told Morgenthau to organize
a committee to study the facts, determine their legal implications, and
tell him what should be done.[31]

That did not please O'Connor. Later that day and in days to come,
he heard from a friend at the Treasury that "many criminal irregulari-
ties" appeared in Crowley's record. He also heard that Jones was defending Crowley and had talked to Wheeler, "trying to have him pull
off," that Jones did not believe Crowley's actions, "even if criminal,
should be investigated," or that the Treasury committee should report
in writing, and that he had won McIntyre to his way of thinking.[32]

Some of this information came, somewhat strangely, from Morgenthau. When O'Connor told him that he would demand a written
report, Morgenthau at first implied that it was unlikely. He had gone to
the White House again and heard Senator Glass "protesting against
the outrageous behavior of O'Connor and [saying] what a fine fellow
Crowley is and that this thing has to stop." It also seemed that the
president was not ready to force Crowley's resignation without more
facts. Morgenthau reported that when "Bert Wheeler said to the President: 'When are you going to get rid of that crook, Crowley?' the President said: 'Better go slow, Bert, in calling people names.' " On the

other hand, Morgenthau added, McIntyre had told him the president wanted the Treasury's report on his desk Tuesday morning, May 11, and he had agreed.[33]

But the secretary had second thoughts after speaking to his general counsel. When Morgenthau told Oliphant on Monday that a written report was necessary "to keep myself clear," his counsel warned that the secretary would be legally protected only if the report's distribution was limited and Crowley was given a chance to answer it. That prompted Morgenthau to postpone finishing his report. Worried about his own position, he phoned O'Connor, asking again for the report O'Connor had allegedly held since March 1935. The comptroller answered that he had nothing that required action against Crowley. O'Connor, too, was cautious.[34]

Once again, Morgenthau went to the White House, at first for a session with Jones and McIntyre. He found that both men wanted to quash the proceedings. Though acknowledging that Crowley had "violated many criminal statutes" and made an "awful mess," they thought he was no longer liable: the statute of limitations had run out. Morgenthau replied that the matter was "too serious" to be dropped just because of legal technicalities: Crowley should not keep his FDIC chairmanship unless he could disprove embezzlement and fraud at the State Bank. Perhaps, but Morgenthau would have argued more strongly had he been aware that only the federal statute of limitations had run out while Wisconsin's remained in force. Even so, the president, who had just arrived, instructed Morgenthau to tell Crowley he must resign as FDIC chairman, as of June 30, but "with a promise that if he wants a job he can have it."[35]

Morgenthau made an appointment to speak with Crowley May 21. That very morning, however, he conferred with the committee the president had asked him to form. Staff counsel then informed him that Wisconsin's statute of limitations remained live, and they thought the case against Crowley should be given to the attorney general. He could decide whether it should be given to Wisconsin authorities. Morgenthau was upset; he had misled the president. Now he would have to speak to him before he spoke to Crowley.[36]

The next day Morgenthau advised the president of what he had just learned. He found that the president did not care for turning Crowley's case over to the attorney general. "That is very, very unfair," he told Morgenthau. "It puts him on the spot." The president may have been right, but he had few if any qualms about putting Morgenthau on the spot, telling him to ask Crowley if the Wisconsin authorities had cleared him. If he said they had, Morgenthau was to tell him that either he must provide "some documentary evidence" or Morgenthau would have to have a "verbal conversation with the District Attorney of the State of Wisconsin." The president did not tell Morgenthau what he should do about Crowley if he were not cleared by either means, and the secretary saw problems for himself. Hoping to get off the spot, he told the president that the examiner who in February 1934 had cleared Crowley's record was now an FDIC supervisor handling the Ann Arbor, Michigan, reorganization, which gossip said, was not "straight." But Roosevelt was unrelenting. Tackling Crowley was Morgenthau's job.[37]

For a month Morgenthau tried to avoid a direct confrontation with Crowley. In mid-June his administrative assistant, William McReynolds, phoned Crowley. Where were his answers to the president's demand for evidence that Wisconsin authorities had cleared him? Crowley first sputtered that he had been too busy preparing a speech, then spoke of references to his transactions in Madison "as a sort of blackmail proposition." He insisted that they were handled properly, were personal, and were "entirely irrelevant to my position here in Washington." He did not say who was creating problems for him. Possibly he meant presidential press secretary Stephen T. Early, who, he said later, "set this thing in. . . . " It is more likely that he meant O'Connor, who had hunted him for two years, gathering reports, spreading gossip, explaining to one and all that Crowley had "betrayed" a "voluntary" patronage agreement with him during his confirmation battle. But Crowley did not explore O'Connor's rumormongering with McReynolds. He said that he would not answer the charges spelled out in Morgenthau's report: "It's a matter of my own personal life." Of course, he added, "I don't want to cause any trouble . . . for the President," but if no one was "pressing this thing," he hoped it would "blow over."[38]

No one was pressing. When Morgenthau finally called Crowley to his office July 2, he advised him that "many of the statements contained in the report and represented as facts looked bad," but he did not tell Crowley he must resign. Further, Morgenthau specifically denied responsibility for the report. Then, when Crowley asked him if he should resign, Morgenthau weakly said yes, he thought so. Crowley's work at the FDIC was "eminently satisfactory," but "so many bankers and others, particularly in the Chicago district," knew about his banking problems as to invite "a great danger of criticism against the President for holding him." Even so, if Crowley decided not to resign, the secretary said, he "did not propose to do anything further about the matter." It was the president's responsibility; Crowley should discuss the situation with him directly.[39]

With that, Crowley ended the meeting, advising the secretary that he would "go home and think the matter over and then decide what to do." He could not at the moment; he was too shaken; indeed, if Morgenthau's secretary's observations are fair, "hysterical." As for her boss, he had spoken quietly, with consideration, and "showed no feeling of agitation during the discussion." In fact, Morgenthau was seething but, by choice or presidential order, unable to act.[40]

And so Crowley recovered from a second deadly threat to his federal career. Wheeler, whose threat had resurrected his transgressions at the State Bank, did not launch an investigation. He told Morgenthau in December that "some people suggested to me not to take the matter up until the election anyway." He had agreed, he said, because Crowley announced that he would resign after the election. Now, ignoring his own threat in May to investigate and his ability do so when Congress reconvened, Wheeler asked Morgenthau: "What are you going to do about that bird? Are you going to keep him there?" The question was almost rhetorical. If the president had wanted Crowley's resignation, or had members of his administration—most notably Morgenthau—demanded action, Crowley would have been forced out. Both men knew it. And any number of senators—Vandenberg, LaFollette, and Glass, as well as Wheeler—might have spread the story in the press, forcing the president's hand. But all had balked at the last, killing move.[41]

They had refrained for various reasons. Some, like Oliphant in the Treasury, could not credit the reports they saw. They saw and preferred the warm, engaging, and devoutly moral Crowley they knew. As for O'Connor, whose desire for power and fear of losing it had spawned the Treasury's investigation two years earlier, he was so compromised from his part in Crowley's confirmation battle that he could only hope, as he so often told Morgenthau, that the chairman of the FDIC would leave quietly. Then, there was Jones, defending Crowley and "so much interested," as O'Connor reported, "in quashing all the proceedings."

Understandably, believed one senator: his RFC had bailed out several Wisconsin banks to which Crowley was indebted.

No administrator except possibly the president was more compromised than Morgenthau. He had promoted Crowley; he had asked him to give his nephew a job with the FCA in St. Paul, then name him the FDIC's chief statistician; and he may not have warned the president of the Treasury's harsh reports in January 1935. But even had Morgenthau been less involved, he could not pursue Crowley against the president's wishes. He could only resign himself to damning Crowley among close subordinates and hoping the president would, one day, see the light and fire him.

By 1936, and perhaps earlier, Roosevelt saw as well as Morgenthau the case against Crowley and the administration's moral obligation to give its evidence to Wisconsin authorities or fire Crowley. But there were grave political and economic dangers in doing so, for him and perhaps the country. If the president ever considered giving the Treasury's report to Wisconsin authorities, by May 1936 it was too late. Soon the American people would go to the polls, and their knowledge that the administration covered up the Treasury's reports for more than a year could cripple the president's prospects for reelection. This he dared not chance. Neither did he dare it after the election; it would cripple his second term.

Probably there never was a "right time" for the president to hand the Treasury's reports to Wisconsin authorities. The impact on those in Washington who had connived at Crowley's confirmation aside, the President's political support, that of Phil LaFollette and the Progressives, and that of the New Deal in Wisconsin would have been shattered. Most people would conclude that LaFollette must have known about Crowley's methods at the State Bank when he named him chairman of Wisconsin's Banking Review Board. Further, his brother, Bob, supportive of the New Deal in the Senate, would be implicated. Finally, there was grave danger to the country in indicting Crowley. It could shatter confidence in the FDIC, the deposits it protected, and the economy. On that basis alone, the president might have decided that withholding the Treasury's evidence was the lesser evil.

The president might have asked Crowley to resign quietly, no more. But would Crowley have done so? He had said that he would not cause trouble for the president, but reporters would question him, and Morgenthau's secretary had twice seen him become hysterical under pressure. Who could tell what he might do if asked to resign? On the other hand, Crowley was a valuable asset, and his FDIC chairmanship the least of it. Beyond his friendships on the Hill, his influence among Democrats and independents in Wisconsin and Minnesota would help decide whether the president won or lost those states in 1936. And Roosevelt knew it. He had recognized it for some time, but never more so than in 1934, when Crowley's insights revealed his knowledge of three-party Wisconsin's labyrinthine politics.

5

Banking and Politics

In 1936, Franklin Roosevelt needed more than a personal victory. To solidify the New Deal, he needed a triumph large enough to preserve and even extend his coalition in Congress. Crowley's critical assignment as November's elections neared was to tighten the support of a new bloc of Wisconsin Progressives and Minnesota Farmer-Laborites to the president and the New Deal without losing many unhappy, old-line Democrats there in the process. Capturing those states was important; establishing a model for progressives elsewhere in the country was no less so.[1]

The president had recognized Crowley's skills in 1934, if in a somewhat unusual manner. In June, Crowley had learned that the president wanted Wisconsin to reelect Senator Robert LaFollette, even though he would run on the new Progressive party ticket. He had even urged the state's Democrats to slate him. Crowley found the president's wishes to that point unpleasant but acceptable—the senator was unbeatable as well as cooperative—what he feared was the impact on Schmedeman and other Democratic candidates of a presidential endorsement of the Progressive senator in Green Bay in August. He decided to warn him and suggest alternatives. Because Roosevelt was vacationing on the cruiser *Houston* "somewhere in the Pacific," on July 20 he sent the White House a long memorandum for forwarding. In so doing, he revealed much of himself.[2]

The first section of Crowley's memorandum—a letter—began with "deference to your surpassing astuteness," and ended in much the same obsequious manner. His mother had bred him to reverence authority, but he was also a novice in Washington; given time, he would address Roosevelt confidently and soberly; and still later, he would challenge Roosevelt's successor as his equal, if not his inferior.

What a colleague one day would say of Henry Kissinger fit Crowley, also bred in an authoritarian background—"obsequious to his superiors" and "devious with his peers," as Roosevelt, Morgenthau, and O'Connor knew; and, as others would say in later years, "domineering with [at least some of] his subordinates."[3]

Once past his deferential introductory words, Crowley boldly described the situation in Wisconsin. He placed Democratic prospects that fall at 60 percent if Roosevelt did not endorse Senator LaFollette at Green Bay. And he hoped he would not, because "any gesture of approval" would be viewed by Wisconsin voters as endorsing Philip LaFollette's newly formed Progressive party and, also, help him win back the State House from Governor Schmedeman. Moreover, it was unnecessary for the president to praise Senator LaFollette to ensure his reelection. Crowley pointed out that in 1928 when LaFollette was ill, he had secured the withdrawal of "real Democratic opposition." He could do that again now. Then the president could inform "Bob" and take the credit. That way, Crowley concluded, "you could accomplish your desires and enable us to keep the Party intact in this campaign and also in 1936."[4]

Crowley left no doubt about his feelings. For him, the battle between Schmedeman and Philip LaFollette was central and both personal and political. Even from Washington he was Schmedeman's friend and mentor, and he lengthily explained the governor's many achievements and their consistency with the president's program. He expended more passion, however, denouncing Philip LaFollette. He seems to have decided that the president was more likely to be moved by fear of Philip's influence if governor in 1936 than by a concern for Schmedeman and Wisconsin's Democratic party.

Venom fueled Crowley's words as he warned the president that Philip LaFollette was selfish, domineering, a man of "overweening ambition," whose goal was nothing less than a new national party. That spring he had forced "Bob" and other progressive Republicans into his Progressive party and, though he spoke of supporting the New Deal, he was condemning Agriculture Secretary Henry Wallace's farm program "as morally and economically wrong," and instructing Progressives in the House to sponsor radical proposals that would embarrass the administration. Philip wanted to be governor again to secure a base from which to snipe at the New Deal and create a new national party strong enough to offer its nomination and program to the president in 1936.

Crowley did not limit himself to Philip LaFollette's threat; he knew he had to broaden the political problem and make positive suggestions. He hoped Roosevelt would bypass Green Bay and so advised. If he did, Crowley insisted, the Democrats would win and absorb the Progressives. If, however, the president felt he must endorse Senator LaFollette, he should "also endorse the Congressmen who supported him 100 per cent, and the state administration that followed his lead." Then some Democrats might survive. He noted, however, that any mention of Senator LaFollette meant certain defeat for most Democrats, and he pleaded with the president to inform them if that were his intention, so they could withdraw quietly, gracefully.

Crowley's analysis was trenchant and prophetic. It was also biased. He did not tell the president that Schmedeman's rhetoric was angling to the right or that Philip LaFollette's campaign reflected many real grievances. Of course, it is not clear whether the president read the twenty-page message. Upon his return from the Pacific, Roosevelt traveled first to Minneapolis where, publicly, he was flanked by Governor Floyd Olson and Senator Henrik Shipstead, both Farmer-Laborites. No Democrat was near. It was another story, though, when he spoke in Green Bay on August 9.[5]

Roosevelt did not ignore Senator LaFollette; he had said too much to the press in June for that. But he expressed his "gratitude" for the cooperation of Senator Duffy and Senator LaFollette in the same breath, labeling both "old friends of mine." More to the point, from Crowley's point of view, he then praised Governor Schmedeman, "another old friend of mine, for his cooperation with the national administration." Seemingly, Crowley was pleased; a few days later he congratulated Schmedeman on the "good publicity on the President's visit" and insisted that the governor must "take advantage of his endorsement." And at least one journalist agreed that the president had boosted Schmmedeman's prospects and handed Philip LaFollette "a slap on the wrist."[6]

Unhappily for the governor, it was not enough. Crowley had mentioned in his summary of July 20 that Schmedeman "had done an outstanding job under existing circumstances." Unfortunately the "circumstances" had involved necessary budget reductions and the chaotic milk strike. And Schmedeman's handling of the strike had bought him the wrath of William Rubin, the farmer's counsel. Now challenging Schmedeman in the Democratic primary, Rubin condemned the governor as a "reactionary" and "mouthpiece for Leo Crowley." Yet Schmedeman might have won but for failing health, the result of an accident which, by late September, required the amputation of a leg.[7]

During the summer Crowley had noticed that his friend looked "very, very badly." Only in mid-September, though, did he learn from a "confidential source" that the governor was seriously ill. Quickly, he wrote to Schmedeman's wife, expressing regret that he had come to Washington because he and the governor had previously divided the work in Madison. Sincerely and deeply compassionate, he advised her to make her husband rest and allow "those who perhaps have been critical . . . assume responsibility for the party." When Schmedeman could not speak to the Democratic convention, the Republicans argued that he was dying, and the president suggested that Crowley himself take his place, but Crowley wrote Schmedeman that everyone was ready to "assist you." He had lunched with the Uihleins, their financial angels since 1928, and they "will give you any further aid that you may need." He was optimistic, Crowley then assured the governor, and he wrote reassuringly again in early October when doctors finally amputated his friend's injured leg. He told Schmedeman he would get the sympathy vote, but not to worry. Should he lose, "between all of us fellows we can certainly find a connection for you somewhere."[8]

Schmedeman did lose—to Philip LaFollette—by a slim margin, while Senator LaFollette won by a landslide, and Progressives obtained two Democratic and two Republican House seats. Schmedeman was but one victim, however, of a sweeping liberal, even radical, tide that fall. Minnesota's Governor Floyd Olson and his Farmer-Labor party gained strength; so did labor-supported liberal Democrats from Pennsylvania south and west across the country. For a traditional Democrat like Crowley, this victory of the "left" was hardly an unmitigated blessing. That spring, he had told a crowd celebrating his birthday in Milton Junction that he believed government should help people to save their homes and farms and find jobs, "but after that we'll have to pull ourselves out individually." Now, he dreaded the emergence of a labor-dominated, radicalized, second New Deal powered by the very forces he warned the president about in July. But

Crowley buried his fears. He knew that the president now recognized that it was essential to manage the forces on his left, and not least those of Philip LaFollette in Wisconsin and those of Floyd Olson in Minnesota. And he knew that the president needed his political savvy—and his mastery in the upper midwest—as never before.[9]

Looking toward 1936, Roosevelt was soon seeking the support of Governors LaFollette and Olson and their parties. In 1932, he had captured Wisconsin and Minnesota only with their help, and he would need it again. Moreover, endorsements by both men, as well as Senators LaFollette, Shipstead, and Ernest Lundeen would aid him with many farmers and workers, intellectuals and independents throughout the country. Finally, it would lessen the danger from a third party unifying the followers of such panacea-peddlers and critics as Louisiana Senator Huey Long, Father Charles Coughlin, and Dr. Francis Townsend. But it was one thing to seek alliances with Wisconsin's Progressives and Minnesota's Farmer-Laborites, it was another thing to secure them. To transform possibilities into realities, Roosevelt needed Crowley. Obviously, Crowley was familiar with the labrinythine channels of power in Wisconsin and trusted by Progressive and Democratic leaders; less obviously, he had acquired a somewhat similar familiarity and influence in Minnesota, apparently during his tenure with the Farm Credit Administration in St. Paul. As in Wisconsin, he had developed friendships with essentially conservative federal administrators, bankers, and Democrats, but he had also struck up a relationship with Minnesota's radical Farmer-Labor Governor Olson so close that, in August 1935, Olson would advise federal relief administrator and Roosevelt intimate Harry Hopkins to inform the president "that he has regard for Crowley and he thinks the Democratic Party should use him in dealing with those Middle Western States."[10]

The president was already using Crowley's reports and advice regarding both Minnesota and Wisconsin. In June 1935, he named former Governor Schmedeman federal housing administrator for Wisconsin on Crowley's recommendation; he asked Crowley's views on a Minnesota banker proposed for the Federal Reserve Board and other political appointments; and he even sought his advice on pardons. Crowley seemed to be the primary federal patronage dispenser for Wisconsin and Minnesota.[11]

Indicative of Crowley's new role as the president's agent in the upper midwest is a memorandum he sent back while on a weekend scouting trip there. No longer was he defending Wisconsin's Democrats or damning Philip LaFollette and the Progressives; coolly, he advised the president that Governor LaFollette was in "quite a strong position" despite legislative setbacks at the hands of Republicans and "reactionary" Democrats. Further, he had spoken with LaFollette at length, and the governor "had promised very definitely that he would go along in 1936 and take an active part in support of the President." They had "discussed the possibility of organizing a Roosevelt Progressive Club in the State." Crowley told the president he advised waiting a year to create one. Nothing should be done that might further alienate Democratic leaders already upset about critical federal appointments given Progressives, at least not until "it is definitely shown that the LaFollettes were going along."[12]

Obviously, Crowley was still wary of the LaFollettes, Philip in particular; but the White House took his caveat less seriously than the advantages he laid out. Presidential Secretary McIntyre reviewed the memorandum, urged the president "to read it," and a few days later Roosevelt hosted both LaFollettes at his Hyde Park home. According to the press, they had come to discuss the "Wisconsin relief situation." Naturally, Wisconsin Democrats thought otherwise and quickly phoned for a conference with the president. Put off, they turned to Crowley, who told McIntyre that the president must see them. Tokens would do: ten minutes each with the president in the Oval Office for the state chairman and national committeeman. Thus honored, they would return to Wisconsin with word that the president himself had blessed their organization.[13]

Crowley's single goal now was the president's reelection in 1936, emphasizing Wisconsin. If the LaFollettes demanded a weak, anti-New Deal Democratic ticket, leaving liberal Democrats little option but supporting the Progressives, he dealt with it. When the White House was not certain whom the president should see, he left no doubt. In May 1936, when McIntyre wired him in Madison that W. B. Rubin was "requesting appointment behalf liberal Democrats, Wisconsin. Any suggestions?" Crowley shot back: "Under no circumstances. . . . He will only cause trouble out there in the setup." Even if Duffy urged it, there must be no appointment, as Rubin wanted to put the president "on the spot." Otherwise, "the situation will take care of itself and is working out all right." Accordingly, McIntyre put Rubin off."[14]

Stopping egocentric gadflies like Rubin was only one of many delicate problems Crowley handled that election year. August saw him advising the president on the stops he should make during his "non-political" swing to survey the drought in the upper midwest, talking with Governor LaFollette about the wisdom of meeting with the president alone, and warning that Democratic leaders believed their meeting would invite serious defections to Alf Landon, the Republican presidential candidate.[15]

Throughout 1936, Crowley attended to the logical but fragile alliance that bound Wisconsin's Progressives and Minnesota's Farmer-Laborites to the president. He realized, as Progressives and Farmer-Laborites did, that they could win few congressional races or state races against a Republican and a strong Democrat boosted by the president's coattails. But with the possible exception of a solidly urban, ethnic district, Democrats could not win without the independent, usually rural voters from which the Progressives and Farmer-Laborites drew so heavily. Divided, Republicans would conquer, threatening the New Deal. Crowley's task was to prevent this, to prod Progressives, Farmer-Laborites, and Democrats into cooperating, trading off districts and endorsing the president's policies. Roosevelt had told reporters in 1934 that "the party label does not mean so very much," that "I am trying to get the right kind of people." He meant it in 1936, too, and probably with greater emphasis. Personally, Crowley could not have been pleased with the president's tactics. They involved sacrificing Democratic candidates, and this in order to strengthen a "Presidential Party" that would preserve if not strengthen a New Deal Crowley felt had gone too far already. But whether from loyalty, hopes for an even better future in Washington, or fears that his earlier banking practices might come to light, Crowley worked on forging the alliances the president was seeking in 1936.[16]

Roosevelt's emphasis on strengthening a "Presidential Party" extended beyond Wisconsin and Minnesota to the building of a national coalition. And Crowley was closely involved. On September 8, he informed the White House that he had spoken with the LaFollettes. They would meet with Minnesota Farmer-Laborites and progressive-minded independents from other midwestern states in Chicago on September 11 to endorse the president. Possibly Crowley reported soon after that the Chicago conference launched a Progressive National Committee to be chaired by Senator LaFollette; that Labor's Non-Partisan League had associated itself; and that together they formed an umbrella under which John L. Lewis of the newborn Committee for Industrial Organization, and labor's other allies, could cooperate in the campaign for the president and his policies. But Crowley was primarily concerned with executing the strategy necessary for the president and his allies to carry Wisconsin and Minnesota that fall.[17]

By September, Crowley had Wisconsin well in hand. One Progressive congressman, who had castigated the New Deal in 1935 as "charity capitalism," was now calling it a "net gain" and running without major Democratic opposition. And elsewhere in the state, the LaFollettes and Broughton were rounding out other trade-offs that aided Progressive congressional candidates and the president alike. Crowley had more difficulties in Minnesota, despite major assets. Some leading Democrats had developed a working relationship with Governor Olson some years before, and he had associated himself with the President in 1932—"Me and Frank," he had told voters. But two problems developed in the first half of 1936: a Farmer-Labor faction, led by Senate candidate Ernest Lundeen, began a dalliance with William Lemke's Union party; worse, Crowley learned on February 29 that Olson was dying of cancer. He could do nothing about either, however; he could only advise the White House that key appointments in Minnesota should be delayed until the situation there cleared.[18]

Fortunately for Roosevelt, Governor Olson's death created a vacuum that the Farmer-Labor party could fill only by supporting his campaign. By October 1, Crowley, representing the president, had arranged for the Democratic candidates for the United States Senate and for governor to stand aside in favor of their Farmer-Labor opponents, and soon Elmer Benson, the Farmer-Labor candidate for governor, was speaking of "our new deal." So were other Farmer-Labor leaders, resulting, as in the Iron Range surrounding Duluth, that the Democratic candidate for the United States House dropped out and endorsed Farmer-Laborite Johnny Bernard.[19]

Crowley did his work well in Minnesota as in Wisconsin. In November, both states gave Roosevelt their electoral votes. This in itself was not exceptional—only Vermont and Maine went Republican that year—but Roosevelt's popular vote percentages in Minnesota and Wisconsin exceeded his national average, itself skewed skyward by the heavily Democratic South. But even those numbers do not adequately measure Crowley's contribution. Although Roosevelt carried forty-six states, his popularity in rural areas had ebbed. Surely some of that vote which he did retain in Minnesota and Wisconsin owed more than a little directly to the lingering tradition and continuing organizational strength of Farmer-Laborites and Progressives and indirectly to Crowley's superb management of their alliances with the president and co-ordination with local Democrats. He had harnessed the energies of rival politicians to the president's wagon. Roosevelt's triumph was his as well.[20]

Crowley appears to have told the president immediately after that he wanted to leave Washington. He had told a friend in June that he would leave "sometime in the late fall"; he had discussed it with Morgenthau in early July; it was rumored now that he had solid offers from business; and the FDIC was in good shape. But he did not leave. Why cannot be documented. Probably, the president persuaded him to stay on. And with good reason. Campaigning and governing are twins in a symbiotic, never-ending game, and few knew this better or were more expert at it than Roosevelt and Crowley. The president knew there would be a continuing need for Crowley's political talents. He knew, too, that Crowley had gained the confidence of many bankers and state bank supervisors, businessmen, and politicians. Consequently, he must have stroked Crowley's ego, insisting that he needed his administrative skills at the Federal Deposit Insurance Corporation and his feel for the labyrinthine politics of Minnesota and Wisconsin. At least nothing more was heard about a successor at the FDIC.[21]

In almost three years at the corporation's helm, Crowley had compiled an impressive record. Few banks had failed since it was created, and even then there were no runs; depositors had waited quietly, knowing they would be paid promptly. Of course, fortune had aided Crowley's efforts. Most truly insolvent banks remained closed in the wake of the 1933 Banking Holiday; and the RFC and a slowly improving economy had bolstered most others. But Crowley had done his part, too. He had worked with the RFC's Jesse Jones and with bankers everywhere to recapitalize weak banks; he had secured stringent conditions for FDIC membership; and he was then working with the Federal Reserve and Treasury to toughen examinations for FDIC membership. Perhaps he was too tough. Arguably, constantly warning bankers against too liberal loan policies was unnecessary and undesirable; badly burned bankers already looked closely at new loans when more credit might have boosted a slowly growing economy. But managing the economy was not Crowley's job; guaranteeing bank deposits and safeguarding the FDIC's integrity was. In this he won the highest marks from bankers, state supervisors, politicians and, where he and the FDIC noticeably aborted bank runs, the public. Ironically, though, for one who made his way politically among Progressives and Farmer-Laborites, he found his loudest cheerleaders among primarily conservative bankers and politicians.[22]

Of course, good fortune favored Crowley's staffing. Lacking jobs in the private sector and sensing opportunity in Washington, more bright, motivated, and superbly educated young men and women came to the FDIC than otherwise would have been the case. Morrison G. Tucker, an Ivy Leaguer and friend of Rockefellers, had not gone to Wall Street, then under fire, but to the RFC and then the FDIC. For him and others, public service in a young and flexible agency prompted exchanges with such economic experts as Professor Jacob Viner of the University of Chicago; other sharp discussions of theory and practice with their boss; and a bonding common with mutual respect. By late 1936 they had emerged as a trusted team on which Crowley could depend then and later when war came.[23]

Crowley's good fortune was also Roosevelt's. With a skilled staff at the FDIC, he was largely free to help the president deal with the shattering of the New Deal coalition early in his second term. In 1937 and 1938 most conservative and some moderate Democrats joined Republicans to block Roosevelt's requests to enlarge the Supreme Court and to streamline the Executive Branch; in condemning the Congress of Industrial Organizations; and in hunting for "Reds" disguised as New Dealers. They charged that the Democratic party had been theirs before 1932, even before 1934. Now New Dealers had taken over. The president had stolen the patronage and power of regular Democrats; he had given both to radicals in Wisconsin and Minnesota, in the labor movement, and in his administration and Congress.[24]

New Dealers laughed bitterly at this caricature of their influence. In 1937 and 1938, with the economy in a deep recession, the president's dithering and refusal to consult undermined their already slight impact on policy. Most pleaded with the president to act, and hoped; but Governor LaFollette challenged him openly. In April 1938, he launched the National Progressives of America, at root attacking the New Deal for "scarcity economics" that provided "spoonfeeding relief," not "real jobs." The governor had a point, but as Crowley had warned the president four years before, Philip LaFollette wanted national power.[25]

Attacked now on his right and left, Roosevelt struck back at both. That summer he campaigned openly against conservative Democrats, chiefly Southerners, who had betrayed their party's "liberal" 1936 platform. This highly publicized "purge" (a term that evoked the deadly Soviet purge going on then) clouded the president's broader strategy in 1938. While he hoped to replace "Copperheads" in the South with loyalists, he wanted to rid himself of publicly condemned radicals in the upper midwest (and elsewhere), but subtly. A compliant Congress was not his ultimate objective. That centered on 1940, possibly a third term, surely the strength to name his successor.[26]

Running from Farmer-Labor Governor Elmer Benson in Minnesota was a crucial element in Roosevelt's policy in the upper midwest. Benson had been elected in 1936 as Olson's heir and with moderate Democratic support. Since then, he had marched leftward. Now, Crowley reported, he had been renominated, but rural Farmer-Labor elements were shifting to the Republican party in protest; urban, Irish-Catholic Democrats were collaborating with the Republicans; and the president's strength was slipping with Benson's. Crowley thus advised the president not to endorse Benson until he escaped the Communist millstone and embraced the New Deal. And Roosevelt agreed. In early September he gave Benson that message; however, the governor did not respond until Crowley spoke to his secretary a few days later. Only then did Benson speak warmly of Roosevelt and the New Deal and condemn alleged Communists he had formerly indulged. Even so, Roosevelt endorsed him only in a half-hearted last minute statement, seemingly in an effort to mollify Benson's friends among nationally influential intellectuals without alienating moderates in Minnesota and elsewhere in the country.[27]

Benson went down, the victim of a conservative reaction, and with him the coalition of Farmer-Laborites and Democrats that had supported Roosevelt in 1932 and in 1936. Thus, for the president to capture Minnesota in 1940 required the emergence of a moderate Farmer-Labor party and the building of Democratic support. Crowley did what he could from Washington. Job requests from radical Bensonites he filed away, those from moderate Farmer-Laborites he usually dealt with more favorably; he advised the president which Democrats were loyal and should be "recognized"; and he suggested signs of renewed Farmer-Labor and Democratic cooperation. Beyond that, he could not help the president in Minnesota. The chairman of the Democratic party there blamed him for the "destruction and demoralization" of his party and the Farmer-Laborites, as well as the Progressive and Democratic parties in Wisconsin.[28]

The Democratic state chairman's indictment could hardly have been more damning. Perhaps needless to say, Crowley was not welcome in Minnesota's Democratic party politics after 1938. And he was not in Wisconsin politics either except where his assets were plentiful. He could expect some information and support from New Deal loyalists, but he depended most heavily on the state's postmasters and other recipients of the patronage he managed. And he needed every one. In Wisconsin as in Minnesota, Roosevelt wanted to control the Democratic delegation to the party's 1940 national convention and, if he ran then, Senator LaFollette's endorsement. LaFollette not only dominated Wisconsin politics, he had achieved national influence. The problem, for Roosevelt and Crowley, was the senator's two commitments in 1938: first to help Philip, his administration-bashing brother, secure another term as governor; second, his support for the Progressive Senate candidate against Duffy, a loyal Democrat Roosevelt did not want to offend. As in Minnesota, Roosevelt and Crowley had to move carefully in 1938.

In February, at Crowley's suggestion and perhaps his design, Roosevelt gave him a letter which he read at a testimonial dinner for Senator Duffy. Roosevelt praised the "loyalty" and "liberal viewpoint [of] our good friend Ryan Duffy," and he expressed hope that "his home folks [are] as proud of him as we are." It was an endorsement, the *Milwaukee Journal* reported the next morning; and the guests had responded "enthusiastically" to every word Crowley read; but warm words were not enough. Duffy needed tangible help from Roosevelt, either in securing Progressive endorsements or in appointing his friends to federal positions held by LaFollette's men. He got neither. In May, Duffy wrote McIntyre that Evjue's *Capital Times*, "the big daily LaFollette newspaper," had attacked the governor's launching of the National Progressives. McIntyre got the hint—with Roosevelt's encouragement the newspaper might endorse Duffy—and suggested to the president that Crowley speak to Evjue, as "it should be handled indirectly." Roosevelt, after speaking with Senator LaFollette and, perhaps Crowley, decided to "let this ride." So, too, in July, when Duffy wanted an "openly hostile" federal administrator in Wisconsin replaced with his own man. McIntyre told Crowley the president wanted him to tell the senator his request must be denied, and he "did not want any correspondence on it unless absolutely necessary." Further, Crowley was to inform "Bob" LaFollette of the decision, "confidentially." Roosevelt was determined to retain the senator's support, without totally alienating a Democratic party he would need in 1940.[29]

Roosevelt achieved his two major objectives in Wisconsin in 1938: Philip LaFollette was defeated by a Republican and, hardly less important, his brother was not alienated. Crowley played a useful role. In August he had suggested to McIntyre that a power project Governor LaFollette wanted should be "held in abeyance," and McIntyre saw that it was done. And while hard evidence is lacking, it is reasonable to believe that Crowley helped induce the Democratic nominee for governor to withdraw and support the Republican candidate. In Wisconsin, conservative Democrats and the New Dealer in the White House shared a common goal in 1938, drumming Philip LaFollette out of politics. They succeeded, but there was a price to be paid. Duffy lost, perhaps because Roosevelt sent him only a tepid last-minute endorsement, but he was not alone. Almost every Democrat and Progressive went down.[30]

Soon after the disaster, the administration began working on the messes in Wisconsin and Minnesota. Crowley hoped to consolidate moderate Farmer-Laborites and Democrats in the latter state, and he successfully fought the nomination of former Governor Benson to the Interstate Commerce Commission. He might have opposed the appointment of former Progressive Congressman Thomas Amlie to the ICC in Benson's stead but did not. Amlie was repudiating his radicalism and eagerly preparing to stand on the "firing line" as a Democrat. Moreover, his appointment would please *Capital Times* editor Evjue and other moderate Progressives. But Crowley argued that such gestures had to be balanced with appointments appealing to Wisconsin Democrats. When, in May, he learned that a federal judge in Wisconsin would resign, he wrote the president, requesting an opportunity to discuss Duffy's qualifications; and in June Duffy's name went to the Senate.[31]

While Crowley was ever ready with political advice, he could not ignore his official position as chairman of the FDIC. In the late thirties, he and the agency remained immune from the growing anti-administration sentiment in Congress and the country because he pursued policies that were politically and financially prudent and sound. In

1937 and 1938 the FDIC conducted numerous bank examinations, but it avoided stepping on the prerogatives of other federal institutions and state agencies, as well as costly duplication, in the process. Crowley was also careful to avoid gratuitous affronts to bankers and quietly straightened out banks engaging in unsafe practices or guilty of violating FDIC specific regulations. Banks continued to fail—approximately seventy-five in 1937 and in 1938, both recession years—but the failures were isolated; depositors and banks nearby had no cause to fear. As one commentator fairly enthused in 1938, "In the mind of the 'man in the street' the two most commendable projects of the Roosevelt Administration are the CCC [Civilian Conservation Corps] and the FDIC."[32]

Crowley took pride in the FDIC's stabilizing influence. New visitors to his office were shown a picture of patient depositors queued before a bank and proudly told that they had been paid off two weeks after it folded. But by 1938 his public assurances hid more closely expressed fears of the impact of a contracting economy—the FDIC could save dozens of small banks; it could not deal with a general collapse—and he warned supervisory authorities to "act vigorously" if bankers did not maintain "sound banking practices." Crowley wanted bankers to reduce salaries and dividends, strengthen their capital structures, and improve their liquidity. Again he seemed solely concerned with the FDIC's "mandate to protect depositors," not with the dangers of a credit crunch.[33]

Most bankers heeded Crowley's admonitions or were favored by circumstance. But there were striking exceptions requiring swift action by the FDIC, a few by the chairman himself. Perhaps Crowley would have attended personally to the most threatening in any case, but in some his intervention incidentally strengthened the president's position, in others he acted purposefully to save the president from embarrassment.

The most significant interventions took place in New Jersey. Crowley's decision to work with Jesse Jones and the RFC to assist the Camden Trust Company to absorb an insolvent bank rather than let it go under was lauded by the *Camden Courier Post* as a "shining tribute to the New Deal," and the paper thanked both men for their "genuine assistance." Crowley enjoyed the tribute; he kept a copy in his files. But his decision—saving the insolvent bank rather than paying off its depositors—was only incidentally political: it was cheaper, and it saved a neighborhood bank.[34]

A more complex and dangerous problem threatened a year later when the New Jersey Title Guarantee and Trust Company, the second largest bank in Jersey City, closed. Informed on a Saturday, the FDIC staff was on the scene Monday morning, evaluating assets and appraising deposits. That was the usual scenario. In this case, Crowley appeared to assure depositors that they would be paid off in two weeks, and that he had arranged with other banks nearby to provide advances to businessmen so they could deal with immediate expenses.[35]

Crowley's quick action—he flew to Jersey City—stemmed from his fear of a widespread panic. Rumors were circulating that the Title Guarantee's failure resulted from the tax policies of Democratic Mayor Frank Hague, which threatened runs on other banks in the city if the FDIC did not act decisively. Moreover, as Title Guarantee held the deposits of another city and of the state, the legislature was likely to investigate, and an investigation might lead to "Boss" Hague and, perhaps by extension, to the president. Political as well as financial dangers loomed heavily over Jersey City in early 1939.[36]

Thanks in large part to Crowley those dangers did not materialize. A week later, after the FDIC announced that over a dozen banks in Hudson County (Jersey City) would be merged, he was back and on the radio, assuring the public that the consolidated banks would be stronger than ever, and insisting that there would be no loss to any depositor, "no matter what the size of his deposits." And no panic ensued. Indeed, the *New York Times* pointed out that the succession of bank consolidations, including several in March that followed hard upon the Title Guarantee and Trust Company's failure, aroused "little interest." Because of the Federal Deposit Insurance Corporation, "the public has regained its confidence."[37]

Crowley was elated with the FDIC's success in New Jersey—he kept key newspaper clippings attesting to it—but he worried as September 1939 approached and no word came of his reappointment. He may well have had "Potomac Fever," but he surely needed money. His income from the family's General Paper Company and a few pitifully limited dividends had to cover more than $11,000 in annual interest on his large debts, leaving little for the quite elegant if quiet lifestyle he enjoyed. No wonder he was worried and that his usual sinus problems became more noticeable to those visiting his office. Once he had asked visitors not to smoke; now he had removed the ashtrays.[38]

In late July Crowley phoned the Treasury to set up a meeting with the secretary about his "possible reappointment." Not coincidentally, perhaps, he chose the same morning to write the president about salient facts that would appear in the FDIC's annual report soon to be released. In the past such brief abstracts had stressed the growing strength of the banking community and of the FDIC in very general terms. Not this time. Crowley stressed the corporation's necessary "extensive rehabilitation of banks in the State of New Jersey," the last major area of "concentrated hazard to the Corporation." He pointed out that the FDIC had protected 466,000 depositors there, more than half the total throughout the country that year, an emphasis which suggested that the gratified depositors constituted a major portion of the electorate in a key state. He might have added that he had handled the case there so smoothly as to save "Boss" Hague, and perhaps the president, some embarrassment. But there was no need. Roosevelt would have read that message.[39]

Crowley's coup in New Jersey impressed the president (and Morgenthau, who acknowledged it). Roosevelt not only reappointed Crowley forthwith, he wrote him a buttery note. It may have been the first time the president addressed him as "Dear Leo." In any case, it was far from the last. What struck the president "most forcefully," he wrote, was Crowley's and the FDIC's "flexibility in meeting its few major problems speedily and effectively. The example of the State of New Jersey . . . is what I have in mind."[40]

Crowley may have been relieved at his reappointment, but he had fretted overmuch. Even before his exploits in New Jersey, a crescendo of approval had been accorded his leadership. Bankers and reporters, as well as senators and congressmen, applauded the FDIC and praised him, often directly, often personally in letters congratulating him. But had it not been so, the president surely would have found him another place close at hand. In three years Crowley had turned the tables on those who had condemned him as a liar and a liability. Not only had he demonstrated great ability at the FDIC, he had demonstrated impressive political skills. In 1939, with a possible attempt to secure a third term a year away, Roosevelt could well have believed the latter more important. If so, Crowley would soon prove him justified.

6

Private Enterprise and Public Service

By the fall of 1939, Leo Crowley had established himself as a force to be reckoned with in Washington. Since "Jefty" O'Connor left the year before, Morgenthau was his only enemy of note. The Treasury secretary could not forget his department's findings against Crowley four years earlier. He still told his staff that Crowley was a crook and a liar, but he had to be careful outside his office. Crowley was one of the president's fair-haired boys, even "Dear Leo."[1]

Crowley reveled in his job and in the president's favor. He was managing the FDIC and handling the political interests of the White House there and in the upper Midwest with the quiet effectiveness the president demanded; and he received tangible evidence of the president's great respect for his skills in September when he was named to a new six-year term as chairman of the FDIC. But much as he appreciated the recognition, Crowley found his $10,000 salary limiting; even supplemented by a second salary he received from the family paper company in Madison he could not reduce his still-huge debts. Fortunately, for him, that and more were about to change dramatically. He had the many bureaucratic skills and savvy, as well as the financial expertise and political influence the president and others required in a world that had just gone to war.

Crowley's second career began to emerge on December 1, 1939, when he told reporters he had "tentatively accepted"—subject to speaking with the president—the chairmanship of Standard Gas and Electric, a giant public utility holding company. The *New York Times* discussed Crowley's appointment at some length, but wrongly tied it to his experience in Wisconsin, perhaps because Standard Gas had a subsidiary there. The *Times* ignored the financial and legal problems of

Standard Gas and why Victor Emanuel, its chairman, chose Crowley to handle them in his stead. For the "real story," with its various implications for Crowley, readers would have to turn back the clock.[2]

In 1929, Victor Emanuel, known on both sides of the Atlantic as a speculator and playboy, had organized the Standard Power and Light Company. A holding company, he used it to seize a controlling interest in Standard Gas, which, also a holding company, controlled other holding and operating companies in twenty states and Mexico. Emanuel's highly leveraged foray collapsed with the coming of the Great Depression. By 1933 Standard Gas, the linchpin of his system, paid no dividends, and by 1935 it was in receivership. Emanuel kept control of Standard Gas and Electric then and after it emerged from bankruptcy three years later. But he could not expect a return on his investment (through Standard Power and Light) until Standard Gas's subordinate companies registered profits. Worse, in March 1938, the Supreme Court declared the Public Utilities Holding Company Act of 1935 constitutional.[3]

The Court's acceptance of the PUHC Act created a major problem for Emanuel. It prohibited "third degree" holding companies such as Standard Power, effective January 1, 1940. Thus, Emanuel had to divest—or appear to divest—control of Standard Gas without surrendering ownership. Naming Crowley chairman just a month before the effective date solved that problem. Crowley was to be his surrogate. Standard Gas would have to simplify its corporate structure and, as Crowley later said, clean up its balance sheets to comply with the law. He brought his business skills; more important, he brought his bureaucratic connections and skills. The PUHC Act was riddled with ambiguities. As one utilities analyst noted a few years before, "How far holding companies may be disturbed will depend entirely on the leniency of . . . the [Securities and Exchange] Commission." Crowley could expect his good friend, Thomas "Tommy the Cork" Corcoran, one author of the PUHC Act, to help him find its ambiguities and loopholes. He could also count on his own contacts and influence—including his friendships with commission members—that went with his years as a bureaucrat and as an adviser to the president. He was uniquely suited, then, to obtain a sympathetic hearing—and "leniency"—from the SEC.[4]

Emanuel never spoke of his expectations of Crowley. Perhaps he hoped Crowley could persuade the SEC to permit Standard Gas to retain operations in two geographical areas—in the Minnesota and Wisconsin region as well as in and west of Pittsburgh—but it is equally if not more likely that Emanuel believed it sufficient if Crowley bought time for Standard Gas to restructure. Given time, the company could sell off its weaker properties and reduce its bonded indebtedness; and given the stronger economy which war in Europe now almost ensured, it might cover the arrears on its preferred stock and, possibly, pay a dividend on its common. One day Emanuel and Standard Power might recoup their investment. As for Crowley, now fifty, he had to be very pleased with Emanuel's offer: a starting $50,000 salary; a readiness to move Standard Gas's headquarters to Washington; and, it was rumored, a promise of the presidency as well as the chairmanship of Standard Gas at a later date. There was only one possible problem, Crowley said at his December 1 press conference: he could not give Emanuel a firm answer until he spoke with the president, who was resting at his spa for polio victims in Warm Springs, Georgia.[5]

Crowley later recalled phoning the White House the following Monday and advising the president, "I'd like to drop over to talk about a personal matter," and Roosevelt saying, "Delighted, come over at 2:00." He also recalled not specifying what he wanted to discuss and worrying as he entered the White House, how will the president react when I tell him of Emanuel's offer? Will he want my resignation? Crowley further recalled that he did not sense a conflict of interest, that federal laws did not prohibit working for a private corporation and the government simultaneously, and that he intended returning his salary as chairman of the FDIC.[6]

Such is Crowley's story. Whether he really worried that the president would make him resign as FDIC chairman is doubtful. He had quit the boards of the Lehman Corporation and of Pan American Airways earlier that year because the president feared the United States might become involved in a European conflict and asked him to remain—"until after the war." Now, it would seem, the president approved in principle his acceptance of Emanuel's offer and his remaining at the FDIC before he examined Standard Gas's books and before the president left for his Warm Springs retreat. Why the president made this turn about is a matter for speculation in due course. But it is almost certain that Crowley informed Roosevelt of his intentions. Not to have advised the president first would have been rude if not impolitic, as Crowley implied when he apologized to Morgenthau for not having informed him earlier. In any event, Crowley's fears, if any, were gone just one hour after he entered the White House. Outside, he informed newsmen that he would join Standard Gas, but remain at the FDIC for a bit longer. Asked how long, he replied: until "certain matters" are satisfactorily completed—"for a few months, put it that way."[7]

Crowley was convivial as always with the newsmen; he enjoyed chatting with them while walking from the Mayflower to his office at the National Press Building, though he was always cautious and never more so than when questioned about his discussions with the president. Now, though, when reporters asked about a conflict of interest, he sideslipped. Heading up Standard Gas would "in no way conflict" with chairing the FDIC; the FDIC, he said, did not regulate utilities, it insured bank deposits. Crowley was rather transparently playing with words; the reporters had obviously implied that he might use his position at the FDIC to influence the SEC or markets in which Standard Gas would disgorge its subsidiaries. They did not press him on that crucial question, though. They asked whether his federal salary would continue, to which he replied that it would not. Finally, they wanted to know what else he and the president had discussed, to which he replied that they had talked about "the whole banking situation." Again, the reporters did not press. They knew he considered his talks with the president "privileged."[8]

On the face of it, Crowley added little more when responding a few days later to notes from two old nemeses, William Rubin and William T. Evjue, congratulating him on the Standard Gas appointment. He replied that the president had asked him to "remain in Washington for the next few months. Naturally," he continued, "I am interested in the future success of the President." What that meant, he did not hint. Neither did he suggest why the president wanted him at the FDIC when almost anyone could have run it, when its politically astute general counsel usually testified when the Hill called, and when his own duties consisted chiefly of ritualistic speeches to bankers' forums. In a memo to Morgenthau just after seeing the president, he admitted only that he had agreed to stay on in Washington "until the [bank] problems now confronting us are disposed of."[9]

In retrospect, it appears that Crowley intended to remain at the FDIC through the Democratic National Convention the following summer or, perhaps, through the November election. The president wanted him to stay. Quite probably Roosevelt had decided to seek a third term, but at the very least he wanted to control the Democratic party's nominating process. Any incumbent would want as much. But the circumstances were especially compelling. In September, Britain and France had challenged German agression, they needed American aid, and Roosevelt had already made it clear (by obtaining legislative modification of the Neutrality Act) that he would help as much as he could. At the very least, that required nominating a Democrat candidate for president equally sympathetic to the Allied cause and capable of winning in November.

Actually, only one man fit that bill of particulars—Roosevelt himself. No one has found a "smoking gun" that might reveal when Roosevelt decided to seek the nomination himself. Yet there are tenuous but striking clues that Roosevelt decided by December of 1939 to seek the nomination himself, and that he had seriously considered the idea for some time. Otherwise, why had he courted Senator LaFollette the last two years; why was he now extending a warm hand to a Democratic outsider like William Rubin and a former Progressive like William Evjue; and why did Crowley write both men, both troublesome in the past, that he would stay in Washington "for the next few months. Naturally, I am interested in the future of the President." What future, if not a third term.

Roosevelt faced a special problem in 1940: no president had won a third term. Even seeking it was unseemly. But there was a solution—a united Democratic party claiming that with the world in chaos Roosevelt must run. Thus, Roosevelt had to be drafted—or appear to have been. Crowley and other loyalists in Wisconsin and elsewhere must secure the delegates he needed, and carefully. Roosevelt's name could not be invoked, at least not directly, and Postmaster General Farley, who was staunchly opposed to the third term concept and himself a probable contender for the nomination, had to be handled delicately; otherwise he might defect and wreck the president's chances in November. Delegates would have to be corralled by Crowley's invisible badge as a member of the administration, by the prestige it suggested, and by the patronage, perquisites, and power it implied, not by overt promises and pressure. Securing delegates for Roosevelt required the very political skills Crowley had honed so long and so well.

Roosevelt required Crowley's help for reasons ranging well beyond the help he could provide in securing the Democratic nomination. The anti-third-term tradition aside, 1940 would not be a reprise of 1932, much less 1936. Even a convention "draft" would not restore the president's original coalition; New Deal programs and policies, and the perceived influence of Wisconsin's Progressives, Farmer-Laborites, Progressive Republicans, "radical" Democrats, and the CIO, had estranged many traditional Democrats. For Roosevelt to win a third term, he would have to regain their support, but especially that of Catholics and small businessmen.

Crowley was not a spokesman for Catholic Americans, but as a main street businessman and banker who had gone to Washington and done well, he was a distinguished figure with whom many Catholics could identify. Besides the party leaders, delegates, and voters he might personally and directly influence, he was a magnet Roosevelt very much needed, the more so if Farley turned on him. And permitting him to take the chairmanship of Standard Gas was not a drawback but an asset. It not only enhanced Crowley's attraction among Catholics, it strengthened the administration's opportunity for a much-needed reconciliation with decision makers in the business community. The president did not expect them to contribute to his reelection; he wanted their influence in the media and on the Hill, obtaining support for rearmament and aiding the Allies; he wanted their investment directed to armaments; and, sometimes, he wanted their administrative expertise in Washington. All this required a trade-off: signaling a moderation of the New Deal and a commitment to stopping the Axis.

Permitting, indeed probably encouraging, Crowley to take the chairmanship of Standard Gas while remaining at the FDIC was one of the first signals Roosevelt offered business leaders. Personally, Crowley was not beloved on Wall Street; he was an outsider, and he was associated with Victor Emanuel, who was viewed by many as a scoundrel in the mold of Samuel Insull. But Crowley favored rearmament; he had said that publicly earlier that year. He used his position as chairman of the FDIC in ways major banks and big business approved—among them the reduction of assessments in the Banking Act of 1935—and, though he publicly defended the administration, he used conciliatory language. No wonder *Barron's*, the financial weekly, noted when commenting on Crowley's appointment: "Although a supporter of President Roosevelt, he is not and never has been a New Dealer. His relations have been with the conservative wing of the Administration."[10]

Such considerations, primarily political, apparently induced the president to ask Crowley to remain at the FDIC. The *New York Times*, however, explained the decision on simpler grounds: Crowley was "one of the President's closest personal friends," though the two explanations are not mutually exclusive. *Time* commented favorably, if later, that "with apparent White House approval Leo the Lion took the job." Not so the *Chicago News*, however. It chastised Crowley as just one of several New Dealers who could be heard "hurling impassioned invective at trembling businessmen one day and more than likely be found a few months later on the payroll of a similar corporation." It was a caustic, damning charge but, in Crowley's case, inaccurate. Doubtless, he commented privately on the practices of some of the bankers whose institutions the FDIC had to salvage, but there is no indication that he vilified them. Such was not his style. The *Chicago News* would have stood on stronger ground had it condemned Crowley's determination to take Standard Gas's chairmanship while remaining at the FDIC, not to mention the president's agreement that he might do so.[11]

Somehow, Crowley escaped charges of conflict of interest. He was able to focus on bank problems that he told Morgenthau and the press required his personal attention. A disaster threatened in Philadelphia. Crowley had learned two months earlier that the Integrity Trust Company was "in an unsound condition" and must be closed if a remedy were not found. And that could not be allowed to happen; the Integrity Trust held too many deposits exceeding the $5,000 maximum the FDIC guaranteed, and several nearby banks held similarly large deposits. Crowley had feared that a general panic should larger depositors in Integrity Trust lose their savings in excess of the maximum guaranteed by the FDIC, and he had talked two Philadelphia banks into assuming both the assets and liabilities of Integrity Trust, provided the FDIC loaned them the difference. The plan was by no means new—it reflected the views of the FDIC's monetary theorists that the corporation protect all depositors, whether their accounts exceeded the guarantee or not, and Crowley had embraced it earlier in dealing with Jersey City's banking problems. Even so, he had written the president at Warm Springs on December 1 to indicate how he was handling the problem at Integrity Trust.[12]

The Integrity Trust situation was discussed again by Crowley and Roosevelt at their conference at the White House the Monday following, but within a larger and obviously political framework. The president had just heard from an ally, New York Governor Herbert Lehman, that one bank in Syracuse, another in Utica, would close if they did not get help. That would mean problems for both cities; it could also embarrass both of them. Lehman was deeply concerned; so was the president; and he told Crowley to see what could be done to prevent both banks from going under. At the same time Crowley was to proceed with his plan to save even the largest accounts in Philadelphia's Integrity Trust Company.[13]

One event surrounding the Philadelphia episode revealed that the president trusted his FDIC chairman completely. During their conference Crowley warned the president that when Integrity Trust was closed, its stockholders would be left in the cold, and some would probably ask the White House to find some way of saving the institution. Three days later he learned that one or two stockholders had talked to Grover Whalen, the New York City politico, about speaking to the president on their behalf. Crowley sharply disapproved; he did not want any interference with his plans for the bank, but equally he had no sympathy for bankers who took excessive risks or for stockholders who let them. More than a bit self-righteously and hypocritically, he insisted that they should have learned from events earlier in the decade. He was right, though, and he phoned General Edwin "Pa" Watson, now the president's chief aide, to ask that Whalen not be given an appointment if he called.[14]

Watson must have agreed. In the weeks that followed, Whalen phoned the White House repeatedly, only to have Watson inform him that the president's time was filled. "Senators [are] clamouring at our doors," he said. And Crowley had a free hand; he was able to proceed with his Philadelphia plan unimpeded. As a result, he was able to tell the president on January 1 that all arrangements were complete: a public announcement would be made in two days, and the transfer would follow shortly. And when it did, on January 14, the president penned a memorandum for Watson, "Will you tell Leo Crowley I am delighted that this was done."[15]

Crowley always enjoyed the president's warm words; otherwise he was too busy to ponder congratulations or do much else. Dictating letters to several Standard Gas directors, he spoke of his duties at the FDIC but stressed the time he spent analyzing Standard Gas's corporate structure, attending SEC hearings, and preparing for the "show cause" order soon to come. He wanted the directors to understand why he must turn down their dinner invitations. As he wrote one of them, "My dual job . . . will be somewhat of a tax on my energy."[16]

Crowley did not mention a third commitment that would absorb much of his time and energy that winter and spring, even probably until November—politics. He wanted to contribute as much as he could to the president's bid for a third term, giving special attention to Wisconsin. He saw at least two serious problems there at the moment. Not only was the Democratic party divided into at least three factions, but even united it could not hope to carry the state in November without Progressive support, and that meant Senator LaFollette's endorsement was critical. As an opponent of aid to the Allies in the European war, LaFollette's support might well influence those Progressives who were torn between the president's New Dealism at home and his interventionism abroad. However, at the very least LaFollette had a price; he wanted Roosevelt's support for his candidacy in November 1940, and his share of federal patronage.

Roosevelt and Crowley were ready to pay the senator's price; so were national committeeman Broughton, former congressman James Hughes, and a new member of the Roosevelt faction, Crowley's nemesis in years past, William Rubin. They argued that simple realism required the usual biennial trade-off with the Progressives; Democrats were highly unlikely to win any state offices whatever their course; securing Roosevelt's reelection offered their only hope of producing the patronage on which they subsisted. And if jobs had to be split with the Progressives, something was better than nothing. Expediency as well as loyalty to the Boss and the New Deal motivated Crowley, Broughton, Hughes, and Rubin as they got ready for their party's state conference in mid-February. It was crucial; at Wisconsin Rapids they would be slating delegates for the presidential primary in April.

Their preparations greatly angered another, emerging element of Democrats led by Outagamie County's chairman, Gustave Keller, and his Milwaukee County counterpart, "Boss" Edward Curry. Also claiming to be Roosevelt loyalists, this faction, which labeled itself "The Democratic Party Organization of Wisconsin," or DPOW, spent much of January denouncing Broughton, Crowley, and company for the years in which they had traded off with the Progressives and split patronage with them. Keller and Curry insisted, probably accurately, that these bargains had crippled the state's Democratic party in the past and, if they continued, would destroy its chances of becoming a liberal force in Wisconsin for years to come. For the moment, however, what mattered was the DPOW's public refusal to support Senator LaFollette unless he ran as a Democrat, and their announced decision to boycott the party's February conference at Wisconsin Rapids and to run their own Roosevelt delegates in the spring primary.[17]

The DPOW's challenge threatened Crowley's plans—and presumably Roosevelt's—for forging an alliance with LaFollette and the Progressives in the fall. It also created an immediate problem. Anti-Roosevelt Democrats, open collaborators with the Republicans in the state races in 1938, intended to slate Vice-President John Nance Garner for president in the April primary, and the threat was obvious: if the Crowley-Broughton and Keller-Curry factions split the Roosevelt primary vote, Garner could get a substantial number of delegates. Further, a split in Wisconsin could lead to similar divisions elsewhere, destroying Roosevelt's prospects for an apparent draft and nomination by acclamation, and damaging his chances for a third term. It was a distinctly dangerous prospect for the Crowley-Broughton regulars, and it became real when, on February 8, the DPOW filed its slate for the April primary.[18]

Three days later Crowley arrived in Wisconsin Rapids for the Democratic party conference Broughton had called. Expecting DPOW dissidents as well as regulars to attend, he had in his pocket a "New Deal harmony message" from the president and Farley. But he would not read it. The DPOW had not sent delegates; it was ridiculing the meeting as the "Broughton-Hughes-Crowley postmasters' conference," and though there was truth to the claim, Crowley saw no reason to appeal to them for reconciliation and united support for the president. He already had most of the delegates pledged to Roosevelt or a successor the president named; and he had Senator LaFollette's concurrence with his approach. Two weeks before he had advised the president, "It is apparent that Bob LaFollette will go along and I am going to . . . talk with him." And he had on the Sunday he arrived at Wisconsin Rapids; "Bob" had then agreed to Progressive support for the slate selected there. And Crowley had felt comfortable discarding his "harmony message" in favor of a fighting speech that might galvanize the delegates.[19]

At the conference's banquet that same Sunday evening Crowley did exactly that. He scourged the DPOW for destructively "silly bickering," which by itself denied them any right to lead the party. Besides, they had no authority. The "national committeemen are . . . the only persons authorized to pick delegates for the national convention," he reminded the crowd; and he told the regulars they could rest assured that the administration would deal only with them, not the DPOW, and "route all business through the national committeemen." And, Crowley concluded, he felt assured that the convention would select delegates "truly in favor of the things President Roosevelt stands for," and then they would go on to victory in April and in November.[20]

Crowley achieved one objective early that evening. He awakened the eight hundred delegates. But that was fairly easy; they were already smoldering at the DPOW's belittling charge that they were attending a "postmasters' conference," and they enjoyed having the Keller-Curry crowd hammered and their place in the administration's heart confirmed. But Crowley found it tougher trying to reach a consensus on a second name on the primary slate should Roosevelt not run. Despite previous pledges to let the president decide, many delegates wanted Farley. William Rubin proposed the label "Roosevelt or Farley—New Deal," only to meet with strong opposition from delegates he called "timid Irishmen," afraid that Farley's name on the slate would stir religious prejudice. Crowley and Broughton agreed, but they had other reasons for opposing Rubin's proposal. They explained that Farley's name on the slate would alienate Progressives and other voters who knew he was not a New Dealer and believed that he was tainted with the corruption of big-city politics. They did so carefully, however, well aware that some delegates might defect if Farley were not on the slate. At the same time, they satisfied this gathering of party regulars by agreeing to drop the words "New Deal" from the slate. Eventually, the conference titled its slate "Officially Endorsed Roosevelt-Farley Delegates," suggesting that the postmaster general was to be Roosevelt's running mate. It was a label which, Rubin noted, was "approved with hesitancy . . . by Leo and Charlie."[21]

Crowley's and Broughton's fears were soon confirmed. Voters were confused, and Progressive leaders entered the campaign later than Crowley had hoped. For weeks he worried that Senator LaFollette might find in Farley's name on the slate a reason to reject it. Worse, if possible, placing Farley's name on the slate might prompt the *Capital Times*'s Evjue to endorse the DPOW in the April primary and, by splitting the Roosevelt vote, result in a Garner victory. For almost two years

Evjue had been praising the president as the "greatest liberal in the country today"; he had endorsed both his domestic and foreign policies; and he had pleaded with him to run again; but he could not stomach Farley. He blamed him as much as Crowley for the many reactionary Democrats sitting in the Wisconsin legislature. Furthermore, he did not like the delegates Crowley and Broughton had slated at Wisconsin Rapids; they were not New Dealers.

Crowley was not oblivious to Evjue's hostility; he had been aware at least since 1933 that the editor disapproved of his and Farley's conservative views and saw them as opportunists; but he recognized the depths of Evjue's hostility and its dangers for the president only at February's end. Then Rubin warned him that Evjue had told him he might endorse the DPOW slate.[22]

A few days later Crowley called the powerful editor. He did not beat the drums for the Wisconsin Rapids slate; he argued that the Keller-Curry faction had rebelled merely from dissatisfaction with his patronage agreement with Bob LaFollette. Evjue answered that his argument was not acceptable. Both slates were comprised of "reactionary Democrats" who were simply using Roosevelt's name to further their own purposes. According to Evjue's recollection Crowley then said he would be satisfied if the editor "maintained a hands-off policy and did not support the Keller slate." Evjue responded that he would consider it, but he promised nothing.[23]

On March 18 Crowley spoke with the president and then with Broughton. He asked the Sheboygan editor to "clarify" the label adopted at Wisconsin Rapids. And the next morning Broughton editorialized in his newspaper that the conference had been called "because of the demand for a 100 percent Roosevelt ticket." He pointed out Crowley had spoken with the president the day before the conference and, with the president's blessing, "announced his support for the officially endorsed Roosevelt-Farley delegates and predicted their election." Consequently there should be no doubt in any voter's mind that the Wisconsin Rapids slate was for Roosevelt first and last; "there can be no second choice."[24]

Broughton's editorial did not still Progressive criticism of the Roosevelt-Farley slate, but Evjue kept silent, and Senator La Follette worked with Crowley and Broughton behind the scenes. By March 26, the three persuaded former Progressive Congressman Gerald J. Boileau to endorse the Wisconsin Rapids slate, in part at least by agreeing to endorse him for a slot on the Securities and Exchange Commission. And that evening Boileau delivered a statewide radio message. He asked Progressives to "join with liberal Democrats in support of the candidate under whose name appears the words 'Officially-endorsed Roosevelt-Farley delegates.' " He argued that not doing so might "send delegates to the [national] convention who are hostile to Roosevelt." He meant the delegates slated for Garner.[25]

Boileau's endorsement did not produce the strong Progressive support for which Crowley had hoped. Several Progressive leaders told the press that Boileau "put his foot in it." They said they had "more use" for the DPOW's slate than that chosen at Wisconsin Rapids. Indeed, such was their hostility that even a last-minute Crowley appeal (at a Knights of Columbus banquet) did not seem to rally them. The Wisconsin Rapids slate captured only fourteen of the twenty-four delegates in the next day's primary. This was a far cry from the clean sweep Crowley and Broughton had predicted and wanted, and the DPOW, which won seven seats, was not subdued. Moreover, it soon met in Fond du Lac and issued a resolution condemning the regular slate as illiberal and undemocratic. After the spring primary, then, prospects for the Wisconsin Rapids regulars, the DPOW, and the Progressives cooperating to capture Wisconsin for the president that November looked very bleak.[26]

Crowley saw the problems inherent in the splintered primary vote. He understood that between the spring and fall some means must be found to secure Democratic unity and cooperation with the Progressives. What could be done, however, he did not know, and he could not give much time to pondering it; he was too involved with his new duties as chairman of Standard Gas and Electric.

On March 5, the SEC had warned Standard Gas that it had not complied with Section 11 (b)(1) of the Public Utilities Holding Company Act. Along with six other holding companies receiving similar notices that winter (including the better known Commonwealth and Southern presided over by Wendell Willkie, also cited that day), Standard Gas had neither simplified its corporate structure nor restricted itself to a single system. Thus, it was instructed to "show cause" for its noncompliance by April 16 and to get ready for hearings set for May 6.[27]

Hurriedly Crowley had reviewed Standard's books, consulted with its directors and lawyers, and visited its far-flung subsidiaries. He had attempted to determine which systems could best be divested, which one, or possibly two, should be kept. Section 11 (b)(1) could be interpreted by the SEC or by the courts to allow two systems, though the SEC had not to date. Actually, Crowley hoped to retain three holding subsidiaries. The Philadelphia Company, which was in fact a major holding company that controlled holding and operating companies in western Pennsylvania and eastern Kentucky, was one, the most profitable, and Crowley believed it was the key to Standard Gas's future. But Crowley also hoped the SEC would permit Standard Gas to retain Northern States Power and Wisconsin Public Service, two other major holding companies, as a second system, and he thought it might if they were merged and demonstrated sufficient efficiency and geographical contiguity. To further this objective, Crowley had just hired George C. Matthews, a Republican member of the SEC as vice-president of Northern States Power; Crowley believed no one was better suited to restructure that company along lines acceptable to the commission. But Matthews and Crowley needed time to fully develop and formalize such a plan.[28]

On April 10 Standard Gas asked for sixty days extension, and two days later the SEC agreed. Crowley quickly told newsmen that hearings would begin just after the July 4 holiday. He wanted it known publicly that Standard Gas was ready to make "partial compliance" with the SEC's "show cause" order before hearings began. Soon it would dispose of two Pacific coast companies and a Rocky Mountain company, leaving only its core Philadelphia Company and three other subsidiaries in the Midwest. Crowley further implied the later paring of some of Standard Gas's midwestern companies, cleverly suggesting other moves he thought would improve Standard Gas's public image. But he carefully entered a caveat. All the divestitures then planned could affect the value of properties to be divested in the future, and all, then and later, had to be "in the public interest." They must be, as the PUHC Act stipulated, "fair" to investors and consumers alike.[29]

Crowley's press statement was studded with such caveats. It implied that Standard Gas knew better than the SEC how to protect the many interests that would be affected by its divestitures; it pointed out that plans for disgorging its three western companies would require approval by regulatory bodies other than the SEC; and it strongly suggested later complaints that commission orders requiring "forced sales" would injure innocent stockholders. In sum, Crowley's specific points recaptured what his first, conciliatory statements had conceded. Thus he gave nothing. However, he achieved a substantial public-relations coup. The *Wall Street Journal* confirmed it, pointing out that Crowley's response to the SEC's order was "sharply divergent" from that of the United Gas Improvement Company, which attacked the SEC's order as procedurally defective and the PUHC Act itself as unconstitutional. And the *Journal* was not alone. The *Little Rock Gazette* asserted that "Standard Gas is the first of the nine major companies to offer even partial compliance with the holding company act's 'death sentence.' "[30]

Crowley was frankly pleased with his coup, as doubtless the president was. Politically, it suggested that the expected conflict between the SEC and the holding companies—and, implicitly, other conflicts between the government and business—might be resolved fairly amicably and without undue harm to business. Where Standard Gas led, other holding companies were likely to follow: their image demanded it, and, properly handled, some divestitures at a "fair" price would enable them to slice their top-heavy debt structures and make the back dividend payments on their preferred stock. Then, too, as Crowley advised his stockholders, their investments would be more valuable when integration (the legal name for restricting holding companies) was complete. Perhaps; no one could know for certain. But Victor Emanuel surely hoped so. He knew that his capital tied up in his preferred stock in Standard Gas could be employed more advantageously in the shipbuilding and aircraft industries that now interested him; and in the frantic atmosphere following Germany's recent conquest of Norway and Denmark other major players apparently agreed. In the month following Crowley's announcement, the value of utility stocks shot up, and the other holding companies faced with "show cause" orders agreed to cooperate.

Crowley had devised a brilliant strategy. Perhaps it leaped at him as obviously serving the interests of both the White House and Standard Gas, even the public interest, but it also reflected his own pragmatic temperament. He was very comfortable, then, asking other utility managers to work closely with the SEC, not to fight it, as he urged when addressing the Wisconsin Utilities Association. Cooperation would benefit both, he asserted. "Are not our aims and those of the Securities and Exchange Commission fundamentally identical?" The commission could help them achieve the "basic reform" and "drastic financial reorganization" they knew were essential to pay their "huge preferred stock dividend arrearages." Certainly they had made little progress on their own; they needed help and should seek it, as bankers had earlier from the FDIC and with fine results. But a cooperative attitude promised more than simply aid in their financial rehabilitation. The SEC might then recognize that "an open-minded attitude . . . , as well as much commonsense interpretation," would be needed to make the Holding Company Act as "useful to the public, to the industry, and to the investor as it can be made." Everyone profited, Crowley argued, when a "mutual understanding could be reached quickly and advantageously by two groups of reasonable men."[31]

What Crowley meant by a "mutual understanding" was clarified June 14 when he filed Standard Gas's answer to the SEC's "show cause" order of March 5. Its plan suggested that the company was going to divest six fully controlled systems and sell minority holdings in five peripheral companies, give up several hundred millions in income-producing properties, halve the twenty states in which it operated, reduce its debt, and simplify its capital structure. It was a magnificent plan, stressing Standard Gas's "voluntary compliance" with the SEC, but it was surely designed less for realization than public consumption.[32]

Crowley's capacity for public relations perfumed a plan that gave nothing while asking all. Actually, Standard Gas's response proposed divesting four, not six, fully controlled systems, "as soon as feasible," and the remaining two at some later, even less specific time. Even then, disposal of the last two would be contingent on the SEC's permission for Standard Gas to merge Wisconsin Public Service and Northern States Power (in Minnesota) into one system, which it could keep along with its main Philadelphia system. Also, Crowley wanted to retain Standard Gas's minority holdings in several utilities and in an engineering firm used by its operating companies. And there were more caveats. The most significant, Standard Gas's demand for obtaining "maximum values" for its properties, could mean endless postponement of any sales. So, too, with Standard Gas's emphasis on debt reduction. Neither numbers nor dates were given for these transactions. Crowley was playing for time. Even so, the *New York Times* congratulated Standard Gas for "voluntary compliance."[33]

Crowley's strategy was working—for Standard Gas, for the president, and for himself; whatever came of Standard's Gas's response, however the SEC responded in its turn, he had time to clear his desk at the FDIC, help the president secure nomination for yet a third term, and if successful help him win reelection. He would then have fulfilled his December 1939 agreement with the president. Roosevelt had agreed, perhaps even encouraged him to accept the chairmanship of Standard Gas. He, in turn, had helped obtain endorsements from Senator LaFollette and other prominent Progressives in Wisconsin that spring; and, against the critical background of the administration's determination to rearm and aid the Allies, he had worked hard to sell business leaders generally, and utility managers in particular, on cooperation with the administration. Whether he had succeeded in his various missions only time would tell. But he thought he could resign that summer with a ringing "well done" from the White House.

7

A Third Term for the President

By late June 1940, Leo Crowley was ready to resign from the Federal Deposit Insurance Corporation. The president had asked him to deal personally with bank problems in Utica and Syracuse, New York, indicating that they were embarrassing Governor Lehman and could embarrass him. He had done so. In March, he had told the president that the Syracuse bank could be saved immediately, the "problem case in Utica" in six weeks, and the president had thanked him. In fact, Crowley underestimated the Utica problem, and it was almost summer before it was properly resolved. Even so, Roosevelt thanked him again, and Lehman was obviously grateful.[1]

Crowley wanted to leave the FDIC, then, at June's end, after he signed the corporation's annual report. But he did not. The president needed him. He could "fix" possibly embarrassing bank problems, and he had friends and allies from Wall Street to Main Street and on both sides of the congressional aisle. More immediately important, he might be able to unite Broughton's regulars and Keller's rebel DPOW at July's Democratic National Convention; and most important, he alone might be able to secure Senator La Follette's endorsement and reactivate the Democratic-Progressive coalition in Wisconsin the president knew he would need in November. Crowley had to be persuaded to stay, at least for a while. And when Roosevelt asked, he could not refuse.[2]

That June, on the eve of the Democratic National Convention, helping the president meant working with Broughton to retain control of the Democratic party machinery in Wisconsin, and bringing the DPOW delegates into the party fold. Securing an overwhelming majority for the president at the convention was not the problem; all but three Garner delegates seemed safe. The problem lay down the road, in re-creating the Progressive-Democratic alliance that had carried the state for the president twice before and would be absolutely essential this year. Unfortunately, the DPOW's agenda threatened that alliance. Keller and Curry were still insisting that the party slate strong rather than nominal candidates in the September primary—which would preclude a Progressive-Democratic coalition. To that end, they hoped to gain control of the party. The key was unseating Broughton as a national committeeman.[3]

Crowley did not need to have the danger pointed out. Handed a tough Democratic opponent, Senator LaFollette would not endorse the president, many Wisconsin Progressives would not support him, and Roosevelt would not capture the state's electoral votes that fall. Worse, lacking the senator's progressive and isolationist seal of approval, Roosevelt might lose other industrial states he needed in order to win nationwide. The danger inherent in the DPOW's threat to the president's reelection was not to be underestimated. Thus, unifying the Democratic party under Broughton's aegis was absolutely essential. Both he and Crowley understood that; it was foremost on their minds as they left for Chicago and the Democratic National Convention. What could or should be done about it was another matter.

Crowley had gone to Wisconsin Rapids five months before with a harmony message and attacked instead. In Chicago, on July 14, speaking at a pre-caucus dinner for Wisconsin's delegates, he did the same. He began cooly enough, saying that Roosevelt would run and he, Crowley, would manage the campaign in the Midwest; but as he first praised Broughton, then argued that the president "wants him," and, finally, called Keller's faction "troublemakers," the cheers turned to boos. The delegates knew what was at stake, and one stated the issue bluntly, "Is Mr. Roosevelt going to support Bob LaFollette or [is he going to support] the entire Wisconsin Democratic ticket, including the senatorial nominee?"[4]

Crowley was not happy with the question. Sensing danger, he first tried a jest, responding that, if Democrats could collaborate with the Republicans two years earlier, why not with the Progressives this year. But when the room began to rumble again, he asserted—truthfully or not—that he really did not know what the president intended. Quickly, Keller broke in: "Here is something you do know. Did you write a letter . . . insisting that Bob LaFollette be reelected? Are you personally going to support [him]?" Crowley tried to answer, but his response was drowned in the crosscurrents of invective that filled the room, and he scurried from the hall.[5]

Crowley did not regret his caustic remarks. He had seen no need to mollify the Kellerites; their primary votes had come from the most fervent Roosevelt enthusiasts, who would support him regardless of, perhaps even because of, a deal with Bob LaFollette. In fact, condemning the Kellerites as "troublemakers" was useful. Crowley knew it was essential for control of the party machinery and a deal with LaFollette that Broughton be reelected national committeeman, and that, it seemed, rested on securing the support of Garner's three delegates. He knew also that the conservative Garnerites, whatever their opposition to the president, were more worried that the liberal DPOW would grab the party machinery and spirit it out of reach. What he had done, then, in flogging the Kellerites was attempt to persuade the Garnerites that they had a common enemy. And he succeeded. Broughton was reelected, and he and Crowley retained control of the party. Crowley's biting precaucus words, surely well thought out, had served their purpose.[6]

But if Crowley's remarks were deliberate, he did not have to manufacture the spirit that animated them. Reporters had noticed earlier that he was in an "irritable" mood and attributed it to a long, tiring train ride and a hotel room saturated with a Chicago summer's heat and humidity. But Crowley's head had been spinning the past week, thinking of his most recent conversation with the president. Roosevelt had stated the obvious: Farley was almost certain to announce his resignation as chairman of the Democratic National Committee either at the convention or a few weeks after. Would Crowley consider replacing him? No more had been said, and Crowley did not know how seriously to take the offer. Obviously, there was a major obstacle to his chairmanship of the Democratic Party—his chairmanship of Standard Gas. Crowley knew that this could hurt the president's reelection prospects, particularly if his opponent was Wendell Willkie, in the past a spokesman for the utilities in battling the Holding Company Act. But he also had heard Roosevelt ask his help. The conundrum had been on his mind ever since.[7]

But that was not all that kept him awake. The president was seeking a running mate to replace Vice-President Garner, but who? Crowley recalled years later that the president asked him to take five names to his office and analyze them as running mates and as cooperative vice-presidents. Then, later that day, Roosevelt had phoned, "Come over and let's go over those names again." And he had gone back to the White House to tell the president, "I think the one fellow that can help you would be Henry Wallace." And he recalled the president asking him to go to Chicago and "work with the fellows and nominate Henry Wallace if you can."[8]

How accurate Crowley's recollections of this discussion were remains a question. Unfortunately, in the course of reminiscing, he tended to filter in discussions which could only have occurred before the 1944 convention. Even so, it is very likely, as Crowley recalled, that the president phoned him after his dinner with the Wisconsin delegation to say that Wallace was still his choice as a running mate. Whether Roosevelt then said, conspiratorially, "I haven't told anyone else about Wallace," is another matter.[9]

What Roosevelt probably discussed with Crowley was publicity about his choice of the secretary of agriculture, as that evening Crowley gave the story to a good friend and political ally, J. D. Ferguson, associate editor of the *Milwaukee Journal*, who saw that it appeared the next morning under the headline, "Wallace Likely Prospect for a Place on Ticket." It seems unlikely, though, that Roosevelt had not told anybody else about Wallace, as Crowley recalled him saying, or that Crowley needed reminding; Wallace fit too neatly into Crowley's plans for carrying Wisconsin and Minnesota. Certainly Ferguson stressed the advantages. The secretary of agriculture might not appeal to conservative Democrats, but he would to southern sharecroppers who "never before had heard the clink of hard money in their jeans," to midwestern farmers determined to get their "conservation checks," and to progressives and "footloose mavericks." Wallace was a "natural." The president's choice proved again "the 'boss's' political astuteness."[10]

Crowley hoped the *Journal* story would strengthen support for Wallace in the Wisconsin delegation. Wallace on the ballot would attract Senator LaFollette, and his endorsement would produce the much-needed alliance with Wisconsin's Progressives and, possibly, Minnesota's Farmer-Laborites. However, many members of the Wisconsin delegation thought Wallace was radical and impractical. On Thursday afternoon, even after he officially became the president's choice, only nine of the twenty-four-member Wisconsin delegation were ready to vote for him, and at the first roll call that evening his total reached only fifteen. Eventually, Wallace received twenty-two votes but only under pressure. For most Wisconsin delegates, Wallace was still not a "real Democrat"; he was that New Dealer hybrid—of Progressives, progressive Republicans, and Socialists—who had taken over and transformed the Democratic party they believed their legacy. Only the president's magic at the polls and the plums it promised had brought them into line.[11]

This shifting political culture was clearly reflected in the coverage Wisconsin's major newspapers gave their Democratic delegation. The *Wisconsin State Journal* and the *Milwaukee Journal*, which just a few years earlier praised the state's Democrats, and Crowley in particular, now usually ridiculed them. Except for J. D. Ferguson, they mercilessly chided his speech and exchanges at the precaucus dinner and his later efforts to strengthen support for Broughton, the president, and Wallace. Only Evjue's *Capital Times*, soon to endorse the Democratic ticket, commented favorably on the delegation, including Crowley. And during the convention, it called him "a possible choice for the Democratic national committee chairmanship," now that Farley had announced that he would refuse another term. Whether Crowley would take the post was the question, Evjue wrote. As the convention closed, Ferguson at the *Journal* agreed.[12]

The following Saturday, July 27, Crowley paid an unexpected visit to the White House. He had spent the week with Standard Gas's lawyers and accountants in New York, reviewing the company's proposal to divest its San Diego Gas and Electric subsidiary, and he was tired. In fact, he had not been feeling well, and he was going to the Mayo Clinic in Rochester, Minnesota, for a checkup as soon he cleared his desk. Now he advised the president that his health would not allow him to accept the chairmanship of the Democratic National Committee, and he must resign as chairman of the FDIC. He suggested that the president name his general counsel, James Markham, to succeed him at the FDIC. Markham, he said, was a superb administrator and, significantly, a very close friend of John McCormack, the Irish-Catholic Democratic majority leader in the House. Crowley did not have to add that the president needed McCormack's support for aid to Britain.[13]

Crowley had thought his appointment with the president would be brief, that the president would quickly agree to his resignation on Tuesday, when he released the FDIC's's annual report. But Roosevelt did not agree, insisting that they put the matter aside until Crowley returned from Mayo's. Also, he seems to have asked Crowley to reconsider taking the party chairmanship then, too, as Crowley wrote Evjue, "I want to be . . . helpful to him on the campaign, but I can hardly go along with him on the Democratic Chairmanship as my health will not permit it." And he wanted to leave the FDIC for the same reason. Or so he advised. In fact, he had a second, critical reason; in August he was to assume the presidency as well as the chairmanship of Standard Gas, and he thought he could not couple those jobs with his chairmanship of the FDIC, much less the chairmanship of the Democratic party. As for leaving Standard Gas, he did not intend giving up the salary and perquisites, not even for the president.[14]

Later that day, back in his office, Crowley drafted a formal letter of resignation to become effective August 15. Well aware that Roosevelt might put him off again, he devised a bargain. If the president let him resign, Crowley told Evjue, he "was willing to take charge of the Chicago office and work throughout the Middle West." Crowley did not explain how his willingness to manage the president's midwestern campaign was compatible with his ill-health or his responsibilities as chairman of Standard Gas, headquartered a day's train ride away. Perhaps he still believed the president had a claim on him. In any event, he closed his letter to Evjue by asking his onetime and future arch-critic, now "Dear Bill," to keep it and his enclosed draft resignation to the president confidential "until you hear from me."

Crowley's letter to the president can better be described as a plea than a bargain. He reminded the president of his attempts to leave on earlier occasions, and that he had "deferred during the formative years of the Corporation and until the solution of several serious situations among the banks." Now the corporation was financially "sound," functioning "smoothly," and the banking system was "in excellent condition." His work was done, and the president should let him resign.[15]

But Crowley did not resign. Why not, is unclear. Possibly the president "put him off" again. He had every reason to do so with an election at hand. Roosevelt was well aware of the FDIC's public favor. Republicans as well as Democrats credited it with renewing the nation's faith in its banking system and stabilizing the banks and the monetary system. Even then, both major parties were claiming credit for creating the corporation seven years before; and Evjue had just placed the guarantee of bank deposits at the very pinnacle of the president's achievements in an editorial endorsing him for reelection. It was one of the few elements in that record almost every American could applaud. It was not only a smashing success, it was a bipartisan achievement.[16]

So the FDIC appeared to the millions who remembered bitterly what had happened to their deposits earlier in the decade or when many banks failed during the otherwise golden twenties. It meant even more to people who more recently had seen the FDIC's agents come to town, closing or merging their failed bank but redeeming their hard-earned savings. And if the bank was critical, Crowley had probably appeared, his picture, his name, and his efforts to save it gracing their newspapers for days and even, in some circumstances, weeks. In their minds he was the FDIC. And both had preserved the savings of Republicans as well as Democrats. They were nonpartisan.

This was Crowley and the FDIC publicly, and in some part accurately. But there was another, partisan side to the story that he and the president knew well. It was the story of banks saved, most obviously in New Jersey and New York, by methods which would least embarrass the president, his friends, and political allies. It was the nonpartisan but politically significant story of other banks Crowley told subordinates to nurse through difficult times. His motives in those cases and others, where he endorsed requests for help from the Reconstruction Finance Corporation, was preservation not only of the banks and the FDIC's funds but sustenance of the surrounding economies. But however pure Crowley's motives—and they appear to have been that—this policy strengthened him and the president politically. So did his readiness to cooperate with state banking supervisors; they appreciated his sympathetic, even deferential manner when working with them and, in turn, provided information the administration often found politically valuable. Crowley was, then, a political asset the president could ill afford to lose. He had made that clear when he congratulated "Dear Leo" on his "splendid" annual report earlier in the summer. Crowley had to stay.[17]

Roosevelt could be very persuasive, and he may have used his magic to persuade Crowley to withdraw his resignation; it is more likely, however, that Crowley decided, at last, not to submit it. Writing Evjue, even drafting his resignation, provided the needed catharsis. Otherwise, how explain his decision to remain at the FDIC after Roosevelt's reelection, when his departure would have gone unremarked and the president would have had an opportunity to appoint an acceptable replacement. In fact, Roosevelt's needs and Crowley's were hardly incompatible. The president's foreign policy required reconciliation with the business community; Crowley wanted the chairmanship, presidency, and salary Standard Gas provided; and there is good reason to believe that Victor Emanuel made his federal job and influence with and proximity to the SEC a condition of his Standard Gas appointment.

In early August, while Crowley worried about his forthcoming visit to Mayo's and whether he should remain at the FDIC, the *New York Times* was reporting on "excellent authority" that he was the "most probable choice" to replace Farley as chairman of the Democratic National Committee. Or he would be, the *Times* emphasized, if he were not the "head of a public utility corporation, holding a position similar to that of Wendell Willkie, Republican nominee for President." The *Times* argued that Crowley's private position was an insurmountable obstacle. So, also, Supreme Court Justice James Byrnes, the president's primary adviser on domestic policy and politics then and later, would say the following year, "He, being an Irish Catholic and coming from Wisconsin would have been fine, but I told the President he couldn't do it [because of his position at Standard Gas] and . . . that was why Leo Crowley didn't become Chairman." "Ed" Flynn, Democratic boss of the Bronx, was named to the post. At the same time, the president, not knowing whether or when Crowley could return to the FDIC, began checking out Markham as interim chairman.[18]

Still in early August, Crowley underwent a colon resection at the Mayo Clinic. Difficult though it was, by late that month he was once more commuting between Washington and New York. But his presence was noted only at month's end, when reporters saw a letter Standard Gas had sent its stockholders on the twenty-sixth. It revealed that, despite Crowley's health problems, he had been named Standard Gas's president as well as its chairman eleven days before; also that the SEC had just signed off on the company's plan to divest San Diego Gas and Electric.[19]

Newsmen who had attended Crowley's press conference the past December when he was appointed chairman of Standard Gas were not stunned by his assumption of its presidency. *Business Week*, however, was shocked at having to "discover" Crowley's appointment. It argued that Standard did not meet the test of "full disclosure of material facts" the SEC demanded and noted that its spokesman at its hastily called press conference was "a former employee of the Commission." But *Business Week*'s critique was an exception. The *Chicago Herald-American* happily reported that Standard Gas would move its headquarters from New York back to Chicago after November to accommodate Crowley, who "plans to spend all his time here [devoting] full time to the utility system." It added that Crowley had told the president he would stay at the FDIC until then since pending legislation required his attention.[20]

Actually, the only issue Crowley had to worry about then was the election. The legislation mentioned was minor and could have been handled by Markham or whoever succeeded Crowley as chairman, while the SEC had just accepted Crowley's June 14 plan for divesting San Diego Gas, calling it "fair and equitable." Of course, that was only the first step in Standard Gas's program. The SEC had not approved Standard Gas's total plan for integration which called for keeping its major systems in the Minnesota-Wisconsin region and in the Pittsburgh area as a quid pro quo for divesting its many other, far-flung properties. On the other hand, it had not rejected the plan. Either the commission wanted more time to study Standard Gas's plan or it was awaiting the outcome of the November elections. In either case, Crowley had time to focus on the president's reelection campaign in the slightly more than two months before the polls opened.[21]

Yet, contrary to what he had told the president, Crowley did not take charge of his campaign in the Midwest. Very likely, his health did not permit it. As for Wisconsin, apparently he played only a sporadic and superficial role. But in Crowley's case, and especially in political matters, appearances could be deceptive. As the *Wisconsin State Journal* noted in early August, only "telepathy" could account for recent Democratic maneuvers. It seemed that the Crowley-Broughton regulars had agreed to support Frances McGovern, once a Progressive Republican governor, now the DPOW's gubernatorial candidate in the Democratic primary. And the DPOW, in turn, had accepted a conservative Democratic Senate candidate. That opened the door for "Bob" (LaFollette) to endorse the president. Such were exactly the arrangements Crowley had been fashioning for a dozen years, and the *State Journal* did not doubt his hand in these.[22]

Until that summer, Crowley's trade-offs had assumed Senator LaFollette's support, and thus essential Progressive support, for the New Deal's domestic program. But the Nazi conquest of Europe and air attack on Britain were even then altering those patterns. Progressives, in particular, were dividing sharply over the president's ever-stronger support for Britain. To attract those who feared the German threat, Evjue organized the Wisconsin Committee of Independent Voters for Roosevelt and Wallace, and by September 24 it was the fulcrum of like-minded organizations in twenty-two states. But Senator LaFollette's endorsement remained critical. In September, nationally syndicated columnists Drew Pearson and Robert Allen reported that both LaFollettes were "cooling off on their isolationism and were seriously considering a public declaration for Roosevelt." Perhaps this was wishful reporting, but a DPOW leader was even then willing to echo, "If Bob would declare himself in favor of Roosevelt, liberal Democrats will throw every ounce of their support to him." Prompted, perhaps, by statements such as these, "Bob" endorsed the president a few days later and, following his lead, the Progressive party convention came up with its endorsement on October 1. Whether and when liberal Democrats would respond with an endorsement of Senator LaFollette remained to be seen, but the seeds sown by Crowley and Evjue the previous winter appeared to be flowering.[23]

Meanwhile, the Democrats had done their part in a state convention the *Chicago Tribune* called a "LOVEFEAST." Later, pundits would recognize Crowley's skillful hand behind the scenes, but at the time the harmony was attributed to Broughton. After supporting Keller for attorney general, he blocked the DPOW leader's bid for the state chairmanship and, supported by the Garnerites, managed to elect a centrist leader of his own and Crowley's choice. At the same time, Broughton rejected the Garnerites' demands that the party openly support James Finnegan, the Democrats' candidate for the Senate; but neither would he endorse Senator LaFollette. He argued that the senator had endorsed Roosevelt halfheartedly, failing to affirm his support for the president's foreign policy. Broughton hoped this tactic would mollify those DPOW members hostile to the Progressives, but it served primarily to anger Evjue. Worried about Senator LaFollette's reelection, Evjue denounced Broughton as an "appeaser," comparing his refusal to endorse Senator LaFollette to former British Prime Minister Neville Chamberlain's sellout of Czechoslovakia at Munich two years before, but the analogy was outrageous on its face. Moreover, Broughton was engaged in a sound if delicate balancing act, focusing totally on the president's reelection.[24]

Such, also, was Crowley's emphasis, as he addressed the convention. His speech was as tactful as Broughton's diplomacy, employing the generalizations that would bind Democrats, eschewing the touchy points which might divide them. Cleverly, he avoided the controversial aspects of the president's foreign policy. He did not mention aiding the victims of Nazi aggression. Rather he called for strengthening the army, navy, and air forces, and rigorously enforcing the Monroe Doctrine. So, too, Crowley handled domestic issues and politics in a manner to which none could take exception: "We are proud that so much of what was begun experimentally in Wisconsin by way of improving the general welfare has been tried, found good, and adopted on a national scale . . . under the vigorous leadership of our great President, Franklin D. Roosevelt." It was time, he concluded, to end the "squabbling within the ranks . . . and carry our platforms to victory—a glorious Democratic victory for the Nation and for this State."[25]

Crowley entrained for New York right after his speech, leaving to Broughton, Evjue, and Rubin the business of sustaining the convention's harmony and solidifying the coalition between Roosevelt and LaFollette. It was not an easy task. On October 5 and 8 the *Capital Times* featured Broughton's announcement in his *Sheboygan Press* that the paper "will not support an anti-New Dealer, and that goes for Mr. Finnegan." But he did not mention supporting Senator LaFollette, either. As Rubin wrote the president, he had just met with Senator LaFollette and told him that while "the greater number of Democrats will not vote for Mr. Finnegan," they would not vote for the senator either, not "until his endorsement of you is less equivocal than at present." Neither, Rubin added, should the president endorse the senator until he expressed faith in the president's "declarations . . . that you will not send any of our boys to either Europe or Asia." It would "embarrass those of us who . . . have made our position clear on the subject."[26]

A few days later Rubin wrote Crowley of his concerns, though he emphasized Crowley's promise to obtain aid from national labor leaders in getting out the vote in Wisconsin. Crowley wrote back that he would soon speak with Teamsters Union President Dan Tobin and would get in touch with Rubin when he was in Milwaukee a week or ten days later. Then, that October 11, he wrote Evjue that he had planned on leaving for Madison that day, but had to remain in Washington until Monday. Apparently the president wanted to discuss what Henry Wallace might say in a forthcoming speech in Madison, specifically how Wallace might then extend the president's endorsement to Senator LaFollette without offending too many Democrats.[27]

If so, Crowley had a superb opportunity to discuss the problem at length with Wallace the following Sunday, when he hosted a dinner for him and a dozen Wisconsin notables at his home in Madison. What they decided, if they did discuss the problem, would not become apparent for two days more, until Wallace spoke at the University of Wisconsin's Stock Pavilion. Meanwhile, that afternoon, Wallace met with Senator LaFollette and Democratic gubernatorial candidate Frances McGovern, then issued a simple statement to the press: "I had not intended and I am not authorized to endorse any political party other than my own." Reporters did not have an opportunity to ask whether his statement precluded an endorsement of Senator LaFollette personally.[28]

They found out Tuesday evening. In the opening paragraph of his Stock Pavilion speech, Wallace destroyed the harmony that was achieved at the state convention little more than three weeks before. "Let me express my appreciation of the untiring support we in Washington have received from Democratic and Progressive congressmen in Wisconsin and from your senior senator, Robert M. La Follette," he blurted. It was a fair statement of the facts, but with it four Democrats on the platform walked out, among them the nominees for governor, senator, and attorney general. Later that night they agreed to remain in the race—what else could they do—but McGovern warned, "An endorsement of that kind at Green Bay in 1934 split the party and it will do it again." As for Keller, years of frustration exploded in disgust at the treatment he felt loyal Wisconsin Democrats had been getting from the president for some time. He blamed Crowley and Broughton. So did other dissident Democrats and even Progressives, who went on the radio later to denounce the "betrayals" by the president and Crowley. They argued that, in 1936, Roosevelt and Crowley had sold out the Democratic candidate for governor to Philip LaFollette; that earlier in 1940 they had made their deal with Robert LaFollette; and now, to complete the deal, James Finnegan, the Democratic Senate candidate, was "being sold down the river."[29]

Both the *Milwaukee Journal* and *Chicago Tribune* did their utmost to widen the cracks in Democratic ranks, castigating Broughton as well as Crowley and the president. Broughton answered, if weakly, that Wallace's words were misunderstood—and Crowley said nothing—but the *Capital Times* responded strongly. Its political columnist satirized the "walkouts" as "four feathers" who were so lightweight they were "blown off the stage"; stated that Wallace so admired LaFollette that he would have praised him more highly if allowed; and scoffed at the attacks on Broughton and Crowley. Not that the *Capital Times* had changed its mind about Broughton; it still scorned him as an "appeaser," but that had been known a long time, and it was silly and stupid to attack him now. As for Crowley, the columnist pointed out that he was "the only Democrat who has stuck solidly with Roosevelt since 1932. [He] has brains which is more than can be said for most of Wisconsin's Democrats. Had [they] stuck with Roosevelt, . . . they would not be in a leaking boat today."[30]

Crowley must have found it more than a bit amusing that the *Capital Times*, which so often had attacked him (and would again), was now praising him; and he might have found it sad if not dishonest that the newspaper's political pundit had labeled Broughton an appeaser. Crowley knew, and the writer should have, that the difference between himself and Broughton was in large part a reflection of the constituencies they served. Crowley knew that he could speak sharply to Wisconsin Democrats because he did not have to pick up the pieces or face the barbs they returned. Once he spoke, he could run back to Washington and the bracing glow of the president's favor. Broughton was not so fortunate. Whatever happened, he remained in Wisconsin, there day after day having to cajole aggrieved leaders and mediate between their factions, trying to hold the deeply divided Democratic party together.

Crowley, Broughton, and the *Capital Times* knew why there was so much factionalism in the party. Personal ambition and diverse group interests always made some inevitable, but Wisconsin's also flowed from deep-rooted religious and ethnic characteristics and conflicts. Irish and German Catholic leaders, from the New Dealing Keller to the conservative Finnegan, represented groups which had often enough felt threatened by the Protestantism of the Progressives. Thus most resisted an alliance that would place Progressives in a dominant role. Then, too, Irish and German Catholics, though probably the former more than the latter, resented the intrusion of the federal government and the transformation of the Democratic party in the past eight years. They had enlisted in the Democratic party a century before to preserve their ethnic and religious values; now it seemed to belong to secular progressives who were expanding federal power in ways that one day might threaten those values. And if that were not discouraging enough, the president was aiding England, the Catholic Irishman's mortal enemy. Understandably, the Finnegans, Clancys, and Callahans had fled their Democratic heritage or were threatening to do so.[31]

If Crowley's future behavior is any indication, he shared a number of the values, fears, and antipathies of his fellow Irish Catholics. Five years later he would break with President Truman for several reasons, but probably the most crucial was his losing fight for traditional, religiously oriented individual and family values against the intrusive power of the state. Possibly, too, he had heard stories of persecution by the British in the Ireland of his ancestors, but such slight evidence as exists—essentially memories of a younger sister—suggest that such stories, if told, made little impression. Certainly, they did not affect Crowley's support for the president and his policies in 1940, and there is no serious evidence that they did so later.[32]

The press often noted, as *Barron's* did when Crowley accepted the chairmanship of Standard Gas, that he was conservative but "a supporter of President Roosevelt." There is no necessary contradiction, of course. Many prominent members of the administration were not New Dealers, if that term described, among other things, a commitment to the redistribution of wealth. And that included the president. Partly because the FDIC guaranteed bank deposits, Crowley was a monetary conservative; surely he was also a fiscal conservative, and certainly he was not antibusiness. But as his first federal job, as Farm Credit administrator in St. Paul suggests, Crowley could transcend the apparent conflict between the interests of bankers and farmers; pragmatically he sought answers to the crushing impact of deflation on both. Government must aid both. It might also, as he said in Sheboygan in May 1939, regulate some businesses to correct past abuses and prevent new ones. But as he emphasized soon after taking the chairmanship of Standard Gas, the public interest and that of holding companies such as Standard were not antithetical; reasonable men could reconcile them. Much as the president, then, Crowley was both a New Dealer and a conservative, recognizing that one must "reform in order to preserve." And he acted on these assumptions when he battled for the president's reelection in Wisconsin and elsewhere in 1940.[33]

Happily, Crowley heard from Rubin in mid-October that likely losses among Irish and other conservative but normally Democratic voters would be somewhat compensated for by the recent formation of a large new group, "Republicans for Roosevelt." Also, Broughton had just walked the extra mile to coax McGovern, the party's gubernatorial candidate and one of the "four feathers" who had stalked off the platform in Madison, to introduce Wallace at Platteville. All in all, if Crowley were able to get more labor support more quickly, the president should carry Wisconsin.[34]

During late October the president's coalition came together, and on November 5 he carried Wisconsin by a narrow margin. Crowley's efforts could not have been more important. He was chiefly responsible for obtaining Senator LaFollette's endorsement, which (with the exception of strong backing from Nebraska's independent Senator George Norris) was the only one Roosevelt received from a progressive Republican bloc in the Senate that had once supported him almost unanimously. He also obtained money and workers from the Teamsters Union. And, working with Broughton and Rubin, he kept most Wisconsin Democrats in the fold. Beyond that, Crowley contributed to the president's success nationwide. As chairman of the FDIC, he had saved or strengthened many banks, making the corporation one of the New Deal's two most popular achievements; and, as chairman and president of Standard Gas, he had explained at every turn that the interests of the utility industry and, by extension the business community generally, were not incompatible with the interests and policies of the administration. Quantifying Crowley's success in this effort and in his others to secure Roosevelt's reelection is not possible, but he could hardly have done more to help the president secure a third term.[35]

November 1940 might have marked the end of Crowley's years in Washington. He had organized the FDIC so efficiently and supervised its banks so effectively that he might have left his post with the president's blessing and the country's gratitude. Moreover, it was doubtful that the president would find a major need for his political skills in Wisconsin again. There, Progressives were continuing to split over the president's foreign policy, so-called internationalists moving toward the Democratic party, and isolationists returning to the Republican party. Now more easily than at any time earlier in the year, Crowley might have resigned his chairmanship of the Federal Deposit Insurance Corporation and devoted full time to his posts as chairman and president of Standard Gas.

Why Crowley remained at the FDIC is not recorded. Later he would explain that he treasured his chairmanship, and that Roosevelt said it was his as long he remained in the White House. But it must be assumed that he enjoyed more than the routine. He was privy to the bureaucratic grapevine and probably in a position to secure foreknowledge of SEC decisions, if not influence them. He could also enjoy a certain status his relationship with the president afforded. Reporters joined him during daily walks from the Mayflower Hotel, and Wisconsin newspapers emphasized his powerful influence within the state. In January 1941, when Broughton resigned as national committeeman, they commented in understandable but nonetheless curious usage that the "fine Italian hand" of Leo Crowley was responsible for the Sheboygan publisher's replacement by a "regency" of Crowley's friends, strengthening his control of patronage in Wisconsin. And there were some things reporters did not reveal of Crowley's influence; later that year, he suggested that the president name Evjue minister to Iceland, and the president agreed, though (unhappily for Crowley's peace of mind) Evjue rejected the offer. Finally, and probably of greatest importance in Crowley's decision to stay at the FDIC, the president asked.[36]

Crowley's dual position, as chairman of the FDIC and chairman and president of Standard Gas, as well as his Irish Catholic lineage, had assumed an importance beyond its electoral significance. The Axis dominated Europe, threatened to invade Britain, and endangered American interests and ideals; yet American businessmen, distrusting New Dealers they had fought for years, were only reluctantly shifting production to rearmament. Crowley was well positioned to persuade businessmen of the new reality, that their interests and the views of the administration were not incompatible. One week after the election he had repeated earlier messages, telling utility executives "that our aims and those of the Securities and Exchange Commission [are] identical"; reasonable men could find "mutual understanding," much as the FDIC and American bankers had. But Crowley was more than a spokesmen for reconciliation between the administration and business; he was a respected, trusted liaison with many conservatives and isolationists on the Hill. Finally, rumor had it that he was a financial advisor to the papal nuncio and, as the British ambassador noted later, "the most prominent Catholic layman in the United States." Thus, Crowley's presence in the administration could only strengthen the president's efforts to aid Britain and to spur businessmen to contribute to rearmament. The president knew it, and when he asked Crowley to stay, Crowley knew he had no choice.[37]

8

Alien Property Custodian, I

During most of 1941 Crowley enjoyed a very comfortable year. The FDIC ran so smoothly he easily found time to fill the void in Wisconsin's Democratic leadership left when Charlie Broughton resigned as national committeeman; he completed Standard Gas's SEC-sanctioned divestiture of San Diego Gas and Electric; and, though much of his debt from the early thirties remained, he was better off than at any time since the depression began. He returned his federal salary, but Standard Gas paid him $65,000 a year, and investments brought in another $2,000 annually. He lived well. At the Christmas season just past, reporters had seen him leave with a train compartment sagging with gifts for his extended family in Wisconsin; and daily they noted his hand-tailored suits, that he ate at Washington's best restaurants, and that he loved the racetrack. Much of this they reported. They did not write about the many nights he played poker or talked politics on the Mayflower's balcony. They did not write about the many evenings he spent in his suite answering requests for favors from folks in Wisconsin. Perhaps they accepted such work as the natural burden of the politician, too banal to report, but Crowley found writing more than a political act. He personalized his responses. He enjoyed this opportunity to interact with and help people. Like the president he served, perhaps more so, he cared.[1]

Crowley's world, as that of most Americans, changed with the Japanese attack on Pearl Harbor on December 7. Many years later, Crowley recalled an intense discussion with the president in the Oval Office that crisis-ridden evening. "Leo, I've got a job for you," the president had told him. "The only scandal in Woodrow Wilson's administration was with the alien property custodian in World War I. I want you to take it on."[2]

114

Crowley recalled telling the president he would have no part of a persecution of German-Americans similar to that when A. Mitchell Palmer was custodian during World War I. And the president had responded, "You'll deal only with Germans, not with German-Americans, and no one will interfere with you." Crowley recalled rejoining that it would be a "nasty job" handling German property and patents, but he would take it if the president wished.

There are problems with Crowley's reminiscence. His discussion with the president did not occur on Sunday evening, December 7. He refers to German property only, although the United States was attacked at Pearl Harbor by the Japanese. This problem could be explained away: war with the western Axis powers was expected shortly, German technology promised the greatest contribution to the war effort, and Germans constituted the second largest ethnic group in the country. But Crowley was not in Washington December 7. More important, his reminiscence telescopes and greatly oversimplifies a lengthy process and a complex issue, naming an alien property custodian.

Crowley strongly implied that in his post-Pearl Harbor talk with the president, he reluctantly agreed to be named alien property custodian. Actually, he and the president reached at most a tentative understanding, and that followed from a complex process that had begun more than a year earlier and would continue three months longer. Some facets of that winter's drama are missing—the FBI burned the stenographic notebook of a "sophisticated" and "well informed" person that it found at a New York nightclub—but even the existing evidence clearly reveals a struggle over policy, power, and turf so bitter that it rocked the president's official family to its core. The evidence also reveals that Crowley found a powerful new patron in Supreme Court Justice James Byrnes, now a key presidential adviser.[3]

The first step in controlling alien property came in April 1940, when the president authorized Treasury Secretary Morgenthau to freeze the assets of Norway and Denmark, both just overrun by German armies. Policy differences within the administration precluded further action until June 1941, when the president froze Axis assets. These went to the Treasury's Foreign Funds Control section (FFC), but with a compromise providing for supervision by a State, Treasury, and Justice Committee. However, this arrangement did not remain static. By the autumn, new Attorney General Francis Biddle was expressing fears about espionage and sabotage in frozen properties and asserting that Justice not the Treasury should supervise alien property. He was arguing also from precedent, that the Trading with the Enemy Act of 1917 had placed the alien property custodian's office in the Justice Department, and it belonged there again.[4]

On October 22, Biddle asked the president to appoint Crowley alien property custodian within the Justice Department. He noted that Crowley already represented Justice on the interdepartmental committee supervising Foreign Funds Control (prompted by Justice Byrnes who saw in Crowley not only a competent administrator but, much like himself, a regular Democrat and administration loyalist who would keep him, thereby the president, apprised of the political implications of FFC policies). Biddle boldly suggested that Crowley's methodical approach to issues would offset Morgenthau's often impulsive directions to FFC. Finally, Crowley could handle the custodian's job; chairing the FDIC had given him exactly the right experience, and he could bring a superb cadre with him.[5]

The president was obviously impressed with Biddle's case, as his aide, "Pa" Watson, quickly wrote a memo as a reminder: "Next week Leo Crowley re discussion between President and Attorney-General on Alien Property Custodianship." However, the president momentarily at least had second thoughts about any delay; he saw Crowley that morning at 11:15, but nothing was decided. Crowley did not want to take the job, especially if it meant surrendering his salary at Standard Gas. However, it is equally possible that before Roosevelt saw Crowley he spoke to Morgenthau and heard him speak glowingly of Foreign Fund Control's performance and condemn Crowley for his links to Victor Emanuel. Then, too, it was characteristic of Roosevelt to procrastinate when he faced difficult decisions.[6]

By late November, however, the United States was fighting an "undeclared war" in the Atlantic, it was on the brink of war with Japan, and the president recognized that it was essential to name an alien property custodian. Possibly, he was prompted by a note from Byrnes, who argued that it was essential to have clear lines of authority, then "get the best man you have on the team and let the heathen rage." At bottom, the president, too, understood the need to place one man in charge and hold him responsible. He recalled the many moral, legal, and political problems associated with alien, and especially enemy, property during and after World War I. He remembered the excesses, the scandals, and that a custodian had gone to prison; and he wanted to avoid a repetition on his watch. On Sunday, November 30, he called Byrnes to the White House to discuss what he called "a difficult decision."[7]

The justice understood the president's fears. A congressman during World War I and after, he shared the president's memories. Tongue in cheek, he soon said he would like to see a glass-walled alien property office located centrally on "Pennsylvania Avenue," where its employees and lobbyists would be readily visible to the public. The president chuckled at Byrnes's remark, then asked whom he would put in charge. The justice records himself answering: "Leo T. Crowley, chairman of the Federal Deposit Insurance Corporation. He had proved to be an efficient administrator, had the respect of leaders in the world of business and finance, and his relations with Congress were excellent," though Byrnes would have used a different tense and probably said: "Why not Crowley, as I recommended to Biddle earlier." As for Roosevelt's reaction to Crowley's name, Byrnes records him as rejoining: "I have been thinking of the same man but don't like to move him from his present post. Can we work on some plan giving him both offices."[8]

Where the president intended placing Crowley's second office —in the Justice Department or in an independent agency under the supervision of the White House—Byrnes did not record. Both knew that the question was delicate and bound to be troublesome. Morgenthau wanted alien property in the Treasury, Biddle in Justice; one or both would be offended if the president placed Crowley's office elsewhere than in his department, and Morgenthau would be unhappy even if Crowley was named alien property custodian in the Treasury Department. But a decision had to be made.

On Friday, December 5, the president made two decisions that appear to confirm Crowley's ties to Biddle, but more likely again reflect Byrnes's influence. Roosevelt named Crowley the attorney general's alternate on the Economic Defense Board, soon relabeled the Board of Economic Warfare, and chaired then and later by Vice President Wallace. Crowley was loath to take on this job—he had enough responsibilities—and he would have been more doubtful had he been able to see beyond the horizon, but with a "shooting war" in the Atlantic and an imminent conflict in the Pacific he could not reject the president's plea for help. "Dear Leo," Roosevelt penned, "I know how many duties I have already imposed on you, but in this emergency you simply have to take on one more."[9]

But that was not all. That same day Biddle wrote the president that he wanted Crowley to head up a new division in Justice to handle the patents and other property of Axis nationals, which he seemed to believe might be separated from the monetary assets FCC would continue to control. The attorney general argued that it was critical that the "new division be set up by a businessman who has had experience with the application of governmental regulatory procedures on a nationwide scale and whose acquaintance with business leadership is on the same broad scale."[10]

The president's return memo met Biddle's requests, agreeing that Crowley's "success in both business and government make him uniquely qualified to cope with new problems . . . regarding the patents and property of Axis nationals." As of December 5, then, the president had apparently decided to give Crowley a second hat as alien property custodian in the Justice Department. But Pearl Harbor, two days later, upset that decision. Meeting for lunch, Crowley, Biddle, and Morgenthau agreed that the "state of war" and pertinent legislation then being drafted made it necessary to postpone the appointment of an alien property custodian.[11]

This gave Morgenthau more time to stress the Treasury's case for continuing to manage all enemy assets. Privately, he advised his inner circle that he wanted to inform the president that Foreign Funds Control was doing an excellent job, and that placing a custodian in Justice would divide responsibility and make management more difficult. Further, he wanted to tell him that Crowley was uncooperative; in the thirties he had generally refused to go along with Treasury and Federal Reserve initiatives; he had shown bad judgment in distributing patronage; and now, worst of all, he was tied via Standard Gas to such wheeling-dealing businessmen as Victor Emanuel. And there lay danger. Morgenthau felt he had to warn the president that Crowley would name Emanuel's friends and his own allies, not competent business executives, to manage the properties he, if custodian, would control.[12]

What Morgenthau wanted to tell the president, and did, was quite different. His own hands were not clean. Condemning Crowley's handling of patronage smacked of hypocrisy, overlooking his nephew's position at the FDIC; and scourging him as an embezzler overlooked his own part in burying the Treasury's indictment. As for Crowley's ties to Standard Gas and Emanuel, the president had approved the former, and apparently he thought the latter a plus. In any event, a Washington newsletter was headlining: "Leo Crowley: His Popularity at the White House Grows." Thus, Morgenthau was cautious when he saw the president on December 15. He argued that the FFC was doing a "swell job," but was threatened by a few "bright young men in the Department of Justice . . . [who] want more power." It was best to keep the present arrangement: the interdepartmental committee supervising the FFC. At last, Morgenthau heard the president say, "Sounds fine to me," and he left believing he had saved alien assets for the Treasury.[13]

But the struggle over management of alien property had only begun. On December 18, Crowley entered the fray. Learning that the attorney general intended to press his department's position at the White House that afternoon, he phoned a confidential ("Do not let the A.G. know it comes from Leo Crowley") message for the president. Its elliptical and convoluted language largely defies translation. Apparently he wanted the president to know that he could "get along very well with Morgenthau," although he had told Byrnes that he would not serve as custodian in the Treasury. And he did not want to work in the Justice Department either. He had phoned to prevent just such an order Biddle was preparing. Crowley said he wanted "most" that there "be no disagreement between the Treasury and the Attorney-General on this matter." By elimination, then, as well as a later clue (rejecting cooperation with the Justice Department when custodian), it seems clear that Crowley was prepared to serve, if at all, only as an independent custodian operating directly under the White House.[14]

Meanwhile, Byrnes had assigned Oscar Cox (a lawyer and presidential assistant in the Office of Emergency Management) to draw up three alternative executive orders, providing for placing the Alien Property Custodian's office in the Justice Department, the Treasury, or as an independent agency under the OEM in the White House. And two days after Crowley's phone call, Byrnes sent the president the alternative orders, along with an analysis supplied by Cox. They argued that, whether Crowley was named custodian in the Justice Department or in an independent agency, all or most of the assets frozen and managed by the Treasury would have to be transferred, and Morgenthau would be seriously offended. On the other hand, the present arrangement, adding only more supervision by the interdepartmental committee, "would not be satisfactory as the Department of State," which lacked a direct interest, "would have the controlling voice." In diplomatic language but forceful argument, Cox and Byrnes insisted that the president should determine where the custodian's office should be placed and give it all the authority essential to carry out its responsibilities.[15]

But the president did not want to decide, not then at least. He did not want disharmony in his official family at any time but assuredly not when Prime Minister Winston Churchill was visiting. Neither did he want to offend Morgenthau. Temporizing again, he asked Byrnes to consider the idea of making Crowley custodian in the Justice Department "with full responsibility," but giving him an assistant from the State Department "with relatively little to do," and another from the Treasury with "supervision over the assets which are now or would hereafter be run through the Treasury machinery." Possibly the president proposed to place Crowley in charge of the patents and property of enemy controlled firms and leave the Treasury with its frozen alien and enemy bank deposits, but he did not say so, and other interpretations are possible.[16]

Roosevelt's flim-flam did not sit well with Byrnes. He told the president Crowley would not serve if alien assets were split. He "is very emphatic." And Byrnes agreed. Dividing responsibility would result in conflicts the president would have to resolve or provide the custodian or the Treasury with alibis for failure. Byrnes then recommended placing Crowley in the Justice Department for "housekeeping purposes" and giving him all property and full responsibility. But he acknowledged that there were some obvious reasons for not giving Crowley full responsibility at that time. If a compromise were necessary "to preserve peace in the family," he suggested that the funds of alien firms might be left with the Treasury until Crowley required them. The gradual transfer would salve Morgenthau's pain. Or so Byrnes argued. Surely he did not believe it. He had obtained Crowley's and Biddle's approval; but he had not discussed the matter with the Treasury secretary.[17]

Early on December 31 Byrnes phoned Morgenthau. After a bit of humorous chatter, the justice asked if he could see the secretary "right now." He wanted to "save the Boss some headaches on this alien property custodian." Morgenthau agreed and, as Byrnes wanted to avoid any lurking newsmen, invited him to use the East Executive Avenue entrance and his private elevator.[18]

Upon his arrival Byrnes brought up the president's plan making Crowley custodian in the Justice Department but giving him an assistant in the State Department and in the Treasury. He began tentatively, reluctant to tell Morgenthau that Biddle and Crowley would accept the plan only if they chose the two assistants. But he did not get that far. No sooner did he say that Crowley would be custodian in the Justice Department than Morgenthau broke in. "Jimmy," he exploded, "how can a man who is getting fifty to seventy-five thousand dollars as chairman of Standard Gas . . . , and is the personal front and representative here for Victor Emanuel, be Alien Property Custodian."[19]

The secretary's blast appeared to catch Byrnes offguard—he was apparently unaware of Morgenthau's personal hostility towards Crowley—but he soon rejoined with a strong endorsement for Crowley: "Well, I will tell you something, Henry. The President was ready to make Leo Crowley Chairman of the National Democratic Committee . . . , but I told the President he couldn't do it."

If Byrnes expected Roosevelt's evident regard for Crowley to influence Morgenthau, he was quickly proved wrong. Calling Crowley unethical, Morgenthau said Byrnes should tell him he was not qualified to be custodian. "You know the President won't." Someone, though, had to stop Crowley. He was a merely a "front" for Emanuel, who now controlled New York Shipbuilding, Vultee and Consolidated Aircraft "with between five and seven hundred million dollars . . . in war contracts." Finally, Morgenthau argued, Biddle wanted Crowley "to look after political appointments for him," and the custodian "won't be any better than A. Mitchell Palmer during the last world war."

Byrnes responded sympathetically, "That is the most outrageous thing I ever heard." So, too, Byrnes referred to Crowley's link with Emanuel, "He ought to give it up." Wishfully, Morgenthau rejoined, "Well, if you make this a necessity on Crowley's part he will resign from the Alien Property Custodianship." But Byrnes could only respond that "the President had promised [Crowley] the job." Morgenthau again said he hoped Crowley would prefer Emanuel to the custodian's post. Then "our boys can run this thing . . . and there will no trouble or scandal."

Again Byrnes tried to soothe Morgenthau—"I agree with you," he replied—but he also returned to his explanation of the president's plan to give Crowley two assistants, and Crowley's insistence that he and Biddle name them. This angered Morgenthau. At first, he insisted on retaining Foreign Funds Control and naming the Treasury's assistant under Crowley, then that Crowley might serve as custodian in the Treasury, only to have Byrnes say that Crowley told him, "I won't come to the Treasury." Bitterly, Morgenthau reiterated his opposition to the president's plan, but if Crowley was made custodian, he wanted no part of the responsibility.

Byrnes agreed, then handed Morgenthau some salve—he could keep the funds of alien firms until Crowley sought them. At that point, Morgenthau caved, Byrnes left, and the secretary called in Ed Foley, his general counsel, to explain what happened. Or try. Byrnes, he said, had been "leaning" on him, asking him if he were "not going to let me, a Justice of the Supreme Court, settle this thing" without taking the president's time. And he had given up. Crowley would "get the whole works" one way or another. He could not allow Crowley to say that "he made a failure of the business because the Treasury wouldn't give him the money." On the other hand—Morgenthau said he was thinking more clearly now—"the battle isn't lost." The president would do nothing until Churchill left town. He had two weeks to change the boss's mind.[20]

The secretary recognized that to have any chance of winning Foreign Funds Control must deal successfully with the most important German-owned companies within its grasp: General Aniline and Film and, allegedly, its sister company, General Dyestuffs. General Aniline manufactured a variety of products essential for the war effort: the best dyes and photographic equipment, a critical resin, and Atabrine, a substitute for quinine. In some chemical fields GAF was the only manufacturer, or the only important one. But that only begins to measure its significance. It was a major American subsidiary of the dreaded German chemical combine, I. G. Farbenindustrie. Commonly known as I. G. Farben, this cartel was dangerous for reasons other than mere size. During the past decade it had taken the lead in conspiring with key American corporations to stifle the United States's technological development and ability to defend itself. Further, the cartel dominated the Latin American market for chemical products, in part through General Dyestuffs, another of its American subsidiaries and GAF's sales agent.

All this was revealed by Justice Department investigations, but most Americans became aware of it through dramatic articles in newspapers and periodicals. *Fortune* condemned I. G. Farben and other German cartels as "the direct politico-economic instrument of the Nazi party at home and abroad," welded by a totalitarian system into a "single instrument for total war."[21]

The significance of the cartel problem was clear, but how to handle its complexities was not. Use of the patents and domestic factories of German cartels to win the war was taken for granted. What should be done with the American subsidiaries of German cartels after the war, and how they should be handled during the war were the questions then being debated. The first was a legacy of the First World War and events since. During that war, the alien property custodian told a Senate committee that German control of the dyestuff industry in the United States had been broken—his office had sold hundreds of German patents to American companies. But in short order he was proved wrong. Before President Woodrow Wilson left office, German chemical companies dominated the Latin American market for all drugs except aspirin, and that the German Bayer Company licensed. About that time, too, Sterling Products, which had bought many German patents during the war, sold them to the Grasseli Chemical Company. Shortly after, Grasseli and Bayer assigned their patents to a new company, Grasseli Dyestuff, which was renamed General Dyestuff and became a component of I. G. Farben. Also in the twenties, I. G. Farben organized I. G. Chemical Corporation, an American subsidiary whose real ownership it would attempt to hide after the outbreak of war in 1939 by renaming it General Aniline and Film and transferring its shares to a "dummy" neutral Swiss firm, I. G. Chemie. Thus, it appeared, Germany had recovered its pre-war dominance of critical producers and patents in the American chemical industry and won control of Latin America's markets.[22]

Even before Pearl Harbor the Justice Department's antitrust division had unmasked I. G. Farben's beneficial ownership of GAF, and, since, it had secured an indictment to sever their relationship. Further, it was about to take similar legal steps to sever General Dyestuffs and other American subsidiaries from their German owners. Again, as twenty-odd years past, the Justice Department was cutting the bonds between Germany's cartels and American industry. What would happen after the war then became a critical question. Were "Americanized" German assets private property the custodian must employ carefully, as a trust, so they might be returned intact to their owners after the war? Were they war booty to be kept after the war and, meanwhile, used by the custodian as best served American business and the American people at home and abroad? Or were there more complex answers?

The State Department was quiet on the subject, but there can be little doubt that it favored the return of private enemy-owned property after the war. This position is suggested by some legal briefs and journal articles then in preparation; the traditional cautious and legalistic position of the department; and its obvious efforts in the past quarter-century to universalize the rule of law. Beyond that, the State Department wanted a fairly "soft" peace, emphasizing the symbiotic twins, democracy and prosperity, in the Axis states after the war. This, too, suggested that the United States employ enemy assets carefully, conserving them for eventual return to their owners after the guns fell silent.[23]

The position of the Justice Department and Treasury differed sharply from that of the State Department. They believed a tough policy was necessary to ensure that, after the war ended, Germany did not rebuild its cartel system, return to the economic warfare it had waged so effectively before Pearl Harbor, and threaten the world again. The custodian must treat enemy assets—property, patents, and markets—as captive property. At a press conference the president first seemed to agree, but on a larger scale: German cartels must not be allowed to recover their subsidiaries and markets in the Western Hemisphere. Then he drew back; there was nothing to be gained and even grave danger in a rigid, harsh policy. Roosevelt was equivocating, but he was placing a premium on the flexibility that would permit the greatest productive effort, while postponing a decision that was far from critical and would be needlessly divisive. Given this emphasis, Crowley was, Byrnes and Biddle had often noted, an effective administrator especially well-suited to the post of custodian; mechanically, the tasks of the custodian did not differ greatly from Crowley's present tasks as chairman of the FDIC. Further, though no one said so, Crowley was an administration loyalist who could be expected to staff the former German subsidiaries with businessmen who were not only effective in their fields but Democrats sympathetic to the administration. Finally, he had collected so many friends on the Hill, Republicans and

Democrats alike, that he would have some immunity from criticism. Crowley had political assets that Morgenthau and Foreign Funds Control lacked.

While Roosevelt and Byrnes worried about how and where Crowley might be named custodian without unduly offending Morgenthau, the Treasury secretary was attempting to root out subversives at General Aniline and Film and growing angry with the resistance of John Mack, its acting chief and a friend of the president, to his orders. He also felt that Mack's salary was excessive. And both thoughts brought Crowley to mind. He feared that Crowley as custodian would keep the same personnel, men who owed their loyalty to I. G. Farben, and that he would name "political directors" to the boards of GAF and other companies he would control, men with more influence than experience and very likely Victor Emanuel's friends. Then there was Crowley's large salary at Standard Gas. As Morgenthau saw it, Crowley was Mack writ large.[24]

Morgenthau was correct on one point. He and the men running Foreign Funds Control differed with Crowley, as with Mack, on the handling of alien businesses. In January, Byrnes told the president that Crowley believed Treasury policy on "the supervision of business enterprises is unnecessarily harsh," that it had "nearly a thousand men . . . charged with the investigation of the loyalty of aliens, . . . that the FBI with trained investigators should be relied on." Byrnes did not elaborate, but Crowley's later policies suggest that he believed Morgenthau's handling of managers of German descent at critical, complex industries like General Aniline was too zealous, too rigid, and markedly harmful to production. Subversives must be weeded out, but this must be done surgically and fairly by the FBI, primarily to avoid disrupting production, but also to avoid alienating loyal Americans of German descent. Morgenthau's punitive approach was very likely to do both. So, too, with the Justice Department's many antitrust indictments against the German cartels and their American subsidiaries. Crowley felt they were unnecessary, legalistic, and distracted attention from the priority that should be given the employment of German assets in the pursuit of victory.[25]

Byrnes agreed on both counts, which explains in part his endorsement of Crowley as custodian, but he had to devise a politically satisfactory place for him. He informed the president that he had sent an executive order to Morgenthau after their December 31 meeting, embodying his oral proposal that Crowley be custodian in the Justice Department with two assistants of his choice from the State Department and Treasury, and the secretary had rejected it. Now, as Byrnes saw the situation: "It is useless to try to get an agreement. I think it best that you create an independent agency, having control of all alien property." He had prepared a new executive order to that effect. But there was an alternative if the president wanted to appease both Biddle and Morgenthau: a custodian in the Justice Department, who would be given enemy as distinguished from other alien property, the latter remaining in the Treasury's hands. Byrnes emphasized that it was a cumbersome plan and likely to collapse, but Crowley and Biddle told him they could live with it, and it might just salve Morgenthau's pride.[26]

Byrnes's memo did not move the president toward a decision. Doubtless he was preoccupied with other issues, Churchill's visit and the rapid Japanese advances in Southeast Asia and the Pacific chief among them. But there is reason to believe that the president responded to Morgenthau's harsh policies at General Aniline, and backed him against Mack in his purge of suspected subversives in the company. If so, Morgenthau may have persuaded him for the moment that the Treasury was doing a splendid job and should keep *all* alien property. But the secretary was bitter at his probable loss, and it is reasonable to assume that he harped on Crowley's salary at Standard Gas as sharply and as often as on the Treasury's achievements.[27]

On January 21, Byrnes responded to just such a problem. He seems to have written two notes, but decided to send only one (as the other is undated, unsigned, and not in the Roosevelt Papers, only the Byrnes Papers). Sent or not, the unsigned, undated memo is too revealing to be ignored. After noting that, while Crowley received $50,000 a year from Standard Gas, he returned his salary as chairman of the FDIC, Byrnes first suggested, "If, because he is receiving a salary from Standard Gas, you hesitate to appoint him, you might suggest that he secure a leave of absence from Standard and devote all his time to Custodian Service, paying him . . . $15,000." It is obvious that Crowley was complaining that he could not live on his federal salary of $10,000 unsupplemented by his Standard Gas salary, at least not for more than a few months, as Byrnes further suggested, "Crowley might set up the organization and six months from now, if he wished to . . . , resign." Finally, he told the president that he thought Crowley would accept this compromise "rather than have the Press state you declined to appoint him because of his connection with Standard."[28]

Byrnes's memo is most revealing. He wanted the president to stop dithering and name a custodian; he, and presumably the president, wanted Crowley to serve at least long enough to launch the custodian's office. He had the administrative skills that office required, but, more important, he had political connections and a sensitivity to political issues that Morgenthau and Foreign Funds Control could not match. Thus, Byrnes was prepared to blackmail Crowley if necessary. He believed Crowley would ask Standard Gas for a leave and forego his salary rather than have the president and the press label him a shirker. Crowley would see his compromise—a six-month term—as the lesser evil.

Byrnes apparently used this unsigned memo only as a guide to action. In a second memo, which he *did* send, he mentioned a talk with Crowley that morning. "I volunteered . . . that if you offered him the appointment, he should get a leave of absence from Standard and . . . he might be paid a salary of about $15,000 [and he replied that] if he were paid $15,000 he would get a leave . . . and if you thought it necessary he would resign all connection with Standard." Crowley wanted the president to understand "that he will do anything you desire."[29]

The last sentences in Byrnes's two memos are contradictory. In the first, Crowley appears as self-centered, in the second as self-sacrificing. Which Crowley are we to visualize? It is only fair to state that Crowley was not only being asked to take a pay cut—actually from a $65,000 salary in 1942—but the president also wanted him to take on a role almost as dangerous as that of a soldier in a minefield; and as cautious and skillful as Crowley might be, a misstep could easily shatter him. Crowley knew that; there had been congressional investigations of the custodian's office after World War I, and one custodian had gone to prison. Also, he could hardly ignore the likelihood that Morgenthau, attacking him now, would probe for weak spots after he was named custodian. So would the press. And Crowley knew he was vulnerable: he did not have the shield of status, old money, and solid connections many Wall Streeters and other businessmen had brought to other exposed positions in the bureaucracy in the past year or two; he was associated with the wheeling-dealing Victor Emanuel. Thus, Crowley's reluctance to take the custodian's job is understandable, if less than heroic. But when Byrnes applied pressure and then agreed that Crowley could keep his positions and salary at Standard Gas, Crowley told him he would take the custodian's "nasty job."[30]

Crowley must have had second thoughts soon after. The next morning, walking by the White House, he left a note for the president. He had "talked several times with our mutual friend, Jimmie Byrnes," Crowley advised, and now had a recommendation he believed would settle the custodial matter to everyone's satisfaction. He did not want to burden the president unnecessarily, but "if we can have a few minutes together it will be the easiest way to dispose of the matter. And . . . the sooner . . . the better it will be."[31]

The president apparently agreed. Upon reading the note that morning, he jotted at the top, "General Watson, Have Leo Crowley into lunch with me on Saturday." But what was discussed at lunch that weekend is not clear. Morgenthau heard conflicting reports: Crowley would leave Standard to be custodian. No! He would not. He would tell the president to give all the power to the Treasury secretary. Morgenthau did not know what to think.[32]

Nor did anyone else, apparently, for almost a month. But on February 6, Morgenthau notified the White House that Ed Foley had met with Crowley and Mack, among others, that morning. The three dominated a discussion which "unanimously agreed that the foreign owned stock in the [General Aniline] corporation (approximately 97% . . .) be vested in the Secretary of the Treasury immediately." Morgenthau now admitted that Mack, whom he had liked to portray as an obstructionist and example of what Crowley would be as custodian, had correctly placed the damning evidence of I. G. Farben's control of General Aniline, through the neutral I. G. Chemie of Switzerland, before the group. Now the Treasury should take General Aniline's stock and "Americanize" the company. However, the Treasury needed powers it did not then have.[33]

The president provided the desired authorization on February 12. A brief executive order delegated his powers under sections 3(a) and 5(b) of the Trading with the Enemy Act (of 1917) to the Treasury. Those powers gave the Treasury authority to administer and vest all alien property. And momentarily Morgenthau had some hope that the Treasury could keep alien property. But a few days later he saw that the truth was otherwise. The president's order required the formation of a Vested Property Claims Committee, and the president insisted that

Crowley run that vital operating committee. Even those decisions were temporary, however, apparently designed to deal only with General Aniline and Film. On February 17 Byrnes sent the president an executive order that provided for an independent custodian and for gradually transferring the Treasury's assets and Foreign Funds Control into Crowley's hands.[34]

Just as this last order was officially filed (in the Federal Register), Morgenthau held a press conference. There, a reporter asked him about the Vested Property Committee. Had the secretary delegated to Crowley the authority apparently granted him in the president's order of February 12? Morgenthau hedged, and the reporter pursued, "Well, Mr. Secretary, what all these legalities boil down to is the question of whether you are going to be the alien property custodian or Mr. Crowley." Morgenthau evaded the point, saying that both he and Crowley had advised the president and were "perfectly happy." But the pressure continued, leading Morgenthau to say that the president would give alien property to the Treasury if it did a good job, if not it would go to someone else. But he wanted to make a point; the Treasury did not intend to sell any businesses, favoring a few American companies at the expense of all the others. "If there is no honey, there will be no fly." And in the event the reporters did not understand, Morgenthau repeated his words and asked if they got his meaning. He hoped the reporters would ask what "fly"; then he might mention Crowley's connections with Victor Emanuel and others who would be all too ready to take advantage of property and patents the alien property custodian would control. But no one asked.[35]

Morgenthau's hopes were raised somewhat two weeks later when he heard that the president had told reporters that he was "still studying" the appointment and "there would not be anything on it for a while." Perhaps, he thought, the president had not made a final decision about the placement of alien property or about the custodian. By contrast Crowley was clearly unhappy. On February 27 he wrote the president that he was distressed with the "public discussion [and] confusion and feeling between various agencies" he saw written about in the press. He added that he did not want the alien property custodian's job and was "taking the liberty of suggesting that the administration of enemy property remain with the Treasury and that it be given the additional authority to function properly." Closing, Crowley insisted that he "was motivated solely by a desire to relieve you of at least one of your perplexing problems." He did not remind the president of his earlier reluctance to take the job.[36]

When writing, Crowley was unaware that the president on that very morning was moving in his own way to settle the placement of the custodian. Cagily, Roosevelt suggested at a Cabinet meeting that should the Treasury get alien property, it might include responsibility for handling that of imprisoned Japanese-Americans. "I don't think you should take it," the president advised Morgenthau, hinting that it would be a messy business, and would be for him in particular, when so many Jews were in German concentration camps. And Morgenthau finally agreed. After the meeting, he informed his subordinates that he would abandon his efforts to keep alien property except for the alien funds the Treasury had frozen the past two years. The president had agreed that they belonged in the Treasury.[37]

The struggle for custody of alien property was almost ended. Still, on March 5 the president gave Morgenthau permission to "Go ahead" with the Americanizing process at General Aniline, vesting its stock in the Treasury and replacing its top executives. Morgenthau quickly appointed Robert McConnell, an experienced chemical engineer, to preside over GAF in place of Mack. Then Morgenthau ordered McConnell to replace all suspect technical and managerial personnel "as soon as possible," although dismissals were not to be made on the basis of German birth or extraction alone, and the whole program was to be implemented with a view to maintaining and even expanding company operations.[38]

Morgenthau's decisions of March 5 regarding GAF were, in his biographer's words, "endorsed" by Crowley, but "shaped" is surely more accurate. Morgenthau's instructions to McConnell for managing dismissals reflected Crowley's views. Thus the president had already given custody over alien property to Crowley, though that did not become official for another week. On March 11 the president canceled his executive order of February 12 delegating custodial powers to the Treasury, issued a new one establishing the Office of Alien Property Custodian under the White House's Office for Emergency Management, and named Crowley custodian. As Byrnes wished, and Crowley surely preferred, the custodian would operate independently of the Treasury and Justice departments and control General Aniline and all other alien property the Treasury held at that time merely by asking for it in writing—or so the executive order appeared to stipulate. As of that moment, at least, Crowley had won a striking personal victory. He had taken on a difficult and "nasty job," but he would keep his large salary and positions at Standard Gas. He had found a means of contributing to the war effort, serving the president, and sustaining his life style.[39]

The president's agreement that Crowley could keep his salary and two jobs at Standard Gas is striking. Why the president did so is the question. Did he believe that Crowley's administrative skills were superior to the Treasury's? Not likely. But he may have foreseen less bureaucratic conflict and more accountability with the naming of a custodian independent of the Justice and the Treasury departments, operating directly under the control of the the White House. He could foresee that Crowley would staff alien property with politically sympathetic businessmen. And he could foresee that Crowley would quietly use alien property and patents at home and abroad as he directed. Crowley's appointment, then, reveals, above all, the president's confidence in his loyalty and political skills.

9

Alien Property Custodian, II

On March 13, 1942, the nation's newspapers gave front-page treatment to Crowley's appointment as alien property custodian; and soon there were congratulations from many of the bankers he had known. There was also a warm note from his old friend, "Al" Schmedeman, the former governor half jesting that "the President should appoint me as a member of his Cabinet for the services I have rendered him in starting you in public life"; and there was a nostalgic note from a friend in St. Paul, who recalled "a certain December afternoon in 1932 when I . . . almost insisted that you lend your services to the state of Wisconsin." There was also serious coverage by journalists. The *United States News* impersonally discussed the issues facing the new alien property custodian; Irving Perlmetter, in a syndicated column, spoke of Crowley as "Washington's Champion Officeholder" and titillated with lively descriptions of the properties—diamonds and apartment houses, securities and patents—he would control; and *Time* magazine asserted that Leo Crowley had come to the nation's capital as "a symbol of banking integrity" and was now taking "a job for a Lion."[1]

There were also heartwarming lyrics from Wisconsin's newspapers. The *Wisconsin State Journal* was reminded of "Horatio Alger heroes of fiction." Crowley had risen from poverty to become Wisconsin's "real" governor, chairman of the Federal Deposit Insurance Corporation, and chairman and president of a giant company, meanwhile serving his church so markedly that the pope had knighted him. All this he had accomplished quietly, with an easy smile and a ready measure of Irish humor. And now the president had expressed his appreciation of Crowley's commitment to service by naming him alien property custodian. The *State Journal*, among other newspapers, waxed at some length about Crowley's "commanding presence" and his boundless energy, noting in that connection that on his 44th birthday his FDIC team had given him a cigar box inscribed, "From a deeply admiring but freely perspiring staff." Hard work was not the point, though. The president had appointed Crowley custodian because of his deserved "reputation for diving into a tangled mess and coming out with the solution in a hurry." Neither red tape nor details slowed him, the *State Journal* added; he sliced through the former and delegated the latter. He would handle alien property effectively, quickly, without a scandal.[2]

No sooner did Crowley take over as custodian that March than swarms of job-seekers and of lawyers watching over their clients' interests in foreign-owned or-dominated property and processes, buzzed outside his secretary's door, seeking his attention. However, these were not the huge "flies" Morgenthau, in his February news conference, had warned would be looking for great gobs of "honey." They were gnats Crowley easily fended off by placing a subordinate outside his office to listen to their problems.[3]

Crowley could not rid himself of Morgenthau that easily. On March 23, the secretary sent him a memorandum labeled "Clarification." In essence, there was a conflict between the president's executive order of March 11, establishing the custodian's office, and one of April 10, 1940, assigning to the Treasury authority to investigate and regulate alien enterprises. Morgenthau suggested that the conflict "created certain ambiguities," but he was willing to cede the authority to Crowley if Crowley signed a memorandum to the president endorsing powers the Treasury sought. What those powers were he did not say, but he implied that the difficulty could easily be resolved.[4]

Crowley did not think so. He thought Morgenthau was seeking concessions he could not make, refighting the battle the Treasury had lost that winter. Unhappily, the president would not involve himself in the conflict. Crowley was told to present his case to Budget Director Harold Smith. He had drafted the two conflicting orders and would arbitrate.[5]

Crowley wrote Smith on May 14. He first set forth his clear authority to vest (or hold) all properties of enemy countries and their nationals, including those properties German companies had tried to hide behind dummy companies in neutral countries such as Switzerland. Then he added that, of necessity, the alien property custodian's authority included the investigative powers of the Treasury. And he wanted Smith to order the Treasury to transfer the men his office needed to determine ownership and control. Of course, his office could establish its own investigating system—he had a solid core of trained bank examiners, and he could call upon Justice Department lawyers for help—but the vesting process would be impeded, and any delay would be compounded by the duplication of resources. Consequently, Crowley reiterated, he should get Foreign Funds Control from the Treasury. In return, he would give up authority (which he did not define) he thought essential. He would do so in part because the Treasury insisted, but also he added, with more than a bit of sarcasm, because he was willing to place complete confidence and reliance in the cooperation of the Treasury Department.[6]

Crowley's efforts to strengthen his position while mollifying the Treasury did not move the budget director. Smith could not or would not force the issue, Morgenthau would not budge, and even the president's appointment of his longtime and greatly respected adviser, Judge Sam Rosenman, as mediator, did not help. As June ended and settlement of the vesting process remained unresolved, Crowley decided to write the president, asking him to break the logjam.[7]

His letter is enlightening. It reminded the president that he had wanted enemy property managed "from a businessman's point of view," an approach the Treasury with its "licensing" approach, as in managing General Aniline, would frustrate. Crowley further argued that the Treasury was creating a false distinction between "enemy" business enterprises and "neutral" business enterprises controlled by the Axis powers, "which as a businessman and an administrator I know simply will not work." Indeed, any complicated division of powers would fail; he could not cooperate with the Treasury's "underscrappers," who appeared to think something had been stolen from them and whose honor demanded it back. The best solution, under the circumstances, Crowley concluded, would be for the president to sign an order clarifying more sharply his total custodial powers, thus stifling the claims of the Treasury. He would consider it a "personal favor" if the president assured Morgenthau that there would be no changes in the Treasury's favor so "I can go to work under the order without constant argument."[8]

Crowley never sent this letter. After reading it to Rosenman, he sent the president a more cautious note on July 2. Gone was his earlier fascinating reference to managing alien property "from a business-man's point of view," his blast at the Treasury's "underscrappers," and his request for the rest of the Treasury's powers in the alien property field. Even so, he made his point. An executive order of July 6 set forth the custodian's powers in a manner Crowley found most satisfactory. As James Markham, his deputy, wrote Byrnes the next day: "The President prevented any attempt by the Treasury to get back into the management field. He stood by Mr. Crowley all the time."[9]

Crowley and Markham should have expected no less. It would have been strange had the president just four months earlier entrusted Crowley with a specific assignment, then deprived him of the authority he needed to execute it. And the press would have questioned it as strange. At his April 21 press conference, the president had spoken at length of discussing alien property with Crowley the day before. Publicly, he had emphasized the complexity of Crowley's assignment; after that, the Treasury's loss was only a matter of time.[10]

What the president did not tell newsmen about his discussion with Crowley involved his need for Crowley's help in quieting the antiadministration and antiwar Catholic priest Father Charles Coughlin, the force behind the pro-German weekly *Social Justice*. Postmaster General Frank Walker was even then taking legal steps to make *Social Justice* "non-mailable" under the Espionage Act of 1917, and Attorney General Francis Biddle had asked a grand jury to investigate the periodical. Unhappily for the administration, Coughlin seemed eager to have an investigation. He wanted a pulpit for the very views the administration wanted quashed. Years later, Crowley recalled having warned the president then that the legal action being taken against Coughlin was misguided: "You're making a martyr out of him." Many people would believe Coughlin was being investigated, not because he was pro-Nazi, but because he was damaging the administration. And Biddle, in his memoirs, wrote that, despite his department's efforts to prosecute *Social Justice*, he had always favored a quiet solution: "The point was to win the war—not to indict a priest for sedition." If Coughlin were indicted, the administration would look foolish and subversive of the freedoms for which Americans were fighting.[11]

Fortunately, a solution was at hand. Biddle knew that Crowley was "very skillful at settling rows and cleaning up messes"; and during lunch with Crowley earlier that April he had explained the Coughlin situation, including the dangers in prosecuting him. Crowley had agreed—"You don't prosecute men because you disagree with them"—then said that he knew a better, quiet way of dealing with Coughlin. He would fly to Detroit and ask Archbishop Edward Mooney, Coughlin's immediate superior, to have the publication of *Social Justice* stopped. "I'll bring it back tied up," Biddle recalled Crowley promising. "Then," Crowley had added, "we can tell the President."[12]

No less vividly, the attorney-general recalled that Crowley, three days later, "was again in my office, smiling and rubbing his hands at the success of his mission." He reported that "the Archbishop had sent for Father Coughlin and told him that he must stop all his propaganda, on the air or by pen, for the duration. . . . The Archbishop wanted his word now. The alternative was being unfrocked. The priest agreed." And that, Biddle noted, "was the end of Father Coughlin, much to F.D.R.'s delight."[13]

Biddle wrote later that he knew of no conditions attached to silencing Coughlin. In that regard and others, he amply praised his emissary: "Crowley, who did these things with finesse, never asked me for an assurance that no action would be taken against Father Coughlin if he were silenced." And Crowley did not advise him of what he had said to Archbishop Mooney except that no guarantees were given; it was simply understood that "the whole point of the arrangement was to avoid a trial."[14]

There is more to the silencing of Coughlin than Biddle knew—or, at least, recalled. Mooney's threat to defrock Coughlin if he did not desist occurred on May 1, after Crowley left Detroit. Further, Coughlin insisted years later that Mooney was "doing as he was instructed to do." These clues and others provide reason to believe that Mooney was "instructed" by the apostolic delegate in Washington. Four years earlier, the delegate had reversed his order to stop Coughlin's broadcasts, and Mooney would have almost certainly spoken to him before ordering Coughlin to stop publishing *Social Justice*. If so, he had little reason to worry. Crowley, who reputedly was the delegate's chief adviser on financial issues, had returned quickly to the Capital to assure his support for silencing Coughlin. Also, two years later, when Crowley was able to do the Vatican a favor, he acted promptly. There remains only one puzzle. Biddle's memory, twenty years later, of Crowley sitting in his office, "smiling and rubbing his hands" after his success in silencing Coughlin, seems incompatible with Crowley's devotion to his church and his recollection that he strongly disapproved the administration's political motives. Yet Biddle had no reason to concoct Crowley's demeanor in his office; and when, two decades later, Biddle asked Crowley if his manuscript recollection of the event was accurate, Crowley answered only that he hoped Biddle would not publish it. How Crowley really felt about his mission at the time we shall probably never know.[15]

Fortunately for Crowley, or perhaps a sign of his abilities, his offices in Washington ran smoothly when he was away. He had developed a devoted, superbly trained staff at the FDIC, and some members were doing double duty in the custodian's office. Among the major figures were James Markham, the FDIC's general counsel, now also deputy custodian; Henry Riley, the FDIC's chief operating officer; and Forbes Campbell, publicist at the FDIC. Others, less prominent at the FDIC, came over to manage departments with similar characteristics, while Morrison G. Tucker made the jump to handle the Division of Chemicals, Pharmaceuticals and Special Services, for which he had little background but where he quickly took hold. Probing corporate records for enemy ownership or control, no matter the field, involved research that was methodologically quite similar to examining bank records. And there was no problem of time lost because the FDIC and the custodian's office shared the same headquarters on the fourth floor of the National Press Building.

Crowley went outside the FDIC in some instances. He culled Monroe Karasik from the Justice Department to work with Tucker in the Chemicals, Pharmaceuticals, and Special Services Division; A. Matt Werner, a Democrat, lawyer, and old friend from Wisconsin to serve as general counsel; and, finally, his youngest brother, S. James, came from Chicago to take charge of business operations. Withal, Crowley turned to men whose expertise and loyalty he knew and trusted. Thus he believed he had time to complete a mission for Biddle and to handle his governmental responsibilities even while managing Standard Gas.[16]

There were also opportunities to mix pleasure with business. In early April Crowley had given his annual speech to the Wisconsin Bankers Association. Mindful of his time, the convention was shifted to Madison so that he could visit longer with his family, which for Crowley most meaningfully meant his two older brothers, Will and Harry, with whom alone he was comfortable discussing his problems in Washington. Then, in May, he traveled to Milwaukee, where

Marquette University awarded him an honorary doctorate of laws, the first of many he would receive. Almost simultaneously, Catholic University of Washington, DC, gave him the distinction of delivering its commencement address. It was his first, and he enjoyed it immensely, but it was the first of many, all, it must be noted, at Catholic schools. At those he was now a role model. But for Crowley, such honors precious though they were, had to be fitted within the time he could spare from his many responsibilities, including those as chairman and president of Standard Gas and Electric, which now paid him a handsome $65,000 annually.[17]

Fortunately for Crowley, Standard Gas required little of his attention in 1942. That little, though, was roundly applauded by *Barron's*. It pointed out that Crowley used the proceeds from the sale of San Diego Gas and Electric to strengthen Standard Gas's major income producers rather than slicing Standard's debt. This tack, *Barron's* argued, meant better future benefits for Standard, and Crowley had coupled this promise of better prospects with the then depressed market value of Standard's stock to argue before the SEC that temporarily and probably for the duration of the war it should not, and could not by reasonable interpretation of the law, attempt to break up the utility. He had reminded commission members that they were responsible under the Holding Company Act to protect investors as well as consumers. And his argument had proved successful; Standard would remain intact through the war. But the outcome was thought to have a broader significance. The *New York Times* noted that similar remarks by the president of a more powerful holding company were ignored by the SEC. The *Times* regarded Crowley's prominence as a result of being recently named to "the extremely important wartime job of Alien Property Custodian [and being] high in administration circles, . . . of prime importance" in the SEC's decision. His pronouncements could not be ignored.[18]

While Crowley's superb headquarters staff and well-organized examiner-investigators enabled him to spend some time on Standard Gas's problems and a few days on the road addressing a convention or a commencement, he could not avoid his ultimate responsibility for the policies of the Alien Property Custodian's Office and, of course, the FDIC. There was no question, though, of the priority required by the custodian's office. Although some aspects of its methodology were not substantially different from the FDIC's, its objectives, its policies, and some of its methods were. Indeed, Crowley soon decided that some problems were so novel and complex as to justify bringing in a small group of men with experience in vesting alien property during and after the First World War. And some other issues were potentially so controversial that prudence prompted him to form a second, independent committee of prominent businessmen and lawyers for consultation and protective coating.[19]

The complexities of Crowley's task were not clarified by the first accounts of the items the custodian would control. Popular stories emphasized the glitter, even the gold, while they grossly exaggerated and, paradoxically, understated because they misread the value of the property seized. Of the estimated seven billion dollars in enemy property taken after Pearl Harbor, only slightly over half a billion were in physical assets; and little of that—stocks, trading companies, and banks, even gold—could possibly contribute to the war effort. Even the highly publicized General Aniline and Film was not a large-scale manufacturer. Indeed, the entire list of property seized was absent even a single manufacturer of size. The real nuggets were to be found elsewhere, among patents owned by German-dominated companies. Of these, however, Americans learned little except for a few dramatic highlights; the scientific complexities of most formulas were not susceptible to the capabilities of the nation's popular press.[20]

Only the quaintly titled *Oil, Paint, and Drug Reporter* kept a weekly watch on the custodian's handling of confiscated enemy patents, and its coverage was usually so technical or so skimpy as to defy all but the most highly trained and concerned readers. *Business Week* filled in some pieces, bringing an essential bit of drama and the prospects for business to its coverage of the technology involved. It pointed to the many important patents, once jointly owned by Standard Oil and I. G. Farben, General Electric and Krupp A. G., that had been liberated by actual or threatened antitrust proceedings. They were now vested in the custodian's office, and they would soon be released royalty-free to American firms able to use them. Further, The *OPD* reported that, by April 20, the custodian had "Americanized" (or replaced the alien managers) of the Schering Corporation, prominent in pharmaceuticals. Crowley had also seized Schering's common stock, which was being held in a special account "pending [his] further determination." What that meant was not specified, but a plan was even then germinating for using Schering for purposes beyond war production.[21]

Also in April, Crowley was promoting legislation that would empower his office to seize domestic as well as foreign patents crucial for the war effort. He had to proceed without the White House's support, however, as the president did not want to fight conservative opponents on this issue. Testifying before the Senate Patents Committee on April 27, Crowley stressed his need for the bill. He also stressed a balanced concern for the interests of business and the imperatives of war production. But there was little new in what he said. What counted were years of building his credibility with liberals and conservatives alike. It was an important asset to an administration facing an increasingly balky and distrustful Congress, and it helped Crowley obtain the legislation his office needed to seize crucial domestic patents.[22]

By mid-June, three months after Crowley was named custodian, his leadership was producing solid results in the Alien Property Custodian's Office. It had absorbed such major German-dominated companies as American Bosch and Rohm and Haas, and equally, even perhaps more important, it had vested more than a thousand enemy patents.[23]

As the vesting process quickened and the significance of the companies seized became apparent, magazines such as *Business Week* raised again the issue of the disposition of enemy property after the war. Did the authority to "vest" mean confiscation or merely supervision? If supervision, was the custodian authorized to return the property to its former holders? Further, if the custodian was merely a trustee, was he obligated to protect the capital value and earning power of the property? If so, what, precisely, did that mean for the property's use? The president had stated emphatically that April that enemy patents must not be permitted to "slide back" to their former owners, but was his word the last word? *Business Week* did not think so; eventually the legal system would determine the disposition of all enemy property?[24]

Lawyers in the custodian's office were even then considering the future of enemy property. Crowley, himself, though, was more concerned with retaining Senate support for his present policies. By late August, he was preparing testimony for the Senate Patents Committee, explaining the progress made by the custodian's office through the first half of 1942 and its plans for the near future. He would say that his office had vested "approximately 7700 enemy owned patents, . . . about 20% of the estimated total" it expected to acquire within the next two months. Then it would publish a list of its patents and applications for patents, which it would make available to American industry. There would be no general policy for a while—his office did not have enough experience—with one exception: exclusive licences would be issued rarely and, unless military secrecy required, not without a public hearing. Crowley wanted it known that, while his first concern was the war effort, his second was the maintenance of a competitive economy.[25]

Crowley went on to say that he wanted to transform what had been the Treasury's previously "essentially passive" handling of enemy property into "forceful activity against the enemy." What he had in mind was an aggressive program for Schering, the drug company whose common stock the custodian's office had placed in a "special account" that April. At that time, Monroe Karasik, the young lawyer Crowley had taken from the Justice Department (probably because Karasik caught his ear with a solid idea) suggested using the newly vested Schering to drive its former German parent company from its Latin American market. There would be political as well as economic benefits. Having just returned from the region, Karasik reported that German firms, such as Schering, served German foreign policy; their officers and salesmen peddled German propaganda, and part of the company's profits paid the bills. He wanted permission to devise a plan that would drive Schering out, a plan which might later be broadened to drive all German pharmaceutical and chemical firms out of Latin America.[26]

Crowley thought Karasik's idea had tremendous possibilities. Its successful implementation would not only contribute immensely to the struggle against the Axis but also create new markets for fledgling Americans pharmaceutical and chemical firms just liberated from German control—and not merely for the duration. Thus, in May, Crowley told Karasik to work on a proposal with Morrison Tucker, chief of the Pharmaceuticals, Chemicals, and Special Services Division, and other long-trusted associates he had borrowed from the FDIC.[27]

In June, Karasik presented "A Program for Schering in Latin America," elaborating on what he had told Crowley orally earlier. This time, however, he placed less emphasis on the program's contribution during the war than on its economic and political benefits after the fighting ended. "From the standpoint of postwar trade," his report read, "the situation is ominous, as the names of the German products are being kept alive, and the trade channels . . . are kept open for the resumption of complete German domination after the war." And that should not be permitted. Germany's urge to dominate "must be aborted."[28]

Crowley found Karasik's proposal extremely exciting. It explained that Mexico and Brazil could be persuaded to seize Schering A. G.'s patents, that a holding company could be formed, and that the profits could be split three ways. Reading it, Crowley thought the plan for Schering might be expanded. Turning to Karasik, he told him to work with the office's legal staff to draft a proposal for the Mexican government providing for cooperation between a Mexican and an American holding company, the latter to include General Aniline, General Dyestuffs, and Afga-Ansco, along with Schering and, perhaps, other companies later. Crowley visualized at least one American cartel, but he knew the "Program for Schering" alone required the cooperation of the State Department, the Board of Economic Warfare and, not least, the president. For that he needed more hard facts. Someone in his office must go to Latin America and bring them back.[29]

That someone was Morrison Tucker. However, fact-finding was not his only or chief mission. Japanese conquests in the Pacific had cut off traditional sources of the cinchona bark, from which quinine was derived, and Atabrine as a substitute was not proved; but the custodian's office controlled CAPCO, a coffee plantation in Guatemala that also contained many acres of unworked cinchona trees. Tucker's mission was to appraise their condition and, if sound, negotiate their use with Guatemala's president. And this he did. However, the trip exhausted him, and he did not make it to Mexico. From what he heard, though, Tucker could tell Crowley that German pharmaceutical and chemical companies could no longer supply their outlets in Latin America. Schering and other "American" firms could fill the vacuum.[30]

Meanwhile, the custodian's office was expanding nation-wide, investigating, vesting, administering, and sometimes liquidating enemy properties. In October, *The New York Post* financial columnist, Sylvia Porter, pointed to a policy "diametrically opposed to the policy followed by the custodians of the first World War." Properties seized would be managed, not sold; and, she noted, in the cases of Schering, General Aniline, and Magnesium Development Corporation, but expecially Schering, Crowley's policies appeared extremely sound. "Since

[Schering] was vested," she reported, "a huge market has developed for its products." She attributed this partly to its Americanization, which had brought its old American customers back, but she also pointed to its strong new management and its absorption of Germany's Latin American markets. Crowley could not have asked for a more favorable piece had he written it himself.[31]

In one respect, Sylvia Porter's report was unduly favorable. She missed the mark altogether when ascribing a success like that at Schering to General Aniline and Film. General Aniline was not thriving. Neither, for that matter, was its sales agent, General Dyestuffs. These problems came to Crowley's attention in August. General Aniline's board sent him a memorandum asserting that Dyestuffs was not cooperating and that the two firms should be consolidated under its aegis. This clearly was the type of complicated and delicate problem Crowley was appointed to solve. Not only was the welfare of General Aniline and General Dyestuffs at stake, but also the reputations of their managements and of those responsible for appointing them. In this instance, it may be recalled, Morgenthau had named General Aniline's board the previous March; while Crowley, since then, had appointed Dyestuff's board. Now, with the stakes running high, Crowley asked a member of his consulting committee, Boston attorney John J. Burns, to review General Aniline's charges and make recommendations.[32]

On October 20, Burns reported back. The two companies faced disaster if drastic remedies were not made. General Aniline had blamed General Dyestuffs unwillingness to cooperate. Burns, however, blamed the "incompetence of the present officers and directors of General Aniline." Beginning with Robert McConnell, the firm's president, they lacked essential technical knowledge. On the other hand, all but two of General Dyestuff's executives were well qualified, and one, Ernest K. Halbach, is "generally ranked . . . as the outstanding dyestuff executive" in the field.[33]

There could be no mistaking the thrust of Burns's report—or what it required. But Crowley did not act on it for months. The primary, if not the only, reason was Halbach. General Aniline's board was charging, privately to date, that Halbach was a German agent; and Crowley had lent credibility to the charge, if indeed he did not originate it. In June, when his office vested General Dyestuffs, he had taken Halbach's stock and, exaggerating the significance of his forty year connections with German firms, fired him as the company's president. Then, however, just after Burns's report seemed to discredit General Aniline's charge, and his own earlier judgment, Crowley recognized a desperate need for Halbach's expertise at Dyestuffs and brought him back to the company as a "special consultant" and de facto president. Even so, Crowley worried that there might be a measure of truth in General Aniline's charge, and its board would publicize it and damage him if he discharged them without thoroughly checking it. His determination to protect himself was, then, the major, if not the only reason, he did not get rid of General Aniline's board in 1942, or for several months into the new year. Halbach had to be investigated and, he hoped, cleared a second time.[34]

Meanwhile, Crowley, busy though he was, played a critical if narrow role in Wisconsin's congressional elections in 1942. As a story in the *Wisconsin State Journal* had pointed out the previous winter, "Leo Crowley—in Washington—Wields Influence in Wisconsin." Crowley was "the unofficial liaison man between Washington and Wisconsin. He will know whether a bill or project will receive executive sanction." Specifically, the columnist credited Crowley with obtaining a powder plant for Baraboo in Sauk County. And he had. Why he initiated, and the president approved, a project primarily designed to provide business for a railroad and in a congressional district held by a Republican is curious. Crowley never explained, but despite the rapidly diminishing strength of the Progressive party he had once used to such great advantage for the president's benefit, it is obvious that he had real clout at the White House in 1942. Later, Crowley would only say of the powder plant and other prizes the White House approved, that the president "was nice to me."[35]

That fall, the *Capital Times* assumed that Crowley was speaking for the president when he endorsed Progressive candidates for governor and Congress. So did the Democratic gubernatorial candidate who lamely argued that Crowley "has misled President Roosevelt with respect to Wisconsin politics." Of course, Crowley had done nothing of the kind. He had adopted the only strategy which might defeat the state's Republican governor and, simultaneously, win Senator LaFollette's support for a Green Bay Democrat running in a Republican congressional district. And Crowley's trademark trade-offs succeeded as usual: Both Progressive candidates won; so did the Green Bay Democrat. Partly as a consequence, Crowley was again mentioned for Democratic national committee chairman.[36]

It was just talk. Byrnes had already pointed out that Crowley's position with Standard Gas disqualified him; both Roosevelt and Crowley knew he had enough burdens already; and, in any case, he could help the president more in his essentially or at least ostensibly apolitical jobs than as a political manager. In fact, this was more true after November 1942 than before. The president had not dominated Congress since 1936. Since then, a southern Democratic–Republican coalition had blocked his domestic program. But it was only after the 1942 congressional returns that it was strong enough to carry its own agenda; and that meant more than legislation; it meant hostile investigations.

Acute politician that Crowley was, he would not have ignored the election's results or implications. It is probable that they contributed to his postponing revisions in the officers and board at General Aniline. However, his own position was ambiguous. It might be remembered that Crowley had endorsed Morgenthau's choice of Robert McConnell as General Aniline's president in March, just prior to assuming his custodian's post. Not only had he affirmed then that McConnell was a "capable administrator" but, as Morgenthau would be quick to recall, he had told the Treasury secretary "he would not interfere with anything which we had done and would leave in General Aniline and Film the men we had installed." During the late fall of 1942 and the first half of 1943, then, Crowley was caught in a trap partly of his own making. He could only hope that General Aniline's board would study Burns's report and quietly resolve its feud with General Dyestuffs.[37]

Such dramatic problems occurred rarely; daily, Crowley found himself bombarded by businessmen anxious to learn how the patents liberated from enemy control could improve their products or processes. Their first hint—and the public's—came, finally, almost a year after Pearl Harbor. In November 1942, scientists, patent attorneys, and journalists were permitted to see thousands of patents at the National Chemical Exhibition in Chicago. There was no licensing policy, however, until December 7, when Crowley formally handed a memorandum on patent policy to the president.[38]

Within two weeks, it was revealed that 50,000 patents would soon be generally available. Crowley said that American industry could then obtain patents from "the most important center of scientific research outside the United States." Catalogues could be seen in Washington and Chicago or obtained by mail. However, the bonanza was largely ignored. Six months later, *Business Week* reported that American industry had applied for only a fifth of the patents seized, and almost half of the applications had come from one firm. Crowley, the story said, was "puzzled by the delay."[39]

Perhaps he should not have been. One business leader, coincidentally Robert Wilson, a General Aniline director, argued that there was no profit advantage to a company in spending large sums on machinery to utilize a patent when competitors could do likewise. As Louis Johnson, Dyestuff's president, wrote Crowley, "I do not believe he agrees with your patent policy." Obviously, and perhaps justifiably. Yet there was little Crowley could have done. Giving a single firm an exclusive license—and profits—would have led to shrieks of "special privilege," an especially serious charge when equality of sacrifice was demanded at home as well as on the battlefield. Possibly Crowley had run afoul of a problem for which even he had no solution.[40]

By July 1943, however, Crowley had a solution to his difficulties with General Aniline's board and its year-long feud with General Dyestuffs: GAF's board was replaced. According to its outgoing president, Morgenthau appointee Robert McConnell, he and the board were forced out for only one reason: his "serious objections" to a "new policy which it is proposed to adopt for this company's operations and which the new board selected by Mr. Crowley will be expected to carry out." That new policy, he pointed out, was "predicated on permanent Government ownership of General Aniline and Film Corporation, with a view to utilizing [it] as a spearhead in Latin America and other foreign countries to further . . . the Government's political or good neighbor policy." Explaining further to Morgenthau and three board members, McConnell said he was "entirely sympathetic to [Crowley's objectives]"; however, he opposed his means—he was "a firm believer in the principle of private enterprise"—and in any case he "could not conceive that such a venture would have the remotest chance of success." Therefore his decision to resign.[41]

Of course, McConnell was forced out. During the spring and early summer of 1943 Crowley had found new directors for General Aniline's board. The search had been difficult, perhaps because those asked lacked time (as they complained); but they could not have ignored the fact that serving on GAF's board actually meant doing the custodian's bidding. In the end, most of those accepting were, as the *New York Times* noted, "associates of Mr. Emanuel . . . of Standard Gas and Electric Company, of which ... Mr. Crowley is president and chairman of the board." The *Times* further noted that among those associates of Emanuel named to General Aniline's board were two officers of General Dyestuffs, a vice-president and president Louis Johnson. Perhaps unaware of the lack of cooperation, even the feud between General Aniline and General Dyestuffs, the *Times* did not stress Crowley's neat solution when he de facto merged the two companies. So, too, it either failed to see or failed to point out that, while technically Crowley's and Emanuel's friends would run both companies, they would be guided by the same Ernest Halbach identified the previous autumn in the Burns report as the guiding genius at Dyestuffs.[42]

By July 13, Crowley's plans for General Aniline and General Dyestuffs had matured. The stockholders of both (meaning for all intents and purposes the custodian, who had vested the stock) met that midsummer day in 1943 to elect, in fact to confirm, the new board Crowley had chosen. With that, McConnell's resignation was accepted and Morgenthau's remaining influence broken, while Crowley's influence, through the expert Halbach, was firmly in place. Crowley had achieved another smashing coup, or so it seemed that summer. If there were weak links that might be exploited, he had no time to think about them. Even then, the president was asking him to assume an additional and, surely, a heavier burden.[43]

10

The Nation's # 1 Pinch Hitter

The second week of July 1943 saw Crowley wearing his three hats—as alien property custodian, as both chairman and president of Standard Gas, and as chairman of the FDIC—as if they had been shaped for him alone. Old friends learned of his long hours, his miles traveled, and his major responsibilities, and worried about his health, but Crowley shrugged off such concerns. There was so much to do, and doing it was his pride and pleasure. He had just "consolidated" General Aniline and General Dyestuffs, he was putting the last touches on another plan to strengthen Standard Gas, and that spring he had written the president that New York's "ultraconservative" mutual savings banks, which had left the FDIC a few years earlier, had finally admitted its soundness by seeking readmission. He would have been happier, though, had Roosevelt's reply, after thanking "Dear Leo," attributed the decision of the banks to the FDIC's policies rather than "the soundness of this Administration."[1]

By the early summer of 1943 Roosevelt needed tributes to his administration's "soundness." His generals and his admirals were not the problem; neither was his diplomacy; rather, he confronted a conservative, increasingly hostile Congress and two threatening war-related problems. The most complex involved interagency conflict in managing American and Allied economic activities abroad, but it was not politically dangerous, and its resolution could be postponed. Such was not the case, though, with a public conflict involving two members of his official family; it was politically damaging and had to be resolved quickly.

The president himself bore measurable responsibility. Previously, he had appointed his vice-president, Henry Wallace, chairman of the Board of Economic Warfare, and authorized the board to control the

148

export of strategic materials and to develop, import, and stockpile the same. To Wallace and his deputy, Milo Perkins, this directive meant that the supplying of American troops must take precedence over the price paid. It also meant to the vice-president and other New Dealers in the BEW that its purchase contracts in Latin America must favor labor there. This would give meaning to the administration's "Good Neighbor" policy and improve productivity. Unhappily from this viewpoint, the BEW was not the only agency authorized to negotiate in Latin America, and it did not control the funds to implement contracts it made.[2]

The president had placed those funds in the hands of Secretary of Commerce Jesse Jones, who supervised a number of agencies involved in securing critical raw materials. Jones refused BEW's requests for funds on two grounds: that BEW purchasing agents in Latin America duplicated his agents, who were first in the field; and that BEW contracts there included prolabor clauses and were too costly, as was its undue stress on speeding shipments. Needless to say, Wallace and Perkins became ever more frustrated and ready to fight for the funds they required.[3]

Wallace and Jones battled off camera until June 1943. Then Wallace manuevered Jones into surrendering his purchasing agency, the United States Commercial Corporation, to the BEW. But Jones quickly struck back. He advised the newly dominant conservative coalition of midwestern Republicans and southern Democrats in the Senate of the 78th Congress that the BEW's prolabor Latin American contracts represented international "do-goodism," an undesirable extension of the New Deal to the world. Wallace countered that Jones's "bankerminded" grip on the BEW's purchasing hamstrung its capacity to import critical war materials and possibly prolonged the war, but without positive effect. Southern Democrats such as Tennessee's Senator Kenneth McKellar and Virginia's Harry Byrd were relaying Jones's tale of wasteful utopianism to the press and public.[4]

Perkins and Assistant Secretary of Commerce William Clayton, who often acted for Jones, joined the battle, but it might have remained a limited skirmish excepted that, at June's end, Wallace publicly charged Jones with "obstructionist tactics" which could prolong the war. This open feuding angered the president—he had earlier warned that any members of the administration submitting quarrels to the press should "send to me a letter of resignation"—but he merely asked Jimmy Byrnes, his "Assistant President," as the press labeled him, to patch the quarrel between the two men.[5]

Byrnes's effort the next day did not still the public feuding; and on July 6 he wrote the president: "I am satisfied there is no way of reconciling the differences between Mr. Wallace and Mr. Jones." The president should put an end to the conflict by "withdrawing authority from both Wallace and Jones and creating a new organization" that would embrace both their agencies. There was congressional criticism of the "dissension and lack of coordination on the home front"; combined with a growing anti-New Deal strength it could cripple the administration if the president did not act.[6]

On the afternoon of July 14, Byrnes handed the president detailed proposals. The two of most immediate political importance spoke to what Byrnes called "the Wallace-Jones fight." He called for renaming the BEW the Office of Economic Warfare, providing it with a new director, and handing it Jones's agencies. But he did not suggest a director for his newly conceived OEW until the next day. Then, he noted, "I recommended Leo T. Crowley." Then, too, he jotted in his diary, "Work was started on the preparation of letters to Wallace and Jones [explaining the former's firing and the latter's demotion], . . . to the heads of agencies [warning them again about public feuding], and the Executive Order [outlining Crowley's authority as head of the Office of Economic Warfare]."[7]

On paper, Crowley could end the discord between his proposed OEW and the procurement agencies Jones controlled. He could integrate the agencies into the OEW or control them by appointing new boards of directors. He could also direct the Reconstruction Finance Corporation to provide the OEW with the funds it needed for its operations. However, the *New York Times* quickly pointed out that until Congress handed the RFC new funds, Jones as federal loan administrator "would continue to hold the money bag." In truth, Jones's influence with Congress, so critical in prompting the president's executive order, insured that for the moment it would prove cosmetic.[8]

Years later, Crowley recalled that he was at the White House when the president said he was going to let Wallace and Jones go. "He was tired of their disagreeing publicly." More to the point, Crowley recalled his own sentiments; he had thought that Wallace and Perkins had been wrong as to the substance of their feud with Jones and too aggressive in pursuing it; he had believed that he, sharing many of Jones's concerns and more conciliatory in temper, could secure the federal loan administrator's cooperation without much difficulty. He had also advised the president that July day that his new assignment would require his personal attention, the more so as he could not draw much on the loyalists who had worked closely with him at the Federal Deposit Insurance Corporation and later at the Alien Property Custodian's Office; they were already stretched thin. Further, he reminded the president that he had taken the job as alien property custodian for organizational purposes only, and asked that he be allowed to resign. But he was turned down. As for surrendering his job as FDIC chairman to focus on his new assignment, Crowley had no such intention; even then a newspaper was praising him for transforming "a gasping baby" into a solid guarantor of banking stability. He finally told the president he would ask Standard Gas for a leave, at full pay, of course.[9]

At the president's press conference the day after the shake-up, reporters were satisfied when he said that Crowley would take a leave of absence from Standard Gas; they did not ask whether he would continue to receive his salary, now $75,000 annually. They did ask sharp questions, though, about the newly named OEW. Milo Perkins, as much a firebrand as Wallace, had remained at his post to encourage experienced Wallaceites to stay. Now newsmen, after asking the president how long Perkins would remain, heard him say it was up to Crowley. It was the reply they might have expected. The president was shielding himself from liberal attacks for Perkins's dismissal by publicly handing the decision and its timing to Crowley, one of whose functions was taking blows which otherwise would threaten the White House. Curiously, though, the *New York Times* gave the story a Machiavellian twist; accordingly, the president and Crowley had arranged the day before that the president give him a "green light" to get rid of Perkins, thus himself absorbing liberal attacks that might otherwise impair Crowley's effectiveness in his new job.[10]

Crowley was not around for the president's press conference. He spent most of the day in New York, where he persuaded Standard Gas to grant him leave at full pay. On the train that day or the next when he returned, he must have reflected on the notes he had drafted for Perkins and Jones before leaving Washington the morning before. That to Perkins answered the question reporters were then asking the President. Crowley asked him to remain "at least until July 30 . . . to advise and familiarize me with respect to the problems of economic warfare."

As for Jones, Crowley asked "Dear Jesse" to have his four RFC agencies affected by the president's executive order of July 15 "carry on until I have had time to acquaint myself with their various operations." Meanwhile, he foresaw "no changes in the corporations affected except [formalities] such as may be required by the order." The cynic might see a bit of ambiguity in that sentence, especially when coupled with Crowley's closing line. After reminding Jones of their decade of friendship and cooperation, he wrote: "I know now that I can count on you to cooperate with this program."[11]

As for Jones, he was then publicly promising "every possible assistance" to Crowley, and adding, "The President could not have selected a better qualified man." He probably meant it, too, but personal as the feud between Wallace and Jones had become, it was always fundamentally institutional. Honeyed words could not dispel differences in perspective and interest. Even before Crowley left for New York (on July 16), he had issued OEW Order # 1, ratifying every action "previously prescribed or executed by . . . the Board of Economic Warfare." His order, though absolutely proper, obviously irked Jones. At the bottom he penned, "Should exclude Wallace Order # 5," referring to a February attempt by Wallace to transfer all policy-making power from Jones's agencies to the BEW. For obvious reasons. Wallace's February order had inflamed Jones, who had defied it. Now Crowley, including it in his Order # 1, had given Wallace's action new, undeniable force.[12]

There are other signs of friction during these early months. An OEW officer called an RFC subsidiary and said that Crowley had called from New York and wanted action on a pressing matter, only to be told that Jones's agencies would act as determined by Jones "until further action was taken by Mr. Crowley or Mr. Byrnes [in person]." Crowley then personally insisted that Jones execute an OEW purchase order instantly. But these clashes were exceptions. Crowley soon fired the OEW officer and other Wallacites who upset Jones and his subordinates. He wanted Jones's cooperation. This was not because Crowley lacked authority; that was established in the executive order appointing him OEW director; but he knew the president had appointed him to deal with a political problem, and to do it quietly, without arousing Jones's nest of allies on the Hill. The president knew he could. Years later, New Deal Brain Truster "Tommy" Corcoran would tell Lawrence Eklund that Crowley "had a very personal relationship with Roosevelt, who trusted him for his adroitness in handling a delicate political situation. . . . He was the best internal diplomatist of the entire Roosevelt Administration." Corcoran was a close friend of Crowley and might have been guilty of some exaggeration, but a St. Paul banker who knew Crowley from his tenure with the Farm Credit Administration summed up what he meant to the president when he wrote: "You are the Nation's # 1 Pinch-Hitter."[13]

Crowley understood that though the executive order creating the OEW gave him the authority to force the compliance of Jones's agencies that must be his last resort. He had been appointed to defuse the open conflict that had prompted Wallace's removal and, on paper at least, Jones's loss of authority. Crowley thought he could, too. Years later, despite differences with Jones, Crowley would speak warmly of him and his faith that he "could go to him with a problem and . . . sit down and talk it over. He'd understand it." Jones was "sound"; Wallace's people had not been. However, Crowley knew he could not employ a heavy hand even had he been so inclined. He held the markers and could count on the friendship, respect, and trust of many powerful senators and representatives, but so could Jones. Unfortunately for the administration, those now-dominant congressmen, Democrats as well as Republicans, were overtly sympathetic with Jones's conservative positions (as Crowley privately was). It had been obvious in their devastating attacks on Wallace and Perkins; it was obvious now in notes Crowley received after his appointment: two contained warnings.[14]

Senator McKellar, perhaps the sharpest critic of Wallace and Perkins in their feud with Jones, wrote Crowley that he was sending him Perkins's testimony for his reading. What the Tennessean meant was clear: firing Perkins would strengthen Crowley's famed reputation for "splendid diplomacy and good sense." Alternately, the threat, were he to retain Perkins, was clear. And if Crowley needed another jolt, he received a note from McKellar's brother, praising him as a man with "common sense who would get rid of the crackpot professors." In fact, Perkins was not a "crackpot professor"—he was a businessman from, ironically, Jones's Houston—but the writer had made his point.[15]

Crowley understood the delicacy of the problem. He answered Senator McKellar's telegram with the grace which had so obviously marked his first note to Jones, but with a tactful added touch of deference. He did not remind the senator that with more patience he would have heard him say that Perkins would stay on until July 30, but only in a "consultant capacity." Rather, he added honey, writing that he would "make a complete analysis of the executive personnel and I am sure you will be in full accord with whatever action is taken." Finally, Crowley informed the senator that he wanted very much to talk with him when he returned to Washington. Crowley's tone could not have been more conciliatory, yet he set no topics for discussion and no names for dismissal; in fact, he conceded nothing. Every word reflected his belief that McKellar, if not coddled, could impair the effectiveness of the OEW, not to mention his own reputation; conversely, a little bit of deference could bank the senator's support and that of some of his friends. Indeed, Crowley's reply exemplified the shrewd political judgment which many in Wisconsin and Washington had already witnessed, and to which Corcoran would later allude.[16]

Surely Crowley obtained more pleasure from the purely laudatory letters which stressed his dedication, sympathized with his new headache, and worried about his health. Best, perhaps, there was a note from the British Embassy. It addressed his new status and his appointment's significance for Britain as an ally. While the Wallace-Jones feud had focused exclusively on the procurement of critical raw materials, of importance to the British as potential lend-lease, the OEW was also significant as it controlled exports to neutrals and made preemptive purchases abroad. Suddenly, British representatives viewed Crowley as an administrator to reckon with, and they were not alone; other Allies acknowledged his new power and prestige. But Crowley's significant new post and these heady accolades did not protect him from the criticism of William Evjue, his sometime ally at Madison's *Capital Times*.[17]

After July 16 William T. Evjue could be heard running around Madison telling everyone who would listen, "I am damn sore about the way they treated Wallace. . . . " But he did not editorialize on the issue until July 21, and then circuitously, after the *Chicago Tribune* published numbers from Crowley's state income tax returns for 1939, 1940, 1941, and 1942. First, Evjue wrote a "news" article for his Sunday edition. Printing what he labeled the "right numbers," he noted that they seemed to refute prior reports that Crowley "has been receiving no money from the government" since he became chairman of Standard Gas. But Evjue made little of the issue until the following Wednesday, when he printed an editorial that clumsily employed innuendo to couple Crowley's business ties to Wallace's fate.[18]

"Leo T. Crowley has led a charmed life in politics," but no longer,

Evjue began. He "has risen to a new place of power over the mangled body of Henry A. Wallace." Then the innuendo began. Evjue reminded his readers that "Crowley has been a protege of an international banker named Victor Emanuel, who represents the so-called Lowenstein interests in Europe. . . . " That had led to Crowley's chairmanship and presidency of Standard Gas and Electric, a "Byllesby corporation," and there he had been receiving $75,000 a year in salary. Guilt by association was Evjue's thesis, but not with the little-known Emanuel and probably unknown, distant "Lowenstein interests." The guilty party was the relatively familiar "Byllesby empire" of nearby Chicago. Evjue reminded readers that it was in "considerable disrepute during the depression," when it spent $123,000 "to . . . corrupt Wisconsin public officials." Evjue did not mention that the linkage between Standard Gas and the "Byllesby empire" was severed before Crowley's involvement with the utility. He wanted to indict Crowley and focus on one issue: why "Henry A. Wallace, who held unflinchingly to New Deal principles and ideals, is on the scrap heap while the Jones-Crowley type of New Dealism and the Tory Southern Democrats seem to be in the ascendancy." Evjue had chosen the locally well-known Crowley to vent his frustration with the rising anti-New Deal tide.[19]

Crowley ignored the *Chicago Tribune*'s report of his sources of income and the follow-up article and editorial in the *Capital Times*. He reacted, however, after Evjue published another blast on August 15, castigating him and the administration for firing John Bovingdon, an OEW economist charged by Martin Dies, Texas's right-wing Democratic Congressman, with Communist leanings.[20]

This incident first became public on July 31, when Dies told the press that seven years earlier Bovingdon had presented a rhythmic dance program to alleged "Communist groups" and previously had visited the Soviet Union. The OEW officer Crowley told to look into the charges of Communist sympathies reported that Bovingdon was "doing a good job" and that his dancing "may have been an avocation." But Dies was unrelenting, and on August 3 Crowley politely asked Bovingdon to resign "for the best interests of the Office of Economic Warfare." Bovingdon then released a letter to Crowley refusing to resign, calling himself a "victim of an anti–New Deal offensive," and adding that he would not "retreat before the Dies un-American Committee." Immediately after that, according to the *Chicago Tribune*, Crowley booted the "toe twiddler."[21]

Crowley's dismissal of Bovingdon is understandable given the pressure he faced. Even the usually temperate *New York Times* saw totalitarian meaning in a remark about rhythmic dancing Bovingdon made nineteen years earlier. And Henry Wallace had earlier fired a BEW employee Dies exposed. Even so, Evjue also denounced Crowley for firing Bovingdon and the president for permitting it. He saw surrendering to the Un-American Activities Committee or Dies, its chairman, not as an isolated act, but as a reflection of the administration's disturbing new readiness to buckle before right-wing pressure. Thus his editorial of August 15 scourging Crowley and the president.[22]

Crowley reacted, but probably only because he was in Madison for his fifty-fourth birthday. According to Evjue, Crowley asked friends to arrange a meeting because he was afraid of a rebuff if he asked himself. If so, it is understandable that Crowley was cautious when they met. So was Evjue. The editor reiterated his fears about "the trend of affairs in Washington." He told Crowley that Bovingdon's dismissal revealed anew a "distinct tendency in the Administration to appease its enemies," and coming so soon after the Wallace affair "shocked him." He viewed the incident as another sign that the president no longer seemed interested in the New Deal. According to Evjue, Crowley rejoined that the Wallace affair was a "big mistake" on the president's part, then he attempted to explain it on the ground that the president was not paying sufficient attention to matters on the home front because he was "tremendously interested in winning the war." He denied that the president was heading toward the right or that he was trying to appease the right.[23]

In retrospect, Evjue's fears much more closely resembled the truth than Crowley's excuses and denials. And at year's end the president would admit it, advising reporters and the country that "Dr. New Deal" was no longer needed, that what the country needed was "Dr. Win the War." These statements surprised no one who had kept tabs on the administration. The coalition of Progressives, Farmer-Laborites, and the CIO which had colored the New Deal had been shattered five years earlier. Reality in 1943 and after was the president's power resting on the pre-New Deal Democratic base supplemented by internationalist, often export-oriented Republicans. Reality was the president's replacing Wallace, who had enraged conservatives, with Crowley, who would mollify them. It was, in part, the price for the free hand the president wanted in order to manage the war and to shape the

postwar world. This was a price—these in sum were realities—
Crowley seems to have justified feebly at best—but Evjue might not
have accepted them under any circumstances.[24]

Many liberals could not. But the president's action on July 15 and
Crowley's actions following were realistic and effective. The *New York
Times* and other newspapers always designated Crowley a "conservative New Dealer," and the New Deal legislation he said he had
favored—and did—justified that oxymoron. He was neither a conservative nor a radical. He had not favored the WPA (the Works Progress
Administration), but he acknowledged approving the creation of the
FDIC, the Securities and Exchange Act, the Social Security Act, the
Farm Home Act, and the RFC's policies under the New Deal. Whatever else in the New Deal he had supported or disapproved of or how
strongly he was too prudent to state, though he admitted that once
policy was made, as with the WPA, loyalty to the administration required him to go along with it.[25]

As a "conservative New Dealer," Crowley could trim his sails to
the increasingly strong conservative winds without difficulty. And
without challenge. After July 15, congressional criticism of the OEW
ended, at least for a few months. But Crowley's appointment did more
than mollify such critics as McKellar and Dies. It soothed the State Department, which had complained bitterly about the BEW's interference
with its charter overseas; it offered hope to Latin American businessmen, who had been angered by the BEW's interference with the wages
they paid; and it offered hope to the American businessmen seeking
relief from the BEW's control of exports and its competition for raw
materials. All thought Crowley might adopt the minimalist course favored by his friend Commerce Secretary Jesse Jones and by conservatives in Congress. And had they heard Crowley discuss the president's
priorities with Evjue, they would have been even more sanguine.[26]

Crowley did not elaborate on the president's emphasis on the war
and disinterest in domestic matters for Evjue, and the editor did not
challenge him to do so. Rather, he asked Crowley to tell the White
House that "liberals . . . are becoming somewhat skeptical of
Roosevelt." Then he jotted a reflection on their meeting that day,
"Crowley's real concern over the editorial centered in the revelations . . . concerning [his] connection with the Standard Gas and Electric Co."[27]

Except for Evjue's editorials, Crowley received favorable if generally shallow attention from the press, as if what he wore or how long he slept were significant. Among all the reporters suddenly interested in Crowley, only one penetrated the surface of his personality and politics. Robert L. Riggs, Washington bureau chief of the *Louisville Courier-Journal*, neatly sized up Crowley as "four-fifths Jones and one fifth Wallace." Crowley and Jones used the same "banker" language; Wallace's "kind of thinking and rhetoric left Crowley completely cold." Riggs accurately pointed out that "Crowley's liberalism was of the Community Chest variety [centering on] sympathy for the underdog . . . , raising money to see that no one in Madison, Wis., lacks food and clothing [and to pay for] a new hospital. But he has no interest in making over . . . our social and economic system."[28]

There was a disparaging tone in Riggs's characterization, as if the virtues he mentioned were stigmatized by their inadequacy. But he shrewdly fastened on the reasons the president chose Crowley to succeed Wallace. "There is one thing about Crowley that you can gamble on, he is not going to get into any public brawls with any other officer of the government." Leo Crowley knew what Wallace had never learned: that a tightly buttoned lip, a measure of manipulation, and easygoing ways were essential for an administrator. Riggs hammered the point: those qualities were "making [Crowley] a far more powerful figure in the New Deal than is generally realized . . . close to James F. Byrnes, the President's No. 1 man, [and] on friendly terms with practically every member of Congress. He knows as much as any man in Washington about the Administration's plans for the present and future."

As Riggs could have predicted, that summer Crowley provided reporters with little insight into his plans for the OEW. Asked about likely staff changes at the OEW and the future of the OEW's satellites still functioning under Jones, Crowley said only, "It would be foolish on my part to go in and start immediately to disrupt an established set-up." In fact, though, he was considering major changes within the OEW and between it and Jones's agencies. Possibly, too, he was afraid that the president would ask him to take on another, even greater task than bossing the OEW. Either from Byrnes or from the president, he might have learned that the White House was considering how better to coordinate the nation's economic agencies operating abroad; it had been discussed at some length on July 14 and again the next day, perhaps, in its earlier stages, while he was there.[29]

On July 28, just two weeks after taking command at the OEW, Crowley wrote Jones that "his first efforts [would] be . . . to take over such activities [as purchases abroad] and consolidate them in the OEW organization." Meanwhile, Crowley informed Jones, his agencies must act on the purchase orders drafted by the OEW. And the next day, either as a matter of form or because Jones balked, he sent the War Mobilization Committee his "Statement of [OEW's] General Economic Program." More Wallace than Jones, it used such forceful language as "maximum speed" and "vital to the enemy" in demanding the compliance of all agencies involved in the purchase of strategic war materials abroad without regard to cost. Doubtlessly, Crowley had earlier cleared the document with his friend and patron Jimmy Byrnes, who chaired the WMB, as it was promptly approved. Now he had greater authority to make Jones act on the OEW's orders, should the need arise. But the "Statement" was not formally registered for another four weeks.[30]

The month's delay might be attributed to Crowley's desire to avoid an open rupture with Jones and Jones's allies on the Hill. But charges that equipment was "lying idle" and "hours were being lost" because Crowley was making "no decisions" strongly suggest that he lacked confidence in the OEW's staff until then. Indeed, he was slow to find a new ramrod. It was August 31 before he replaced Milo Perkins with Laughlin Currie. He probably did so on White House orders. Currie, a presidential assistant, would provide close liaison; also, as a New Dealer, he might quiet carping from Wallaceites like Evjue. Even so, he was a curious choice for both the president and Crowley. Coming from Harvard University's faculty, he personified the "crack-pot professor" the McKellars so detested. Yet neither reacted. Perhaps they were sufficiently pleased that Crowley flushed out Deputy Director Morris Rosenthal and General Counsel Monroe Oppenheimer, both New Dealers and both outspoken critics of Jones and, now, of their new boss. Crowley had had reason to fire them whatever their political beliefs, as both men spread what Oppenheimer later recalled as ribald, derogatory stories about his management of the OEW, the least damning him as "the leader of the wrecking crew." Crowley believed such attacks from staff members impaired morale. He wanted deputies who were supportive as well as competent.[31]

Until the summer of 1943, the OEW had focused almost exclusively on procuring strategic materials and on denying them to the

Axis. Now, since the Allies liberation of North Africa and seizure of Sicily, Crowley's OEW faced new, broader, in some respects more complicated problems. New regulations were required to deal with leakages of strategic materials from North Africa, but these the OEW could develop alone. Providing food and shelter for liberated North Africans and Italians was something else. Temporarily, the American Military Government for Occupied Territories (or AMGOT) dealt directly with these problems, though it was supported by several civilian agencies. These included Crowley's OEW, the Office of Foreign Relief and Rehabilitation Operations, the Office of Lend-Lease Administration, and the new, much needed but ineffective Office of Foreign Economic Coordination, the latter three known in short as OFFRO, OLLA, and OFEC.[32]

The Army had fought civil involvement in the occupied territories. It claimed that it alone was competent to administer aid properly, that involving civilian agencies would mean "inevitable confusion." And the previous winter Budget Director Harold Smith had warned the president that several civilian agencies, plus the Army, all involved in planning, financing, procuring, and administering, must "produce confusion in the basic war jobs." But the president was insistent. He wanted civilian involvement, if not control. Still, he had admitted serious confusion among the various civilian agencies. In June he had sent a plan to Secretary of State Cordell Hull that he argued would eliminate that problem and conflict with the Army by placing the civilian agencies under the control of the State Department.[33]

The president's plan was immediately implemented, but with a crippling change. The Office of Foreign Economic Coordination it established embraced what was then the Board of Economic Warfare, the Office of Lend-Lease Administration, the Office of Inter-American Affairs, and the Office of Foreign Relief and Rehabilitation Operations; but it was not given real authority. OFEC was just an interdepartmental policy committee, and Assistant Secretary of State Dean Acheson, who chaired the committee, could not achieve even a semblance of agreement simply by asking for it.[34]

All this was apparent to all but (possibly) the president by mid-July. Byrnes had seen it and, among his various proposals in the Wallace-Jones feud, suggested consolidating the many civilian agencies operating overseas into one agency under a strong chief. Perhaps he intended Crowley to be that chief, but he did not say so. Neither did Budget Director Smith, though he heartily agreed with Byrnes's proposal and argued it at length. The sole result, however, was to irritate the president. He saw serious political problems in moving or removing Edward Stettinius at OLLA; Herbert Lehman at OFFRO; and, in particular, Nelson Rockefeller at Inter-American Affairs. At the same time, in contrast with the threatening criticism that broke during the Wallace-Jones battle, there were no cries now from Congress or the press to end confusion and conflict in American civilian agencies operating overseas. There was internal clamor to deal with a real problem, but there was no pleasant solution. Dealing with it could wait.[35]

Probably no one was more aware of the confusion and conflict than Crowley. For the record, he covered up. When newsmen asked him soon after his appointment as OEW director and again in early August if he had any difficulty following the foreign policy lead of the president and secretary of state, he replied sharply: "No need to coordinate me and Cordell Hull. There isn't anything we can't settle in a one minute talk." This last was apparently the case—Crowley's relations with Hull were sound—but reporters had asked the wrong question. They should have asked him how he felt about Acheson's management of OFEC, as Crowley was soon "telling the same tale of woe that had been told by Wallace, Perkins, Nelson Rockefeller, and Lehman, about the 'interfering' tactics of the State Department."[36]

By early September, Byrnes sensed the widening dimensions of what may have appeared to Crowley as a bureaucratic problem. The British, Byrnes recalled later, were complaining of difficulty in dealing with "conflicting jurisdictions" in North Africa; and the *New York Times* was emphasizing "uncertainty regarding the representative spheres of OEW, Lend-Lease, and OFFRO; . . . friction between OEW and the War Food Administration as regards foreign food purchases"; and Lehman's unwillingness to subordinate his agency to the State Department "to the extent [the latter] desired." At last the press was snapping at the administration's heels.

Years later, Byrnes would recall that he had "feared a real scandal would result from the constant pickering [sic]," and that he quickly began planning a unifying agency, the Foreign Economic Administration. However, Byrnes leaves no doubt that he believed the crux of the problem was conflicting personalities, not institutional cohesion and authority. In drawing up his plan, he saw as his most trying task "trying to keep the various directors in good humor." He specified Stettinius and Rockefeller, who viewed the idea of a superagency as so "humiliating" and "objectionable" "they could not sleep," and he deliberately kept the obstreperous Lehman in the dark. Of course, the unassuming Crowley was not on his list of troublemakers. Indeed, Byrnes now expected him to be the proposed agency's chief.[37]

Probably Crowley knew that Byrnes was designing a new unifying agency, possibly even that he would propose him as its chief. In any case, on September 21, Crowley sent Byrnes his assessment of the conflict and confusion among the economic agencies operating abroad. His lengthy memorandum argued that the major culprit was the State Department, which interfered with (or micromanaged) the execution of policy when it should only formulate and coordinate it. That led to problems in the field, ranging from wasteful duplication to the more critical problems of needless delays and confusion. On the other hand, the State Department provided "no help" on major policy issues such as what was to be shipped by private exporters as opposed to lend-lease, or the restoration of private trade in the liberated areas. In sum, Crowley advised Byrnes, the operating agencies needed broad guidelines, not close supervision and interference. Unfortunately, Secretary Hull, who agreed with his views, had abdicated responsibility.[38]

Crowley then suggested a relationship between the operating agencies and the State Department which, he believed, would permit the former to perform their tasks "expeditiously" within the framework of State's lead. First, agency directors would submit their programs for a specific time in the future; second, if the secretary of state did not show that the program was contrary to the national interest and where it required modification, agency directors might proceed; third, agencies should be deemed competent to implement their programs without State Department interference except in unusual circumstances; and, finally, the Bureau of the Budget should review the personnel of the agencies and the State Department to eliminate duplication and insure proper working relations.

Without knowing it, Crowley had forecast the "hands-off" approach he would bring to the Foreign Economic Administration that Byrnes was designing. Based on his own success in Washington, he had concluded that sound administration meant clearly demarcating lines of authority beween agencies and, within each, finding the right staff and giving it only the most basic guidance and coordination. Whether that was the best method of managing the agency Byrnes had in mind only time would tell. But in September 1943 Byrnes and the president must have thought it was: they decided that Crowley should run it, assuming direct control over the OEW, OLLA, and portions of other agencies; indirectly supervising the OFFRO (soon UNRRA, the United Nations Relief and Rehabilitation Administration); and coordinating their operations with the State Department and, in the case of OLLA, the Treasury. The Office of Foreign Economic Coordination would be eliminated as superfluous.

Clearly, Roosevelt and Byrnes recognized that even Crowley, though often labeled the the president's "friction remover" and "peacemaker," might have a hard time supervising men as powerful and self-important as Rockefeller, Stettinius, and Lehman. Thus they decided that it was just as critical to move their chairs as to find a chef to head the table. Fortuitously, a tragic personnel problem at the State Department, coupled with a Soviet agreement to form UNRRA, paved the way for the changes the White House wanted. Stettinius, who had eased Crowley into discussions with the British over lend-lease two months earlier, was to be jumped to the State Department as undersecretary. There, with Acheson, he would be the department's liaison with Crowley. That, Byrnes said, would "greatly lessen if . . . not put an end to the intolerable conflicts abroad." There would be less conflict in Washington, too; Lehman's pride would be saved, and Crowley's problems lessened, by transferring the former New York governor from OFRRO to UNRRA, where he would have larger responsibilities. Finally, conflicts Crowley might expect with Rockefeller would be obviated by leaving his Office of Inter-American Affairs outside the new grouping.[39]

The president announced the new setup on September 25. After briefly mentioning who had been removed, promoted, and moved, he praised Crowley as "one of the best administrators in or out of government, [whom] I find great satisfaction in promoting . . . to a position which will centralize all foreign economic operations in one operating agency." The background stories he left to the press.[40]

The next day's papers accurately ascribed the forming of the Foreign Economic Administration to numerous "complaints, particularly from the Army, that too many agencies have men abroad operating in the same economic field." This had prompted "delays and much bickering over 'who has authority over what.'" Fortunately, it now ap-

peared that these problems would cease. Consolidation, drawing together "all the economic threads," was the key to ending conflict and
confusion, duplication and waste."[41]

Time magazine approved both the machinery and the man chosen
to run it. "On paper, Franklin Roosevelt's long-needed overhauling
looked good. At least responsibility and authority have been centered
in one man." And the president had said he could do the job. The
magazine called Crowley "Washington's newest Czar" and pointed
out that unofficially he was called "Secretary of State for Economic Affairs," which probably "means as much as this tremendous title
sounds." Did it? No one actually knew. This was obvious, though—the
president had again turned to "the Nation's # 1 Pinch-Hitter."[42]

11

Global Diplomat

On September 25, 1943, Leo Crowley reached what would be the pinnacle of his public career. For almost a decade he had worked effectively but on the periphery of the Roosevelt administration. Now foreign economic administrator, he would be a major player, a member of the president's cabinet. British representatives found him worth reporting on to their home offices. And newspaper features reflected his new status. Previously they had focused on his personal habits; now they stressed the lights shining nightly in his National Press Building office, his search for more space in an already overburdened Capital, and the potential he brought to the complexities of his new task.

Early commentaries, as in *Time*, glowed over his appointment. Crowley had a superb reputation as a savvy politician and administrator. He was, one commentator wrote, the president's "manager par excellence." He would reorganize American agencies operating in the economic field abroad and coordinate their work with State Department policy. Supposedly Crowley's new task was temporary—organizational: when the president's # 1 pinch hitter completed it, he could return to the bench.[1]

This last was not the president's intent. True, by mid-fall Crowley had devised a flow chart for the Foreign Economic Administration. It appeared, in brief, in the *New York Times*, November 7, 1943, at the end of John McCormac's feature article, "Diplomat of Global Economics." Crowley was proposing a complete reorganization of the agencies he controlled and those still technically, and probably effectively, run by Jesse Jones. OEW and OLLA would cease to exist. A geographically organized bureau of areas would be responsible for distribution abroad, and a bureau of supplies for purchases at home and abroad, and the directors of both would report to Crowley. So would various other officers, most notably his two deputy administrators and general counsel. Also, Crowley told McCormac, he was creating an Executive Policy Committee that would meet weekly to coordinate the FEA's activities.[2]

In fact, six months—and sharp criticism from within the FEA and without—would pass before Crowley reorganized the agency and established his Executive Policy Committee. Breaking up the OLLA and OEW as independent entities involved revising job categories, which required considerable preparation. Reorganization also involved absorbing the agencies Jones controlled, inviting the very attacks from congressional conservatives the president wanted to avoid. Finally, reorganization required naming bureau chiefs and Executive Policy Committee members, crucial decisions Crowley was reluctant to make hurriedly. Rather, he thought he could operate the agency through his deputy administrators and general counsel, Laughlin Currie, Henry Riley, and Oscar Cox respectively. These were men he knew and valued, Currie and Cox as White House staff, with easy access to the wishes of the president and Byrnes; Riley as the FDIC's executive officer, whom he thought could manage the FEA's division heads and lower ranks. Only time would tell. And Crowley needed time to handle the one problem which probably most influenced his appointment as foreign economic administrator. It appears unlikely, though, that he told McCormac the president was counting heavily on his "peacemaking" ability to dampen emerging congressional criticism of lend-lease. He had told him enough.

McCormac was more than satisfied. He applauded the FEA plan as "a graphic illustration of the Crowley administrative method." More important, as his article's rather bloviose title suggests, he had discovered that Crowley was not merely an interim manager, he would run the FEA and help make policy for countries liberated from Axis domination. That meant, Crowley had told him, "helping stricken countries to help themselves." His administration's aim "must be to assist the devastated nations to their feet, not to tell them where to go and take them in a wheel chair." Modestly, and surely with a banker's eye, Crowley added, "I don't think I know enough to run the world." And with that, he fixed the philosophy that would guide his two years as foreign economic administrator.

Crowley prized McCormac's piece, especially as the president sent him a copy. But he also enjoyed the recognition he was getting from Catholic monthlies and weeklies. The *Sign* flavored its paean to his rise by noting that the pope had said years earlier, and Marquette University more recently, that Crowley was "endowed with a genius for administration which he has devoted to the service of his Church and his State." It then implied that Crowley, like the pope, could speak authoritatively on other matters, citing him as favoring a Catholic education, advising Catholics that they could aspire to state and federal posts without fear of discrimination, proclaiming that faith in God provided the strongest protection against authoritarian tendencies, and stating that "we are each and every one of us our brother's keeper." Crowley, the *Sign* concluded, was in every sense a role model, paying him tribute by any definition.[3]

There were other tributes to Crowley's new status that fall. British observers in Washington studied him very closely, stressing that he offered "something for everyone"—Catholics, moderate Democrats, Progressives in Wisconsin—and now as a big spender in his new job he would need every bit of their support in Congress. Rumors spread that Crowley advised the papal nuncio on financial matters; and the *Notre Dame Alumnus* informed Catholics nationwide that the university gave Crowley an honorary doctorate that fall. Further, several congressmen, as well as the *Washington Post*, applauded his plan for reorganizing the FEA. And in Madison, Evjue wrote that, when Crowley labeled his reorganization "the most far reaching consolidation of government agencies in the war," he did not exaggerate. But Evjue obsessed that Crowley might be receiving salaries from both Standard Gas and the government and asked a reporter in Washington to look into the matter.[4]

Questioned, Crowley replied unhesitatingly that he was still chairman and president of Standard Gas. But he spoke cautiously about his salary situation. He first said that he received none from any of Standard's subsidiaries (which was untrue); then when asked about the mother company, he paused before replying, "I'd rather not answer the salary question if you don't mind." He did not either, and Evjue decided to drop the issue until he obtained Crowley's state tax records and, perhaps, until a more propitious time. That fall the lend-lease program was facing serious criticism for the first time since Pearl Harbor; harassing Crowley, whose FEA managed the program, could only render this essential program more vulnerable.[5]

Evjue probably exaggerated the threat to lend-lease, but the crisis which had inspired the program two and a half years before had disappeared. In March 1941, a truly frightened Congress had supported the president's insistence that the Axis threatened the United States, and that Great Britain constituted "our first line of defense." The United States would "lend" and "lease" Britain and others fighting the Axis such materials as would enable them to defend themselves and, the Lend-Lease Act stipulated, "Promote the Defense of the United States." Even then, however, criticism abounded. Perhaps the most telling criticism then, and certainly later, was that Britain was not broke—she could sell her investments abroad and tighten her belt. Americans should not be taxed to sustain her living standard, and American manufacturers should not have to compete abroad with British exports that were in any way dependent on lend-lease shipments.[6]

In 1941 only Crowley's old enemy, Secretary of the Treasury Morgenthau, spoke effectively to most of these arguments. He had used British and Treasury statistics to explain Britain's desperate financial straits. But at last most congressmen relied less on specific statistics than on Morgenthau's reputation for fiscal conservatism and integrity. Thus he persuaded them that the British could not afford the guns or the butter they needed to fight, but they would get only such lend-lease as their needs justified. He would keep a sharp eye on British exports (that might threaten American exporters), on reverse lend-lease (reciprocal aid), and on their dollar balances. Britons would not prosper at American expense. In fact, Morgenthau promised lend-lease on a basis that even conservative congressmen might live with—the Treasury would keep Britain (and other recipients) on a short leash with a choke collar.[7]

The State Department, which would also influence lend-lease, was more flexible and more forthcoming than the Treasury. It saw lend-lease as a means of prodding Britain to limit its commercial exports during the war and to abandon its imperial discriminatory tariff system after it. In September 1941, Assistant Secretary of State Dean Acheson had secured Britain's agreement to restrict its exports; and, in February 1942, he had won their agreement to cooperate in creating a postwar world free of tariff barriers. But the first agreement, the only one of immediate significance, was so vague as to become the focus of constant negotiation.[8]

OLLA monitored and restricted Britain's civilian exports and imports under lend-lease, and with the Treasury and State Department kept a sharp eye on the relationship between all lend-lease, reciprocal aid, and British dollar balances. British representatives in Washington argued that limits on their exports should be loosened—they had to pay for goods and services bought elsewhere in the world; they argued that their lend-lease requests should not be monitored, as those of the Soviet Union were not; and they argued that, as Allies, the United States and Britain should simply pool their resources as needs required, not meanly count what each supplied and each might owe. The British could count on the president and State Department for support. They could not count on Congress. And they could not count on Morgenthau. He continued to seek restriction of their dollar balances and linked their lend-lease shipments and exports to those balances.[9]

Actually, the British had little to fear until the summer of 1943. As long as the Axis threatened, British exports and dollar balances could and did rise sharply, and there was no open criticism. However, as the balance of power shifted to the Allies, and the United States bore more of the war's burden, sympathy for Britain had declined. In Congress and out, there were now voices insisting that Britain not prosper at America's expense. It was time to tighten lend-lease.[10]

This new mood was first recognized within the administration in August 1943. OLLA and the Treasury argued that Congress soon would demand more reverse lend-lease to limit British dollar balances, and the State Department gave ground. Following, in early September, the president for the first time suggested postwar repayment of lend-lease. This readiness to bend before a critical, tight-fisted Congress went unnoted by the press. So did the significance, later that month, of Crowley's appointment as foreign economic administrator. McCormac's feature in the *New York Times* examined Crowley's vision of America's postwar role, not of lend-lease; and Richard Stokes of the *St. Louis Post-Dispatch*, though he wrote of a "Roosevelt Shift from the Left to the Right," only reiterated Robert Riggs's "one-fifth Wallace, four-fifths Jones" analysis in the wake of Wallace's debacle. Neither reported the September shuffle as a turning point in American lend-lease policy.[11]

Some forty years passed before a British historian correctly assessed the importance of the president's order of September 25. Alan Dobson wrote that it marked the end of a two and a half year period in which few if any restraints marked aid to Britain; and that it initiated a period of increasingly limited lend-lease and increasingly onerous restraints. However, he holds Crowley singularly responsible—his "business values" and "anti-British sentiments"—for these limitations when there is compelling evidence that Crowley's management of lend-lease during the last two years of the war reflected domestic and global politics beyond his control.[12]

Crowley was not the free agent Dobson portrays; he was first and foremost the instrument of a president who had shown time and again during the summer of 1943 that he wanted potential problems defused before they became public and exploded. Crowley had precisely the right talents for the job. If at times he was dubious about lend-lease, he was still the president's man, ready to promote and defend the administration's policy. But Crowley's value to the president stemmed from two other factors without which his readiness to follow where he led would have been relatively meaningless. First, his faith in Roosevelt's authority and judgement was matched by his obvious respect for Congress and, in turn, its faith that he would honor the intent of its work. Further, Crowley was a relatively conservative Democrat, Irish Catholic, and a midwesterner: he had some natural protection against ever louder charges that lend-lease was in part a cover for extending the New Deal abroad and giving its recipients, but Britain in particular, more aid than their needs warranted. At the very least the president knew that Crowley would get a fair hearing when he defended lend-lease on the Hill.[13]

Appointing Crowley was a preemptive step Roosevelt took none too soon. In early October, after five senators returned from an inspection of lend-lease, two Republicans in the group criticized the FEA's management of the program and some of the recipients. Britain, they said, was getting luxurious linen cloth when cotton fabric would suffice; Australian farmers were getting more trucks than American farmers; and the Russians would not permit American planes to use their bases in Siberia, at a cost of many American lives.[14]

Some of the charges were patently false and easily answered. But Crowley had to deal with the fact that British exporters were reshipping lend-lease to the Middle East, benefiting at American expense from the publicity as well as the trade balances. He had no choice but to eliminate the offensive items from British shipments. And he had to deal with the charge that "the British were "refraining from supplying oil . . . to preserve their reserves in the Middle East." This prompted him to meet with Byrnes, who was then able to explain the problem to the president's satisfaction. It also prompted him to order the FEA to reallocate resources "to increase the movement of gasoline and distillates from Abadan to points previously supplied from Western Hemisphere sources." The results were to draw the fangs of those who insisted that Britain was preserving its oil reserves at American expense and, also, to preserve American and Latin American resources for future use.[15]

Two weeks later, Crowley found himself defending lend-lease before a subcommittee of the Truman Committee on Defense Expenditures. In his opening statement, he insisted that errors were bound to occur in so "huge" a program, but the FEA would correct them "as fast as any . . . are disclosed." The FEA wanted to cooperate; he hoped Congress did. But he was disturbed by "groundless and unsubstantiated charges that have been made concerning the administration of foreign economic affairs." Lend-lease had "saved the lives of many of our boys and the boys of our allies." Coupled with reverse lend-lease, which Americans should value as "mutual aid," it would "hasten the day of final victory."[16]

Crowley's mixed language—seeking cooperation but criticizing those making "groundless and unsubstantiated charges"—played well with the public but not with the full Truman Committee. On November 5, a Truman Committee report emphasized that "lend-lease was originally authorized by the Congress solely because the British and others whom we desired to assist did not have sufficient American exchange to purchase materials needed by them. [It] was never intended as a device to shift a portion of their war costs to us." This, however, was what the British were doing. Taking advantage of the FEA's soft-headed liberality, they were securing lend-leased capital and consumer goods and raising their exports and living standard at the expense of American exporters and taxpayers.[17]

Crowley did not ignore the Truman Committee's criticism. He knew that it marked Congress's intent to restrict what previously had been open-ended lend-lease. Thereafter, the FEA must tighten Britain's leash in some degree or Congress would act drastically. Thus the day the report was released he spoke to the president. Who said what is unknown, but the result, soon after, was an FEA quarterly report that gave greater stress than previously to British contributions in goods and services than before. Both Crowley and Roosevelt apparently thought stressing reverse lend-lease would protect both the program and the administration.[18]

The immediate results were gratifying. Cox brought Crowley

countless news stories that stressed item by item and dollar for dollar what the British were providing in lend-lease. Some newspapers also emphasized intangibles. The *Pittsburgh Post-Gazette*, for one, insisted that "bookkeeping comparisons" were "odious" if pressed too far. It asserted, as Crowley had when testifying before the Truman Committee, that "profits from mutual aid will be enough for all when the United Nations ... have won the war." But such support notwithstanding, by mid-November Cox, though himself very friendly to lend-lease, was telling Crowley that politically sensitive items must be removed from the lend-lease list.[19]

Specifically, Cox advocated the removal of capital equipment that enabled the British to manufacture consumer goods they sold abroad in competition with American manufacturers; civilian products that might be reexported to the Middle East; and sugar, oil, and fish the United States purchased offshore, lend-leased to the British, and which their government *sold* to its public. The last had the broadest appeal, as the powerful *Chicago Tribune* insisted that items such as Iceland's fish had "no military significance," and, worse, enriched the British government at the American taxpayer's expense. But as Cox knew, and Crowley and Morgenthau agreed, the graver threat to lend-lease came from organized manufacturers and exporters worried about losing opportunities they had expected to seize during the war. In mid-December Secretary of State Cordell Hull reluctantly endorsed the FEA's report to the White House advocating restrictions on lend-lease. However, he asked the president to withhold judgment until Acheson informed British representatives in Washington.[20]

Acheson felt that Crowley and Morgenthau were taking a "legalistic" view of lend-lease; they would not accept Britain's need to earn export dollars to cover her war expenses in her colonies, much less to improve her financial posture in the postwar period. He was right. But Morgenthau felt constrained by his commitments when promoting lend-lease in 1941, and Crowley by the politics of the possible. Cox and Currie, even the president, discussed Britain's needs and what Congress would accept, but none were better placed than Crowley to assess the latter. Famed British diplomat and economist John Maynard Keynes noted this, albeit caustically, when he said that Crowley had his ear "so near the ground that he was out of range of persons speaking from an erect position." In fact, Crowley roamed the Mayflower nightly, mixing with congressmen who might have both ears to the ground, but could in any case impair Anglo-American relations.[21]

Given the need to restrict British lend-lease, Crowley's negotiations with their representatives were not always smooth. On January 7, 1944, he responded somewhat sharply at first when they asked him to consult before removing items from their list of requests. He recovered soon enough, but he was unusually irritable that day. He was just then feeling the blast of recent criticism from the press, from within the FEA, and even from his patron and good friend Jimmy Byrnes. The criticism was not directed at his handling of lend-lease; it focused on what Marquis Childs of the *St. Louis Louis Post-Dispatch* called the "near-breakdown" of the FEA, involving delays in securing strategic materials, confusion, and demoralization. The Wallace-Jones feud seemed to be erupting again, if with different contestants.[22]

In three articles at the year's end, Childs had blamed Crowley for the FEA's problems. He had not absorbed Jesse Jones's procurement agencies into first the OEW then the FEA. Thus Jones still controlled the United States Commercial Corporation, the FEA's purchasing agent abroad. As to the consequences, Childs quoted a memorandum that, he was careful to point out, came from a FEA executive "who is not a New Dealer but a businessman." It focused on delays in procuring materials and building plants, of a resultant inability to plan and, consequently, bewilderment, boredom, and low morale. Subordinates blamed Crowley; they could seldom find him; they had to see Henry Riley, one of his deputy administrators.[23]

Childs, who was one of Washington's premier journalists, had checked his story before going to press, and Crowley had admitted that there were disgruntled people in the FEA. He had added that he hoped they would leave quickly. They were responsible for the low morale Childs spoke of. As for Jones, he had been allowed to retain some powers "solely on a service basis," to avoid dislocations. Crowley wanted Childs to know that the FEA would soon absorb the United States Commercial Corporation, but he added, "You can't order up such a consolidation on Saturday and deliver it on Monday."

Childs admitted the point, but he was not satisfied. He had seen a barbed memorandum from Paul Nitze, chief of the Metals and Minerals Division, charging that there were "inexcusable" delays stemming from the United States Commercial Corporation's failures to pursue the policies set forth by the OEW, and they were a "disgrace to the

United States Government." Childs took Nitze at his word, and fairly so. Nitze was hot-tempered and self-righteous, but he was a highly successful recruit from a Wall Street investment firm and had well-placed Washington allies, which gave him both credibility and protection. Now, though he criticized the United States Commercial Corporation's failure to cooperate with the OEW, he called Crowley the real culprit. Nitze blamed Crowley for not integrating the USCC into the FEA, thus leaving Jones with a veto over FEA policy. In so doing, Nitze endorsed Childs's argument that the FEA was not the strong organization the president had promised the previous fall, and that Crowley was responsible. He operated, Childs wrote, "as the head of a holding company with subsidiaries operating more or less on their own." And that was not good enough.[24]

One week after Childs's column appeared, Evjue's *Capital Times* reprinted a *Washington Post* editorial. Apologizing for its endorsement of Crowley's projected reorganization in October, the *Post* asserted, "Three months have passed, and now we must confess that we had mistaken the blue-print for the real thing." Some weeding was to be expected, but some specialists were left "thumb-twiddling" after their jobs were eliminated, while others, equally skilled, were replaced by "appointees who are either temporary or who commute from jobs in New York." This did not make sense. Neither did problems the FEA was specifically intended to resolve: internally, overlapping jurisdictions; externally, lack of cooperation with the State Department. Foreign missions often received conflicting orders. In sum, the *Post* concluded, Crowley had failed. The FEA was, as Childs had argued, "near breakdown." It must have "the intervention of the Office of War Mobilization as the over-all coordinator."[25]

Crowley responded to the *Post*'s criticism and that of Childs via an interview with John McCormac, who had written so favorably about him and his plans in the *New York Times* two months earlier. And he chose well: McCormac first asserted that Crowley would be responding to recent newspaper attacks inspired by "the New Deal wing of the Administration," then he lobbed the specifics at him so that Crowley could easily hit them out of the park. Had Crowley failed to cooperate with the State Department? No, he said; he had acted "to coordinate our foreign economic activities with the approval of the heads of the State Department, whether or not this has been understood by its lesser officials everywhere."[26]

Other lobs and easy answers followed, until at last McCormac reminded Crowley of charges that he had failed to consolidate the FEA; that Jesse Jones, who had once frustrated the BEW, was still "largely running the show"; and that the result was bitterness, demoralization, and a torrent of resignations. Crowley reacted sharply: he had tried to coordinate the foreign economic activities of the United States "in such a way as not to interfere with the day to day prosecution of the war. . . . I have never conceived it my duty to carry on the original disagreement between Vice-President Wallace . . . and Mr. Jones. I have coordinated the activities of Mr. Jones' foreign corporations in such a way as to make the maximum use of RFC's trained personnel." He told McCormac he was satisfied, especially now that he had placed his men and some from the State Department on the boards of Jones's corporations.

Crowley meant it. As Riggs had seen, he was more Jones than Wallace. Thus he had told Childs: "Some of those people out of the old Office of Economic Warfare don't realize that a contract has to be looked over. They're spending the Government's money." But he could not ignore the growing criticism. He knew very well that the president had appointed him first head of the OEW, then foreign economic administrator, only partly for his administrative skills; he had counted on his political savvy to staunch the flood of criticism from Congress and the press as it involved the conflict between the OEW and Jones's agencies. This Crowley knew he must do now. Indeed, the storm in the press provided him with the political cover he needed to do what was now essential.[27]

On January 6, Crowley sent the president a memo stating that he intended taking over the USCC, if the White House did not object. The president did not. He was relieved that Crowley was responding to Childs's articles of the week previous. But he was even then worrying about another critic of the FEA. Drew Pearson had just blasted the FEA as a "flop." Echoing some of the charges made in Childs's columns the week before, Pearson informed a national audience that the president had burdened Crowley with too many tasks, especially as Crowley had another job running one of the biggest utility corporations in the country. Accordingly, there was a leadership vacuum in the FEA's top post. "Things are bound to break wide open soon," Pearson predicted.[28]

They did not, perhaps because the president saw a memo from Currie that day. He argued that most "criticism was coming from people Crowley had eased out of both the OEW and L-L." True, the RFC had "procrastinated," as Childs had charged, but "Mr. Crowley has worked this out patiently, believing that controversy should be avoided." Currie implied that Crowley was doing just what the president had in mind when he appointed him, avoiding fights with Jones that might create trouble on the Hill. Finally, Currie advised the president that the FEA's situation was improving."[29]

The British had their own view. A Washington-based member of the Foreign Office noted perceptively: "A pincers movement seems to be converging on [the FEA] from liberal and conservative quarters— pro-New Dealers Drew Pearson and . . . the Scripps-Howard press and Washington Post have vied with each other in telling stories of its lack of method and control." Crowley's "chickens have come home to roost in unprecedented quantities this week," and he "appears to have lost most of his friends in the press."[30]

But the press was not the White House. The president recognized Crowley's problems and their threat to the White House, but he was reluctant to remove him. He knew no one smoother at dealing with both the British and Congress on lend-lease. Both found him open, frank, his word his bond; the British found him cordial even when disagreeing; Congress and its crucial foreign relations committees found him prudent as well. The British Embassy cabled the Foreign Office that in December, after Crowley testified for UNRRA, a House Foreign Affairs Committee member told him "that it was a pleasure to know that matter was in such solid and capable hands." But however effective Crowley might have been then, that was prior to the press attacks. Now, in early January, the president instructed Byrnes to investigate.[31]

On January 11, Byrnes turned in a page and a half memorandum with his findings and advice. First, he had found "the same old differences that existed between State and Lend-Lease and State and OEW" and had asked both Hull and Crowley to insist on "tactful cooperation" by their subordinates. Second, he had listened to a wide range of criticism from within the FEA, not only from partisans of Perkins. He meant men such as Nitze, who claimed that Currie and two or three others stopped the division chiefs from presenting Crowley with problems he could easily dispose of. At root, though, Byrnes agreed with Childs and Pearson: "Leo has a tremendous job demanding six days a week and still has to give time to Alien Property Custodian and FDIC." It was too much, as Crowley himself readily admitted, but he and

Crowley had come up with a solution. In two weeks, Crowley would send the president his alien property report, and then "will recall that he was to continue for only a while, and he will ask that you make another appointment." Further, Crowley said "he will suggest a man to be appointed as head of FDIC."[32]

This last statement measures Crowley's distress and, likely, the reason for the arrogance the British found so irritating and unusual at their January 7 meeting. He was ready to give up his treasured chairmanship of the FDIC, as well as the alien property custodianship, to remain foreign economic administrator. Apparently, running the FEA had become the ultimate test of his public service. Should he leave a failure, his prior achievements would become meaningless; he would lose his Cabinet rank; and he would betray the values—service, honor, obedience—his mother and his church had inculcated and to which, excepting a single misstep, he had always been committed. Reporters who wrote critically of his "passion for power" did not know him. He had tried to avoid the job of alien property custodian, and he had not sought those at the OEW or FEA. If those jobs added status, they also brought criticism. He had accepted them only to serve his president and his country.

Happily, as Byrnes informed the president, Crowley was "over the worst troubles" at the FEA. He recognized "the necessity of improving his housekeeping," but he had made "great improvements in the last month," and he thought there was one means of really coping with it: he wanted to "get Milton Eisenhower to serve as General Manager. I have promised to help him and shall take the liberty of using your name if necessary to get him to accept."[33]

The president did not take immediate action on Byrnes' memo. And Crowley found time for matters other than "housekeeping." On January 17, he spoke to the Commerce and Industry Association of New York. After brief mention of his administrative problems at the FEA and stating that they were "pretty well behind us," Crowley told the industrialists what they had wanted to hear: there would be no "unnecessary encroachment upon . . . private export and import trade." The FEA was planning to provide exporters "every assistance" it could then and beyond the war. Crowley said he was thinking not only of consumer goods but of the plants, dams, and railroads to be rebuilt from France through the Soviet Union to China. Withal, Crowley concluded, exports should double within a decade if the United

States maintained a free trade policy, and the result "will be a future of peace and prosperity."[34]

Crowley meant what he said. In October he had told the old OEW and OFFRO agencies in the FEA to "direct their activities towards the immediate resumption of private trade with French North and West Africa." In early December, he had asked Hull to emphasize private trade in forthcoming talks with the French National Committee of Liberation. And he himself brought the subject up with the FNCL's representative in Washington. But all to little effect. Hull and, even more the French, preferred lend-lease to private trade.[35]

Several factors had focused Crowley's attention on restoring private trade with French Africa. Personally he favored it, but it was more important that American exporters were demanding it. Further, supported by their congressmen, they were claiming that the British were securing that business and other business in the Near East unfairly, exporting relabeled, finished lend-lease products or products manufactured with lend-lease capital equipment. Whether true in whole or part, these claims added to the problems Crowley foresaw when he sought lend-lease extension that spring.

Selling lend-lease to Congress was the single issue on Crowley's mind when he spoke with Ben Smith, the chief of the British Supply Council in North America and members of his delegation, in his office on January 20. One Briton, who had heard that Crowley was arrogant and irritable at his meeting with the delegation two weeks earlier, commented later that Crowley was "frank" and "more friendly than I had imagined." Crowley appeared eager to please, but he feared that the British did not understand American public opinion. He warned Smith that "anti-British sentiment, like the anti-Morgan and anti-public utility sentiments he had heard as a boy in Wisconsin, was based on ignorant watchwords like imperialism, colonies, cartels, and monopoly, but it did exist and must be recognized."[36]

The British also understood Crowley to say that they should "sit down and in their own interests help F.E.A. to get over the difficult period ahead." He advised them "that a lot of window-dressing was necessary in order to keep Lend-Lease out of American politics in the Presidential Year, and to ensure a smooth passage on the 'Hill' next June." Specifically, that meant eliminating a "long list of small things, which appeared big" to the politician. Later, Crowley advised Smith, "once window-dressing had been done, . . . [meaning after Congress acted] he stressed that he would be the first to cooperate in finding ways and means of restoring the position and so allow our dollar balances to be restored."

Crowley also stressed his political problems when responding to a complaint made earlier by the British ambassador. Lord Halifax had mentioned that the FEA did not monitor Soviet lend-lease requests, why did it monitor theirs, and implied that Crowley and the FEA preferred the Russians. Crowley's answer did not mention American manufacturers' fears of competition with British exports or the technical and political problems involved in attempting to monitor Russian requests. Rather, he said the British knew that, "politically speaking, the mass of public in America had become 'Russia minded' and the magnificent show put up by the Russians had appealed to their hearts." In sum, Crowley told the British, the policy question was out of his hands, but "if he had to have a bedfellow, he would much prefer England to Russia."

Crowley's digression continued. He hoped the British would understand some special problems he faced within the FEA (though his references were to his appointment to the OEW). He said that he had "taken on the F.E.A. much against his better judgement and at the special request of the President . . . to act as a catalyst in the row between Jesse Jones and Wallace." What he had found was "the most virulent hatred between the Wallaceites and the Jonesites." Even now, they caused him problems, "but there was a good deal of sniping from the outside" as well. That "made it all the more important that the English should sit down and in their own interests help F.E.A. to get over the difficult period ahead."

At this point Smith said he appreciated Crowley's problems, and they should get their people together to discuss the items to be removed from the lend-lease list. Crowley agreed. Obviously, he had made his point, but he pounded it again, although now his tone could not have been more friendly: he would tell his people to negotiate with the British "as partners," the "only objective being to get Lend-Lease through Congress without having the subject dragged into internal party politics." And he meant it. In ending the day's discussions, he agreed with the British minister that if their representatives "deadlocked," the two of them would have to "come together straight away and settle the problem."

Smith's record of his discussion with Crowley is enlightening, but his marginal notes and those of others in the delegation are hardly less valuable. Smith's secretary thought Crowley was "frightened to death of personal attacks. He even alluded to his own vulnerability in being a Public Utility president with a salary of $75,000 a year. His reputation appeared to depend on getting Lend-Lease extended without causing the President any sleepless nights and he wanted us to help him." Smith agreed, telling associates even more bluntly that "Mr. Crowley shd. add an R. to the initials of his organization." Yet curiously, Smith's cable to the British War Cabinet presented a picture of American public opinion—"a primeval chaos" in which the administration must "tread delicately"—coupled with assurances that the White House had the moral courage to ensure that Britain was treated fairly, that at last actually substantiated Crowley's accent on the FEA's problems and real and realistic efforts to deal with them.[37]

It was with that understanding that British and American representatives negotiated the items to be taken out of lend-lease. The FEA publicized that items such as Iceland fish and Caribbean sugar (which the *Chicago Tribune* had criticized so sharply in the fall) were stripped; thereafter, the British would have to pay. And the British did not complain, though they thought they had a good case. They recognized that trying to explain their lack of dollars and need either to sell such items as fish and sugar or tax their people more heavily would not work. Few would read the explanation, and most of those would scoff. If there were doubt, they heard protests from American meat exporters who learned that the British were selling their products in the Near East with the British flag imprinted on them. They knew, too, that as American forces played an increasingly large role in the European war and the American public foresaw a quick, early end to the war, Americans would display ever stronger opposition to shipping them capital goods or anything that could be labeled "non-essential" for victory on the battlefield.[38]

Crowley could not ignore these pressures. Although they did not threaten the extension of lend-lease—then and for at least a year to come Congress and the public would acknowledge that American money saved American lives—Congress might enact restrictive amendments. Further, attacks on lend-lease, if unanswered, could endanger the reelection of the president and of Democratic congressmen friendly to its unrestricted extension. This last Crowley understood very well. He knew that "Bertie" McCormick's *Chicago Tribune*, so strongly hostile to the administration and Britain, played upon an apparently receptive public miles beyond its urban hub. He had heard from informants in the Midwest that they were worried about Democratic prospects that year. Consequently, the FEA let it be known on Sunday, February 13, that the British would be paying cash for fish and sugar; and just four days later it gave the *New York Times* solid reason to believe that British supply officials in America had agreed on the "virtual elimination" of capital goods under lend-lease, explaining that it was "one of many adjustments being made to keep lend-lease exports geared to military needs." Further, the FEA pointed out that it was taking steps even then to return exports to regular commercial channels. Finally, the *Times* headlined a February 20 column, "Flag Imprint to go on Exported Foods." Thus, Crowley's FEA began taking public steps to deal with those aspects of lend-lease that were likely to be most vulnerable to attack when House hearings began in early March.[39]

Ironically, just as Crowley was stressing the FEA's moves to protect American exporters and taxpayers, he was himself becoming the focus of the most damaging publicity he had ever known. Perhaps he foresaw it. Monday morning, February 14, he turned up at the White House. Apparently he asked for the meeting to discuss his forthcoming annual report as alien property custodian, but he also obviously reminded the president that he took the post two years before on a temporary basis. Now he wanted out so he could "devote his energies more fully to the FEA task." And by Friday, the story was also out. At the president's press conference that day, a reporter asked if Leo Crowley "will soon give up his post as Alien Property Custodian?" And the president answered, "That has been on the card for a long time."[40]

So it had, for more than six months. And that day the president had agreed that Crowley could resign as soon as a successor was found. He could then focus more closely on his increasingly critical and demanding job as foreign economic administrator. Or so it appeared on Friday, February 18. But just the day before, fate or, more likely, Crowley's past and present connections had intervened. I. F. Stone, an investigative reporter writing for the *Nation* and *PM*, had inaugurated a series of articles charging him with numerous derelictions as custodian. And overnight the first articles were pounced on by liberal editors throughout the country, among them, of course, William Evjue, Crowley's oldest critic. Always seeking new evidence, he used his *Capital Times*'s Sunday paper to headline, "Resignation of Crowley as Custodian Is Due to Administration Concern."[41]

Suddenly, Crowley found himself facing a much more personal and dangerous attack than that in January. Then his competence was challenged; now Stone was condemning his ethics, and in Madison and across the country. Stone's first piece in the *Nation*, reprinted in the *Capital Times*'s Sunday edition, strongly suggested that some of Crowley's most important decisions as alien property custodian had not been inspired by the public interest but by his corporate connections. The charge, in short, was corruption.

Crowley recognized the implication that he was resigning because of the press attacks stressing his ties to Emanuel, and he thought it unfair and untenable. He had accepted the custodian's job reluctantly and pleaded with the president ever since to let him resign, only to be refused. The linkage Stone implied—with Emanuel—did not exist. Even so, Crowley did not want to resign under fire, and on Tuesday he wrote Byrnes, asking that he speak to the president about deferring his resignation for a while. He asked because of "attempts by a few individuals to reflect on his record as Alien Property Custodian." Given time, Stone's attacks would stop for lack of substance.[42]

12

Embattled

For Leo Crowley the late winter of 1944 was the darkest period he had known for many years. Columnist I. F. Stone's assault on his policies as alien property custodian imperiled his career and reputation. Yet he was not the victim of a personal vendetta but of Stone's larger ideological focus. The previous July, when the columnist saw Wallace "betrayed," he had placed Crowley among a "right-wing quadrumvirate" which, aided by Roosevelt's "flaccid retreat before [his party's] Bourbons," was killing the New Deal. In October, after Crowley became foreign economic administrator, Stone was only a bit kinder. Crowley would probably "leave alone the progressives under him, provided only that there is peace and quiet." That need explained how Crowley "managed to keep several jobs and his health," and why he lacked "the hard, gemlike flame" Stone thought essential to cope with big business. (Dean Acheson later wrote that Crowley reminded him of Talleyrand's admonition: "Above all, no zeal.") Still, Stone admitted that the FEA "could have a much worse boss than Crowley."[1]

After the new year, Stone began to attack Crowley more often and more sharply. First, he mentioned Crowley's role at Standard Gas, and that Standard had ties to the J. Henry Schroder banking firm of New York and London, which *Time* magazine said was, before 1939 at least, "an economic booster of the Axis." After implying that Crowley might have pro-Axis sympathies, Stone quickly denied that he believed it. But the allegation (which he would make and refute in later articles) had to cast doubt on Crowley's ability to act properly as alien property custodian and attract attention to later articles attacking him. And Stone made it clear that he intended to do such that. In an article on February 12 he wrote: "I hope next week to tackle the task of naming the men and influences in Washington which already make it seem an almost hopeless task to achieve full employment after the war and to prevent revival of the cartel system."[2]

As promised, on February 19, Stone cited "The Cartel's Washington Friends," Jesse Jones and Leo Crowley. Stone charged that Jones would not permit the postwar use of government-financed war plants as "publicly operated yardsticks" and weapons against cartelization. But Crowley was his main target in that *Nation* article and in his concurrent five-part *PM* series. Stone blamed him for not making critical patents available generally. Crowley had left "these basic essential monopolistic devices" in the hands of the worst carteleers, among them General Aniline. He had failed to take the steps needed to prevent Germany from recovering major industries in the United States and Latin America, thus repeating mistakes made during and after World War I.[3]

Stone explained Crowley's failure in terms of his "attitude and personal relations." Crowley was "a small town banker taken into the big time," shrewd but "impressed by the big businessmen now cultivating him, . . . and obligated to one of them for his livelihood." Consequently, he had handed these businessmen, and Victor Emanuel and his friends in particular, directorships in major companies such as GAF and General Dyestuffs. And those businessmen did not view "a directorship in General Aniline . . . as a foray into economic warfare but as just another trusteeship." They believed it their responsibility to enhance profits and sustain the rights of property, so they would not disturb existing, cartelizing patent agreements; and Crowley would not order them to do so. He was a "subordinate of Victor Emanuel."

Again, as in his January piece in the *Nation*, Stone explored Standard Gas's links with the banking house of J. Henry Schroder, again by implication impugning Crowley's patriotism, then denying any such intent. But that was for dramatic effect. Stone emphasized Crowley's appointment of "five Emanuel business associates to the board of General Aniline & Film and of Emanuel himself and one of his associates to the board of its key sales subsidiary, General Dyestuffs." Stone also named the new directors of these companies, revealed Crowley's salaries from Standard Gas and, he believed, from the government; and he hammered hard at Crowley's representation of what Stone described as conflicting interests. It was a story that could only have fascinated and appalled progressives and purists, but it was hardly news and of little concern to the White House.

Stone and Roosevelt operated from different premises. The president could not afford Stone's moralism. Always the realist, he focused on winning the war as quickly as possible and at the lowest possible cost in life; he, Biddle, and Byrnes had agreed that cooperation with business was essential to those ends; and they had further believed that Crowley's association with Emanuel would facilitate that cooperation and therefore speed production in former German subsidiaries. In fact, Crowley's appointments to the boards of GAF and General Dyestuffs in the summer of 1942 had apparently done just that.

Crowley's achievements did not impress Stone. He viewed the war ideologically. It should be fought not merely to win, but to overthrow what he viewed as a Fascist-oriented system of monopoly capitalism at home as well as abroad; and he attacked Crowley for not fighting it in that way in his role as custodian. There were two reasons he did not, as Stone saw it: Crowley failed to sever the former German subsidiaries from their parents because he was dependent on Emanuel and because he "lacked an unconventional and original mind." But Stone ignored a vital point. Ultimately, it was the president's responsibility to decide how German subsidiaries should be handled. Probably Stone did so deliberately. He could not admit the president's responsibility with an election a few months away, and a Republican the bleak alternative to Roosevelt. Before long, he would puff the president he had previously pilloried, labeling Roosevelt a leader of "stature and vision." His assault on Crowley, then, was among the last shrill gasps of a dying progressive tradition.[4]

After Stone's earliest blasts, Crowley and Roosevelt seem to have believed his charges were not dangerous unless the president lent them substance by accepting Crowley's resignation. Treasury Undersecretary Daniel Bell told his boss that Crowley's influence was undiminished. He reported that at a Cabinet meeting February 19 Crowley dominated the discussion of lend-lease, persuading the president that British dollar balances were too large, and "something ought to be done to jog the British along" to reduce them.[5]

But Crowley's influence with Roosevelt seemingly diminished by early March. Stone had followed his series in *PM* with further blasts. Some were old news, but a column on February 25 reported that Crowley had used his great influence as both alien property custodian and foreign economic administrator to secure advantages for General Aniline in its competition with American Cyanamid and Eastman Kodak in Latin America. This promised immediate benefits for Crowley's patron, Victor Emanuel, as well as his friends; and would, if I. G. Farben later regained control of General Aniline, enable the German cartel to recover its earlier dominant position in Latin America. So Stone argued. And the president, weakened by severe coronary problems and tired from persistent bronchitis, may have begun succumbing to the now almost daily barrage. Crowley, previously always a political asset, was now viewed as something of a problem.[6]

Suggestive of Crowley's diminished influence, on March 1 the president asked Byrnes whom he believed should succeed Crowley as alien property custodian, and Byrnes did not name the candidate Crowley had proposed. Then, on March 4, *Labor*, the powerful weekly of the railway unions and crucial for Democratic prospects in the autumn elections, began syndicating Stone's *PM* series, and Charles Broughton's *Sheboygan Press* did the same. Now the president had to recognize that Crowley was no longer the subject of criticism by a small element of Wallaceites and intellectuals who read the *Nation* and *PM*; he was now the butt of politically potent unions and at least one loyal Democratic newspaper that tended to reflect mainstream America. Which probably accounts for Roosevelt's memo to Byrnes on March 6: "Do you know when Leo Crowley expects to get out as Alien Property Custodian? The more I think it over, the more I think we should take action soon—and I think Francis J. McNamara is the best choice." The president, with his formal reference to Crowley and his readiness to appoint McNamara rather than James Markham, Crowley's deputy and choice, seemed to be distancing himself from his beleaguered alien property custodian.[7]

But the chill between Roosevelt and Crowley, if such it was, seems to have lasted just two weeks. On March 20, the president asked the Senate to confirm Markham, Crowley's deputy and choice, as Crowley's successor as alien property custodian. Roosevelt's request is part of the official record. How Crowley regained (or strengthened) his influence with the president is explicable only in part, and then from small scraps of testimony, rumor, hearsay, observations then, and reflections later. All suggest his still-strong prestige on the Hill and thus his crucial ability to overcome obstacles to the extension and funding of lend-lease.[8]

In February, when Stone's series first appeared, Crowley was giving the press statements stressing the Foreign Economic Administration's achievements and his own, which primarily focused on closely restricting British lend-lease. Crowley's press releases may have distracted attention from Stone's attacks, but they were actually designed to strengthen support in Congress for extending lend-lease authority as free of congressional encumbrances as was then the case. The extension of lend-lease was the crucial issue facing the FEA as officers of the formerly independent Office of Lend-Lease Administration and lawyers on loan from the State Department prepared Crowley to testify at hearings that were to take place in early March.

Among those prepping Crowley that February, and sitting with him when he appeared before the House Foreign Affairs Committee a few weeks later, was George W. Ball, a young lawyer from Chicago, then a disciple of Dean Acheson, later undersecretary of state in the administrations of Presidents Kennedy and Johnson. Writing a half century later, Ball recalled thinking that Crowley performed dismally in the hearings. He and others advising Crowley cringed as he "mumbled" and "bumbled" through the statement they had prepared for him, repeatedly referring to himself as chairman of the *Federal* Economic Administration, even though the FEA's proper title was printed clearly on the paper before him. Also, Crowley blamed mistakes the FEA might have made on the impossible task of finding "first rate people to work on these matters," crudely impairing the morale of his staff and colleagues. Then and later, Ball wondered how the president, when he appointed Crowley to run the FEA, could describe him as "the best administrator in or out of government" when he was "spectacularly unequipped by training, comprehension, or temperament for the job." Roosevelt, Ball concluded, must have been "in a puckish mood."[9]

Ball's charges cannot be dismissed lightly. His credentials do not permit it. And he is not alone in recalling and castigating Crowley's qualifications. Paul Nitze, who in 1943 had criticized Crowley's management of the FEA's economic warfare section, would also condemn him forty-odd years later, labeling him "thoroughly incompetent and corrupt," an administrator who "used politics and his political connections to further the personal ambitions of his former business associates." But though the price be a moment's digression, Nitze's vitriol and Ball's charges must be placed in context. Doing so will contribute to understanding all three men.

According to Ball, Crowley's "bumbled" opening statement and ignorance of the "philosophy" of lend-lease so worried him (about troublesome comments Crowley might make to the committee in later testimony) that he secured Chairman Sol Bloom's agreement to hear a witness who would soon be available to give "secret testimony." There are solid reasons to believe that Nitze was Ball's witness. In any case, Ball admits that his witness, "Rather than telling the committee anything secret, . . . gave them a bland, rather halting . . . description of his activities. . . . It was a lamentably bad show. I paid a high cost . . . in terms of my relations with Chairman Bloom." Apparently, Ball could not find "first-rate people," or even people who could make the case for lend-lease when "fully coached," as his secret witness was. The problem lay partly with the coach. Ball, whose elitism, like Nitze's, is prominent when discussing Crowley, underestimated the difficulties in persuading some on Bloom's committee that the civilian lend-lease goods paid for by the American taxpayer were a worthy investment. In either case, Ball's critique of Crowley's handling of the Foreign Affairs Committee is, at the very least, suspect. So is his criticism of the president for appointing Crowley chairman of the FEA.[10]

Roosevelt had known Crowley for a decade, and he knew why he had named him to chair the FEA. The president's effusive remarks about Crowley as "the best administrator in or out of government" notwithstanding, he had not appointed him chairman of the Federal Deposit Insurance Corporation, alien property custodian, or chief of the Office of Economic Warfare because of his technical expertise, eloquence, or manners; he had done so because Crowley had a well-earned reputation for organizing an agency and managing men, and that because he was a politician with few peers. Crowley had demonstrated for almost a decade that he could secure the cooperation of state bank supervisors, work easily with Jesse Jones and other agency heads, mediate disagreements over lend-lease between Morgenthau and Acheson, and, of the utmost important, broker differences between the administration and Congress. That was Crowley's primary task at the moment, taming the barons on the Hill. And in that context lend-lease did not suffer when Crowley muffed his lines at a committee hearing. Indeed, minor slips might have been positive. Certainly it did not hurt to remind House members that he, Leo Crowley, was still chairman of the highly successful *Federal* Deposit Insurance Corporation. Neither, probably, did it hurt lend-lease extension when Crowley mumbled his opening lines. Probably few committee members listened to such statements. They knew that important differences over lend-lease would be thrashed out in private conferences between Crowley and committee leaders. The hearings themselves consisted of easy give and take about the duration and purposes of lend-lease.

When those issues arose during the hearing, Crowley answered succinctly, "I agree that lend-lease is a war emergency measure." What "emergency" meant could be interpreted liberally to sanction lend-lease after the actual fighting ended, but no one challenged Crowley (or Acheson, who pushed the same line). Congressmen were soon asking Crowley other questions, but none highly charged. He told them FEA would turn over its civilian responsiblities in the liberated areas to UNNRA as soon as possible. He told them again and again that the FEA was "tough" with the British, ending shipments that did not contribute directly to the war effort and protecting American exporters and taxpayers. No one challenged him. Over a decade, he had earned their respect as nonideological and fair. Besides, in contrast with the aristocratic, Episcopalian, and Anglophile Acheson, Crowley, as an Irish Catholic businessman from the Midwest with a meager formal education, was as immune as any administrator could be from congressional suspicions of pro-British sentiment.[11]

Crowley supplemented words with deeds. British representatives could vouch for that. Reporting home, they called Crowley an "astute custodian of American interests at home and abroad." He had given critical places in the FEA to "hardheaded businessmen" who regarded the agency as a "spearhead for protection and promotion of American business," he had handed others to "a number of Roman Catholics," while he had eased the Anglophiles into insignificant posts which they quickly left. Crowley was cleaning house in the FEA just as he had after taking over the OEW in July. So noted the British ambassador, and if he exaggerated the "move to the right," many congressmen were favorably impressed.[12]

Crowley's reputation with Congress was never greater than in March 1944. Morgenthau had heard that Crowley had given Federal Reserve Board chairman Eccles "an awful licking on the Hill." He was corrected by Undersecretary Daniel Bell, who said that it was not Eccles, but asserted that Crowley had always been "very popular" on the Hill and "is riding on the crest of the wave now. He is very shrewd . . . in giving out appointments and so forth. They think he is a great administrator up there." Byrnes agreed, too, saying, "Crowley was the best administrator in the Executive Department."[13]

Morgenthau scoffed, "Doesn't he ever read the papers." But Bell knew better. He might well have told Morgenthau that Byrnes and Congress were not praising Crowley as a great housekeeper but because he understood the system in which they worked; because he treated them as decent but flawed men like himself; because, coming from the same America, and still in touch, he respected their values and views. What I. F. Stone said of Crowley, that he was a small-town banker brought into the big time, applied to most of the men on the Hill. Fundamentally, they were much the same. He like them had come to Washington for its power, perks, and recognition. He spoke their language; they understood and trusted him.

Crowley's influence on the Hill extended beyond his personal relationships. Tactics were also crucial, as Morgenthau's diary clumsily suggests. On March 11, the Treasury secretary told Bell and a few others in his office he could not really understand how Crowley won support for the president's policies; perhaps someone might "find out from Oscar Cox." He had heard, however, "and you musn't repeat this, please—that Crowley has been spreading stories to make a breach between the President and Churchill." A few days later, after Morgenthau told the group that Crowley was giving reporters "verse and chapter" about the breach, his secretary chimed in, "That is no gossip, either; that is factual." Morgenthau and his subordinates were implying that Crowley was stirring up trouble for the British. It is much more likely, though, that Crowley was leaking a story that would warn some troublesome congressmen that threatening lend-lease was undermining Roosevelt's relations with Churchill, which would prolong the war, and they would not want that known back home.[14]

During March, Crowley played a complex game as he fought for the extension of lend-lease. Nothing he said or did would matter much, however, unless he were viewed as acting for the president. And that inference would quickly disappear if the president named anyone other than his deputy, James Markham, to succeed him as alien property custodian. Roosevelt understood this. Passage of the lend-lease program was his immediate priority, as on March 20 he sent Markham's name to the Hill for confirmation; criticism of Crowley's associations and policies could be handled later.

At a press conference on March 24, Roosevelt announced Crowley's resignation as alien property custodian, saying that he had "justified abundantly [his] confidence." And surely Crowley had. The criticism of the past month notwithstanding, Crowley had done his job—a "nasty job" they had once agreed—as the president had prescribed, employing enemy patents and property in a productive, businesslike manner, stressing their contribution to the quickest possible victory, while leaving in abeyance the question of their postwar ownership. Now, Roosevelt stated, he had written Crowley that he wanted to "lighten somewhat [his] burden [to] permit you to devote all of your time and . . . superior abilities to your work as administrator of the Foreign Economic Administration and as chairman of the Federal Deposit Insurance Corporation. Those are big jobs, and their importance will continue to increase."[15]

The president's last words could not have been closer to the mark. The battle to extend lend-lease was not yet won. Only the day before, the House Foreign Affairs Committee had approved an amendment which appeared to forbid the president's making final lend-lease settlements or assuming "any obligations on the part of the United States with respect to postwar economic or postwar policy except in accordance with established constitutional procedure." Actually, the amendment, drafted by the State Department and FEA, added no meaningful restrictions to lend-lease; it had been required in order to head off truly restrictive amendments.[16]

Roosevelt had mentioned one such threat when he was announcing Crowley's resignation as custodian. Responding to criticism that farm machinery, needed at home, was being shipped abroad, he stressed a letter from Crowley stating that less than 2 percent had been exported under lend-lease since the program began. Perhaps, but farm bloc congressmen knew that the machinery was now shipped under the UNRRA program. And UNRRA was in some respects within Crowley's purview. Although ex-New York Governor Herbert Lehman directly managed this newly established program, obtaining the funds for it was one of Crowley's newer "big jobs" whose "importance," the president said, "would continue to increase."[17]

That spring the FEA was asking Congress to supply UNRRA with an outright appropriation of $450,000,000 immediately and another $350,000,000 out of lend-lease funds when needed later. And Congress was balking. The farm bloc in the House feared that, while farm machinery might not be shipped directly under the lend-lease program, the FEA would ship it under the UNRRA program. Crowley did not deny that one day that might be the case, but he tried to assuage the farm bloc's fears. Perhaps military operations might not progress as rapidly as hoped, in which case shipments of farm machinery would be delayed and American farmers receive the benefits. Crowley offered curious comfort but apparently enough for worried members to take home to their constituents.[18]

Even so, the Defense Aid Appropriations Bill for FY 1945, as the bill providing funds for both lend-lease and UNRRA was known, moved slowly through Congress. It was June 30 before the president approved it, and it was July 6 before he sent Crowley final instructions regarding the FEA's relationship with UNRRA. In the interim, he gave Crowley discretion to transfer lend-lease funds to UNRRA should Lehman need them, and further, he "counted on Crowley [to act] as "guide, counsel, and friend to the United Nations Relief and Rehabilitation Administration."[19]

Crowley did just that. When a congressman carped at UNRRA's expenses for clothing, Crowley ordered a Park Avenue skating rink converted into a factory which, Drew Pearson told the nation, re-worked old army uniforms into clothing that UNRRA distributed in the liberated areas. Briefly, Crowley had national recognition. Of course, such opportunities for close cooperation between the FEA and UNRRA were rare, but during the year and more he and Lehman worked together, Lehman persistently praised the FEA's "cordial cooperation."[20]

Crowley's clothing coup marked the end of a year in which he was fully engaged as foreign economic administrator. As might be expected, however, he never forgot domestic politics. The previous July he had spoken confidentially with columnist Drew Pearson "about the importance of keeping the President and [former presidential candidate Wendell Willkie] on friendly terms," as Willkie was closer "than any other Republican candidate to endorsing the President's foreign policy." If the president did not run again, Willkie might be willing to cooperate with him, in return for a Roosevelt blessing, toward world peace. In return, Willkie was not to criticize the president's domestic policies until the following June.[21]

Pearson, aware that Crowley was speaking for the president, agreed to "follow this matter up," and did. But he wrote Crowley in August that Willkie, while "interested," would make no "definite commitment," so "the net result of my conversation was negative." Even so, Pearson added, he was "optimistic" that Willkie was "anxious to keep the good will of the President" and would "continue to support his foreign policy 100%." Which was enough for Crowley to reply, briefly, that they should meet and discuss the matter further.[22]

During 1943 and 1944, Crowley's political activities appear to have been limited to such insider gossip with Pearson, Ickes, Byrnes, and the president. Ironically, he was now labeled "Boss" of Wisconsin's Democratic party, but as most Progressives had returned to the Republican fold, his speciality, forging coalitions that could help Roosevelt capture the state, was obsolete. Crowley knew this, but until and even during the Democratic National Convention in 1944, he continued to see himself as an important factor in the scrimmaging that crystallized in the nomination of the president's running candidate.[23]

Ten years later, exchanging letters with Byrnes, Crowley recalled that the president called him to the White House twice on the Tuesday before the Democratic National Convention. He wanted help selecting a running mate. Crowley recalled Roosevelt's saying first that "Byrnes would make the best vice-president" but saying the next moment that "the colored question would come up and then we'd have a lot of trouble." Crowley remembered, too, that after the president advanced Justice William O. Douglas and Missouri Senator Harry Truman as possible running mates, he told him to go to Chicago and "work with the fellows and nominate Henry Wallace if you can."[24]

Crowley was upset by the president's rejection of Byrnes and ran over to his patron's office to inform him. Thus he violated his code against relating discussions with the president. And he paid a price for his indiscretion. The president struck his name from a dinner for Democratic bosses that night. Even so, Crowley continued to think it possible that Byrnes would receive the Democratic nomination. First, he heard Chicago's Mayor, "Ed" Kelly, inform Byrnes that the president "has given us the green light to support you," then he heard DNC Chairman Robert Hannegan echo the mayor: the president wanted Byrnes.[25]

Monday evening, at the convention, Crowley learned, at last, that the president had abandoned both Wallace and Byrnes for Truman. Even so, he asked Wisconsin's Democratic party chairman "to tell the delegates that they are morally bound to support Mr. Wallace. If later this week it is found that he cannot be nominated, I wish you would ask the delegates to consult with me before they pledge themselves to anyone else." A Wisconsin columnist found it peculiar that Crowley, "who is known to be allergic to Mr. Wallace, had suddenly jumped aboard the Wallace choo choo . . . which apparently is puffing no place at a very, very fast rate indeed." Two explanations are possible: first, that Crowley remained faithful to the president's instruction to "nominate Henry Wallace if you can"; second, angered by Roosevelt's rejection of Byrnes, he hoped to derail Truman.[26]

Crowley's disappointment, and possibly anger at Roosevelt's rejection of Byrnes and eventual choice of a vice-president, may well have influenced his attitude toward Truman after the senator from Missouri became president, but clearly it did not interfere with his work during Roosevelt's presidency. Returning to Washington after the Democratic National Convention, Crowley was soon tightening administrative controls at the FEA, collaborating with the State Department on plans for the occupation of Germany, and thinking ahead to the president's reelection.

During the spring Crowley had made some progress in tightening his control of the FEA. He had little choice. The many complaints from within the agency the previous December and January had been confirmed by a critical Bureau of the Budget study, and in late April he had acted. He had asked "Lock" Currie to organize an Executive Policy Committee, including Henry Riley, Oscar Cox, and himself. The committee would thrash out and make policy under his guidance; and, independently, it would supervise bureau chiefs more closely to coordinate their operations and consolidate some divisions. Crowley hoped that forming this Executive Policy Committee, however belated, would "materially improve the FEA's effectiveness."[27]

Cox, for one, had immediately applauded his boss's decision. But within a month problems developed. Crowley's memo establishing the Executive Policy Committee was so loosely drawn that its members felt they could bring assistants; meetings proved cumbersome; and restricting attendance did not help much. Also, Crowley seldom met with the committee. He preferred to have Riley, Cox, or the committee secretary summarize the issues discussed and relay his decisions. Moreover, he indicated that he expected "all major policy matters resolved" before they were sent to him to sign.[28]

Those policy matters ran the gamut of economic issues worldwide. Some were old: repetitive conflicts with the British and French over lend-lease, their exports, and their dollar balances. And there was a new twist to lend-lease. That summer, after discussion in the Execu-

tive Policy Committee, Crowley sent the president a memo suggesting
that the shipment of capital equipment be limited to the "immediate
war effort," and twelve months might be sufficient. Finally, that summer saw the first interdepartmental planning for the occupation of
Germany.[29]

The president had suggested a "tough" position on Germany at
Casablanca in January 1943, when he demanded "unconditional surrender." The State Department, on the other hand, argued that a
"peace of reconciliation" was essential for a prosperous, peaceful,
democratic Germany, which was, in turn, a prerequisite for a prosperous, peaceful, democratic Europe. As for Crowley and his Executive
Policy Committee, there was no discussion of the issue until the spring
of 1944, months after the State Department circulated a proposed executive order calling for an indepartmental committee to study postwar commercial policy.[30]

Crowley played a leading role in the formation of the State-Trea-
sury-FEA Executive Committee on Economic Foreign Policy. He could
visualize its significance for the FEA. A defeated Germany would need
economic aid if it were not to fall prey to anarchy or communism. And
the FEA, as the civilian agency best equipped to provide every function required—from food to intelligence—would be expected to do so.
Consequently, on May 19 the FEA requested, and the ECEFP adopted,
its proposal to put discussion of economic policy for ex-enemy countries on the agenda.[31]

Despite the reference to ex-enemy countries, the ECEFP never
seems to have discussed a governing policy for Japan. On June 9, the
State Department presented the committee with two draft proposals
for the occupation of Germany, one titled "General Objectives," the
other "Post-Surrender Problems: Immediately after Surrender: Policies
Essential to Guard Against Internal Collapse." Both drafts stressed
moderation, not punishment: Germany must be deprived of her war
potential, pay reparations, and be integrated into Europe's economic
system. But Currie argued that the drafts did not solve the central
problem: how Germany could be deprived of the means to make war
yet retain enough heavy industry to pay reparations. Indeed, throughout June and July, it was FEA representatives who asked the hard questions. But when the committee approved final drafts of the State Department proposals—known as ECEFP 31/44 and 32/44—on August
4, it left the FEA with the task of providing specificity.[32]

On August 8, Crowley asked James W. Angell, an economist on loan from Columbia University, to form a German Working Committee to design the "specific economic controls" that would be required by Allied authorities in Germany to provide against aggression in the future, but also to assist in delivering reparations in the immediate postwar years. The GWC was to be guided by the ECEFP's two drafts calling for a "peace of reconciliation." Curiously in some respects, despite Crowley's call for "specific economic controls," Angell's committee was given two months to come up with a broad-gauged study. The details could be filled in later.[33]

By early September the GWC finished more precise versions of the ECEFP's drafts, but they did not get at the root of the problem, how a defeated Germany should be treated. One critic within the FEA scored the revisions as "disturbing," "unrealistic," and if adopted "disastrous." Germany, his memorandum insisted, was "diseased, lethal, psychopathic." Its industry must be rigidly supervised or cannibalized for reparations.[34]

Meanwhile, Morgenthau had reached the same conclusions. In mid-August, Harry Dexter White, the secretary's economic adviser and representative on the ECEFP, had warned him that the committee's August 4 drafts called for leaving German industry intact. In that case, White argued, Germany would dominate Europe again. Morgenthau had agreed. On August 17, he told White to devise a tougher Treasury plan for Germany's occupation, adding that the president would be receptive. The president had just balked at the Army's *Handbook*, providing guidance for a moderate treatment of Germany. He had told Secretary of War Stimson that the guide was "pretty bad" and must be revised so that the Germans would be allowed no more than "a subsistence level" of food and other basics. But the *Handbook* was a guide for the war's immediate aftermath. For the longer term, the president stated that a combined State, War, and Navy committee should develop an acceptable plan for Germany. Where the aftermath would end and the longer term begin was never clarified and created not a little confusion.[35]

After that, Morgenthau had the Treasury frame a tough "Post-Surrender Program for Germany." Completed by September 2, it advocated dismemberment, complete disarmament, and payment of reparations out of existing resources. And it appeared to exert some influence. When the newly formed State-War-Navy Committee met on

September 5, the State Department had moved to a somewhat tougher posture than earlier that summer. Stimson, however, continued to stress the moderation he called essential to stability in Germany during the immediate post-surrender period, while American forces were being moved to the Pacific. On September 6 and 9 the State-War-Navy Committee, unable to find common ground, conferred with the president. However, Roosevelt would not commit himself.[36]

But in Quebec the following week Morgenthau secured the support he required. Not only the president but his conferee, Prime Minister Winston Churchill, signed on to the Treasury's plan. At the same time Morgenthau promised Churchill $6.5 billion in lend-lease for fiscal year 1946 (beginning July 1945), almost half in civilian goods. This promise was a problem Crowley would have to deal with that fall. So were other consequences of Morgenthau's "success" at Quebec.[37]

Crowley soon became aware of those consequences for him personally. Between September 21 and 23, the press sometimes criticized the Army's moderate position on Germany, but more often the president for taking Morgenthau, rather than Hull, to Quebec, and for agreeing, with Churchill, to Morgenthau's ideologically harsh and counterproductive plan. The barrage unsettled the president. He postponed a press conference scheduled for September 28. That in turn prompted journalists to write that he was backing away from the Morgenthau Plan. They were right.[38]

At a press conference on Friday, September 29, the president explained his new position. He referred to a letter he had written Crowley, in which he had ordered, among other things, that he have the Foreign Economic Administration "accelerate" its ongoing study of controlling Germany's future capacity to make war "under the guidance of the Department of State." Exactly what he meant, Roosevelt did not say, but newsmen could draw some fairly obvious conclusions. The president had read the newspapers and his mail; he had recognized that endorsing Morgenthau's plan might endanger his reelection; and he had taken a cautious step toward disassociating himself from his Treasury secretary's harsh proposal. How far he would go reporters could only wonder; his reference to his letter to Crowley and the FEA had been too limited.[39]

Reporters found the Morgenthau Plan and the administration's waffling fascinating copy, but they missed a portion of the story they might have found no less fascinating and, perhaps, more significant.

They did not know that the president's letter to Crowley originated not in the White House but in the Foreign Economic Administration, and not as a flash response to burgeoning hostility to the Morgenthau Plan, and that it was in fact written three weeks earlier.

On September 7, Oscar Cox, as Crowley's general counsel, had drafted an FEA agenda for its new year that he thought the president might want to release "publicly in the near future and possibly at his Press Conference tomorrow." It mentioned eight major policies that Crowley, acting on the president's orders, expected the FEA to "put into effect when the military resistance of Nazi Germany is overcome." Actually, only a single phrase in one policy problem was significant: Section 7, dealing with "Control of the Warmaking Power of Germany," did not mention "the guidance of the State Department," as the president's letter of September 29 did.[40]

Neither was there such a reference in the small but critical revision suggested by Harry Hopkins that evening. Hopkins simply told Cox he believed the letter would be more effective if turned around so the press and public would think the president wrote it to Crowley. And Cox made the changes the next day. However, as noted, the letter was not released then; it was sent to the State Department where, after two weeks, the words "under the guidance of the State Department" were added to the FEA's responsibility for studying control of Germany's future warmaking powers. The phrase was redundant—the FEA was already bound to act under the State Department's guidance—and doubtless reflected Hull's pique when the president did not take him to Quebec. In any event, the revised letter was returned to the FEA on September 23, whereupon Hopkins advised the president to release it three days later, the day after the FEA's annual report went to Congress.[41]

But it was not released on September 26, either. Doubtless the president learned that the Morgenthau Plan was getting mixed reviews at best; he might need the escape hatch afforded by the FEA's letter. However, possible complications were then arising. On September 25, the FEA's Executive Policy Committee discussed the revised letter at Crowley's request, then decided that in light of the State Department's revision it should be withdrawn. The committee saw nothing to be gained by being drawn "into the dispute which exists currently between the Treasury, State, and War Departments concerning what to do about Germany." Even so, the EPC eventually agreed that Crowley should make the final decision as to whether or not the letter should be withdrawn.[42]

When Crowley was advised of the EPC's position, he discussed the letter and how it should be handled with Cox, who then phoned the White House. Cox advised Presidential Secretary Steve Early that his boss was "concerned about Point 7 of the proposed letter from the President"; that, "in view of all the public talk about a split between State and Treasury . . . , the reference to the 'guidance of the Department' should be omitted." Cox might have added that his boss was afraid of being trapped in a fight between the State Department and Treasury. However, he merely asked Early to prevail upon the president to postpone announcement of the letter so that he could discuss it with the secretary of state. Crowley would discuss it with the president after that.[43]

Whether Cox spoke to Hull between September 25 and 28 is not known. What is clear is that Crowley spoke to the president, and that Roosevelt was less concerned with Crowley's worries than his own political problem. The FEA's letter served his purposes; he could get on with his reelection campaign free of the millstone the Morgenthau Plan had become. Crowley, a comparatively obscure bureaucrat, and the FEA, an equally obscure agency, could wear it.[44]

Newspaper reactions nationally and from abroad revealed that the president had succeeded as well as he could have hoped. Perhaps the headline on a *Roanoke* [Virginia] *Times* editorial put his coup most vividly, "It's Now Leo Crowley's 'baby.' " Exactly how Crowley would care for his "baby," in particular whether he would do so, as he was instructed, "under the guidance of the State Department," was disputed by the many commentaries Cox collected in the month following. All agreed that the FEA was devising "technical" economic controls for Germany. Beyond that, some asserted that the FEA favored rigid controls and, as one put it, scrapping German industry "designed for war-making purposes." On the other hand, the *Wall Street Journal* asserted that the views of Crowley and his subordinates would produce a "middle ground" between the "soft peace" the Army and, perhaps, the State Department, wanted, and Morgenthau's plan. But no one knew what Crowley and the FEA would and could do. Nor would they learn for some time to come.[45]

13

Germany, Politics, and Lend-Lease

Late September 1944 marked the end of Crowley's first year as foreign economic administrator, a time for reflection whatever the circumstances. But its punctuation by the president's letter on Germany gave him special reason to look both behind and ahead. In the year past, he had been criticized publicly more often than in his previous ten years in Washington—unfairly it would seem. Lend-lease was extended and new appropriations obtained, critics of other economic warfare programs were no longer heard, and the FEA was consolidated and reorganized. As for the agency's second year, the outlines were clear. Crowley foresaw problems involved in the extension of lend-lease flowing from Morgenthau's promises and the approaching end of the European war. And he saw another problem stemming from the president's letter ordering the FEA to "accelerate" its planning to control Germany's future warmaking power. The press said, "It's Now Leo Crowley's 'baby,' " but he knew he would not have a free hand. Finally, that fall he hoped to contribute in some manner to the president's reelection campaign.[1]

The highly public manner in which the president told the FEA to "accelerate" its planning for Germany and his phrasing, "under the guidance of the State Department," leave little doubt that he was backing away from Treasury Secretary Morgenthau's harsh plan. But the FEA's German Working Committee, formed in August to flesh out the ECEFP's policy of August 4, was uncertain what that meant for its work: there was no "authoritative direction."

Crowley could not provide it. Shortly after Quebec, the president had written him that the "German people must feel defeat"; then came his letter of September 29; and, after that, a statement in mid-October, "I dislike making detailed plans for a country we do not yet occupy." Crowley could only ask the German Working Committee to develop mechanisms that would permit the FEA to implement the president's policy when he set it; and, also, to establish firmly the FEA's advisory authority in Germany.[2]

On October 9, Crowley told his Executive Policy Committee to consider establishing a new "German Branch" with two offices, one in London that could provide on-the-spot advice to the United States Group of the Allied Control Council for Germany, the other in Washington to provide the data and reassessments that would be required to "backstop it." Crowley's order reflected his recognition that the Army would manage Germany in the immediate post-war period and exclude the FEA from decision-making, impairing its assigned role in controlling Germany's war-making capacity later. However, the Army might find the FEA was too useful to exclude if the FEA were on the scene and able to provide sharply focused advice on managing Germany. Thus Crowley told the EPC to instruct GWC chairman James Angell to report quickly on his committee's progress.[3]

The next day Angell turned in a plan for Germany, but it was sketchy, and the EPC instructed him to produce a detailed plan by October 24. Now there was a new sense of urgency. It had little to do with the European war or White House policy: Allied forces were stalled on Germany's border, and the president had no desire to present a plan during the election campaign. But the Army had just drafted a tougher, new directive for the immediate post surrender period (JCS 1067) than its previous "soft" guideline which the president had rejected, and with it available the Army seemed likely to cut the FEA, as well as the State Department, Treasury, and Navy out of policy-making for Germany altogether. But despite the EPC's urging, the German Working Committee did not produce a detailed plan. Part of the problem was the failure of the State Department to provide the FEA with the "guidance" required in the president's letter to Crowley of September 29. It was the end of October before Acting Secretary Stettinius told Crowley he had assigned an officer "to deal with . . . the treatment of Germany and to work with the Foreign Economic Administration."[4]

Fairness suggests that the GWC's sloth reflected in part the great complexity and controversial nature of the German problem, in part the failure of the State Department. But by late October the FEA's Executive Policy Committee had decided that Angell had too many jobs and that the composition of the GWC was unsuited to its charge. Further, by November 2 the EPC saw dire consequences in the GWC's failure: their boss was not "adequately informed as to the potentialities of the FEA's contribution to German control work" and would "have no basis on which to discuss [it] with Hull and the President" when, as scheduled, he met with them after the election. Crowley would be embarrassed; moreover, the FEA might be excluded from later planning for Germany's occupation. Thus Angell was given one week to provide the EPC and Crowley with a summary of its "proposed economic policies towards Germany" and the FEA's "functions" in applying them.[5]

Angell's failure to report by November 9 sealed his fate and that of the GWC. An exasperated Crowley approved an EPC proposal that established a new, German Branch in the FEA. Then he looked for a lawyer from outside the FEA to run it. His network helped. William "Bill" Batt, whom he knew from the Combined War Materials Board, suggested Henry Fowler, who had worked for him and was now with the War Production Board. Then another phone call to Julius Krug, the WPB's chairman, prompted him to loan Fowler to the FEA. Thus Crowley obtained a director for the Washington office of the German Branch, and one he would never regret. As for Fowler, he would recall a different Crowley from that demonized by Nitze and Ball. Forty-five years later, he remembered that, at their first meeting, Crowley "turned the German Branch over to me to handle." This might suggest Crowley's obvious and oft-criticized tendency to delegate. But Fowler insisted, "In time I learned that Crowley found qualified people and delegated responsibility; then he backed them up." For the moment, though, "I knew only that I was to pull together a unit that would analyze Germany's industry and economy as they affected her ability to launch another war or to dominate the economies of the rest of Europe. And there was little time."[6]

There was more time than Fowler recalled. And he arrived in November, too late to prepare Crowley for his postelection meeting at the White House. Crowley knew this would be the case. He knew, too, that the president was focusing then on issues just as critical as the occupation of Germany, and more immediate: there was the connected issue of the amount of lend-lease to be negotiated with the British and later asked of Congress; and, even more immediate, the president had an election to win.

Crowley played a useful role in the president's victory over Republican challenger Thomas Dewey, in part using his position as foreign economic administrator. During the spring he contributed to the president's image as commander-in-chief, clearing a letter to the president stressing highly successful strong new steps the FEA was taking to prevent German purchases of strategic materials from neutrals Spain, Sweden, and Portugal. These steps, he wrote the White House, the president could point up the next day at his press conference.[7]

D-Day in France supervened. But Crowley turned the delay to advantage, sending the president a more sharply worded, even perfervid version the White House made public on June 13. Then, as spring turned to summer, Crowley saw great political advantage to the president in sending Colonel William O'Dwyer, the influential New York politician, to Rome to represent the FEA, but as a brigadier general. When Secretary of War Stimson balked at O'Dwyer's promotion as "irregular," Crowley informed the president, and he changed Stimson's decision if not his mind. In August, O'Dwyer's promotion was confirmed by the Senate, and soon he was in Italy. Though the president failed to carry New York in November it was not for Crowley's lack of savvy.[8]

Also in August, Crowley himself wrote Assistant Secretary of War John J. McCloy about another matter with political implications. Detroit's Archbishop Mooney, then chairing the War Relief Service of the National Catholic Welfare Conference, had earlier asked the War Department to admit four priests and two laymen to Rome where they could distribute clothing and money. Now, after Crowley heard from Mooney that his request had been disapproved, he warned McCloy that he "would not assume any responsibility if there is further delay in this matter." Crowley might have been repaying his debt to Mooney for stifling Father Coughlin's Social Justice. But presidential politics was foremost on his mind. In September he advised the president, "It would be well to have this cleared up as soon as possible, as several New York newspapers are 'playing up' the Italian situation." The president agreed, and on October 2 the War Department informed Mooney that his group would receive their clearances for Rome.[9]

Crowley contributed to the president's strength that fall in other ways. On September 29, while the president was telling the press of his orders to the FEA to speed its plans for controlling Germany's warmaking capacity, Crowley was speaking in Milwaukee. He said the administration was doing a wonderful job winning the war and would handle postwar problems just as well: witness the creation of the FEA with its ability to pick targets for American bombing raids on Germany and Japan, and the FEA's readiness, now, to plan for Germany's occupation. Deftly he played on the theme of the president's supporters everywhere: "don't change" administrations this year.[10]

Even as Crowley spoke, though, the Republican-oriented *Saturday Evening Post* was challenging the sponsorship of one of the administration's two most popular achievements. Bank deposit insurance was no New Deal gift, the magazine pointed out, reminding its readers of what Michigan residents had known since 1934, that Leo Crowley, chairman of the FDIC, had labeled their Republican Senator Arthur Vandenberg "the father of bank deposit insurance." Moreover, the *Post* stressed, deposit insurance was "stuffed down F.D.R.'s throat" by the Michigan Republican. New Dealers should admit it.[11]

Surely, Crowley and the president were embarrassed. Neither responded, however, until late October, after Dewey repeated the charge in Chicago, now adding a reference to Crowley's letter to Vandenberg ten years before. Asked by the president to respond, Crowley found himself in a serious bind. He could not respond to Dewey without repudiating what he had written Vandenberg. And he could not do that; he and Vandenberg were old, close friends. On the other hand, he could not directly refuse the man in the White House. Thus, he reminded the president that he did not "have any intimate knowledge of the legislative history" of the FDIC (which privately, of course, tended to repudiate his 1934 letter to Vandenberg), but he would have somebody at the FIDC draft one.[12]

What emerged was a statement that the president had favored "sound" bank deposit insurance, that he had opposed an "outright and complete Government *guaranty*," and that he had supported the deposit act enthusiastically since its passage. As for the act's legislative history, the FDIC's letter admitted that Senator Vandenberg had proposed an amendment providing for temporary deposit insurance and supported the bill's passage, otherwise the act was "substantially the work of Messrs. Steagall and Glass," of a Democratic Congress and Democratic president. Such was the essence of the draft Crowley sent the White House. He could hardly have been happy with it; it slighted his good friend Senator Vandenberg. Fortunately for that relationship, the White House decided that his letter was too long and too soft, and a briefer, tougher statement was released over the signature of Speaker of the House Sam Rayburn.[13]

The president had no reason to complain, however, when Crowley spoke for him over the Mutual Broadcasting System just before the election. It is probable, however, that someone at the White House gave Crowley a bit of guidance. His own draft was aimed at independent New Dealers. It reminded them that the president was a great humanitarian and that New Deal legislation originated in Wisconsin progressivism, not socialism or communism. And he knew that at first hand: "I came from the State of Wisconsin."[14]

No one would have known from Crowley's radio address. There was no reference to progressivism and less to Roosevelt as humanitarian than as conservative, reforming to preserve. As Crowley saw it, in the thirties the president had acted "time and again, with courage and vision, to save the jobs, the earnings, and the private property of Americans." He had built a "strong, prosperous, and vital America . . . where Communism cannot live." Who knew that better than he, Leo T. Crowley, "a businessman trained to . . . look after the interests of stockholders."

No speech that fall could have revealed more clearly the New Deal's death. Or perhaps the mythological New Deal. Crowley was asking now-conservative Midwesterners to vote for a president who had saved their property, profits, and jobs once, and who now was saving them and their property from foreign foes, that is to vote for a conservative president. Indeed, Crowley went farther. As the chairman of a major corporation, he could not see how anyone could want to "change a management that has been so successful in serving the interests of the stockholders—all the people of the United States." Mentioning Roosevelt's name but seldom, Crowley stressed the administration's "performance," a "management which has done so well." No one, he concluded, should have any doubt about voting for Roosevelt at the ballot box.[15]

Four days later any doubt was erased. The president secured yet another vote of approval. As for Crowley, he received a note from the ailing Secretary Hull, who wrote that he had read every word of his speech and considered it "one of the finest which had been made." And there was also a commendation from a vice-president of the National Association of Postmasters who was glad that Crowley "brought out that ALL classes of people were benefitted from 1932 on." Many Americans whose investments were saved during the thirties seemed to have forgotten. Crowley had reminded them.[16]

Crowley was pleased with his contribution to the president's reelection, but ten days later he asked the president to relieve him as foreign economic administrator. He was willing to stay on as chairman of the FDIC but wanted to "give more time to my business." Not surprisingly, however, the president asked, in effect insisted, that he soldier on, "at least until the elimination of Germany from the war."[17]

Both the president and Crowley realized that the prospect of victory in Europe the following spring would create new obstacles to obtaining lend-lease extension and still large appropriations. So would rising British exports, competing with those of powerful American exporters. And Crowley and his staff knew it. British complaints about restrictions notwithstanding, those restrictions were minimal. The FEA's senior officer policing them warned his superiors, "I have constantly warned of the danger and indefensibility of our position should details of British nonconformance with the Policy become public knowledge." The solution, if feasible politically, was a change in this "obsolete Policy." But it was not feasible, Currie told the State Department in August.[18]

In mid-September, Crowley learned that the president had not told Churchill he would lift restrictions on British exports, but he had promised some $6.5 billion in lend-lease for Stage II, the first year of the interim between Germany's surrender and Japan's defeat. The details were to be thrashed out by an Anglo-American committee chaired by Morgenthau for the Treasury, with Stettinius representing the State Department, and Crowley the FEA.[19]

The first meeting of the Anglo-American Committee took place September 20. Neither Crowley nor Stettinius spoke that day; Cox spoke for them. He said that the figures for lend-lease to which Morgenthau had subscribed at Quebec assumed proportionately equal contributions to the Pacific war, and that would not be the case. Cox further warned that the FEA was as concerned about munitions as non-munitions in the lend-lease package, because resources the British did not have to employ manufacturing the former could be used to make the latter, thus they could export commercial goods at American expense. Concern over the amount and types of lend-lease was the key word, as Crowley, Cox (and Currie) returned to the FEA's offices and wrote Morgenthau that disagreements on the American side should be settled before further meetings with the British. But the letter was not sent that day or for almost two weeks after. Ever cautious, Crowley wanted to get the president's position first.[20]

Crowley spoke with the president about Stage II the same day —probably September 27—that he pleaded with him not to ask the FEA to plan for Germany's occupation under the State Department's guidance. Later, he wrote Byrnes that the president "did not recall exactly what he had signed at Quebec and regardless of what was signed there, I was to take charge of the thing and handle it in accordance with my commitments to the Congress. He told me to go ahead and negotiate with the British in the regular way. Harry Hopkins and Admiral Leahy were asked . . . to support my position."[21]

Overnight, Morgenthau found himself facing the Pentagon, the White House, the State Department, and the FEA. Hull warned of a "hostile public reaction" if Stage II were not modified; and Crowley echoed him. Repeating Cox's arguments after Quebec, he wrote Morgenthau October 2, "It might not be right or politic for us to supply six and one half billion dollars worth of lend-lease aid," when Britain would be providing only half the resources of the United States in the Japanese war. There were other troublesome issues as well, such as British use of lend-lease to rebuild "their housing that was destroyed by the robot bombing." It was essential, then, that the Treasury, State Department, and FEA get together soon without the British to deal with these issues.[22]

On October 6, the interdepartmental American committee Crowley recommended began what was to be, in the next eight weeks, a fumbling attempt to reconcile Britain's admitted needs with the fears of the State Department and FEA that if the aid were not reduced, it would, as Cox argued, "get blown out of the water in Congress." While Morgenthau spoke of America's moral obligation, Crowley argued from his bias as a banker and his concern for Congress's reaction that Britain should be treated as a "large business that finds itself now in financial difficulty." The United States should help the British get back on their feet, as during the Great Depression it had helped farmers and bankers. That was language Congress might understand. Crowley said he agreed with Morgenthau that aiding Britain was in our interest, but the issue must be handled carefully. The administration must not sacrifice American interests. It could not appear to do so. It could not give some congressmen a stick to beat the administration.[23]

As the autumn deepened and the British specified their lend-lease requirements, Crowley presided over the Executive Policy Committee meetings that evaluated them. It modified most British requests in a very literal manner. The British could ship lend-leased locomotives to India, but not for the cash or equivalents they needed to meet their debts to their colonies. When in mid-November the British asked that such restrictions be lifted as of January 1, Crowley replied that the FEA would recommend no change "until the president has had an opportunity to consider the question." When the British countered that they would pay for materials not under lend-lease that they wanted (to manufacture and freely export), Crowley again insisted that the president must decide.[24]

That very day Morgenthau found that the president would not settle Stage II. He was leaning toward lifting restrictions on British exports after V-E Day, not January 1, and he was worried about Congress, but Admiral Leahy was the man to see and "sell." As for Crowley, presiding over his Executive Policy Committee on the morning of November 20, he indicated that he had not seen the president or Leahy and asked for the committee's recommendations. And that afternoon he got them. The EPC prepared "Mr. Crowley's Statement of Principles," essentially retaining all restrictions on Britain's exports until V-E Day.[25]

On November 22 Crowley took his "Statement of Principles" to a crucial meeting of Morgenthau's lend-lease committee. There he learned that the president opposed a binding program. Morgenthau explained, "He wants to be able to say there was no agreement." Then Stettinius asked why the FEA wanted to postpone easement of Britain's export position until V-E Day, when the British government had a "very acute political problem." Crowley rejoined with his consistent refrain that fall, "I was trying to recognize our acute political problem, too. If the administration allowed the British government to state publicly that they are going to start their export business as of January 1 . . . , it will cause us no end of trouble, Ed, on the Hill and with our general public. Now, that is my viewpoint on the thing."[26]

In fact, it was not quite Crowley's "viewpoint." He quickly added: "We are willing to say that in an administrative way, we will cooperate with them [the British] in between now and VE Day just as much as we possibly can." Crowley seemed to be saying that, as during the summer and earlier, the FEA would police British exports lightly, but there should be nothing in writing or a press release. "I think it would seriously affect our situation on the Hill when it comes to getting our appropriation." Crowley feared that Senator McKellar, who chaired the Appropriations Committee with an iron hand, would block appropriations for Stage II if the administration discussed lifting restrictions on British exports before V-E Day. In fact, to speak of it would be "penny-wise and pound foolish."

Crowley did not have the last word. When American "policy"—it was not an agreement—was announced November 30, it was clear that some materials would be sold to the British after January 1 without restrictions, although subject to available shipping and supplies. As for lend-lease, the dollar amount to be shipped to Britain was not specified, it would be subject to "adjustment . . . in accordance with the changing conditions of the war." However, the New York Times fairly accurately reported the working figure as $5.5 billion, which was slightly more than half the amount for the present year, but enough to help Britain increase her exports and improve her living standards and financial standing. Yet the Times, although aware that the American statement was not a binding commitment, spoke of "the new arrangements" as "locktight."[27]

They were not, of course, and Crowley believed it fortunate. The British program was merely administration policy until it ran the congressional gauntlet, and Congress, though it would be Democratic again in the spring, would also be rebellious. He would have difficulty persuading it that the amount for Britain was required to defeat Japan, a moral imperative, or in America's self-interest. Also, Congress might well insist that lend-lease, set up in 1941 to "promote the defense of the United States," did not cover what must be, in part, postwar relief and rehabilitation.

When Crowley testified before the House Foreign Affairs Committee in February, the last problem emerged first and persisted. Almost immediately, a small Republican group insisted that lend-lease was being used, and would be used, improperly, for postwar relief and rehabilitation. Crowley first rebutted the Republican charges categorically—"It is our understanding . . . that lend-lease is entirely military [now] . . . and that after the war . . . [it] will not be used for postwar rehabilitation purposes"—then he acknowledged that the FEA could not be certain in either case. No one, that day, challenged his sudden equivocation. Neither did anyone challenge his suggestion that Congress might approve the furnishing of supplies to civilians for postwar rehabilitation. Perhaps it was because Crowley confessed his guiding philosophy: "I have never believed . . . that an administrator should interpret legislation under a theory that may be his own. I believe that it is my job to carry out the intent of Congress." And committee members, Republicans as well as Democrats, took him at his word. They had been doing so for a decade.[28]

All in all, these early February sessions were, as Secretary of War Stimson saw them, "a love feast." This was not true, however, after the month's end. Ohio Republican John Vorys, spokesman for the Foreign Affairs Committee's isolationists, had found a chink in the administration's armor; it was about to initial a lend-lease agreement with France that included railroad equipment and other goods that would not possibly be available for shipment until after the war's (approaching) end. The administration was also asking Congress to extend Section 3-C of the Lend-Lease Act, the French agreement's legal basis, from July 1, 1948, to July 1, 1949. Vorys argued that the French agreement violated the spirit of the Lend-Lease Act: Section 3-C had been designed to sell off material intended for use during the war and save the beleaguered American taxpayer. Now the administration wanted to use it as a mechanism for financing postwar foreign relief and rehabilitation through liberal, long-term loans, at the expense of the taxpayer. Thus, on February 27, Vorys and four other Republican members of the House Foreign Affairs Committee demanded extended hearings on "the postwar economic effects of continuing lend-lease beyond the war period."[29]

On March 5, Crowley appeared before the Foreign Affairs Committee to speak for Section 3-C and the French agreement (one of three that included Belgium and the Netherlands). He opened conventionally, saying that the French agreement would enable France to mobilize her resources fully to defeat the enemy. When a congressman interjected that American forces were then crossing the Rhine River, and the war would be over before the equipment could be manufactured, Crowley first denied it, then insisted that the war in Europe was far from over. However he soon argued on somewhat stronger ground that the Section 3-C agreements would enable European countries receiving aid to provide greater support for the American occupation and, also, speed the transfer of American forces to the Pacific. To this he added an argument he must have hoped would strike close enough to home for the committee to win the day: Section 3-C would enable the United States to avoid the crippling surpluses and unemployment that were almost certain if equipment contracted for could not be disposed of for lack of any arrangement for the recipients to pay. The result, Crowley, concluded, could be another Great Depression.

Crowley had a point, but his argument made little impression on congressman Vorys and his four allies on the committee. Their conservatism was a significant factor, but Crowley had begged the question: why contract for and manufacture equipment that could not be shipped for use during the war. No wonder Vorys continued to insist that Section 3-C, if extended for a year, would further open a back door to relief, rehabilitation, and reconstruction; it would not "promote the defense of the United States," which was the test required by the Lend-Lease Act.[30]

Crowley might have rejoined that aiding Western Europe, even after the war against Germany ended, would promote the long-range economic and political security of the United States. And George Ball has faulted him for not doing so. He has charged that Crowley "knew nothing about the economic needs of our Allies" or "the "underlying philosophy" of lend-lease. In effect, he was an isolationist. But Ball's charge is not valid. Crowley was neither isolationist nor internationalist; he was a pragmatist and salesman. In 1948, he would testify that circumstances justified the Marshall Plan; in 1945 he argued for what he believed would sell. He had warned the president the previous September that soundings on the Hill indicated that extending Section 3-C with the French and other agreements proposed by the State Department would very likely fail of passage, unless it was intended, which it was not, that the countries involved would participate fully in the war in the Pacific. When the president sided with the State Department, Crowley had quietly fallen into line. He had worked closely with the State Department. But he was not prepared, in March, to make an argument for postwar aid he knew Congress would not buy. (No one else testifying was either.) He preferred to soothe doubters and congressmen who feared their constituents. Thus he said that if there were a need for American aid during the postwar period, it would be with a "new cart and a new horse." Meanwhile, he emphasized, the United

States would benefit greatly from exporting its war surplus and from supporting, albeit indirectly, its forces in Europe and the Pacific.[31]

Not surprisingly, perhaps, Democratic members of the Foreign Affairs Committee reported out the administration's "extension of lend-lease" favorably the day after Crowley testified. But Vorys and his allies submitted a minority report. Even acknowledging a case for what Crowley had called a "clean-up," they insisted that Section 3-C's extension to July 1, 1949, was "too long," and its discretionary authority was "too broad." Crowley had forseen the latter criticism. He had asked Vorys to trust his "integrity" as lend-lease administrator, only to have the congressman remind him that, frankly, he "was charged with administering something where you do not determine policy."[32]

Crowley moved quickly to overcome the minority's objections. That weekend he and Cox negotiated a two-part amendment that satisfied them. However, it gave nothing away. Both parts spoke to the question of "postwar relief, postwar rehabilitation, or postwar reconstruction," and they canceled one another. Crowley had recognized that Vorys and company would be satisfied with the appearance of a victory; Cox who drafted the amendment quickly notified the president that it was "harmless"; and, although neither they nor the minority said so, Crowley and Cox had secured Vorys' agreement to stifle unfriendly amendments on the House floor. As a result, lend-lease extension, including the extended "clean-up" period, easily passed the House on March 13.[33]

Two weeks later Crowley spoke for the amended extension bill before the Senate Foreign Relations Committee. No one challenged his assertion of the need to equip eight French divisions so near the European war's end, or asked how France would repay what was, really, a twenty-year loan for rehabilitation and reconstruction. Republicans as well as Democrats accepted Crowley's argument that it was in the nation's interest to sell goods in the pipeline on credit rather than cancel production or retain the surplus. However, Senator Vandenberg suddenly produced a "confidential" memo. it referred to the president's agreement at Quebec to "consider" giving Britain $6.5 billion during Stage II, but Vandenberg spoke of it as a "commitment," and asked Crowley, "I would like to know whether there is any truth in it."[34]

Crowley's answer boldly skirted the truth, "Senator, to the best of my knowledge . . . there is no truth in it." In fact, Crowley knew better—Morgenthau had told him of the Quebec agreement immediately after. Though the numbers had been cut since Quebec, Vandenberg's "confidential" memo was essentially accurate. Crowley and Cox fenced, reminding Vandenberg that the president could not commit Congress, but the senator was not satisfied. He asked for a detailed explanation, with dollar signs, of what he was now willing to call "the British understanding." Crowley promised it before the committee's next meeting.[35]

After a few more words about British lend-lease and a brief, later significant exchange about Soviet lend-lease after hostilities in Europe ended, Vandenberg asked about other commitments of which the committee might not be aware. Crowley then advised the committee of pending Section 3-C agreements with the Belgians and Dutch. He said they were not intended to provide postwar relief, rehabilitation, and reconstruction; as with the French agreement, they were being designed to rebuild the Dutch and Belgian railway sytems and otherwise help those countries facilitate the movement of American troops from Europe to the Pacific. Crowley's rationale made sense, and no one challenged it, but Vandenberg warned, "The troublesome thing, psychologically, is that this date, June 30, 1949, sticks out like a sore thumb, . . . it looks as though we are going to be peddling our goods indefinitely."[36]

Crowley was chastened by the warning. The next day he, Morgenthau, and Stettinius notified the president that they believed it best to postpone finalizing of any of the 3-C agreements until Congress approved extension of the Lend-Lease Act. And Roosevelt soon agreed, as the State Department reported on April 5.[37]

It was a prudent decision. The day before the State Department's announcement, Vandenberg had questioned Crowley sharply at another session of the Foreign Relations Committee. First he had pounced on Stage II of the British program. "Suppose," he began, "that Japan collapses 3 months after Germany collapses; are you in a position to call this off?" Crowley answered, "I assume . . . that we would call our lend-lease off and liquidate it." Given the "assume" and the "we," Crowley's answer was by no means absolute, but when Japan surrendered he would act as if he had made a commitment he must honor and persuade the administration to honor as well.[38]

Meanwhile, Vandenberg took off on what he believed Crowley's commitment to stopping British lend-lease with Japan's surrender. "All right," he continued. "Under those circumstances, why is it necessary to have in this extension bill a 3 year post-war period for the liquidation of these accounts?" Crowley squirmed, offering the example of "a power plant which is half-finished," but he did not persuade Vandenberg. Indeed, the senator began hammering at the existing time frame. And Crowley caved. He said the FEA would not make contracts for delivery dates beyond eight, perhaps twelve months. In any event, it would be "bound by what the Congress wishes." That said, the committee approved the lend-lease extension bill with the administration's extended "clean-up" period and with the House's Vorys amendment.[39]

Five days later, on the Senate floor, Vandenberg recommended the extension bill as reported. He argued, as Crowley had during the hearings, the benefits to the United States of getting rid of lend-lease in the pipeline; but his speech is most notable for an extended paean to Crowley himself. And in doing so, he also made a broader point. "Despite all the law we can write," Vandenberg said, "observance of the congressional intent is finally dependent on the discretion of the Lend-Lease Administration [and] I have the greatest confidence in Administrator Crowley."[40]

Vandenberg's faith in Crowley did not persuade Robert Taft, the Ohio Republican now a rising star in his party. He insisted that the French agreement was not a war measure—the war in Europe would be over soon—and that the loan, given its length, was, in fact, a gift. Also, Americans had been saving, and no further stimulus was needed during reconversion. Taft asked the Senate to erase the second and canceling half of the Vorys amendment.[41]

Crowley was probably responsible for the failure of the Taft amendment the next day. Press attention focused on the tie vote, the (unnecessary) casting vote of Vice-President Truman, and the defection of several Democrats. However, the press ignored those Democrats who, as in the case of Tennessee's isolationist Kenneth McKellar, were almost certainly persuaded by Crowley not to vote rather than vote yea. On the other hand, it is significant that Vandenberg, who was even closer to Crowley and had spoken for the administration bill on the floor, succumbed to party pressure and voted for Taft's restrictive amendment. In sum, Crowley may have prevented an administration defeat, but the appearance of a solid Republican phalanx and the crumbling of support from conservative Democrats sounded a warning that echoed loudly through the months following. Truman, who just two days later would find himself in the White House, president on Roosevelt's death, did not forget. And Crowley did not. His testimony in the hearings suggests that he sympathized in some degree with the conservative trend and was wondering how long he could buck it or wanted to do so. This may explain why Morgenthau, Stettinius, and Roosevelt believed he was serious about resigning as foreign economic administrator.[42]

Crowley and Morgenthau had been anything but close since the Treasury secretary learned of Crowley's banking problems in Madison, his debts, and the cover-up at his confirmation. Morgenthau could not forget and did not forgive. Even when no issue divided them, he muttered to his associates about Crowley's perfidy. And since the fall specific issues had arisen: Crowley's readiness to cooperate with the president's retreat from his plan for Germany; Crowley's efforts to restrict British lend-lease during the Stage II negotiations; and Crowley's refusal to ask Julius Krug, at the War Shipping Administration, to give Russian lend-lease a higher priority. But through the fall of 1944 Crowley had been able to confront Morgenthau from a position of strength. Crowley was not only personally confident of his ability to deal with Morgenthau, more often than not he could rely on the support of the president and the State Department. But since the fall the president had been too sick or too far away—in February at Yalta in the Crimea —to afford much support, and an ailing Cordell Hull had resigned from the State Department. Time and the war had taken their toll of two men, who with Byrnes, Crowley had so often found critical sources of guidance and pillars of support.[43]

Crowley now found the State Department increasingly a source of problems for the FEA, and given the phrasing of the executive order establishing the FEA, he could do little about it. Shortly after the Christmas past, his Executive Policy Committee had complained bitterly to Assistant Secretary of State Acheson about a State Department "fait accompli" in naming the chief of a "joint mission" without consultation with the FEA. On February 5, Crowley had spoken angrily to the EPC about having received a letter from Acting Secretary of State Joseph Grew setting forth "an economic policy [toward Argentina] without collaboration with the FEA," and he was not mollified when a committee member said that there had been "informal conversations" with the State Department about the issue. Once he would have spoken quietly to Hull. Now he directed that someone write the State De-

partment, "suggesting that officials of the FEA be included in the for-
mulation of foreign economic policies and that reference be made to
FEA's basic responsibility in this field."[44]

Crowley's anger came as no surprise to Acheson, Stettinius, or
Morgenthau. On January 24, Acheson had lunched with Crowley, and
told Morgenthau soon after, that while walking away from the restau-
rant, Crowley "just exploded all over the place." Acheson warned
Morgenthau: "He's very angry at Ed, chiefly; [but] he's pretty angry at
you. I told him I was probably chiefly responsible so then he turned his
wrath on me."[45]

Crowley's anger stemmed from his increasing isolation from
policy decisions, but especially those affecting Germany. He had taken
the president's order of September 29 seriously. After the German
Working Committee failed to produce, he had found a solid team
leader in Henry Fowler. And Fowler was producing. On January 10, he
had sent Crowley an "Interim Report," listing twenty-seven projects
on which the German Branch was working. He added that preliminary
reports would be ready April 1.[46]

Thereafter, Fowler listed the experts he wanted, and Crowley went
after them, often leaning on old friendships, to do the job. But it was
one thing to engage in planning, it was another to get some grip on the
policy-making process itself. The State-War-Navy Coordinating Committee (SWNCC) exercised some slight influence on the Army; so did
the Treasury independently; but by January, when Fowler was reporting in, Crowley was learning that the FEA had no leverage whatsoever.
Leon Henderson, an economist he dispatched to London to inform the
Army that the German Branch would soon be ready to advise on specifics regarding the German occupation, reported to Crowley that he
received a frosty reception. The Army, it was clear, would not brook
any interference in its occupation policy, at least not then. Thus the
FEA could only continue its planning, as the president had ordered,
and hope that, when faced with the complexity of the occupation's
problems, either he would intervene or the Army would recognize the
great contribution its detailed studies could make.[47]

Crowley felt other disappointments that winter. On March 1, the
president created a Foreign Economic Policy Board, a body for which
the FEA was eminently suited, but the president did not include it.
Then in early April, Crowley wrote "Dear Ed," asserting that the president had signed a State Department memorandum giving the depart-

ment "supervision . . . of [all] civilian economic representatives in foreign countries." Crowley admitted that he did not know all the
particulars, but the memorandum was a "distinct shock." He added,
"I had been under the impression that neither of us would attempt to
rush through such memoranda for the approval of the President without having cleared [them] completely with the other."[48]

Letting off more steam, Crowley reminded Stettinius that he had
taken the post of administrator "with considerable reluctance because
of the confusion that had previously existed." As the secretary knew,
he had been "assured by Justice Byrnes and Secretary Hull [when
clarifying the executive order creating the FEA] that the full responsibility for foreign economic policy within the framework of the general
policy determined by the State Department rested upon the Foreign
Economic Administration." Now, though, "there have been numerous
instances in which representatives of the State Department have not
only failed to comply with the specific provisions of the Executive Order, but have violated completely the spirit of the Order." But Crowley
backed off from an open fight, "I have been reluctant to make an issue
of some . . . , or to bother the President with them." While suggesting
that he would fight, he was, in fact, only pleading.

Crowley was deeply wounded, but there was worse to come.
In mid-March, the president had created an Informal Policy Committee on Germany. IPCOG expanded the State-War-Navy Coordinating
Committee to incorporate the Treasury and FEA, but it was apparently
a sop the president thought would keep Crowley on board, managing
lend-lease on the Hill. Crowley did not want to admit this. On April 10,
the day after his "Dear Ed" letter, Crowley wrote Stettinius again, this
time addressing him formally as "Dear Mr. Secretary." Bitterly, Crowley pointed out that the FEA was not consulted on a memorandum involving the treatment of Germany, this despite the president's September 29 letter and more recently the creation of IPCOG. Now, Crowley
said, he hoped the rumor he had heard that some department wanted
the committee abolished was untrue. IPCOG might modify present
policy if it gave some consideration to Fowler's second report, "A Preliminary U.S. Program for German Economic and Industrial Disarmament." But Crowley might as well have addressed this complaint, as
well as that of the day before, to Mars. Stettinius, with whom he previously had been friendly, either did not care or could not help.[49]

After more than a decade in Washington, and more than twenty years in politics, Crowley realized what was happening even if he was loath to accept it. His influence as foreign economic administrator had diminished significantly. It had rested on a number of legs which had either disappeared or were crumbling. Hull, an ally, was no longer at the State Department; and Stettinius, a caretaker, was surrounded by stronger figures with bolder visions of America's postwar role than he, Crowley, could endorse; Roosevelt's health was failing; and Byrnes had just fallen from grace. Writing the departing Byrnes, Crowley emphasized "his tremendous sense of personal loss," then added that he deplored Byrnes's departure, especially "when your brand of philosophy and ideals are so desperately needed." Crowley was dispirited. He seemed to sense that the end of an era was close at hand.[50]

How close Crowley must have suspected when he saw the president off to Warm Springs, Georgia, on March 30. Crowley recalled some years later that the president discussed lend-lease with him that day as if he would not be alive when the war ended. Perhaps Crowley would have resigned as foreign economic administrator had Roosevelt at least returned to the White House from his vacation. The Senate had adopted the House-amended lend-lease bill; someone else could testify at the appropriations hearings in June. Then, in the early evening of April 12, Crowley was called to the White House, there to learn of Roosevelt's death, there to see Harry S. Truman sworn in as president. Unfortunately, Crowley never wrote or spoke publicly about his thoughts and feelings that night; but he did not forget; he simply chose a different perspective. Many years later he would compare the president he had served so long and faithfully with the president he was about to.

14

The End of Lend-Lease

Five days after Roosevelt's death, Crowley lunched with Sam Rosenman and Oscar Cox in his Mayflower suite. Cox noted, "Leo told us what he expects to do." He wanted to return to Standard Gas immediately, but he knew he could not. Harry S. Truman, now president, had asked key Roosevelt people to stay at their posts. He required their institutional memories, experience, and advice, and the American public and the Allies needed the reassurance that retaining well-seasoned Roosevelt men would provide.[1]

Dutifully Crowley would stay another six months, through the end of the wars in Europe and the Pacific and the collapse of the Grand Alliance. It was a decision he would regret. He would be hurt deeply ten years later when Truman, in his *Memoirs*, charged him with abusing his authority by abruptly shutting off lend-lease to the Soviet Union in May 1945, thus contributing to the collapse of the Grand Alliance, even to the budding Cold War. As Truman put it: The United States gave Marshal Joseph Stalin "a point of contention which he would . . . bring up every chance he had."[2]

Crowley found Truman's charge grossly unfair and attempted a response in the *New York Times*. He pointed out, quite correctly, that Truman did not sign the lend-lease order on May 8, as stated in his *Memoirs*. Otherwise, Crowley argued that it was Congress's intent that lend-lease be discontinued "summarily" when European hostilities ended, except as it would be used in the Pacific, and he included an August 1945 note from Senator Vandenberg stating that he had "literally fulfilled his promises to Congress." What might have been said on the night of May 11, before Truman signed the order, or what was done and by whom the next day, Crowley did not say. Thus, in the pre-Vietnam era, when Congress's influence over foreign policy was usually deprecated and presidential power praised, Truman's charge, that Crowley engaged in "policy-making" by executing the order "literally," remained the accepted version. It is clear now on its face, however, that Crowley was unfairly maligned. He would have engaged in "policy-making" had he interpreted the order Truman signed, but not by executing it "literally," the term used by the president. Further, new evidence turned up since the Vietnam years demonstrates that Crowley was only one player among several key actors in a drama characterized by misunderstandings and a new president operating amidst the pressures of a new office.[3]

Lend-lease to the Soviet Union began in October 1941, when the German army had reached the hills outside Moscow. From then until the Russian victory at Stalingrad a year and a half later, the Soviet lend-lease program enjoyed a privileged status. Nominally, it was managed by Stettinius's Office of Lend-Lease Administration; in fact, it was handled by the president's Soviet Protocol Committee, dominated by Harry Hopkins and General John York, who were totally sympathetic to the provision of "unconditional aid." What the Russians wanted, they got. They were killing Germans and saving American lives. Thus, until 1943, few Americans objected to Russian aid, at least not publicly.[4]

The formation of the Foreign Economic Administration brought only limited changes in Soviet aid policy. That fall, the president signed off on an "eighteen month's rule," asserting that the FEA would approve requests only for equipment that would be operable within that time frame, but the "rule" had been promised the previous spring and applied to every lend-lease recipient. Other than that, the Soviet Union was likely to receive "unconditional aid" as long as the president, Hopkins, and York were in charge.[5]

Meanwhile, the president was getting ample cooperation from Crowley and his general counsel, Oscar Cox, in the FEA. In late 1943, when the president was signing the "eighteen months rule," Cox was explaining to Crowley that Section 3-C of the Lend-Lease Act provided a means of circumventing it. Lend-Lease signatories could *pay* for equipment contracted for during the war but not delivered until after its end; thus recent Soviet requests could be met (as could those of other recipients signing such agreements). Indeed, Cox argued that this method of helping the Russians might "start them well on the road to reconstruction."[6]

By March 1944, Crowley had accepted Cox's suggestion, joining Undersecretary of State Stettinius in sending a memorandum to the president indicating their intention to secure 3-C agreements with the Russians as well as some other recipients of lend-lease. Crowley did so reluctantly, however. Pragmatically, he accepted the 3-C agreements as a "stopgap" that would meet the president's diplomatic needs after the Tehran conference the previous autumn, and, essential as always, as agreements that Congress might buy. But he greatly preferred a more businesslike approach to postwar reconstruction in the Soviet Union and other war-torn countries. Thus that spring he recommended to a congressional committee that the FEA-managed Export-Import Bank be employed to finance postwar reconstruction. The White House agreed.[7]

In January 1945, the president asked Congress to strengthen the bank. Also that month, Crowley sent the president a memorandum warning against open-ended promises to Churchill and Stalin when they met at Yalta, and reiterating his own commitment to the Export-Import Bank. Crowley admitted that "America's financial position was the world's strongest [and] most . . . other countries would be depending on us," but the United States's large national debt and limited resources argued that American interests must be fully protected. The United States could not afford to "finance the postwar reconstruction and reestablishment of the foreign trade of other countries without seeing to it that our foreign trade is protected." The solution to this problem was a greater role for the FEA. It controlled exports, its analysts could determine the needs of the many countries ravaged by the war, and it managed the Export-Import Bank. Thus the FEA could "finance, on a purely business basis, . . . the long-range industrial reconstruction" other countries desired to undertake. Finally, critically, for the administration to employ the FEA and the Export-Import Bank would "sell" with such powerful, hardnosed senators as Vandenberg and McKellar.[8]

Crowley hoped his arguments would strengthen the president's apparent decision to treat postwar reconstruction on a "business basis." Meanwhile he had to sell the administration's lend-lease program. It implied Russian involvement in the Pacific war. The previous fall the president had warned the FEA and all department heads involved not to stop lend-lease when Germany collapsed. An early January memorandum affirmed: "We must . . . continue to support the

U.S.S.R. by providing the maximum amount of supplies which can be delivered to her ports." Although it was clear that victory in Europe was near, the president added: "The U.S.S.R. has been requested to state requirements for a Fifth Protocol to cover the period July 1, 1945, to June 30, 1946. It is desired that . . . every effort be made to meet these requirements."[9]

Crowley replied on January 11 that he had so instructed "the responsible officials of my Administration." And he added, "You may rest assured that . . . every measure possible will be taken to carry out your direction in fulfilling the Fourth Protocol and in preparing for the Fifth."[10]

Crowley did not learn prior to Yalta whether the president's instructions required meeting Russian requests for capital equipment that would only be available after the war in Europe ended. On February 1, General Charles Wesson, who ran the FEA's Russian Branch, handed him a program for the Fifth Protocol that excluded capital goods, stressing that since the Russians had not signed a 3-C agreement there was no legal basis for including them. Crowley told the general to "refrain from raising this problem until the president returns [from Yalta]." He did not intend to usurp the president's role as policy-maker: the capital goods question could be put off until April if need be.[11]

Crowley spoke with the president before that. Later, he recalled their conversation after a March 30 Cabinet meeting. Having just testified and heard senators insist that lend-lease must be used only in the war effort, Crowley warned the president that his request for lend-lease funds "would have to be materially reduced." He said the FEA "could not get [its] commitments . . . for Lend-Lease beyond the end of the German War except the part [each country played] in the case of the Japanese War . . . , and as far as Russia was concerned it was agreed with Admiral Leahy and Chief of Staff [General George C. Marshall] that the only thing Russia would be entitled to was that part of Lend-Lease necessary to keep their commitment in the Japanese War." Crowley added that the Russians had hinted at a $1 billion loan, but he believed it untimely. What did the president want done about this matter and the lend-lease problems he had mentioned? Roosevelt had replied: "You carry out your program and protect your Lend-Lease. . . . You have my approval. So far as the loan is concerned, don't make any commitment to Russia at this time."[12]

The implications of Crowley's recollection are clear enough. By April, the FEA's lend-lease policy was being constricted by a growing consensus spreading from Congress to the military chiefs and, perhaps, Roosevelt himself. Lend-Lease was an instrument of war unless there was a 3-C agreement, and even that loophole was closing. Thus later that month Crowley endorsed restrictions on lend-lease to the Soviet Union similar to those he had opposed in February, then cut British and French requests for civilian lend-lease sharply. He admitted resenting British efforts to rebuild their country at American expense as much as those of the Soviets who "could not understand at all our own great generosity or our immense contribution to the war effort." He felt that Roosevelt, had he lived, would have resented such efforts, too. As for Truman, now president, Crowley thought he saw similar tendencies.[13]

Crowley knew who was now president of the United States, but he did not like it. Years later, he would compare Truman and his predecessor. "Truman," he would say, "didn't have the broad view of world affairs that Roosevelt had." Neither did he have Roosevelt's charm, intelligence, honesty, and warmth. More pertinent, personally, Crowley said, Truman "didn't understand Lend-Lease," did not back him up, did not play "quite square" with him; he was different from Roosevelt, who "had confidence in me and let me go ahead without interference."[14]

Surely Crowley's animus toward Truman preceded their working relationship. The summer before Roosevelt had rejected Jimmy Byrnes, his patron and friend, for the senator from Missouri, and Crowley would have been less than human had he not blamed Truman. It showed, too. Crowley excused Roosevelt's concessions to Churchill and Stalin over the lend-lease they should receive, musing sympathetically that Roosevelt would "butter them up" with a little more. He was not the least sympathetic, however, when Truman "agreed to raise the ante" with the French leader, General Charles De Gaulle. He screamed at Truman about his "great sacrifice" by remaining at the FEA and warned him, "the next time you do anything like that I'm going to quit you, and I'm going to quit you immediately."[15]

That Crowley and Truman would clash was probably inevitable. Truman intended making decisions and acting as president; Crowley typified many who had served under Roosevelt and saw Truman as an accident, and surely no more than their peer. They would operate as they thought their fallen idol would have wished. In fact, in a part of his 1955 letter to the *New York Times* (which it did not print) answering to Truman's charges, Crowley lengthily described Roosevelt's March 30, 1945, approval of his strong commitments to Congress regarding the limitations of lend-lease as justification for his actions. Armed with those commitments, he had moved, as one student of aid to Russia has put it, "into the vacuum left by Roosevelt's death and Hopkins' absence from Washington." Records of the FEA's Executive Policy Committee further show that Crowley asserted himself there as never before. Still, he was not a lone ranger; cautious as always, Crowley was riding a consensus swelling in Congress and felt in the White House, that lend-lease must be sharply modified with the war against Germany all but over.[16]

On April 24, Crowley and Truman discussed that consensus as it involved Western Europe. Truman did not record their words on the time, but he did a few days after a similar discussion with Budget Director Harold Smith two days later. With both, Truman referred to the "growing isolationist spirit" in Congress. He told Smith, "We will open ourselves to a lot of trouble" by any effort to use Section 3-C for "rehabilitation purposes"—even where agreements existed. Crowley, he said, had agreed with his assessment, then suggested using the Export-Import Bank to deal with the problem, and he had strongly agreed: "Lend-Lease should not be used for rehabilitation . . . ; we should get any agreement, such as the French . . . , taken care of through the Export-Import Bank; and . . . other arrangements should be handled through the International Bank."[17]

That Crowley understood his new boss's concern about postwar aid, and believed them similar to his own, can hardly be doubted. It is possible that they discussed it again on May 8, V-E Day, as Truman wrote in his *Memoirs* and Crowley agreed when responding in the *New York Times*. But if they did, it was not because Crowley wanted Truman to sign an order sharply cutting back on aid to the Soviet Union. That crucial meeting occurred on May 11. And even then Crowley was not the policy's prime mover.[18]

The cut-off order of May 11 originated with the subtlety and ambiguity of Ambassador to Russia Averell Harriman's long-stated, now influential advice, that the United States adopt a "firm, but friendly *quid pro quo* approach" to the Soviet Union. Thus President Truman warned Soviet Foreign Minister Vyacheslav Molotov on April 23 that

Soviet-American friendship depended on "the mutual observation of agreements"; it could not last long "on the basis of a one way street." But Harriman's subtlety was ignored then, as it would be in the next month. Truman told former Ambassador to Russia Joseph Davies he had given Molotov "a straight one-two to the jaw," tough talk that was music to the ears of the blatant anti-Soviets now dominant in the State Department and in at least General Wesson's Russian Branch corner of the FEA.[19]

On May 9 Harriman advised Grew that lend-lease shipments to the Soviet Union "should be curtailed." And the day after he won Truman's approval for reducing Soviet aid and making them justify future requests. He wanted to place lend-lease to the Soviets on the same conditional basis that applied to other recipients. But he did not fully comprehend the tougher mood in the State Department and crucial sectors of the FEA. He did not forsee that such powerful policy-makers as Acting Secretary of State Joseph Grew, Assistant Secretary of State William Clayton, Eastern European Branch Chief Elbridge Durbrow, FEA Russian Branch Chief General Wesson, and Crowley, would seize upon the president's sharp words to Molotov as strong endorsement of the abrupt cutoff of aid to the Soviet Union they favored in any case.

According to historian George C. Herring, Crowley "took the lead" in shaping the order that lend-lease that was not designed for Russia's use against Japan "should be cut off immediately as far as physically practicable." However, Leon Martel, who has also studied the aid issue closely, appears on firmer ground in assigning Durbrow and Clayton "the lead" in crafting the order. As for Crowley, he told a Treasury official at the time that the order reflected "a high political decision made by the president and the State Department," but years later he said he had worked on the order with Clayton and Grew. Which of them sharpened the crucial phrasing—to "cut off [aid] immediately as far as physically practicable"—he could not recall.[20]

That Crowley agreed with the wording of the order drafted on May 10 is certain. It was consistent with the recently expressed intent of Congress regarding lend-lease. It was an instrument of war, not of peacetime aid or, as Harriman suggested, diplomacy. Crowley said later, "I had no sympathy or time for people who injected their personal views." He may have meant Harriman, but he certainly meant himself. He also said, as he had so often during testimony on the Hill: "I was old-fashioned enough to believe it was the job of the

Administrator . . . to administrate . . . in keeping with the intent of Congress." He believed that Congress intended a sharp reduction in lend-lease when the war in Europe ended, yet he was surely too cautious to take the lead. His prior record is sufficient evidence. Also, when he phoned Grew on May 11 to discuss their meeting with the president that evening, Crowley asked the secretary if "the president thoroughly understands the situation and . . . will back us up." He reminded Grew that "we would be having difficulty with the Russians."[21]

Crowley's anxious words almost ensure that he thoroughly explained the cutoff order and its almost certain repercussions to the president that evening; and what he did not say others, among them Soviet expert Charles "Chip" Bohlen and Will Clayton, surely would have. Perhaps Truman, under great pressure his first month in the White House, did not assimilate thoroughly what he heard. And he admits that he did not read the order. Unfortunately, the president, who prided himself on taking responsibility—"the buck stops here," read a plaque on his desk—would not for this event. Ten years later he would have the temerity to charge Crowley (and Grew) with "policy-making."[22]

Truman's *Memoirs* make it clear that he recognized later that the order Crowley and Clayton presented for his approval gave the FEA and the Soviet Protocol Committee a green light. "If I had read the order . . . , the incident would not have occurred." But why later? The order was clear. "Deliveries of supplies . . . for the U.S.S.R. should be adjusted immediately to take account of the end of organized resistance in Europe." And the exact meaning of that phrase was further defined as "cut off immediately as far as physically practicable." "Immediately" was twice used and not really subject to misunderstanding. Even so, Truman again indicts Crowley, in this context, for "literally" executing the cutoff order for which, inadvertently or otherwise, he had given a green light the evening before. In fact, the evidence suggests that Crowley was only one member of a consensus that now included the Soviet Protocol Committee's General York, previously a strong advocate of unconditional aid. That concensus had generated an order by the Protocol Committee requiring that ships sailing to Russia return to their ports in the United States. While severe, the language in the president's order—"immediately" and "as far as physically practicable"—appeared to indicate his intent. And if there were any doubt, Truman was talking about tough measures again. He had just told subordinates that Soviet-backed Yugoslav guerrillas must be thrown out of Venezia Giulia.[23]

Today, it appears certain that the cutoff of May 12 was not only consistent with Congress's temper but with the president's—until he heard the Soviets protest and sensed the reaction likely to this disruption of the Grand Alliance. It appears that Truman was embarrassed only *later*; then he used Crowley and, to a lesser extent, Grew as scapegoats. If as Truman charged ten years later, Crowley was actually guilty of "policy-making" and not to be trusted, he would have fired him May 12 or soon after. Or he should have. But that afternoon, after reversing the order to halt shipments to Russia, the president phoned Crowley with what Crowley matter-of-factly told Cox was a "suggestion" that he come to the White House and help draw up an explanatory press release. Further, Crowley was at his office on Monday morning, May 14, and stayed two months beyond the end of the war in the Pacific. Moreover, he participated in Cabinet meetings, met with and acted for the president on major issues, and received warm notes from Truman. These are facts once overshadowed by the Cold War; now they cannot be ignored.[24]

Admittedly whatever Truman may have thought of Crowley, he still needed him. Crowley remained as influential as ever on the Hill, perhaps more so since the action he had taken, or for which he was held responsible. Appropriations for lend-lease had to be guided through Congress, so too, a bill providing for a stronger and more flexible Export-Import Bank. Crowley's support for both was crucial. New Hampshire Republican Senator Styles Bridges was arguing that Congress would have insisted on more stringent lend-lease curbs "had they not trusted Crowley's pledges." Further, after May 12, Crowley could answer Vorys' charge that he had been misled, that aid to Russia was increasing.[25]

Crowley had no problem responding to Vorys. He believed the restoration of aid to Russia temporary. The president had agreed that lend-lease must end with the war. Moreover, Truman had proposed an alternative in his recent request for FY 1946 lend-lease appropriations. He had suggested that the Allies "be assisted in financing necessary equipment and supplies by the Export-Import Bank" after the war. This was the policy Crowley had been urging for some time, but especially since Truman took office. As Crowley saw it, a policy that relied on the Export-Import Bank would rest on the hard rocks of economic self-interest and solid political constituencies; it would strengthen the nation's exports and employment; and it would ensure that America's global obligations not turn into a WPA at the taxpayers expense. It was a policy he could defend and Congress would pass.[26]

It was these considerations, but particularly the last, that prompted Crowley to write the president on July 6. He feared the failure of the Export-Import Bank bill if American officials continued to endorse European demands for aid obviously intended for relief and "postwar use," not the Pacific war. He noted that "many members of Congress have stated emphatically that they had expected lend-lease to be discontinued entirely to countries not participating actively in the Japanese war." He warned, "If we break faith with Congress, we will face insurmountable difficulties in dealing with problems that have yet to be solved."[27]

Crowley saw "a very serious situation" in Eastern as well as Western Europe "that will need to be financed," perhaps "without any reasonable expectation of repayment" in the near future. No isolationist, he believed Europe's rehabilitation essential to a "peaceful, prosperous, and democratic world." But the bank, not lend-lease, was the answer. Further, departing from his argument in January that the FEA should exercise firm control, Crowley was prepared to let recipients solve their own problems, even if that meant loans effectively became gifts. Sounding unusually liberal, he argued that the bank should operate on the premise "that each country . . . has full responsibility for solving its own problems and that its own people must furnish the necessary leadership and initiative. . . . The primary responsibility should not be ours."

Crowley was speaking a language very similar to that of the Marshall Plan he would endorse three years later, but also similar to that he had used when interviewed by John McCormac of the *New York Times* almost two years earlier: "I favor a short term policy of helping stricken countries to help themselves. I don't think I know enough to run the world." Consistently, then, Crowley expressed views that were neither globalist nor isolationist. He recognized that the interests of the United States were linked to those of the world, but he also recognized dangers in American welfarism; and, finally, he recognized that even the best foreign policy must be politically salable at home.[28]

By mid-July Crowley was telling the House and Senate Banking

Committees that the Export-Import Bank could solve the problem of overproduction and unemployment he foresaw in the postwar period. "Fortunately," he advised them, "foreign demand for our products in the reconstruction of war devastated countries . . . will be concentrated . . . on the products of heavy industry." And the United States almost alone could supply such products. Financing was a major problem, but there was a solution. It should be provided, "to the extent that private credit is not available, through an expanded Export-Import Bank." It was the best means of combining assistance to the war-torn countries of the world with the interests of American manufacturers, workers, and taxpayers.[29]

When a senator jumped in to ask whether lend-lease would end when the Japanese war ended, Crowley replied, "That is correct." It was the law: Lend-Lease was an instrument of war, and he had pledged to end it when the Pacific war ended. However, equipment in the pipeline would continue to flow—to American advantage—if the recipients could finance it through Export-Import Bank loans. Further, the bank could finance Allied purchases of American surpluses overseas. This, too, was in the national interest; it was also, Crowley acknowledged, a matter of personal concern that the surpluses be sold. Otherwise, he might be blamed for bad management.[30]

Crowley's fears were soon ended. Indeed, he could not have been more pleased when by early August Congress passed and the president signed the bank bill. When the war ended, he could put lend-lease to bed without any qualms. But he expected time for a smooth transition to bank financing; he did not want a repetition of the confusion following Germany's surrender. Like most Americans, even in early August he believed Japan's defeat many months away at the very least. The dramatic explosion of an atomic bomb over Hiroshima on August 6 only prompted him to form a committee to plan for ending lend-lease. He took no other action until August 10, after a second atomic bomb exploded over Nagasaki. Then he instructed that no ships were to be loaded after V-J Day. He would keep his commitment to Congress to cut off lend-lease at the war's end, unless the Allies financed it.[31]

Shutting off lend-lease always seemed a simple enough matter to Crowley, but especially after consultations with Admiral Leahy on August 13 and with the president on August 14. He came to the meetings armed with a draft directive that authorized the cut-off of civilian lend-lease (which, as opposed to military lend-lease, was FEA's sole respon-sibility) except for 3-C countries, and got preliminary approval. Thus he saw no real problems in ending the program. But circumstances can confound even solid planning.[32]

Word of Japan's surrender reached the White House soon after Crowley left. Effectively it was V-J Day, which day Crowley had planned to stop the loading of lend-lease supplies. However the presi-dent did not officially designate August 14 as V-J Day, perhaps, among other reasons, because of the chaos that would follow a precipitous cutoff of lend-lease. But the outlines of the administration's planning had become well known in Washington, and August 15 found Crowley speaking to the city's press corps about the FEA's plans for terminating lend-lease.

He did not mention a date for terminating lend-lease. There had been no time to notify foreign governments, and there was, as Crowley noted, an American interest in supplying lend-lease under certain cir-cumstances. Thus he emphasized the FEA's desire for an orderly tran-sition from government-controlled trade to private commerce. That ob-jective required the FEA to "adjust" lend-lease to a "realistic" basis now that the war was over. However these words did not mean the end of the program. Crowley said that the United States was obligated to aid those Allies helping redeploy American troops. It was only "re-alistic" and "fair," he advised the reporters, to "help offset the expen-ditures . . . they are making in our behalf."[33]

Crowley's emphasis did not encompass the Russians—they were not helping redeploy American troops then, nor would they be—and the next morning they were informed that lend-lease shipments had ended unless they paid cash or secured credit through the Export-Im-port Bank. This last proposition reflected Crowley's advice to the president and both houses of Congress in July, that the bank extend the Russians a billion-dollar loan if asked. It also suggests that, though Crowley may have been anti-Russian, as Truman insists, he was not sufficiently so to forego the benefits to the American economy of trad-ing with the Soviet Union. Further, when the Soviet Protocol Commit-tee halted the loading of Russian ships the morning of August 17, Crowley reversed the order. He had received no order from the White House, the United States was still at war with Japan, and he did not want a repetition of the chaos that attended the cutoff on May 12. It was time to speak to the president.[34]

Perhaps fortuitously, but quite likely at Crowley's request, the president called a minicabinet meeting that morning. Byrnes, who was now secretary of state, points out that Crowley dominated the discussion, that he reminded those present that he had halted shipments of supplies to Russia in May because it was clearly the intent of the law. Now, if the president agreed, he proposed to comply with the law by informing all the Allies that lend-lease was ended and that further assistance could be secured only as a result of legislation from Congress. "We," Byrnes said, speaking of himself, the president, Director of War Mobilization John Snyder, and Secretary of the Treasury Fred Vinson, all "agreed with Crowley's view and the President authorized him to act promptly." Crowley later recalled much the same scene, though he embellished it somewhat in response to domestic and foreign criticism that he and the president had cut off lend-lease too abruptly. He wanted it known that the decision taken that day reflected the clear intent of the law and the administration's commitments to Congress, that lend-lease stop when hostilities ended. Neither he nor the president had had a choice.[35]

That was not quite the truth. Over the next two weeks, distinctions were made in discontinuing lend-lease, and the Russians were singled out for especially harsh treatment. After the minicabinet meeting of August 17, Crowley, acting on the president's oral orders, ordered that only Russian ships already being loaded were to be filled; their other ships must sail empty. This order may have been deliberate, as the secretary to the Soviet Protocol Committee suggested, "part of a general squeeze . . . now being put on the U.S.S.R." If so, it is unlikely that Crowley contributed to it. Two weeks later, he agreed that the Soviet Union should be able to buy $400 million in lend-lease goods at 2 and 3/8 percent, and that he would recommend a billion more from the Export-Import Bank at 3 percent. This suggests that Crowley was little concerned with Russo-American tensions; he was greatly concerned, as many others were, about America's postwar economy; and he was worried about his reputation as a manager if the war's end found large surpluses in the pipeline. Both these factors would appear to account for his continued urging of a Russian loan for another month, and the consummation of a $400 million credit for the purchase of lend-lease goods on October 15.[36]

Except for divergences in time, the administration's Russian policy mirrored its "general" lend-lease policy of August 18. By August 21, Allied governments were notified of the discontinuance of lend-lease, and Crowley was advising the president that "their reaction . . . was quite favorable." They had expected it, but they also knew he would recommend that the Export-Import Bank provide some of them with credits. In fact, he was negotiating with the French ambassador. Yet there was a major problem; there were no arrangements with the British government, which "undoubtedly will raise more objection than any other."[37]

Crowley understated. The British protested so sharply that, on August 23, Truman extended lend-lease to September 2, the date Japan would surrender in Tokyo Bay. This change quickly included all recipients, including the Russians, and it was so modest that Crowley could not avoid endorsing it publicly as a "natural terminal." But he was not happy; he was embarrassed and angry. Only the day before he had written Senator Vandenberg to thank him for "helpful cooperation" on lend-lease extension in the spring. The senator's efforts had made it "possible to establish very clearly a Congressional and administration intention to terminate lend-lease at the end of the war, and that had made it much easier to deal with the situation which we faced with the sudden ending of hostilities." Vandenberg had quickly responded in the same warm spirit: "You have literally fulfilled your promises to Congress in respect to lend-lease. As usual, your promises proved to be dependable. It is one more reason why I like to do business with you." But Vandenberg's letter notwithstanding, Crowley felt that the president's extension of lend-lease undermined his reputation for dependable promises.[38]

In part, and certainly publicly, Crowley blamed the British for undermining his promises to terminate lend-lease with the end of hostilities, and worse, now asking for an unlimited extension. When Winston Churchill, now in opposition, said bitterly that he could not believe the new terminal date "is the last word of the United States," Crowley responded, tartly, that the president and Congress "have the last word," and President Truman was "standing pat" on his promises to Congress that lend-lease, a war measure, would end on V-J Day. "It is not up to us," he added, "to fight and rebuild the economy of any given nation except our own." On the other hand, hundreds of millions in credit were available to the British as to ten or twelve other governments. The fact was, every country, including the United States, had postwar problems. They must be met and surmounted, Crowley said, "in a brisk, business manner."[39]

Crowley made sure that Churchill's protests and his response ran together, hurrying both to the *Milwaukee Journal*'s Washington correspondent. He was not motivated solely by his commitment to Congress; he was tired of British demands for special treatment. In July, he had written Truman that "he was not for . . . rebuilding the British dollar or sterling position, for the rehabilitation of the war destruction . . . , or for the rebuilding of her foreign trade." He believed the British should live within their means. But he had said that confidentially. Not until August 24 and 25 did he express those feelings publicly.[40]

Crowley's outburst was prompted by news that a British delegation would soon arrive to seek American help in their financial crisis. But if he was unhappy with the British, he was even more displeased with administration leaders. Publicly, he praised the president's "courage" in saying that lend-lease would end September 2, rather than providing a transition period, as new Treasury Secretary Fred Vinson wished. Privately, he was unhappy with the White House and State Department, first for extending lend-lease to September 2, then for undermining the FEA's "brisk, business" approach to ending lend-lease and disposing of surplus property. And there was nothing he could do. In late August, the president told the Treasury to plan for dissolving the FEA. He did not ask Crowley, and Crowley quickly wrote his old ally, Charles Broughton, that he would soon retire from public life.[41]

That Crowley should leave Washington shortly after the war's end was almost inevitable. As the highly regarded columnist Marquis Childs soon emphasized, Crowley had played a uniquely useful role during the war—he was an "honest broker," mediating between the administration and Congress. What Childs failed to point out was that, though Crowley advised Roosevelt, he (apparently) did as he was told once a decision was made. And certainly he never argued with Roosevelt publicly. Such was not true of Crowley and Truman or of Crowley and the Truman administration. In August, but even more so in September, Crowley began taking the "wrong side" on a number of major issues and arguing most of them publicly.

After mid-September, Crowley was making headlines regularly. He protested a month's extension of lend-lease to Britain; he insisted that his old friend Will Clayton was selling Britain American surpluses abroad at below-basement prices; and he said that the administration should demand that the British supply reverse lend-lease, especially when they were seeking a fifty-year loan, interest-free. Indeed, he flatly opposed the British loan under any circumstances; it would justify similar, specialized demands by other countries, when, he believed, they should get interest-bearing credits from the Export-Import Bank. And these are only the most notable issues on which Crowley differed with the administration.[42]

It is curious, then, that Marquis Childs titled his mid-September piece, "Crowley to Stay as Broker," asserting that he "can do business" with Congress. There can be little doubt that Crowley retained the respect and trust of most congressmen, but it is improbable that he could have represented administration policies effectively when he differed with them so sharply and openly. At the same time, and surely more important, Crowley would have been hard put to represent the position of Congress effectively in the administration's councils: the president's advisers, and presumably Truman himself, recognized the depths of Crowley's hostility to its foreign economic policy and, beyond that, his thin to nonexistent loyalty to the president himself. Plainly put, it meant little or nothing that Crowley retained the trust of Congress; he had lost that of the president.

Under the circumstances, there was little reason for Crowley to remain in Washington. The Foreign Economic Administration was about to be dissolved. He might have remained in the capital as chairman of the FDIC—curiously, Truman had just appointed him to another term—but with a sharply reduced status and no prospects. He had a much better option; he could run Standard Gas again. It is hardly to be wondered, then, that on September 24, three days prior to the dissolution of the FEA, Crowley sent the White House his resignation from the FDIC. It was time to go, or it would be when his resignation became effective.[43]

Two days later, Crowley told a reporter for Evjue's *Capital Times* that he would be leaving the administration on October 15; it was natural with the war's end, and he and the president were parting on very congenial terms. He had "done his bit," he just wanted "to become a plain citizen." If "I don't get out now," he told the reporter, "I'll be involved in the postwar reconversion period and it would be unfair to leave then." When told that the president had remarked that morning that he wanted Crowley to remain, had tried to persuade him not to leave, and would again, as as he had successfully some months before, Crowley commented, "I think that was extremely nice of President Truman, and I appreciate his sentiments and confidence, but this time I have made up my mind to get out."[44]

That very day, however, the *Milwaukee Journal* offered a different explanation for Crowley's departure. "The truth is," the *Journal* reported, "that during the last few weeks Crowley has not felt that he has had the solid . . . backing he should have had" in settling lend-lease or negotiating credits with the British. His hands were tied by some members of the State Department and other "high administration officials [who] were proposing more liberal terms for the British." Frustrated, Crowley decided "to call it quits with the government."[45]

In early October, *Time* also implied that Crowley's departure was voluntary, noting that he left his last Cabinet meeting "hopping mad" at the easy credit terms Truman wanted to give Britain. But *Labor* and Wisconsin and other midwestern newspapers were less certain why he resigned. *Labor* pointed to the president's formal acceptance, which saluted: "Dear Mr. Crowley," rather than "Dear Leo," as in the past. "Was Leo Crowley fired?" *Labor* asked. And a reporter attempted to deal with the question at a press conference. He told the president: "There seems to be a mystery about Crowley's departure from the FDIC and FEA." The answer, he had heard, might be in a second letter Crowley sent the president at the time of his resignation, apparently blasting administration policies vis-à-vis Britain. Could the press see the letter?[46]

The president first suggested the existence of a second letter, then said that he had released the only letter received from Crowley, and, finally, supplied what was probably a half-truth, "There is no other letter for release." Crowley had written the president a second letter, however, though whether he sent it is unclear, and it was not on the subject the reporter had in mind. Dated September 26, the letter argued that the president should withdraw his request that Congress establish a system of univeral military training or, as Crowley labeled it, "compulsory military training" or "conscription."[47]

It was not the first time Crowley had expressed strong, even fervent opposition to the plan. He was busy with the termination of lend-lease when the president first proposed the subject at an August 31 Cabinet meeting. But he was alerted when the president incorporated his plan in his "Twenty-One Point" message September 6, and he was quite prepared to discuss it when the president introduced the subject for discussion at a Cabinet meeting the next day. When Truman said he wanted to act "quickly in order to take advantage of public opinion," Crowley blurted that universal military training was just a polite term for conscription. Midwesterners would see it "as a step toward what most left Europe for—to get away from militarism." To him, it implied that the United States would have to "police the world." Why, he asked, was that necessary.[48]

Crowley walked into the proverbial hornet's nest. The president first suggested, a bit fuzzily, that the United Nations was a court, which must have marshals to carry out "a just decision," and that the United States would have to supply them. When Crowley rejoined that international agreements on loans might achieve the same results, the president turned to another metaphor, arguing that at times, "in order to collect monies for county governments, it has been found necessary to employ a sheriff." And his Cabinet appointees quickly echoed him. Treasury Secretary Vinson pointed out that Crowley's attitude dominated the 1920s and "contributed measurably to the cause of World War II"; then Secretary of Labor Lewis Schwellenbach and Secretary of the Navy James Forrestal agreed that Crowley's viewpoint had been heard, tried, and Schwellenbach said, "history proved otherwise."

Crowley could not accept either Schwellenbach's "history" or the president's metaphors as the final word on universal military training. He felt too strongly about the issue, far more so than on any issue he could remember. But he did not mention it at the next two Cabinet meetings he attended; once was enough. Instead, he gave the president an opportunity to consider privately the implications for American youth of peacetime compulsory military training. The result was a lengthy memorandum: "Compulsory Military Training," the other "letter" he intended to send the president when he resigned.[49]

Crowley had decided that compulsory military training was an honest but less harsh description of universal military training than conscription. But he quickly made his point. After acknowledging the need for adequate occupation forces, he attacked the despotic militarism he saw in a compulsory program. It required "involuntary service . . . the antithesis of freedom," which is the "cornerstone of the nation." Compulsion and, regimentation with it, were "foreign principles," hallmarks of the despotic and militaristic countries the United

States had just fought. They were "foreign principles" that had prompted millions of immigrants to leave Europe, millions who had "brought the United States to its present position of eminence."

The "old saws" rolled on a while longer before Crowley began to hit his stride: conscription would weaken the nation's "moral and intellectual fibre" by taking a "precious year from the lives of our youth—a year away from home or from school, or both." It would interrupt the training of the nation's youth "in the so important formative, impressionable period of life." That training occurred in the nation's schools and churches, but its foundation lay elsewhere, in family values. "The family," Crowley insisted, "is the center of decent human living, the developer of character and higher aspirations, the source of better relationships"; and whatever tended to weaken it "was a backward step in the development of our people." Families taught moral principles; military organizations provided training in the use of force and were "essentially unmoral." Now when a war was ending and "the worst instincts of man have had free rein" was no time for compulsory military training. Now there was "need for moral as for physical regeneration."

Crowley's depth of feeling produced a rare eloquence, but it did not produce an answer. Despite persistent requests from the press, Truman did not release Crowley's "second letter." Neither did Crowley. He had sent it as "a strictly confidential paper." Perhaps they spoke about it again, at lunch, on October 16, just a day after Crowley signed the last papers to cross his desk. If so, Crowley did not mention it. The press learned only that the president had asked him to stay in Washington as chairman of the now independent Export-Import Bank and, apparently, left the door open. But no one speculated that he would accept; he had spoken too "bitterly" about the nation's economic policies overseas, and especially about preferences for the British. As for Crowley, he would say nothing directly about his luncheon discussion with the president. He was heading for New York City, then Madison. That much he would say. About his obvious differences with the president, he would say nothing. He would not for a decade, not until the president himself opened the door.

15

Epilogue

Leo Crowley left Washington amidst tributes ranging from the Hill to the Vatican and with a long, useful life before him. For a decade he would advise on matters involving the FDIC; later, he would serve quietly on the Civil Rights Commission created during President Dwight D. Eisenhower's second term; and still later, he would dine at President Lyndon Johnson's White House and send him supportive notes. Essentially, however, Crowley was once more an apolitical businessman. In October, 1945 he returned to Standard Gas. Though he was forced out two years later by a collection of disgruntled bondholders, this was primarily a reflection on their impatience in a difficult postwar era. Better testimony to Crowley's business acumen is to be found in the many years he ran the Chicago, Milwaukee, St. Paul & Pacific Railroad. Named chairman of the bankrupt system in December 1945, Crowley not only took it to profitability, he performed so brilliantly that, after he left in the mid-sixties, its board called him back to handle its takeover of the Northwestern Road. Not until 1970, his work done and almost eighty, did he go home, there to die two years later.[1]

Crowley's funeral mass was remarkable for the sweep of those who attended: bishops throughout the state; nuns he had aided at St. Mary's Hospital; friends from the Milwaukee Road and from the FDIC; and Republicans as well as Democrats. But at least one reporter singled out Thomas Corcoran, the sole member of the Roosevelt administration there to mourn. Few knew Crowley better than this former New Dealer turned lobbyist, and Corcoran spoke of him as "one of the giants of his day." Curiously, this was the same politician, administrator, and businessman columnist Robert Riggs identified in 1944 as "The Nearly Obscure Crowley."[2]

This biography was designed to place Crowley's lengthy service to President Roosevelt and limited service to President Truman in proper perspective. It became, also, a commentary on both presidents, their administrations, Congress, and the print media, as well as state, national, and international politics during the cataclysmic years that spanned the Great Depression and World War II. Implicitly, it also marked that era's ethos and ethics, similar and yet very different from those of today, a half century later.

Ironically, Crowley would not have spent even a few years in today's Washington. He was confirmed as chairman of the FDIC and remained at its helm for almost twelve years despite knowledge of his fraudulent practices as a banker in Madison. That he was not sent back to Wisconsin immediately or as word spread was owing in part to the sympathetic impression he made, but it owed more to a self-serving, bipartisan conspiracy of silence that reached from the Senate to the White House, and to newspapermen who, quite unlike those today, made no serious effort to penetrate his secret. This may testify to lesser political ethics in Crowley's era, and it surely testifies to the journalistic standards of his day, but if his many services under two presidents are a guide, the country was anything but ill served.

Crowley's contributions at the FDIC could not have been more positive. His management not only strengthened the public's confidence in the safety of its deposits, it also secured acceptance of the FDIC by major city banks that had fought the corporation's founding and, ultimately, acceptance by mutual savings banks that had once left its fold. These achievements did not occur without strikingly new and tighter federal controls, but Crowley handled bankers and state banking supervisors with such sensitivity that criticism was limited and praise extensive. He was so successful that Congress would confirm him a second and even a third time, and Republicans would claim sponsorship of the FDIC. To be sure Crowley was favored by an improving economy and prudent bankers; even so, his tenure as chairman of the FDIC must be credited with molding a sharply challenged fragile embryo into a very popular, well-established federal agency.

Except for a few banks Crowley saved at Roosevelt's request, he managed the FDIC as an independent agency whose single concern was prudent banking. But Crowley's independence went no further. Outside his stewardship of the FDIC, he was always ready to serve the president who had brought him to Washington—and retained him despite the Treasury's revelations of his fraudulent practices as a private banker. Indeed, Crowley's primary historical significance lies outside his charge at the FDIC in his various critical roles as Roosevelt's trusted agent, and that precisely because he so faithfully reflected Roosevelt's policies and methods.

During the thirties, Crowley solidified Roosevelt's strength in Wisconsin and Minnesota, but his talents were surely most significantly engaged in winning over political leaders there and in obtaining support from business leaders throughout the country as the decade closed and Roosevelt sought a third term in the midst of a spreading war abroad. In 1938 Crowley helped the president undermine the re-election bids of "radical" third-party leaders in Wisconsin and Minnesota they had previously supported and to position himself nearer the political center. Then he found jobs for supportive Progressives who had lost seats, obtained Senator Robert LaFollette, Jr.'s endorsement, and helped bring Wisconsin home for Roosevelt in 1940. Further, with the president's permission if not his encouragement, Crowley took the chairmanship of Standard Gas while remaining at the FDIC. It is significant today that there was little criticism of Crowley's having public and private jobs and a conflict of interest; it was significant then that the mutually conciliatory relationship that ensued between Crowley, speaking for Standard Gas, and the Securities and Exchange Commission signaled business leaders that the president was seeking an accommodation that would secure industry's greater commitment to rearmament and to aiding the Allies in their battle against the Axis.

The president paid tribute to Crowley's achievements when he practically forced him to take several crucial and perilous posts after Pearl Harbor. But he was not alone. Crowley's appointment as alien property custodian was owing in large part to the advice of Attorney General Biddle and the persistent pressure of Justice Byrnes, both of whom recognized Crowley's political skills, popularity on the Hill, loyalty, and even his integrity. Ultimately, though, the decision was the president's. Roosevelt picked Crowley over Morgenthau's Treasury not because the latter was incompetent but because Crowley would deal with alien property as they had discussed, from a "business point of view," appointing sympathetic businessmen to run the corporations he vested. Whether or not this policy was desirable—and one liberal journalist sharply attacked it for resulting in Crowley's appointment of businessmen who were not only cronies but so conventional that they would not disturb dangerous cartelizing agreements—Crowley was Roosevelt's agent and executing his orders.

Crowley's further assignment as director of economic warfare in the summer of 1943 was another tribute to his political or, as Corcoran would have said, his diplomatic skills. Byrnes was once more at the White House, prompting Roosevelt to name Crowley. In the last analysis, however, Crowley was again Roosevelt's "pinch hitter," sent in to replace Vice-President Wallace and his coterie, whose part in a public feud with Commerce Secretary Jones was strengthening newly powerful conservatives on the Hill. Crowley, a "conservative New Dealer" and friend of Jones, was expected to pour oil on these troubled waters. And he did. But his appointment is more meaningful today because it exemplifies Roosevelt's known tendency to postpone rather than resolve problems, increasingly by mollifying conservatives. And it was not the last time. Little more than two months later Roosevelt answered criticism of other war agencies, including in particular the Office of Lend-Lease Administration, by appointing Crowley chief of an ugly new, all-embracing Foreign Economic Administration.

As foreign economic administrator Crowley held the most complex and critical job of his many years in Washington, and he was castigated accordingly. Within three months centrists in the old OEW were charging him with managing the FEA too loosely and failing to control Jones's agencies. The charges were accurate. But the FEA was a sprawling, politically inspired conglomerate; Crowley lacked the solid staff he had trained at the FDIC and brought to the custodian's office; and, as Byrnes reminded the president, Crowley had more jobs than anyone could reasonably handle. While somewhat unfair, then, the criticism from within the old OEW made it politically feasible for Roosevelt and Crowley to integrate an agency Jones controlled. It also gave the president reason to accept Crowley's often-tendered resignation as alien property custodian. Crowley could then focus on his main charge as foreign economic administrator, handling criticism of the lend-lease program.

Giving Crowley administrative control of civilian lend-lease reflected the president's belief that he could smoothly reconcile differences between the Treasury and the State Department, handle conservative critics, and obtain the best possible deal from Congress. Again Roosevelt had the measure of his man. In 1943 and early 1944 Crowley supported Treasury Secretary Morgenthau's view that lend-lease to Britain should be closely restricted. Personally, Crowley agreed with Morgenthau, but he would have supported him in any case because he knew Congress's temper. For the same reason, FEA officials denied many British requests for goods that were only marginally covered by the spirit of the Lend-Lease Act. However, these concessions to Congress were minor, and when Roosevelt sometimes overruled them, Crowley did not complain; he knew the FEA was an instrument of the administration's larger policy.

Neither did Crowley complain when, in September 1944, Roosevelt instructed the FEA to accelerate its planning for occupying Germany. If Crowley suspected that the president was using him—as he seemingly was—chiefly to escape the political trap created by Morgenthau's plan for Germany, he still responded with all the urgency the order commanded. He used his superb contacts to find in Henry Fowler the right man to form an autonomous German Branch within the FEA. That the branch's work was largely ignored after Germany's defeat was not due to any lack of effort on Fowler's or Crowley's part: the Executive Branch left the Army to its own devices, and the Army's policies in Germany's American-occupied zone were dictated by its own needs.

While Roosevelt's order to the FEA on Germany played out, so did the fortunes of lend-lease the president had bound Crowley to manage. From the fall of 1944 through early April 1945, Crowley argued that lend-lease to Britain should be sharply reduced after Germany's defeat; that, at least publicly, British exports should be controlled until V-E Day; and that the Export-Import Bank, not Section 3-C of the Lend-Lease Act, should be used to rehabilitate and reconstruct Europe after the war. On these and other matters involving the Allies, George Ball has charged that Crowley, "with his limited background . . . a small town banker and politician from Wisconsin—seemed quite indifferent to their problems so long as he avoided trouble with Congress." And a few others then working in the FEA have echoed Ball's denigrating charge to one degree or another. However the evidence weighs in Crowley's favor.[3]

Crowley was neither a provincial nor a Europhobe. The views he expressed to John McCormac of the *New York Times* in 1943 suggest a realist in foreign affairs, a fair counterpart to his moderately conservative domestic position. More concretely, in 1940 and 1941 he remained at the FDIC when he might well have left for Standard Gas, thus implicitly endorsing the president's policy of "all aid short of war"; and in 1944 and 1945 he twice fought successfully to extend lend-lease without restrictions, including in the latter year an extension of Section 3-C. Indeed, after Senator Taft's crippling amendment was killed, Senator Vandenberg ascribed its defeat to "confidence in Administrator Crowley," as he would administer lend-lease strictly as Congress intended. Obviously the president chose well when assigning Crowley to present the administration's lend-lease position on the Hill.

Crowley was effective because Congress knew and trusted him. It knew that he viewed lend-lease with the hard eye of the banker he had been, as strictly a program "to promote the defense of the United States." But as Robert Riggs had noted two years earlier, below Crowley's banker's eye, "four-fifths Jones," beat the soft heart of the civic-minded citizen, "one-fifth Wallace." Thus as lend-lease administrator Crowley agreed to ship the British housing materials to replace homes destroyed near factories that had been or were engaged in war production, but not for every bombed area or at the dollar levels per unit the British asked. Personally he believed his decisions on these points constituted a fair response to British requests; but he also knew that in 1945 lend-lease could not be handled sentimentally; Congress had to be sold on the basis that the British losses to be replaced were suffered in defense of American interests, and that the dollar amounts did not raise British living standards at the expense of the American taxpayer.

Crowley served Roosevelt loyally, discreetly, and skillfully for more than eleven years. He did so even when he opposed major New Deal programs, even when Roosevelt undermined agreements his FEA had reached with British representatives, even when Roosevelt asked him to advocate such programs as Section 3-C about which he was at best dubious. His differences with Roosevelt did not seem to matter. Years later, he remembered Roosevelt's keen knowledge of world leaders and ability to handle world problems, his intelligence, honesty, and personal charm; but what really counted was Crowley's transcendent faith in a reciprocal loyalty, confidence, and trust. Specific pluses and minuses were forgotten, as he remembered that "Roosevelt had confidence in me to do a job and let me go ahead." Even when "people disagreed with what I was doing he always told them that I was responsible to him and . . . to leave me alone." Such was Crowley's memory. Surely, it was slanted by time and his brief service under Truman, but it accounts largely, if not entirely, for his many services to Roosevelt and his country through more than a decade of peace and war.

Crowley's six months service under Roosevelt's successor was anticlimactic, a tribute to his sense of duty. It was almost inevitable, then, that he leave the Truman administration after the war's end. It mattered not that Truman named him to a third term as chairman of the FDIC and offered him the presidency of the Export-Import Bank. The FEA was dissolved, the two great crises of depression and war in which he had served were fought and won; he had done his duty; he could go home.

Surely Crowley would have left Washington whether or not the FEA was dissolved. In the months since Roosevelt's death, he had found himself ever-more at odds with Truman. Truman had not supported him in treating with foreign delegations; and Truman had a vision of the postwar world—seeing the United States as a global sheriff and calling for universal military training and a liberal loan to Britain—which he could not stomach. In the final analysis, however, Crowley's view of Truman—no better than his peer—and of Truman's view of world affairs—limited—probably had less to do with specifics than with Crowley's continuing attachment to Roosevelt.

Understandably Crowley recalled Roosevelt as an unparalleled leader. His fortunes, Roosevelt's, and the country's were intertwined too long, during more than a decade of a bitter depression and a global war, for it to be otherwise. Crowley obviously disagreed with Roosevelt over some programs and policies, and he may well have disagreed with more, but quite unlike his disagreements with Truman they did not breed bitterness and resentment. Except for a critical policy speech or two at the height of the McCarthy epidemic, Crowley spoke of Roosevelt with the greatest admiration for his talents and especially his person. Policies and programs came and went; loyalty and mutual respect were always in fashion. They formed the core of Crowley's credo. Thus, just as Roosevelt always trusted and supported him, he was ever ready to respond in kind. It was this credo and this relationship that earns him the title, "the president's man," Franklin Roosevelt's agent in peace and war.

Primary Sources
and Abbreviations

Notes   Index

Primary Sources
and Abbreviations

Leo T. Crowley Personal Papers,   CPP
   author's possession

Franklin D. Roosevelt Library, Hyde Park, NY
Official Files   OF
President's Personal Files   PPF
President's Secretary's Files   PSF
Miscellaneous Files   FDRP
Henry Morgenthau, Jr., Ms. Diary   MD
Henry Morgenthau, Jr., Farm Credit
   Diary
Oscar Cox Papers
Harry Hopkins Papers
James Rowe Papers

Wisconsin State Historical Society, Madison, WI
William T. Evjue Papers   EP
Frank Kuehl Papers
Albert Schmedeman Papers

National Archives, Washington, DC, and Suitland, MD
Record Groups 34, 103, and 169   RG

Harry S. Truman Library, Independence, MO
Harry S. Truman Papers   HSTL

Clemson University Library, Clemson, SC
James Byrnes Papers   BP

Public Record Office, London, England
Public Records Office

Library of University of Wisconsin at Milwaukee
Charles E. Broughton Papers
William B. Rubin Papers

Bancroft Library, University of California at Berkeley
J. F. T. O'Connor Diary

Library of Congress, Mss. Division
Jesse H. Jones Papers

University of Virginia Library, Charlottesville, VA
Carter Glass Papers

Notes

1. The Plunger

1. Crowley to F. Ryan Duffy, August 28, 1969, CPP, given to the author by John and Regina (Crowley) Doyle, December 1979. Crowley had requests for his "records" from the Franklin D. Roosevelt Library, Hyde Park, NY, as well as the Wisconsin State Historical Society, Madison, WI, both requests in CPP.

2. Interviews with Laurence C. Eklund, side one of three tapes (five sides), made in early August 1969, copies at Wisconsin State Historical Society; ten articles published in the *Milwaukee Journal*, August 17–27, 1969, collected in a pamphlet, *Adviser to Presidents*.

3. For example, George Burns, Milwaukee attorney, to Laurence C. Eklund, August 19, 1969, CPP.

4. Interviews with John and Regina Doyle, December 1979; *City Directories* for Janesville, Beloit, and Madison, Wisconsin; *Milton Courier*, July 1, 1976, pp. 12–15; *Portrait and Biography Album of Rock County, Wisconsin* (Chicago, 1889); *Plymouth County Centennial, 1848–1948*, (Rock City, 1948), 76; *Wisconsin: Its History and Its People, 1624–1924*, (Chicago, 1924), 3: 492–96; Obituaries, April 15 and 16, 1972, from the *Madison Capital Times, Wisconsin State Journal* (Madison), *Milwaukee Journal*, and other newspapers, CPP; also, undated, autobiographical scraps, CPP; Last Wills and Testaments of Leo, Esther (sister), and William Crowley, Dane County records; and Eklund, *Adviser to Presidents*.

5. "Transactions: Deeds and Mortgages," in *Registry of Deeds*, Dane County, Madison, Wisconsin, 205: 289 and 367; 225: 356 and 357; 242: 557; 271: 587; 273: 104. The loans were paid off in 1922 and 1924, 291: 391; and 293: 446. Also, interview with Dr. Harry Purcell, whose father was a close friend and collaborator with Crowley, St. Louis, MO, July 3, 1980.

6. Partial Records of General Paper and Supply Company, August 25, 1919; May 29, 1919; September 15 and 22, 1921; and April 1, 1923, CPP; interview with Harris Allen, Crowley's broker, June 29, 1980, in Milton Junction; *Thirtieth Annual Report of the Commission of Banking on State Banks, Mutual Savings Banks, and Trust Companies, 1925*, lists Crowley as director of Bank of

Wisconsin in 1923; and Crowley began buying real estate by March 1924, if not earlier, *Registry of Deeds,* Dane County, 301: 417.

7. Friends he bought and sold with included, among others, Robert C. O'Malley, later lt. gov., Harry Purcell, and their wives, see *Registry of Deeds,* Dane County, vols. 306 and 320 for 1924 alone.

8. Salary authorization in G. P. and S. records of December 15, 1926; Also, "A Summary and Analysis of Memorandum dated January 15, 1935, Re: Crowley Loans," MD, 3: 105–23; and Records of G. P. and S. board meeting, December 31, 1931.

9. *Milwaukee Journal,* July 8, 1928; and *Sheboygan Press,* September 30, 1932, contain brief sketches of Madison's problems.

10. Ibid.; interview with Thomas Schmedeman, Madison, Wisconsin, June 25, 1980, Leon Epstein, *Politics in Wisconsin* (Madison, 1958), 37–38; and Wayne E. Laufenberg, "The Schmedeman Administration: A Study of Missed Opportunities" (M.A. thesis, University of Wisconsin, 1965), 16–19 and 49.

11. Laufenberg, "The Schmedeman Administration," 16–19 and 49; phone conversation with Thomas Schmedeman, Madison, WI, June 25, 1980; Leon Epstein, *Politics in Wisconsin,* 37–38; *Capital Times,* January 3, 1933.

12. Samuel Lubell, "The Revolt of the City," in *The Future of American Politics* (New York, 1965), 43–68. The *Milwaukee Journal,* July 8, 1928, suggests the enthusiasm of Wisconsin's Irish-Catholic leaders; see *Wisconsin State Journal,* February 4, 1928, for slate.

13. Thomas J. Schlereth, "The Progressive-Democrat Alliance in the Wisconsin Presidential Election of 1928" (M.A. thesis, University of Wisconsin, 1965); James R. Donoghue, *How Wisconsin Voted, 1848–1960* (Madison, 1962); and Richard C. Maney, "A History of the Democratic Party in Wisconsin Since World War II" (Ph. D. diss., University of Wisconsin, 1970).

14. Ibid.; also Epstein, *Politics in Wisconsin,* 35–44.

15. *Capital Times,* September 5 and 9, 1928; also, *Wisconsin State Journal,* December 6, 1932.

16. Schlereth, "The Progressive-Democrat Alliance," esp. pp. 102–8.

17. Interview with Kuehl, in Washington, DC, August 11, 1980.

18. Ibid.; *Milwaukee Journal,* October 29, 1927; *Wisconsin State Journal,* January 23 and February 4, 1928; also, Senator-Elect Ryan F. Duffy to William T. Evjue, January 4, 1933, EP, noted that "Irish-Catholics have for many years been the backbone of the Democratic Party" in the state.

19. *Sheboygan Press,* September 30, 1928.

20. J. Craig Ralston's column, which appeared in the *Wisconsin State Journal,* December 5, 1932.

21. By 1928, Crowley was president of the Bank of Wisconsin and working for Wisconsin Bankshares, a bank holding company dominated by the Kasten family. One member of that family, Walter Kasten, had married an

Uihlein (pronounced E-line) and, according to Harris Allen and Frank Kuehl, could arrange business deals between the Schlitz Brewery and Crowley's General Paper and Supply Company. Also, Jouett Shouse to Crowley, September 28, 1928, Kuehl Papers.

22. Shouse to Crowley, September 28, 1928, Kuehl Papers.

23. *Milwaukee Journal*, September 28, 1928. Also, Schlereth, "Progressive-Democrat Alliance," 112.

24. Affidavit by Frank Kuehl, December 4, 1928; and Financial Statement (Receipts and Disbursements), by James Corrigan, Milwaukee, Wisconsin, April 25, 1930, based on report of special committee investigating 1928 campaign expenses, Kuehl Papers. *Milwaukee Journal*, October 1, 1928; *Wisconsin State Journal*, October 1, 1928; Crowley to Roosevelt, July 20, 1934, OF 300, Wisconsin, FDRP; and Eklund, *Adviser to Presidents*.

25. Eklund, *Adviser to Presidents*.

26. Thirty-fourth through thirty-sixth annual reports of the State Banking Commission show an almost three fold increase in profits, but as early as 1929 that included a merger with the State Bank of Madison. Still, Bankshares' exercising of its option, its employment of Crowley, and his placement on on its board suggest his success at the State Bank before the stock market crash.

27. *Wisconsin State Journal*, February 11 and May 5, 1930.

28. Crowley's Wisconsin Income Tax Return for 1929, EP; and *Wisconsin State Journal*, April 11, 1929.

29. Crowley's Wisconsin Income Tax Return for 1930, EP.

30. Ibid., 1931; and "A Summary and Analysis of Memorandumdated January 15, 1935, Re: Crowley loans," MD, 3: 111–23; and "Memorandum," January 16, MD, 3: 132–34.

31. Records of G. P. and S. board meeting, December 31, 1931, CPP; and Dane County *Registry of Deeds*, 353: 448, and 404: 588. Crowley also initialed a $75,000 mortgage for his brother William.

32. Crowley's Wisconsin Income Tax Return for 1931, EP.

33. Ibid.; the automobile's cost was listed at $4,000.

34. Kuehl interview.

35. Allen interview.

36. *Capital Times*, January 24–February 2, 1932.

37. *Capital Times*, January 30, 1932.

38. Daniel H. Grady, Plaintiff, vs. Leo T. Crowley, Defendant, in Dane County Circuit Court, March 25, 1948.

39. "A Summary and Analysis of Memorandum dated January 15, 1935, Re: Crowley Loans," MD, 3: 111–23.

40. J. Craig Ralston's column in the *Milwaukee Journal*, carried in the *Wisconsin State Journal*, December 5, 1932.

41. Sixty years later his nephew, Dr. William Crowley, would refer to his

uncle's methods in that manner, "shortcuts." And Frank Kellogg interview, Madison, Wisconsin, June 26, 1980.

2. The Richelieu of Wisconsin

1. Interviews with John Doyle, December 1979; and with Frank Kuehl, August 11, 1980.

2. Ibid.; *Wisconsin Blue Book, 1933* (Madison, 1933); William T. Evjue, *A Fighting Editor* (Madison, 1968), 293–94; also George Poundtree, director, Stabilization Division of the Wisconsin Banking Commission to the Banking Review Board, September 3, 1932, Kuehl Papers; and Crowley to Schmedeman, March 28, 1933, *Wisconsin Blue Book* (no page number).

3. Eklund, *Adviser to Presidents*.

4. William T. Evjue to Lowell Mellett, January 31, 1934; and to I. F. Stone, February 16, 1944, EP; also, "Editorial #1," March 28, 1933, *Capital Times*.

5. "Editorial # 1," March 28, 1933, and "Editorial," October 21, 1932, *Capital Times*.

6. Evjue's characterization of Schmedeman was echoed by others, mainly Progressives, see Laufenberg, "The Schmedeman Administration," 15.

7. Laufenberg, "The Schmedeman Administration," 23, 27, and 31–32.

8. *Capital Times*, January 3, 1933.

9. Broughton to Farley, January 28, 1933, Broughton Papers; and Schmedeman to Farley, January 30, 1933, Schmedeman Papers.

10. Farley to Schmedeman, February 8, 1933, Schmedeman Papers.

11. Eklund, *Adviser to Presidents*, and Broughton editorial, "Inseparable in Life," *Sheboygan Press*, April 17, 1945.

12. Sheboygan Press, April 17, 1945; and *Wisconsin State Journal* and *Capital Times*, March 3, 1933.

13. Of the first seven banks to reopen, three were in Sheboygan, Broughton to Schmedeman, September 26, 1933, Broughton Papers; and Schmedeman to Alice Regan, February 2, 1934, Schmedeman Papers.

14. Schmedeman to John J. Korbel, April 24, 1933, Schmedeman Papers; and Crowley, interview of November 5, 1964, with Laufenberg, "The Schmedeman Administration," 47.

15. Laufenberg, "The Schmedeman Administration," 49–52; Eklund, *Adviser to Presidents*; and Schmedeman to H. H. Fielder, Janury 15, 1934, Schmedeman Papers.

16. *Milwaukee Sentinel*, August 15, 1933.

17. *Progressive*, August 5, 1933.

18. Eklund, *Adviser to Presidents*; Laufenberg, "The Schmedeman Administration," 49; *Two Rivers Reporter and Chronicle*, April 25, 1933; and *New Richmond News*, April 29, 1933.

19. Laufenberg, "The Schmedeman Administration," 49; Crowley to Schmedeman, August 13, 1934, CPP; and *Capital Times*, May 19, 1933.

20. Crowley attempted a moderating influence on the milk strike, saying on May 11 that deploying troops "would be a foolish thing for the state to do," *Green Bay Press-Gazette*, May 16, 1933; Evjue, *A Fighting Editor*, 514; and *La Crosse Tribune and Leader*, April 19, 1933; Laufenberg, "The Schmedeman Administration," 42; clippings in Crowley scrapbook; Schmedeman to Major Theodore Lewis, May 25, 1933, Schmedeman Papers; and Crowley to Morgenthau, June 12, 1933, CPP.

21. *Appleton Post-Crescent*, April 3 and 8, and June 12, 1933; *Plymouth Review*, April 4, 1933; unlabeled clipping, Crowley scrapbook; *Milwaukee Sentinel*, April 26, 1933; Crowley to Morgenthau, June 12, 1933, CPP; and *Capital Times*, April 7, 1933.

22. *Wisconsin State Journal*, May 2, 1933; and *Appleton Post-Crescent*, April 8, 1933.

23. *Capital Times*, May 19, 1933.

24. Crowley to Kuehl and to Blaine, September 5, 1933, Kuehl Papers.

25. Blaine to Crowley, September 6, 1933; and Kuehl to Crowley, September 8, 1933, Kuehl Papers. Evjue, *A Fighting Editor*, 522. Wisconsin banking problems were exacerbated because the RFC could not buy the preferred stock of banks in states where stockholders had double liability, as in Wisconsin.

26. National Recovery Administrator, July 25, 1933; *Chicago Tribune*, October 13, 1933; Kuehl to Crowley, August 28, 1933, and September 1, 1933, Kuehl Papers.

27. Haney, "The Record of Wisconsin's New Democrats," *Wisconsin Magazine of History* 58, no.2 (Winter 1974–75), 29–30. Laufenberg, "The Schmedeman Administration," 31–45.

28. *Sheboygan Press*, October 4, 1933.

29. *Chicago Tribune*, October 13, 1933.

30. *Wisconsin State Journal*, October 15, 1933.

31. Morgenthau, Farm Credit Diary, June 12, 1933, 42–43, FDRL. In a memorandum of June 12, 1933, and elsewhere, there is strong evidence that Crowley gave Morgenthau a memorandum with revisions the next morning, and Morgenthau told him to meet with Walter Cummings, his executive assistant, to work out details. See Crowley to Morgenthau, June 12, 1933, CPP.

32. Morgenthau, Farm Credit Diary, June 12, 1933, 42–43; Crowley to Morgenthau, Memorandum of June 12, 1933; Morgenthau to Fred Klauson, president, federal land bank at St. Paul, MN, September 11, 1933, and W. I. Myers, deputy governor FCA, to Klauson, September 25, 1933, RG 103, FCA General Correspondence; and Langer, *Congressional Record*, October 16, 1945.

33. Myers to Klauson, September 25, 1933, RG 103, General Correspondence, FCA; *Minneapolis Tribune*, October 11–14, 1933; *Sheboygan Press*, October

11, 1933; *Marshfield* (WI) *News-Herald*, October 14, 1933; *Milwaukee Journal*, October 15, 1933; and *Wisconsin State Journal*, October 16, 1933.

34. John M. Blum, *From the Morgenthau Diaries: Years of Crisis, 1928–1938* (Boston, 1959) 1: 49; and *Janesville Gazette*, November 17, 1933.

35. Langer to Roosevelt, November 16, 1933, and numerous other telegrams, PPF 27a; Schmedeman to Roosevelt, November 13, 1933, and Duffy to Roosevelt, November 15, 1933, Schmedeman Papers.

36. Telegrams and Letters, PPF 27a.

37. *Janesville Gazette*, November 17, 1933.

38. *Who's Who* for several years; publicity releases, CPP; Crowley corrected many of the misstatements in his reminiscences with Eklund; interview with Paul Nitze, July 9, 1990; also, Nitze, *From Hiroshima to Potsdam*, (New York, 1989), 23–24.

3. Cover-Up in the Capital, I

1. Frank Freidel, *The Launching of the New Deal* (Boston, 1973), 225, 234; Carter Golembe, "The Deposit Insurance Legislation of 1933: An Examination of its Antecedents," *Political Science Quarterly* 75 (1960), 181–200; J. A. Marlin, "Bank Deposit Insurance: Its Development in the U.S.A.," *Bankers' Magazine* 208 (September, 1969), 115–20; "Origin of FDIC Law, 1933–1934," CPP; and *Annual Reports of the FDIC*, 1950 and 1952, 68–101 and 59–72.

2. *Annual Reports of the FDIC*, 1950 and 1952, 68–101 and 59–72. Ironically, given the opposition of large city banks to deposit insurance, the March 1933 debate was initiated by a resolution from the New York state legislature, *Congressional Record*, March 11, 1933, 73rd Cong., 1st Sess. 77, 179.

3. *Congressional Record*, March 11, 1933, 73rd Cong., 1st Sess. 77: 179, and *Congressional Record*, May 19, 1933, 2nd Sess, 76: 3683; also Conference Report, June 13, 1933, 77: 5861; Public Law 66, 73rd Congress; "Original Deposit Insurance Law," Section 12B of the Federal Reserve Act of 1933, inserted by Section 8 of the Banking Act of 1933, *Annual Report of the FDIC for 1934*.

4. J. F. T. O'Connor Diary, June 22, July 12, August 7 and 15, and December 15, 1933; and Marvin McIntyre, assistant secretary to the president, to O'Connor, January 14, 1934, OF 2911.

5. Roosevelt shifted from stubborn resistance to deposit insurance in early June to readiness in August to "insure as many banks as possible." O'Connor Diary, August 22 and 26, and September 6, 7, 12, 16, and 24, 1933; *Annual Report of the FDIC for 1934* (Washington, DC, 1935), 9–14; and Arthur Schlesinger, *Coming of the New Deal* (Cambridge, 1959) 428.

6. O'Connor Diary, December 15, 1933; and Marvin McIntyre to O'Connor, January 14, 1934, OF 2911.

7. Duffy to Roosevelt, January 16, 1933, and Roosevelt to McIntyre, January 23, 1934, Crowley File, FDRL.

8. *Milwaukee Leader*, January 2, 1934; *Sheboygan Press*, October 23, 1933, and January 23, 1934; *Wisconsin Sentinel*, October 24, 1933; *Capital Times*, January 2 and 3, 1934; and *ChicagoTribune*, January 4, 1934; Farley later claimed that Morgenthau recommended Crowley against his advice, see O'Connor Diary, November 27, 1934; and for Morgenthau's claim of responsibility, see MD, February 26, 1934, Box 1.

9. Evjue to Mellett, January 31, 1934, EP.

10. Evjue to Vandenberg, January 31, 1934, EP.

11. Morgenthau had been Acting Treasury Secretary; Crowley to Morgenthau, February 4, 1934, responding to his insistence that he return to Washington, MD, Box 87, and CPP; also, O'Connor Diary, November 23, 1934.

12. O'Connor Diary, November 23, 1934.

13. Ibid., February 6, 1934.

14. Ibid., February 7, 1934; Crowley to Ira A. Moore, president, People's National Bank, February 20, 1934, CPP; Eklund, *Adviser to Presidents*, and Crowley-Vandenberg letters throughout Crowley's tenure in Washington, CPP. Vandenberg might well have been defeated in 1934 but for Crowley's letter, which Vandenberg advertised throughout Michigan.

15. O'Connor Diary, November 11 and 20, 1934, when he admitted that the examiner's report on Crowley was false; O'Connor Diary, February 13 and 14, 1934; and Vandenberg to O'Connor, February 15, 1934, CPP.

16. Glenn Chamberlain to Vandenberg, February 12, Chamberlain to Joseph Dean, February 12, Crowley to Dean, and to F. A. Cannon, February 20, 1934, CPP; W. C. Coopman, secretary to Roosevelt, February 20, 1934, Misc., OF 2911; McIntyre to Farley, February 5, 1934, OF 2911, on Rubin's protest; Rubin to Vandenberg, February 7, 1934, CPP; and Vandenberg to O'Connor, February 15, 1934, CPP.

17. *Milwaukee Sentinel*, February 10, 1934; and *Wisconsin State Journal*, February 13, 1934.

18. Crowley to Rudolph Forster, March 6, 1934, OF 2911; Crowley to Morgenthau, March 8, 1934, and to McIntyre, March 8, 1934, CPP; Farley to Roosevelt, March 5, 1934, enclosing letter of February 28, 1934, from William Kemper, and memo of O'Connor's phone call, March 8, 1934, 21b, FDRP.

19. Crowley to McIntyre, and Crowley to Morgenthau, March 8, 1934, CPP.

20. MD, February 26, 1934, 1; Crowley to McIntyre, March 21, 1934, OF 2911; and O'Connor Diary, March 23, 1935.

21. *New York Times*, February 14 and 15, April 20 and 26, May 5 and 26, and June 1, 1934; Crowley to McIntyre, March 21, 1934, and April 18, 1934, OF 2911, the latter enclosing a "confidential" letter from Wisconsin Congressman

Michael K. Reilly to Crowley, regarding the House Banking Committee's problems; and Crowley, memo to White House, probably May 4, 1934, OF 2911.

22. Ibid.

23. Crowley to Morgenthau, April 19, 1934, Crowley File, FDRP.

24. *New York Times*, May 22, 1934; Crowley to McIntyre, May 21, 1934, OF 2911. The House passed its bill May 24, including the last section which provided for paying as much as one billion dollars to depositors for the period December, 1929–January 1, 1934, despite the objections of House leaders speaking for the president. In the final measure, approved June 11, this burden was shifted to the RFC, *New York Times*, June 12, 1934.

25. *New York Times*, June 1, 1934; and *Capital Times*, June 13, 1934.

26. *Capital Times*, June 13, 1934.

27. Crowley to J. H. Williams, superintendent of banks, Montgomery, AL, June 25, 1934, marked in ink as "Form Used for Investigating Newly Chartered Banks," Records of the Chairman, RG 34.

28. *Wisconsin State Journal*, June 19 and 21, 1934; *Capital Times*, June 19, 1934; and *Chicago Tribune*, June 20, 1934.

29. "Report of the Meeting of September 12, 1934," Office of the Chairman, Box 1, Letters and Memos Folder, Procedure, FDIC, National Archives.

30. O'Connor Diary, July 2 and June 6, 1934; O'Connor Diary, June 18, 1934; *Milwaukee Sentinel*, October 30, 1934; *Baltimore Sun*, September 19, 1934; MD, September 19, 1934, Box 71; O'Connor Diary, September 21, 1934; *Chicago Tribune*, November 24, 1934; and Madison *Capital-Times*, November 24, 1934.

31. O'Connor Diary, September 20, 1934; J. A. Cullen in *Farmers Union-Herald*, October 30, 1934, clipping in CPP.

32. O'Connor Diary, October 5, 1934; O'Connor learned from Crowley the next day that he, Crowley, had recommended a loan to Wisconsin Bankshares, but if he told McIntyre he did not jot it in his diary, perhaps realizing at last that his connection with Crowley's confirmation did not reflect well on him. For Morgenthau's talk with Crowley, and Crowley's reply, MD, October 15, 1934, Box 2, 114 and 118–20.

33. *MD*, October 15, 1934, Box 2, 114 and 118–20.

34. For a discussion, see Blum, *From the Morgenthau Diaries: Years of Crisis, 1928–1938*, I, 345–50.

35. *Milwaukee Journal*, October 23, 1934; and Ralph Hendershot, "Wall Street," in *New York World Telegram*, November 2, 1934.

36. Approved by Stephen T. Early, October 16, 1934.

37. O'Connor Diary, November 17, 1934.

38. Ibid., November 20, 1934.

39. Ibid., November 23, 27, and 30, 1934; and Francis J. Bloodgood to Colonel Louis H. Howe, October 31, 1934, Of 2911, misc., with reference to earlier letter to McIntyre.

40. Glass to Crowley, December 12, 1934, Carter Glass Papers, University of Virginia Library, Charlottesville, Va., hereafter GP.

4. Cover-Up in the Capital, II

1. Glass's record of phone call to Charles S. Hamlin, Dec. 18, 1934, Carter Glass Papers, University of Virginia Library, Charlottesville, VA.

2. Ibid., Crowley to Glass, December 20, 1934, and Glass to Crowley, December 23, 1934.

3. Mortimer J. Fox to Crowley, Dec. 27, 1934, CPP; Crowley to Glass, December 29, 1934, Glass Papers; and *New York Times*, December 30, 1934.

4. MD, January 2, 1935, 3: 11–13. See O'Connor Diary, December 6, 9, 10, and 15, 1934, for belief that Morgenthau was taking his legal staff as a prelude to abolishing his position and making Crowley the "Banking Czar," as the *Chicago Tribune*, November 24, 1934, put it; for learning, from Crowley, that Senator LaFollette would not investigate; and for his effort to have Treasury Undersecretary Thomas J. Coolidge read the "record of Mr. Crowley" and obtain his resignation, which Coolidge refused to do; and O'Connor Diary, January 2, 1935, for his visit to Morgenthau's office that morning.

5. O'Connor Diary, January 2, 1935; and MD, Jan. 2, 1935, 3: 11–14.

6. *MD*, January 2, 1935, 3: 11–14

7. Ibid., Jan. 4, 1935, 3; 34–36.

8. Ibid., Jan. 7, 1935, 3; 15–21.

9. Ibid., Jan. 14, 1935, 3; 105–23.

10. Oliphant to Morgenthau, January 16, 1935, MD, 3: 132–34.

11. O'Connor Diary, Jan. 4, 7, 8, and 9, 1935. MD, Jan. 7 and 14, 1935, 3: 14 and 98–99.

12. Oliphant to Morgenthau, Jan. 16, 1935, MD, 3: 67.

13. O'Connor Diary, Jan. 23, 31, and March 12, 1935; and MD, March 12, 1935, 4: 67.

14. MD, March 12, 1935, 4: 144–144a; and 0'Connor Diary, March 22, 1935.

15. O'Connor Diary, March 22, 1935.

16. Blum, *From the Morgenthau Diaries*, I, 343–53.

17. Ibid., 350; also "K" (for Kannee) to McIntyre, June 13, 1935; and Crowley to McIntyre, June 6, 1935, OF 2911.

18. Crowley to Glass, August 20, 1935, CPP; and William Leuchtenburg, *Franklin D. Roosevelt and the New Deal, 1932–1940* (New York, 1963), 160.

19. *New York Times*, September 14, 1935; *Commercial West Weekly*, August 31, 1935, 70: 20; and Crowley to Morgenthau, September 13, 1935, CPP.

20. *New York Times*, September 29, 1935; Joseph P. Lash, *Dealers and Dreamers: A New Look at the New Deal* (New York, 1988), in which Corcoran is a central figure; Leuchtenburg, *FDR*, 148–49; and Eklund, *Adviser to Presidents*.

21. Eklund, *Adviser to Presidents*.

22. *Milwaukee Journal*, September, 29, 1935.

23. MD, Oct. 25, 1935, 10: 141.

24. Wheeler to Morgenthau, May 1, 1936, MD, 23: 86–88.

25. Morgenthau to Wheeler, May 5, 1936, MD, 23: 85, and to O'Connor, May 5, 1936, 23: 91.

26. O'Connor to Morgenthau, May 5, 1936; MD, 23: 91–92, and 100–104.

27. O'Connor Diary, May 5, 1936; also MD, 23: 100–104.

28. O'Connor Diary, May 4, 1936; and MD, May 5, 1936, 23: 103.

29. Morgenthau to McIntryre, MD, 23: 99.

30. Ibid., 129A, and 109. Jones wanted to avoid the press and had phoned to ask if he could join Morgenthau in taking an underground passage to the White House.

31. O'Connor Diary, May 6, 1936. Morgenthau turned this task over to his executive assistant, William McReynolds.

32. O'Connor Diary, May 7, 12, and 13, 1936.

33. MD, May 11, 1936, 24: 52.

34. MD, May 18, 1936, 24: 189. Three days earlier, however, O'Connor remarked in his diary that "Secretary recommended that Crowley charges be dropped."

35. MD, May 19, 1936, 24: 239, and May 21, 1936, 25: 16–17.

36. Ibid., 17.

37. Ibid., May 22, 1936, 25: 22–24.

38. Ibid., June 16, 1936, 27: 3D, E, F.

39. Ibid., July 2, 1936, 28: 92–93.

40. Ibid.

41. Ibid., December 11, 1936, 48: 109–13.

5. *Banking and Politics*

1. For some perspectives on the rise and fall of the New Deal coalition, see author's "Kent Keller, the Liberal Bloc, and the New Deal," *Journal of the Illinois State Historical Society*, 68 (April 1975), 143–58; "Maury Maverick and the Liberal Bloc," *Journal of American History*, 57 (March 1971), 880–95, and "Thomas Amlie and the New Deal," *Mid-America*, 59 (January 1977), 19–38; and for a recent, penetrating analysis of the Liberal Bloc and within it the Wisconsin Progressives and Minnesota Farmer-Laborites, see James J. Lorence, *Gerald J. Boileau and the Progressive-Farmer-Labor Alliance* (Columbia, MO, 1994). Arguably, the political scene in Washington closely resembled the complexities of Wisconsin and Minnesota politics.

2. President's press conference no. 133, June 27, 1934, for FDR's endorsement of LaFollette. For birth of Progressive party, Charles H. Backstrom, "The

Progressive Party of Wisconsin, 1934–1946" (Ph.D. diss., University of Wisconsin, 1956); Weiss, "Thomas Amlie and the New Deal"; Donald Young, *Adventures in Politics: The Memoirs of Philip LaFollette* (New York, 1970), 204–16; Roger T. Johnson, *Robert M. LaFollette, Jr., and the Decline of the Progressive Party in Wisconsin* (Madison, 1964); *New York Times*, July 14, 1934; Schmedeman to Roosevelt, May 9, 1934, and to Gustave Pabst, June 29, 1934, Schmedeman Papers, reveals that he knew in May that the president might stop in Green Bay and, in June, that he might endorse Senator LaFollette, but that "Leo will be here in a few days and he will probably be able to give us some definite information." Also, Crowley to Roosevelt, July 20, 1934, 300, Wisconsin, FDRP.

3. Leslie Gelb, quoted in Walter Isaacson, *Kissinger* (New York, 1992), 100. For testimony other than Crowley's letter of July 20, 1934, see Chapters 3, 4, and 12, as well as 12, f.n. 19, and author's correspondence with Alfred Eugene Davidson, September–December 1990.

4. Crowley to Roosevelt, July 20, 1934, 300, Wisconsin, FDRP.

5. *Minneapolis Journal*, August 8, 1934.

6. *New York Times*, August 10, 1934; Crowley to Schmedeman, August 13, 1934, Schmedeman Papers; and Young, *Adventures in Politics*, 214.

7. Rubin's attacks in *Janesville Gazette*, August 30, 1934.

8. Crowley to A. G. Schmedeman, September 21, October 1, 4, and 13, 1934, Schmedeman Papers.

9. Young, *Adventures in Politics*, 216; For Crowley's words in Milton Junction, see *Wisconsin State Journal*, April 3, 1934; and for the character and significance of the returns see my "Thomas Amlie" and "Maury Maverick," esp. 882–83.

10. Hopkins to Roosevelt, August 23, 1935, PSF: Hopkins, Box 152.

11. Crowley to McIntyre, June 6, 1935; "Presidential Memorandum for Governor Eccles," March 9, 1936; Crowley to McIntyre, March 4, 1936; and McIntyre to Crowley, January 30, 1936, OF 2911.

12. Crowley to McIntyre, July 29, 1935, OF 2911.

13. see *New York Times*, September 7, 1935, for LaFollette's visit; B. R. (apparently a secretary at FDIC) memo for Crowley, transmitting message from Kannee at White House, no date; and Crowley to Broughton, August 27, 1935, CPP.

14. McIntyre to Crowley, May 16, 1936; McIntyre to Rubin, May 18, 1936; and Crowley to McIntyre, May 19, 1936, Wisconsin File, FDRP, insisting that Rubin's "only desire is to put the President 'on the spot' regarding the Governorship . . . and that situation will take care of itself."

15. Crowley to Roosevelt, August 21, 1936, about swing through midwest and talk with Governor LaFollette, OF 2911.

16. Weiss, "Thomas Amlie and the New Deal," 31; Crowley to McIntyre, September 8, 1936, PPF 1519; and Roosevelt press conference no. 133, June 27, 1934, quoted in Patrick Maney, *Young Bob LaFollette* (Columbia, MO, 1978), 145.

17. Crowley to McIntyre, September 8, 1936, Of 2911; Farmer-Labor representatives included Governor Hjalmar Peterson, Senator Elmer Benson, and Congressman Paul Kvale, reported in Arthur Naftalin, "A History of the Farmer-Labor Party of Minnesota" (Ph.D. diss., Univ. of Minnesota, 1948); *New York Times*, September 12, 1936.

18. Weiss, "Amlie," 31; for Crowley's insights and activities in Minnesota, McIntyre to Crowley, October 7, 1936, PPF 1519; White House Memo of October 8, 1936, Minnesota File, FDRP; and *New York Times*, October 4 and 10, 1936.

19. *Milwaukee Journal*, September 1, 1936; and Naftalin, "History of Farmer-Labor Party," 326.

20. Nationally Roosevelt won 60.2% of the popular vote, while in Wisconsin he won 63.8%, and in Minnesota 61.9%, Edgard. Eugene. Robinson, *They Voted For Roosevelt: The Presidential Vote, 1932–1944* (Stanford, 1947), 41 and 43.

21. Roosevelt to Morgenthau, November 1, 1936, OF 2911; Crowley to William Fawcett, June 29, 1936, that he "contemplate[d] leaving Washington sometime late in the fall." CPP.

22. Joseph Alsop and Robert Kintner, "The Capital Parade," *Washington Evening Star*, September 7, 1938, for Crowley's clash with Eccles; also Frank Wattman, "Looking Forward," *Washington Evening Star*, August 14, 1938, on Crowley's monetary conservatism to protect banks, depositors, and FDIC; and "Silver Lining Called FDIC," editorial, *Washington Evening Star*, August 6, 1938.

23. Author's interview with, telephone conversations with, and several lengthy and solidly informative letters, with capsule biographies of key figures in FDIC, from Morrison G. Tucker, investment banker, Oklahoma City, OK, beginning on February 15, 1984, and continuing through June 1990. Also, interview with Monroe Karasik, Washington, DC, July 6, 1991. The strength of this team is best measured by Crowley's use of its members for other tasks during the Second World War.

24. For conservative reaction, see Leuchtenburg, *FDR and the New Deal*, 231–84.

25. For liberal reaction, see Weiss, "Kent Keller," 151–52; "Maury Maverick," 891–95; and "Thomas Amlie," 33–35; and for LaFollette, see Leuchtenburg, *FDR*, 283–84; Young, *Adventures in Politics*, 252–56; and Evjue, *A Fighting Editor*, 562–64.

26. Reference to "Copperheads" in Leuchtenburg, *FDR*, 267.

27. Naftalin, "History of Farmer-Labor Party." Benson to Crowley, n.d., Crowley to Joseph B. Keennan, July 11, 1938, McIntyre to Crowley, September 11, 1938, and Crowley to McIntyre, September 13, 1938, Minnesota 300 "B", FDRP; McIntyre Memorandum for Crowley, November 11, 1940, with enclosures, and Crowley to "Pa" Watson, November 26, 1940, OF 2911; and for Roosevelt's endorsement and pressure from the left, see Roosevelt to George

W. Kelley, October 29, 1938, which was reworked to insert "liberal" where an early draft used "progressive," and for pressure on Roosevelt from the left, see Heywood Broun to McIntyre, November 6, 1938, Minnesota, 300 "B," FDRP.

28. Presidential Assistant James H. Rowe's quip on Memorandum from "Pa" Watson, April 1, 1939, Minnesota 300 "B", FDRP; Crowley to "Pa" Watson, June 13, 1939, enclosing Memorandum to the President, June 13, 1939, 300 Minnesota "C", FDRP; Crowley to "Pa" Watson, November 26, 1940, to McIntyre, November 19 and 20, 1940, OF 2911; and Joseph Moonan to James A. Farley, November 10, 1938, OF 300.

29. Duffy to McIntyre, May 2, 1938; McIntyre to Roosevelt, May 5, 1938, Wisconsin 300 E, FDRP; McIntyre to Crowley, July 26, 1938, Wisconsin 300 D, FDRP with enclosures: Duffy to Roosevelt, June 23, July 1, 1938, Wisconsin 300 D, FDRP; McIntyre to Roosevelt, June 30, Roosevelt to McIntyre, July 7, and Henry Wallace to McIntyre, July 9, 1938, OF 2911.

30. Crowley to McIntyre, August 17, 1938, and McIntyre to Latta, August 25, 1938, OF 2911; Robert Henry, the Democratic candidate for governor, was replaced by the equally anti–New Deal Harry Bolens, further weakening the Democratic ticket, *Milwaukee Journal*, October 2, 4, and 5, 1938. Roosevelt's last minute endorsement of Duffy in Roosevelt to Broughton, November 1, 1938, Wisconsin 300 D, FDRP, followed by *Milwaukee Journal*'s characterization, November 2, as "weasel words"; and for possible reasons for miscalculations, see William B. Rubin to James A. Farley, October 13, 1938, Wisconsin 300 D, FDRP arguing that Herman Ekern, the Progressive, not Alexander Wiley, the Republican, was the real threat to Duffy and most likely beneficiary should Duffy lose. Farley took the report seriously, attaching it to a note to Roosevelt, October 20, 1938, Wisconsin 300 D, FDRP.

31. For Crowley's opposition to Benson's appointment, see Stephen T. Early, "Classified Memo to the President," April 20, 1939, OF 2911; on Amlie, see Evjue to Edwin C. Johnson, chairman, Interstate Commerce Subcommittee, n.d. but late 1938 or early 1939, endorsing Amlie for Interstate Commerce Commission. Amlie, under fire as a radical, withdrew his name in the spring but ran for Congress in 1941, as a Democrat, with Crowley's blessings, only to lose, CPP; and Weiss, "Thomas Amlie," 37. On Duffy's appointment, Crowley to Roosevelt, May 25, 1939, PPF 1519, "Pa" Watson to Kannee, Memo of May 25, 1939, and Roosevelt to "Pa" Watson, May 27, 1939, 208 G, FDRP.

32. Column of Charles F. Speare, August 17, 1938, newspaper unknown, CPP. See also compliment by Progressive Congressman Harry Sauthoff, *Congressional Record*, June 11, 1938, 183: 11755, also CPP.

33. Clipping, 1938, otherwise unidentified, CPP.

34. *Camden Courier Post*, March 16, 1938, CPP.

35. *New York Times*, February 14 and 15, 1939, CPP.

36. *New York Times*, February 19, 20, 21, 22, March 3 and 5, 1939. For a dis-

cussion of the Hudson Trust Company's problems and of a typical, forceful FDIC response, see Virgil D. Wall, examiner, to William. M. Taylor, supervisory examiner, FDIC, April 17, 1939, records of chairman, RG 34.

37. *New York Times*, March 5, 1939.

38. State Income Tax Return for 1939, EP; and for ashtrays, "Tray Swiper," *St. Paul Dispatch*, May 11, 1939, on which someone, probably Crowley, wrote "For Shame." CPP.

39. C. B. Upham, "Memo to Secretary," July 26, 1939, and Crowley to Roosevelt, July 26, 1939, OF 2911.

40. Roosevelt to Crowley, July 31, 1939, Morgenthau to Crowley, July 28, 1939, and Crowley to Roosevelt, July 28, 1939, OF 2911. This story would see some light in 1942, CPP.

6. Private Enterprise and Public Service

1. MD, 59, 236, and chapter 8.

2. *New York Times, Chicago Tribune, Washington Star*, and *Milwaukee Journal*, December 1, 1939; and clippings, CPP.

3. For Victor Emanuel, *Time*, October 7, 1946, 87–91; *Current Biography, 1951*, 182–83; and senior honor's paper by Edward Frink, Southern Illinois University at Edwardsville (Fall 1983, in author's possession; and for S. G. and E., *New York Times*, March 10 and September 25, 1934; March 15 and August 9, 1935; July 7, 1936; March 3, 1938; March 29, 1940; and April 10, 1941; as well as Owen Ely, "Financial News and Comment," *Public Utilities Fortnightly* (April 25, 1940), 548–51; and, crucially, John Childs, "Assets Behind S. G. and E. Bonds," *Barron's*, April 11, 1940, for classes and value of various bonds, debentures, preferred, and common stock; and, finally, for the Supreme Court's validation of the PUHC Act, *Electrical World* 107 (February 2, 1937), no. 6, for original test case involving Electric Bond and Share; and ibid., 110 (October 15, 1938), no. 16, for the Supreme Court's March 1938 ruling.

4. The complexities and ambiguities of the Public Utilities Holding Company Act of 1935 are spelled out in Robert Blum, "SEC Integration of Holding Company Systems," *Journal of Land and Public Utility Economics*, 17 (November 1941) 423–39; Leslie Fournier, "Simplification of Holding Companies under the Public Utility Holding Company Act of 1935," *Journal of Land and Public Utility Economics*, 13 (May 1937), 138–52; and Robert Charles and Milton Lunch, "Present Status and Future Effect of Public Utilities Act of 1935," 76, *Gas-Age Record* (September 14, 1935), no. 11. For Crowley as surrogate, *New York Times*, January 16, 1940. For Crowley's friendship with Corcoran, *Wisconsin State Journal*, April 16, 1972; author's interview with Corcoran, July 1980; and interview with John and Regina Doyle, December 1979. For Corcoran and PUHC Act,

Lash, *Dealers and Dreamers*. And for Crowley's contacts on the SEC, *Springfield* (MS) *News*, April 20, 1940, and *New York Times* July 17, 1943.

5. *Barron's*, December 18, 1939, *New York Times*, December 2, 1939; and Crowley to Edward Dempsey, February 2, 1940, CPP.

6. The narrative reads as Crowley recalled the Monday following his press conference, but see Grace Tully, "Memo for General 'Pa' Watson," December 4, 1939, OF 2911. Also, Eklund, *Adviser to Presidents*.

7. Ibid.; Crowley to Morgenthau, December 1, 1939, MD, 226: 79; *New York Times*, December 5, 1939; and Crowley to Evjue, November 8, 1940, EP.

8. *New York Times*, December 5, 1939.

9. Crowley to William Rubin, December 12, 1939, William Rubin Papers, University of Wisconsin at Milwaukee; Crowley to Evjue, December 12, 1939, EP; and Crowley to Morgenthau, December 5, 1939, MD, 226: 386.

10. *Barron's*, December 18, 1939; and *Sheboygan Press*, May 16, 1939, reporting a speech in which Crowley stressed the need for defensive armaments and asked professional and business leaders to compare the administration's readiness to compromise with the methods of "single-minded zealots" abroad and to accept its efforts to correct social problems as in their "enlightened self-interest," grappling with "collective misery" before it became grist for zealots at home.

11. *New York Times*, December 5, 1939; *Time*, March 23, 1942; and *Chicago News*, December 5, 1939.

12. *Philadelphia Record*, January 3, 1940; and Memorandum of December 7, 1939, OF 2911.

13. For White House call, Grace Tully, "Memorandum for General 'Pa' Watson," December 4, 1939, OF 2911; Lehman to Roosevelt March 14, 1940, regarding prior conversations about "unfavorable repercussions" which would likely result from the two banks' collapse, OF 2911 and misc. 230, FDRP; also Tully Memorandum cited above.

14. "Crowley" Memorandum, December 7, 1939, covering events involving the Integrity Trust Company from December 1 to January 13, 1940, OF 2911 and misc., 230, FDRP.

15. Ibid; also General Watson to Grover Whalen, January 6, 1940, 1940, OF 2911; Crowley to Roosevelt, January 1, 1940, *New York Times*, January 13, 1940; and Roosevelt to Watson, January 13, 1940, below which Watson noted, "Have done," OF 2911.

16. Elizabeth F. Downey to the Congress Hotel, Chicago, IL, February 2, 1940, and to the Blackstone Hotel, February 27, 1940, CPP; Gift Lists, CPP; and Crowley to Henry G. Wasson, Jr., April 17, 1940, and to Hamilton Pell, December 12, 1939, CPP.

17. Both Crowley and Broughton recognized Duffy's defeat in 1938 exac-

erbated the patronage problem, Crowley to Evjue, March 5, 1940, EP; *Fond du Lac Commonwealth Reporter,* November 10, 1938; Broughton to Crowley, November 16, 1938, CPP; Evjue to Farley, December 12, 1938, and to Senator George Norris, December 28, 1938, EP; open letter in *Capital Times,* December 12, 1938; Farley to Roosevelt, January 1, 1939; *Appleton Post-Crescent,* January 2 and January 13, 1940; *Milwaukee Sentinel,* February 9, 1940; and Stephen Early to "Pa" Watson, November 7, 1939, OF 2911, relaying analyses by Crowley. John Wyngaard, political analyst for the *Green Bay Press-Gazette,* January 12, 1940, noted that it was believed throughout Wisconsin that LaFollette and Crowley "got together to arrange for a 50–50 distribution of Wisconsin political plums."

18. Stephen T. Early to William Rubin, January 7, 1939, Rubin Papers; Early to "Pa" Watson, November 7, 1939, Wisconsin File, FDRP; Crowley to Watson, February 1, 1940, enclosing a memorandum describing the political scene, OF 2911; *Milwaukee Sentinel,* February 9, 1940.

19. Raymond Mobley to Evjue, February 10, 1940, EP; *Milwaukee Journal,* February 11, 1940; and Crowley to "Pa" Watson, February 1, 1940, memo for the President, OF 2911.

20. *Milwaukee Journal, Milwaukee Sentinel,* and *Capital Times,* February 12, 1940.

21. J. W. Martin to Farley, February 14, 1940, Rubin Papers; *Milwaukee Journal,* February 11, 1940. Also, Rubin to Farley, March 25, 1940, Rubin Papers.

22. *Milwaukee Journal,* February 13, 1940; and Broughton to Crowley, March 21, 1940, Broughton Papers; Evjue to Farley, December 12, 1938, EP, and *Capital Times,* same date; *Capital Times,* March 25, 1940; Rubin to Crowley, February 19, 1940, Rubin Papers.

23. Evjue, memorandum of phone conversation, March 5, 1940, EP.

24. Broughton to Crowley, March 21, 1940, Broughton Papers, enclosing his editorial of March 19, 1940.

25. Crowley, Robert LaFollette, and Broughton to Roosevelt, April 4, 1940, recommending Boileau to fill a vacancy on the SEC, 1060-A, OF 2911, to which the President replied on April 18, 1940, "this letter will receive my serious consideration," but Jerome Frank, chairman of the commission had already been consulted, April 17, 1940, and replied that it "would not be so good." See, also, the *Sheboygan Press,* March 27, 1940.

26. *Wisconsin State Journal,* April 5, 1940; *Milwaukee Sentinel,* April 1, 1940; Broughton to Rubin, April 5, 1940, Rubin Papers; and *Milwaukee Sentinel,* April 29, 1940.

27. *New York Times,* March 6, 1940.

28. *Springfield* (MS) *News,* April 20, 1940; also, *New York Times,* July 17, 1943, when George C. Matthews, the vice-president involved, was moved to another subsidiary.

29. *Wall Street Journal* and *New York Times*, April 13, 1940.

30. *Wall Street Journal*, April 13, 1940; and *Little Rock Gazette*, April 14, 1940.

31. *New York Times*, April 25, 1940.

32. *Commercial and Financial Chronicle*, 150: 390–91, June 22, 1940.

33. *New York Times*, June 15, 1940.

7. A Third Term for the President

1. Grace Tully, memorandum for General Watson, December 4, 1939, Crowley to Roosevelt, March 7, 1940, Roosevelt to Crowley, March 9, 1940, Lehman to Roosevelt, March 14, 1940, Roosevelt to Lehman, March 26, 1940, Crowley to Roosevelt, March 26 and June 3, 1940, Roosevelt to Crowley, June 11, 1940, and Lehman to Roosevelt, April 11, 1940, OF 2911.

2. *Capital Times*, June 23, 1940; and Stephen T. Early to General Watson, July 26, 1940, OF 2911.

3. *Capital Times*, June 9, 1940; *Milwaukee Journal*, July 15, 1940.

4. *Wisconsin State Journal* and *Capital Times*, July 15, 1940.

5. Ibid.

6. Ibid.

7. Eklund, *Adviser to Presidents*; James F. Byrnes, talk with Morgenthau, December 31, 1941, MD, 480: 190–92; *Capital Times*, July 16, 1940; and *Milwaukee Journal*, July 17, 1940.

8. Eklund, *Adviser to Presidents*.

9. Ibid.; for the problems with Crowley's reminiscence, see Crowley to Byrnes, March 20, 1956, and Byrnes to Crowley, July 20, 1956, CPP, regarding their memories of maneuvers at the 1944 convention; also, the president's appointment book scheduled Crowley twice the week before the 1944 convention, but not before that in 1940. On the other hand, Crowley's reminiscence fits some known facts too closely to be dismissed out of hand.

10. Byrnes to Crowley, July 20, 1956; *Milwaukee Journal*, July 16, 1940.

11. *Wisconsin State Journal* and *Milwaukee Journal*, July 19, 1940.

12. *Wisconsin State Journal* and *Milwaukee Journal*, July 15 and 21, 1940; *Capital Times*, July 16, 18, and 19, 1940; and Byrnes to James D. Derieux, August 2, 1940, James Byrnes Papers, Clemson University Library, Clemson, SC.

13. Benjamin Cohen to Missy LeHand, July 26, 1940, Stephen Early to General Watson, July 26, 1940, and Crowley to Roosevelt, July 27, 1940, OF 2911.

14. Crowley to Evjue, July 30, 1040, CPP.

15. Ibid.

16. *Capital Times*, June 23 and July 21, 1940.

17. Roosevelt to Crowley, July 30, 1940, OF 2911.

18. *New York Times*, August 1 and 2, 1940; MD, 480: 190–92; Byrnes to Derieux, August 2, 1940, BP; Roosevelt to General Watson, August 3, 1940, asking him to clear the "temporary appointment" of James Markham with Marriner Eccles, OF 2911; and the *Chicago Herald and American*, August 28, 1940, which reported Crowley saying he intended to leave the FDIC as soon as Congress acted on a pending bill, presumably 1941.

19. *New York Times*, August 27, 1940. Interview with Dr. Harry Purcell, July 1980.

20. *Business Week*, August 31, 1940; *New York Journal American*, August 29, 1940; *Chicago Herald American*, August 28, 1940; *St. Paul Dispatch*, August 27, 1940.

21. *Commercial and Financial Chronicle* 151 (August 31, 1940), 1291–92.

22. *Wisconsin State Journal*, August 4, 1940.

23. for further details, *Milwaukee Journal*, September 13, 18, and 19, 1940; *Capital Times*, September 24, 25, and 30, 1940; *New York Times*, September 25, 1940; *Milwaukee Journal* September 30, 1940; and *Capital Times*, October 2, 1940.

24. *Chicago Tribune*, October 1, 1940; *Wisconsin State Journal*, October 2, 1940; and *Capital Times*, October 3, 1940.

25. Transcript of Speech, October 1, 1940, CPP.

26. *Capital Times*, October 5 and 8, 1940; and Rubin to Roosevelt, October 7, 1940, 300, Wisconsin R, FDRP.

27. Crowley to Rubin, October 11, 1940, Rubin Papers; *Capital Times*, August 27, 1940; and Crowley to Evjue, October 11, 1940, EP.

28. *Capital Times*, October 21, 1940. Crowley was not listed as one of the sponsors of Wallace's speech.

29. *Capital Times*, October 23, 1940, includes complete text of Wallace's remarks and description of walkout; and *Milwaukee Journal*, October 27, 1940.

30. *Milwaukee Journal* and *Chicago Tribune*, November 5, 1940; and Aldrich Revell, in the *Capital Times*, October 24, 1940.

31. See Paul Kleppner, *The Cross of Culture: A Social Analysis of Midwestern Politics, 1850–1890* (New York, 1970); Richard Jensen, *The Winning of the Midwest: Social and Political Conflict, 1888–1896* (Chicago, 1971); and Lee Benson, *The Concept of Jacksonian Democracy: New York as a Test Case* (Princeton, 1961), which argues that "ethnic and religious differences have tended to be relatively the most important sources of political differences."

32. Leo Crowley, Memorandum to the President, Subject: Compulsory Military Training, September 26, 1945; see also author's "Leo T. Crowley, Pragmatic New Dealer," *Mid-America*, 64, (January, 1982), no. 1, 47.

33. *Barron's*, December 18, 1939; *Sheboygan Press*, May 16, 1939. See, also, f.n. 10, chapter 6.

34. Rubin to Crowley, October 17 and 23, 1940, Rubin Papers.

35. Robinson, *They voted for Roosevelt*, p. 178. Roosevelt also carried Min-

nesota, p. 110, but comparison with the 1944 election, when Roosevelt did not carry Wisconsin, suggests the importance of LaFollete's endorsement in 1940.

36. "Here's Pie in your Eye," *Wisconsin State Journal*, January 27, 1941; and Evjue, Memo of Long Distance Conversation with Leo T. Crowley from Washington, July 17, 1941, EP.

37. Crowley sent Evjue his speech of November 11, 1940, on November 8, 1940, EP. It was excerpted and analyzed in the *Capital Times*, November 12, 1940. H. G. Nicholas, ed., *Washington Despatches* (Chicago, 1981), 254–55, contains this and other British references to Crowley, most after his July 1943 appointment as director of economic warfare. Many of these also stressed his appeal to Catholics, to middle-of-the-road Democrats, and to moderate businessmen.

8. Alien Property Custodian, I

1. For Broughton's resignation, *Wisconsin State Journal*, January 7, 1941, and Crowley to Otto Stielow, February 6, 1941, CPP; for San Diego Gas and Electric, *New York Journal of Commerce*, January 15, 1941; for income, *Capital Times*, July 18, 1943; and for Xmas gifts, CPP.

2. *Capital Times*, March 22, 1942. Years later Crowley told Eklund, *Adviser to Presidents*, that this talk occurred on the night of Pearl Harbor.

3. See James H. Rowe, Jr., to J. Edgar Hoover, March 23, 1942, and to Crowley, April 6, 1942, enclosing a transscript, Rowe Papers.

4. Ibid., 328 and 335; *Annual Report of the Alien Property Custodian*, March 11, 1942, to June 30, 1943, for executive order 8785, of June 14, 1941; Stanley Coben, *A. Mitchell Palmer* (New York, 1963), 128–49, pointing out that Palmer acted so rashly as to invite a congressional investigation; however, it was Thomas W. Miller, President Warren Harding's appointee, who was sentenced to a federal penitentiary for eighteen months, *New York Times*, March 5 and 9, 1927.

5. Biddle-FDR discussion of October 22, 1941, OF 2911.

6. Roosevelt to Watson, October 22, 1941, and "Index to President's Appointments," OF 2911. For Morgenthau's views, see MD, 480: 194–200.

7. James F. Byrnes, *All in One Lifetime* (New York, 1958) 150.

8. Ibid., 151–52.

9. Roosevelt to Crowley, December 5, 1941, PPF 1519 and Of 2911.

10. Biddle to Roosevelt, December 5, 1941, OF 10.

11. The legislation referred to was the First War Powers Act, enacted December 18, 1941, and for effects on Alien Property Custodian's Office, see Office of the Alien Property Custodian, *Annual Report for March 11, 1942, to June 30, 1943*, 7; also Roosevelt to Biddle, December 5, 1941, OF 10; Grace Tully, Memorandum for the President, January 2, 1942, OF 2911.

12. MD, 480: 194–200; and John M. Blum, *From The Morgenthau Diaries: Years of War, 1941–1945* (Boston, 1967), 4–5.

13. *Washington Banktrends and Backgrounds*, no. 240, December 15 1941; and Blum, *Morgenthau Diaries: Years of War*, 5.

14. Memorandum for the President, December 18, 1942, signed G., OF 77.

15. Byrnes to General Watson, December 17, 1941, OF 77; and Oscar Cox to Byrnes, and Byrnes to Roosevelt, December 19 and 20, 1941, BP.

16. Roosevelt wrote Byrnes, December 23, 1941, "I feel I cannot make a decision until next week for obvious reasons," OF 77; also Byrnes, *All in One Lifetime*, 153.

17. Byrnes to Roosevelt, undated memorandum, persumably late December, responding to the President's memorandum of the 23rd, BP; and Byrnes, *All In One Lifetime*, 153.

18. MD, 480: 192–200.

19. MD, 480: 194–200.

20. MD, 480: 196–200, but especially 198. Morgenthau was furious after seeing a proposed executive order that would bring alien property and the custodian into the Justice Department, and he phoned the White House to ask for an opportunity to speak with the president after the British mission left. Byrnes to Morgenthau, December 31, 1941, BP; Byrnes to Roosevelt, January 8, 1942, and memorandum for the president, January 2, 1942, OF 77.

21. "No Peace with I. G. Farben," *Fortune*, 26 (September, 1942), 104–7 and 144–52; I. F. Stone, five-article series in *Capital Times*, February 22 to February 26, 1944, also in *PM*; and Howard Ambruster, *Treason's Peace* (N.Y., 1947).

22. Ibid.; and I. F. Stone, "Fumbling with I. G. Farben," *The Nation*, January 6, 1945.

23. John M. Blum, *From The Morgenthau Diaries: Years of Urgency, 1938–1941* (Boston, 1965), 326–37; Edward L. Steckler and Warner Rosenberg, "Real Property of Enemy Aliens," *New York Law Journal* of April 21, 22, and 23, 1942, reprints in CPP; and "Treatment of U.S. Property in Enemy Countries," Board of Directors of Chambers of Commerce of the United States, September 17–18, 1943.

24. Blum, *Morgenthau Diaries: Years of War*, 6–8.

25. Byrnes to FDR, January 8, 1942, OF 77.

26. Ibid.

27. Blum, *Morgenthau Diaries: Years of War*, pp. 6–9, reports Roosevelt as "extremely interested" in and strongly approving Morgenthau's report.

28. Byrnes, "As to Crowley," draft memo, apparently of January 21, 1942, BP.

29. Byrnes to Roosevelt, January 21, 1942, BP, and OF 77.

30. Ibid.

31. Crowley to Roosevelt, January 22, 1942, OF 2911.

32. Ibid.; and MD, 487: 388.

33. Morgenthau to Roosevelt, February 6, 1942, OF 4782.

34. "Regulations Relating to Property Vested in the Secretary of the Treasury Pursuant to . . . the Trading with the Enemy Act," as amended by the First War Powers Act, 1941, filed February 15, for which see *Federal Register*, 7: 1021, February 23, 1942, also Treasury Press Release no. 30–43, of same date, in CPP; and Byrnes, *All in One Lifetime*, p. 153.

35. Transcript of Morgenthau's press conference, February 19, 1942, CPP.

36. Presidential press conference, no. 807–8, February 24, 1942, reiterated similar brief comments made a month earlier, no. 801–8, January 27, 1942; also Blum, *Morgenthau Diaries: Years of War*, p. 8; and Crowley to Roosevelt, February 27, 1942, CPP.

37. Blum, *Morgenthau Diaries: Years of War*, 8–9.

38. Ibid.

39. Ibid.; Executive Order 9095, *Federal Register*, 7: 911, March 13, 1942, pursuant to the Trading with the Enemy Act of October 6, 1917, as amended by the First War Powers Act of December 18, 1941; and various newspaper reports.

9. *Alien Property Custodian, II*

1. Schmedeman to Crowley, March 13, 1942, and General Agent, FCA, to Crowley, March 20, 1942, CPP; *United States News*, ca. March 1942, clipping, CPP; Perlmetter, "Seven Billion Dollar Headache War Gift to Leo T. Crowley," syndicated in *Washington Star* and *Capital Times*, March 22, 1942, *St. Louis Globe-Democrat*, March 25, 1942, and other papers; and *Time*, March 23, 1942.

2. *Pathfinder*, April 4, 1942; and *Wisconsin State Journal*, March 29, 1942.

3. *Capital Times*, March 22, 1942; and *Milwaukee* Journal, March 23, 1942.

4. Morgenthau to Crowley, March 23, 1942, CPP.

5. Crowley to Smith, May 14, 1942, CPP.

6. Ibid.

7. James F. Byrnes to Rosenman, May 28, 1942, BP.

8. Crowley, undated draft letter to the President, ca. late June 1942, CPP.

9. Byrnes to Rosenman, May 28, 1942, BP; Crowley to Roosevelt, July 2, 1942, CPP; and Markham to Byrnes, July 3, 1942, BP.

10. Press conference of April 21, 1942, no. 820, pp. 294–96.

11. Biddle to Walker, April 14, 1942, Walker to Biddle, April 14, 1942; and Walker to Postmaster, Royal Oak, MI, and to publisher, *Social Justice*, Royal Oak, April 14, 1942, CPP. Also Francis Biddle, *In Brief Authority* (New York, 1962), 216 and 247; and Eklund, *Adviser to Presidents*.

12. Biddle, *In Brief Authority*, 247; and Eklund, *Adviser to Presidents*.

13. Biddle, *In Brief Authority*, 247–48.

14. Ibid.

15. Eklund, *Adviser to Presidents*.

16. For Crowley's team, see *Congressional Directory*, 78th Congress, 2nd Session, (Washington, December 1943), 312–13; compare with ibid., 75th Congress, 3rd Session (Washington, December 1937), 372; *Annual Report of Alien Property Custodian*, March 11, 1942, to June 30, 1943; and *Sheboygan Press*, November 25, 1942. Also, interviews and correspondence with Morrison Tucker and Monroe Karasik, 1989–90.

17. "Bank Capital Ratios today," Speech of April 7, 1942, and telephone conversations with Dr. William P. Crowley; clipping, unidentified source, June 1, 1942; and Matthew F. McGuire to Crowley, June 12, 1942; and Kuehl to Crowley, June 1, 1942, remarking of his honors, "If you don't soon stop, your family will have to have me when you are gone to properly appraise and preserve them," CPP.

18. *Barron's*, December 14, 1942; and *New York Times*, May 8 and April 30, 1942.

19. The committee included John Foster Dulles of the prestigious New York law firm of Sullivan and Cromwell, *Annual Report of Alien Property Custodian*, March 11, 1942, to June 30, 1943.

20. *Washington Evening Star*, March 22, 1942; *Milwaukee Journal*, March 23, 1942; and *U.S. News*, ca. March 1942, CPP.

21. *OPD Reporter*, April 6; *Business Week*, April 25, 1942; *OPD Reporter*, April 27, 1942.

22. Ibid., also May 4, 1942.

23. Ibid., June 1 and 15, 1942, July 6, 1942, September 14, 1942.

24. *Business Week*, June 6, 1942.

25. "Statement of Patent Policy," August 13, 1942. This policy statement was not given the Patents Committee publicly; possibly it was conveyed in executive session or personally.

26. Conversation with Monroe Karasik, July 4, 1990, Chevy Chase, MD.

27. Ibid.

28. Monroe Karasik, undated staff paper, "A Program for Schering Corporation in Latin America," June 12, 1942, CPP.

29. Ibid.; conversation with Monroe Karasik, July 4, 1990, Chase, MD; and Tucker to author, chiefly January 9, 1988, but numerous other dates; and interview, September 17, 1987, Oklahoma City, OK.

30. Tucker to author, February 4, 1990.

31. Sylvia F. Porter, "Your Dollars and the War," *New York Post*, October 13, 1942, CPP.

32. John J. Burns, "Report to Honorable Leo T. Crowley," October 20, 1942, CPP.

33. Ibid.

34. Burns, "Report to Honorable Leo T. Crowley; also "Excerpts Relating to the Confiscated Property of the Children of Ernest K. Halbach," Hearings Before Investigating and Legislative Subcommittees of the Senate Committee on the Judiciary, Eighty-third Congress, First Session (Washington, 1953), 7–9, 13–21, and 24.

35. Eklund, *Adviser to Presidents*.

36. *Capital Times*, October 31, 1942; *Milwaukee Journal*, November 1, 1942; and MD, 581: 152A.

37. Crowley to John E. Mack, March 16, 1942, OF 77; and MD, March 10, 1942, Box 506, 242, with enclosure.

38. *Business Week*, December 19, 1942; and "Memorandum to the President on the Patent Policy of the Alien Property Custodian," December 7, 1942, CPP.

39. *Business Week*, December 19, 1942; Howland H. Sargeant to Crowley, "Administration of Patents and Copyrights," for Address by the Alien Property Custodian before the Business Advisory Council, June 24, 1943; and *Business Week*, August 21, 1943.

40. Louis Johnson to Crowley, April 20, 1943, enclosing reprint of speech by Robert E. Wilson, "Research and Patents," *Industrial and Engineering Chemistry*, 35 (February, 1943), 177. Wilson's motivation, at least, may have been related to his presidency of a subsidiary of Standard Oil, a firm earlier indicted by the Justice Department's Antitrust Division for restricting its production of synthetic rubber as a result of an agreement with I. G. Farben.

41. McConnell to Morgenthau, July 13, 1943, enclosing memorandum of July 9, 1943, MD, Box 648, 153.

42. Ibid.

43. Ibid.

10. *The Nation's # 1 Pinch Hitter*

1. Progressive Congressman Harry Sauthoff to Crowley, July 16, 1943; Associated Press, August 2, 1943, CPP; Crowley to Grace Tully, May 4, 1943; and Roosevelt to Crowley, May 6, 1943, OF 2911.

2. Edward and Frederick Schapsmeier, *Prophet in Politics: Henry A. Wallace and the War Years, 1940–1945* (Ames, Iowa, 1968), 20–21 and 44–71; Victoria Harrison, "The Wallace-Jones Feud," Senior Honors Paper, Southern Illinois University at Edwardsville (April 1982); and Russell Lord, *The Wallaces of Iowa* (Boston, 1947), 498–517.

3. Jones would not have denied any of this, Jesse J. Jones, *Fifty Billion Dollars* (New York, 1951), 486.

4. Harrison, "Wallace-Jones Feud"; Jones, *Fifty Billion Dollars*, 492–94; and John M. Blum, *The Price of Vision: The Diary of Henry Wallace* (Boston, 1973), 214.

5. Harrison, "Wallace-Jones Feud"; Jones, *Fifty Billion Dollars*, 492–94; Blum, *Wallae* 214; Lord, *The Wallaces*, 506–7; Schapsmeier, *Prophet in Politics*, 62–67; Byrnes, *All in One Lifetime*, 193–93; and the president's warning of August 21, 1942, was partially restated in letters to federal agency chiefs and in a press release of July 15, 1943, BP, and Jesse H. Jones Papers, Mss. division, Library of Congress.

6. Ibid.; Schapsmeier, *Prophet in Politics*, 66 and 67; and Byrnes, *All in One Lifetime*, 193.

7. Byrnes Diary, July 14 and 15, 1943, "Alternative Solution of R.F.C.-B.E.W. Difficulties, and Executive Order 9361," BP; Byrnes, *All in One Lifetime*, 193. The president rejected other options, the most important of which would have consolidated the BEW and several other agencies involved in foreign economic activities into one agency, an option, he would, however, accept in September.

8. *New York Times*, July 19, 1943.

9. Eklund, *Adviser to Presidents*; Clipping, July 16, 1943, EP; John McCormac, "Diplomat of Global Economics," *New York Times*, November 7, 1943; AP clipping of August 2, 1943, CPP; *Green Bay Press Gazette*, July 19, 1943; and correspondence and interviews with Morrison Tucker and Monroe Karasik, both of whom went into the armed forces, as noted in chapter 9.

10. *New York Times*, July 17, 1943; *Chicago Tribune*, July 17, 1943; and Robert L. Riggs, *Louisville Courier-Journal*, July 25, 1943.

11. Technically, Crowley received half his $75,000 salary from Standard Gas, half from a subsidiary, the Philadelphia Company, *Capital Times*, June 26, 1946; Crowley's letter to Perkins in the *New York Times*, July 18, 1943; and Crowley to Jones, July 16, 1943, Jones Papers, Library of Congress.

12. Bascom Timmons, *Jesse H. Jones* (New York, 1956), 329; *New York Times*, July 17, 1943; *St. Louis Post-Dispatch*, July 16, 1943; Crowley to Jones, July 16, 1943, JP; order no. 5 never took effect.

13. Internal RFC memo to Jones, July 16, 1943. The OEW officer, General Counsel Monroe Oppenheimer, was replaced at the end of August, *New York Times*, September 1, 1943. In our interview, June 27, 1990, he said that Crowley fired him because he irritated Jones but offered to help him start a private practice, an offer he refused. He also reinforced the point that the central issue dividing Wallace and Perkins from Jones was that the BEW favored acquiring critical materials whatever the cost, whereas Jones stressed cost. See also Schapsmeier, *Prophet in Politics*, 71 (f.n. 50); Corcoran is quoted in Eklund, *Adviser to Presidents*; also, see Richard C. Lilly to Crowley, July 15, 1943, CPP.

14. Eklund, *Adviser to Presidents*; congratulations ranged the spectrum. See Florida's Democratic New Dealer, Senator Claude Pepper, to Crowley, July 19, 1943; Wisconsin Progressive Congressman, Harry Sauthoff, to Crowley, July 16, 1943; Kansas Republican Senator Arthur Capper to Crowley, July 16,

1943; former senator and at that time Federal District Court Judge F. Ryan Duffy to Crowley, July 29, 1943; Kenneth McKellar to Crowley, July 17, 1943; and D. W. McKellar to Crowley, July 17, 1943, CPP.

15. Kenneth McKellar to Crowley, July 17, 1943; and D. W. McKellar to Crowley, July 17, 1943, CPP.

16. Crowley to Senator Kenneth McKellar, July 19, 1943, CPP.

17. Noel Hall, British Embassy, to Crowley, July 19, 1943; and Edwin E. Witte, University of Wisconsin economist and chairman, Regional War Labor Board, to Crowley, CPP.

18. R. L. (Raby) Hopkins to Crowley, July 23, 1943, CPP; *Chicago Tribune* article of July 16, 1943, reprinted in *Capital Times*, July 18, 1943.

19. *Capital Times*, July 21, 1943.

20. In his editorial of July 18, Evjue reported Crowley's claim to have returned his federal salary, but this does not seem to have been the case. One of Morgenthau's men looked into Crowley's federal income tax returns through 1941 and found they accorded "absolutely with the Wisconsin returns," MD, July 28, 1943, 652: 16–17 and 210; as for Evjue, he was soon searching for evidence of Crowley's involvement in corruption in Beloit, but the stories he read in the *Beloit Weekly*, August 20 and 23, 1943, offered no answers. Meanwhile, *Business Week*, July 24, 1943, and many newspapers reported incorrectly that Crowley had given up his $50,000 (*sic*) a year salary at Standard Gas; and for the Bovingdon story, *Capital Times*, August 15, 1943; and *New York Times*, August 5, 1943.

21. *Chicago Tribune*, August 5, 1943.

22. *New York Times*, August 4, 1943; the employee fired was Maurice Parmalee, who in 1931 had written *Nudism in Modern Life*, for which see Schapsmeier, *Prophet in Politics*, 51.

23. Evjue, Memorandum of Conversation with Leo T. Crowley, August 15, 1943, EP.

24. James MacGregor Burns, *Roosevelt: The Soldier of Freedom, 1940–1945* (New York, 1970), 422–23.

25. *Detroit News*, July 24, 1943; *Newsweek*, July 26, 1943; comment by North Dakota Republican Senator Gerald P. Nye, *New York Times*, July 17, 1943; and John McCormac, "Diplomat of Global Warfare," *New York Times*, November 7, 1943.

26. Evjue, Memo of August 15, 1943, EP.

27. Ibid.

28. Robert L. Riggs, "Crowley is like Wallace and Jones—mostly Jones," *Louisville Courier-Journal*, July 25, 1943.

29. AP clipping of August 2, 1943, CPP.

30. Schapsmeier, *Prophet in Politics*, 71: Memorandum from John Goodloe to Jones, August 27, 1943, calling his attention to the OEW policy "Statement" Crowley submitted to the War Mobilization Committee July 28, which it approved July 29, and which was formally registered August 25, 1943.

31. *New York Times*, September 1, 1943. Interview with Monroe Oppenheimer, former general counsel of the OEW, June 27, 1990, who, with Morris Rosenthal, the OEW's deputy director under Wallace, had ardently supported Perkins and Wallace. Crowley seems not to have fired outspoken critics in the OEW who had connections on Wall Street and in the upper echelons of the administration and were political centrists.

32. "Blacklisting Task Grows," *Business Week*, August 21, 1943; and James P. Daugherty, *The Politics of Wartime Aid: American Assistance to France and to French North Africa, 1940–1946* (Westport, CT, 1978), survey American economic policy in French North Africa, especially after its liberation. Previously, the BEW had exercised some control over shipments to that Vichy outpost, but it is unclear how well or whether it prevented transshipment to Germany and Italy.

33. For Smith's advice, see Burns, *Roosevelt: The Soldier of Freedom*, 342, and James Daugherty, *The Politics of Wartime Aid*, 99–100. Burns mistakenly names James Webb as budget director; see Roosevelt to Hull, June 3, 1943, with enclosed "Plan for Coordinating the Economic Activities of U.S. Civilian Agencies in Liberated Areas," BP.

34. Ibid.

35. Byrnes Diary, July 14 and 15, 1943; "Alternative Solution of R.F.C.-B.E.W. Difficulties," BP; and *New York Times*, July 17, 1943.

36. *New York Times*, July 17, 1943; AP, August 2, 1943; Byrnes to Roosevelt, September 21, 1943, BP: "He [Crowley] is on good terms with Hull;" and "Inside Washington," *Chicago Sun*, undated, CPP.

37. Byrnes to Josephus Daniels, May 5, 1945, BP.

38. Crowley to Byrnes, September 21, 1943, CPP.

39. Byrnes, *All in One Lifetime*, 196; Alan P. Dobson, *U.S. Wartime Aid to Britain, 1940–46* (Dover, NH, 1986), 149; Byrnes to Josephus Daniels, May 5, 1943, BP; Stettinius to Crowley, July 17, 1943, and Crowley to Stettinius, July 22, 1943, CPP; Crowley to Stettinius, November 3, 1943, Foreign Economic Administration Records, Box 689, RG 34; Cox to Stettinius, June 5, 1944, Box 688, RG 34; and Byrnes to Roosevelt, September 21, 1943, BP.

40. *New York Times*, September 26, 1943.

41. Ibid.; *Louisville Courier-Journal*, September 25, 1943, and *St. Louis Post-Dispatch*, September 26, 1943.

42. *Time*, October 4, 1943.

11. Global Diplomat

1. *Time*, October 4, 1943; and "Cornelius Vanderbilt Reports," November 15, 1943, clipping in CPP.

2. *New York Times*, November 7, 1943, clipping in CPP; and Quintin F. Sanger, "Creation of the Staff Offices in the Foreign Economic Administra-

tion," Records Analysis Division, Office of Budget and Administrative Planning, in History of the FEA, Box 855, RG 34.

3. Dick Fitzpatrick, "Crowley of the OEW," *Sign*, October 1943, CPP.

4. Nicholas, *Washington Despatches*, 254–55, following up extensive observations since Crowley's appointment as director of economic warfare in July. *Notre Dame Alumnus* 22, no. 2 (December 1943). Representative Louis Rabaut, November 1, 1943, *Congressional Record*, A 4934; Representative Harry Sauthoff in *Capital Times*, October 7, 1943; *Washington Post*, October 28, 1943; *Capital Times*, January 6, 1944; and Charles Holmburg of the *Capital Times* to Loren Pope of the *Washington Star*, November 30, 1943, EP.

5. Loren Pope to Charles Holmburg, undated, EP.

6. Warren F. Kimball, *The Most Unsordid Act* (Baltimore, 1969), 185–92 and 204–20.

7. Ibid., 184–85; and Dobson, *Wartime Aid*, 129–74.

8. Dobson, *Wartime Aid*, 10, 43–47, and 118, as well as chapter 6, Reserves, Exports, and Reciprocal Aid"; and Dean Acheson, *Present at the Creation* (New York, 1969) 29–33.

9. Dobson, *Wartime Aid*, 25, 126, 147, and 150. Roosevelt quietly shared Churchill's statement when first asking for aid, that "It would be . . . mutually disadvantageous if . . . Great Britain were to be divested of saleable assets, so that after the victory was won, . . . we should be stripped to the bone." Hull and Acheson agreed. Winston S. Churchill, *Their Finest Hour* (Boston, 1949), 566–67; and Warren Kimball, *Churchill and Roosevelt: The Complete Correspondence* (New York, 1984), 1, 108; and Robert Dallek, *Franklin D. Roosevelt and American Foreign Policy, 1932–1945* (New York, 1979), 254.

10. Dobson, *Wartime Aid*, 147–48.

11. Ibid.; Richard Stokes, *St. Louis Post-Dispatch*, October 10, 1943, in a syndicated column.

12. Dobson, *Wartime Aid*, 149; and *Chicago Sun*, September 30, 1943.

13. Dobson, *Wartime Aid*, 149; and H. Duncan Hall and G. C. Wrigley, *History of Second World War: Studies of Overseas Supply*, (London, 1956), chapter 3, but 116–29 especially, is a sympathetic British view of American lend-lease problems, quite at odds with that of Dobson.

14. *St. Louis Star-Times*, October 15, 1943. The two Republicans were Senators Henry Cabot Lodge of Massachusetts and Owen Brewster of Maine; the Democrats Albert B. "Happy" Chandler of Kentucky, Richard Russell of Georgia, and James Mead of New York.

15. *Miami Herald*, November 13, 1943, and more than twenty newspaper clippings of November 12 and 13, CPP; Byrnes to Roosevelt, October 5 and 15, 1943, BP; and Grace Tully to Roosevelt, February 5, 1944, OF 5430.

16. Testimony of Leo T. Crowley before the Overseas Subcommittee of the Truman Committee, October 19, 1943, CPP.

17. *New York Herald Tribune*, November 22, 1943; and extract from memorandum to the president, from Morgenthau and Crowley, January 1, 1944, RG 169.

18. Dobson, *Wartime Aid*, 163.

19. Cox to Crowley, November 25, 1943, clippings in CPP; and *Pittsburgh Post-Gazette*, November 13, 1943. MD, November 2, 1943, 672: 173–209; and Dobson, *Wartime Aid*, 164–65.

20. MD, 679: 91–92 and 684: 267–301; *Chicago Tribune*, October 27, 1943; and State Department Minutes, December 16, 1943, 841.5151/2005, National Archives.

21. Dobson, *Wartime Aid*, 43 and 216. British representatives tended to describe Crowley, Currie, and Cox as "birds of a feather," one commenting that Cox was "willing to subordinate any question of principle to political expediency."

22. Dobson, *Wartime Aid*, 168; MD, January 7, 1944, 692: 2–5; and State Department Minutes, January 7, 1944, 841.2176, National Archives; British Minutes, 145/12/71 and FO 371/40880, British Public Records Office, London; and *St. Louis Post-Dispatch*, December 29–31, 1943.

23. *St. Louis Post-Dispatch*, December 29, 1943.

24. Ibid., December 30, 1943.

25. *Capital Times*, January 6, 1943.

26. *New York Times*, January 5, 1944.

27. Byrnes to Roosevelt, January 6, 1944, enclosing memo from Crowley, which the President approved January 11, 1944, OF 5430.

28. *Capital Times*, January 6, 1944.

29. Currie to Roosevelt, January 6, 1940, OF 5430. Currie had recognized some time before that all as not well in the FEA. Speaking of Crowley's reorganization plan and action on it, he had told a British diplomat in the fall, "We were expecting a surgical operation and were given a couple of aspirins."

30. Nicholas, *Washington Despatches*, January 10, 1944, 304.

31. Ibid., December 10, 1943; Byrnes to Roosevelt, "Memorandum for the President: Subject: Criticism of F.E.A.," January 11, 1944, BP. For Crowley's position on UNRRA, see "Limiting U.S. Contribution," November 10, 1943, Cassie Connor's Memo of meeting between Crowley, Byrnes, Cox, Lehman, and Acheson, CPP; also, Cox to Harry Hopkins, December 16, 1943, on McKellar, Oscar Cox Papers, FDRL.

32. Byrnes to Roosevelt, "Memorandum for the President: Subject Criticism of F.E.A.," January 11, 1944, BP.

33. Ibid.

34. Leo T. Crowley, "Free Flow of Commerce Among All Nations Essential to World Security and Prosperity," January 17, 1944, CPP.

35. Daugherty, *Politics of Wartime Aid*, 146–47 and 150–59.

36. Notes of British Embassy Secretary E. S. Jackson, of meeting between Crowley, Ben Smith, the British resident minister for supply in North America, and Sir Charles Hambro, with commentaries by staff, January 20, 1943, FO 371/38505, British Public Record Office.

37. Ibid.

38. *New York Times*, February 13, 18, and 20, 1944; and AN 148/6/45 Public Records Office, London, England.

39. *New York Times*, February 13, 18, and 20, 1944.

40. *New York Times*, February 18, 1944.

41. *PM*, February 17–21, 1944; *Nation*, February 19, 1944; and *Capital Times*, February 20. 1944.

42. Crowley to Byrnes, February 22, 1944, CPP.

12. *Embattled*

1. I. F. Stone, *The War Years, 1939–1945* (Boston, 1988) 174, reprinted from the *Nation*, July 24, 1943; ibid., 184–85, reprinted from the *Nation*, October 9, 1943; and Dean Acheson, *Present at the Creation*, 47.

2. *PM*, January 9, 1944; and Stone, *The War Years*, p. 210, reprinted from the *Nation*, February 12, 1944.

3. Ibid., 211–13, reprinted from the *Nation*, February 19, 1944. The remaining four articles followed, reprinted also in the *St. Louis Star-Times*, beginning February 21 and in *Capital Times*, beginning February 22.

4. Stone, *The War Years*, 242 and 247, reprinted from the *Nation*, July 8 and 22, 1944.

5. Meeting in Hull's office, March 11, 1944, MD, 715, 3, and March 13, 1944, MD, 715, 127; and Warren Kimball, *The Most* Unsordid Act (Baltimore, 1969), 35–36 and 65–66.

6. Stone's February 25 column was found as a partial clipping in EP; further signs of the president's problems are to be found in Byrnes's threat to resign, Byrnes to Roosevelt, January 26, 1944, BP; and Burns, *Roosevelt: The Soldier of Freedom*, 448–50.

7. Roosevelt to Byrnes, March 1, 1944, BP; letter in Evjue Papers; and Roosevelt to Byrnes, March 6, 1944, BP.

8. Thomas Corcoran to Crowley, March 15, 1951; and Crowley to Morgenthau, March 23 and March 24, 1944, CPP.

9. *New York Times*, March 1, 1944; George W. Ball, *The Past Has Another Pattern* (New York, 1982) 38. Italics are Ball's.

10. Ball, *The Past Has Another Pattern*, 38–39; and Paul Nitze to author, June 7, 1990.

11. Leon Martel, *Lend-Lease, Loans, and the Coming of the Cold War: A Study of the Implementation of Foreign Policy* (Boulder, CO, 1979), 10.

12. Nicholas, *Washington Despatches*, July 18 and October 31, 1943, 266–67.

13. MD, March 24, 1944, 715: 19–20.

14. Ibid., March 11 and March 30, 1944, 715: 10 and 243.

15. *Sheboygan Press*, March 24, 1944; and *New York Times*, March 21, 1944.

16. *New York Times*, March 24, 1944; interview with George W. Ball, June 29, 1990.

17. *Sheboygan Press*, March 24, 1944; and Roosevelt to Crowley, July 6, 1944, Box 772, RG 169, NA.

18. Martel, *Lend-Lease*, 10–11; Crowley, statement before House Appropriations Committee, spring, 1944, UNRRA File, CPP; and Crowley to Sol Bloom, March 21, 1944, Box 875, RG 169, NA.

19. *Milwaukee Journal*, June 13, 1944; *New York Times*, June 23 and 40; and Roosevelt to Crowley, July 6, 1944, Box 772, RG 169.

20. Crowley to Lehman, November 15, 1943, Box 773, RG 169; Crowley to F. J. Bailey, March 15, 1944, Box 719, RG 169; John C. Vincent to Laughlin Currie, December 7, 1943, Box 719, RG 169; House debate, January 20, 21, and 24, 1944, Box 719, RG 169; *Capital Times*, September 9, 1944; and Lehman to Crowley, February 16 and April 21, 1945, Box 773, RG 169.

21. Pearson to Crowley, August 4, 1943, CPP.

22. Ibid., and Crowley to Pearson, August 6, 1943, CPP.

23. Harold L. Ickes, January 1, 1944, unpublished diary, 850, 853, and 854, Library of Congress. John Wyngaard, *Green Bay Press-Gazette*, October 3, 1945; clipping, probably fall 1944, CPP; and *New York Times*, May 10, 1944.

24. Crowley to Byrnes, March 20, 1956, CPP; and Eklund, *Adviser to Presidents*.

25. Byrnes to Crowley, March 14, 1956; Crowley to Byrnes, March 20, 1956, and Byrnes to Crowley, 1956, CPP; Byrnes, *All in One Lifetime*, 221–22, and 226–27; and Burns, *Roosevelt: The Soldier of Freedom*, 505–6.

26. Byrnes to Crowley, March 14, 1956, and Crowley to Byrnes, March 20, 1956, CPP; Byrnes, *All in One Lifetime*, 221–22 and 226–27; and Burns, *Roosevelt: The Soldier of Freedom*, 505–6; *Wisconsin State Journal*, July 18, 1944. Crowley's review of these events in his letters to Byrnes and in his 1969 interviews with Eklund should be read with a large grain of salt given his tendency to confuse some events and words exchanged in 1940 with those of 1944, not to mention his bitterness toward Truman.

27. Crowley to Laughlin Currie, April 28, 1944, Box 1050, RG 169.

28. Cox to Crowley, April 29, 1944; Sidney Sherwood to the EPC, May 20, 1944; and Notes on EPC meeting, August 30, 1944, Box 1050, RG 169.

29. Sidney Sheuer to Crowley, July 12, 1944, with memorandum for the president, Box 1050, RG 169.

30. Paul Y. Hammond, "Directives for the Occupation of Germany: The

Washington Controversy," in Harold Stein, ed., *American Civil-Military Decisions* (Birmingham, 1963), 324 and 329; Stettinius to Roosevelt, February 21, 1944, and to Harold Smith, March 21, 1944, Box 1050, RG 169.

31. Morgenthau to Budget Director Harold Smith, March 21, 1944; Hull to Crowley, March 21, 1944; Crowley to Smith, March 24 and April 3, 1944; and Roosevelt to Crowley, April 5, 1944, Box 1050, RG 169; also Hammond, "Directives," 315, 342–43.

32. Hammond, "Directives," 342–43, also minutes of the meeting of the Executive Committee on Economic Foreign Policy, June 9, 1944, Box 772, and Document D-22–44, June 27, 1944, RG 169.

33. Frank Coe to James Angell, "German Economic Controls," Box 814, RG 169.

34. Joseph Halle Schaffer to Wallace Cohen, Box 814, RG 169.

35. Hammond, "Directives," 349–355; and Warren Kimball, *Swords or Ploughshares? The Morgenthau Plan for Defeated Nazi Germany, 1943–1946* (Philadelphia, 1976), 26–27; and Allan Rosenberg to Arthur Paul, September 21, 1944, Box 814, RG 169.

36. Hammond, "Directives," 355, 361, and 366–67.

37. Ibid., 368–70; and Kimball, *Swords*, 38–41.

38. Kimball, *Swords*, 43; and Hammond, "Directives," 378–79.

39. Roosevelt to Crowley, September 28, 1944, OF 5430; and *New York Times*, September 30, 1944.

40. Cox to Stephen Early, September 7, 1944, enclosing a draft letter from Crowley to Roosevelt of same date, OF 5430.

41. Cox to Tom Blake, September 8, 1944, enclosing revised letter, OF 5430.

42. Notes of EPC Meeting, September 25, 1944, Box 772, RG 169.

43. Cox to Early, September 25, 1944, OF 5430.

44. Crowley to Byrnes, July 7, 1947, BP; and *New York Times*, September 30, 1944.

45. Cox, Memorandum and Enclosures for Judge Sam Rosenman, October 28, 1944, OF 5430.

13. Germany, Politics, and Lend-Lease

1. Crowley had just told the Executive Policy Committee that it must meet twice rather than once a week, and that he wanted to examine every appointment made abroad. See Notes on EPC Meeting, August 30, 1944, Box 1050, RG 169.

2. George S. Pettee to James W. Angell, September 28, 1944, Box 814, RG 169, reference is to ECEFP's 31/44 and 32/44. Notes on Executive Policy Committee Meeting, September 21, 1944, Box 772, RG 169. Roosevelt's post-Quebec

letter in Pettee to Angell, October 2, 1944, Box 814, RG 169, while his later comment is in Robert Dallek, *Franklin D. Roosevelt and American Foreign Policy, 1932–1945* (New York, 1979), 477.

3. The original proposal for a "German Branch" came from Allan Rosenberg (Rosenberg to Arthur Paul, October 4, 1944, Box 772, RG 169), who wanted to enhance the FEA's authority, in large part because, otherwise, he feared that Germany might be treated too gently. See also EPC Agenda, Box 773. RG 169; and Notes on EPC Meeting, October 12, 1944, Box 772, RG 169.

4. Notes on EPC Meeting, October 23, 1944, Box 1050, and Stettinius to Crowley, October 31, 1944, Box 772, RG 169.

5. Notes on EPC Meeting, November 2, 1944, Box 772, RG 169.

6. J. A. Krug to Crowley, November 22, 1944, acceding to his request of November 9, 1944, Box 773, RG 169; and conversation with Fowler (later secretary of the treasury under President Lyndon Johnson) July 6 and 7, 1990.

7. Crowley to Roosevelt, June 5, 1944, Crowley to Elmer Davis, June 1, 1944, and Cox to Crowley, May 26, 1944, Box 814, RG 169.

8. News Release, June 13, 1944, Box 814, RG 169; covering memorandum for the president, June 22, 1944, OF 5430.

9. Crowley to McCloy, August 30, 1944, CPP; and covering memorandum for the president, September 16, 1944, OF 5430.

10. Just before one FEA shipment to Italy, Crowley informed the White House that an announcement would "help in getting out the Italian vote," Thomas Blake to Stephen Early, September 7, 1944, OF 5430; and *Milwaukee Journal*, September 29, 1944.

11. *Saturday Evening Post*, September 30, 1944.

12. Thomas Blake to Crowley, November 2, 1944, and Roosevelt to Crowley, November 2, 1944, OF 2911; and interview with Morrison G. Tucker, September 17, 1987.

13. Crowley's draft in CPP. Roosevelt to Crowley, November 2, 1944, telling him to toughen his letter; Thomas Blake to Crowley, November 2, 1944; "Jefty" O'Connor to Roosevelt, October 31, 1944, and Roosevelt to O'Connor, November 2, 1944, OF 2911, where O'Connor labels Dewey's charge "in error" and informs or reminds the president of Vandenberg's part in Crowley's confirmation. Rayburn's statement in *Washington Post*, October 29, 1944.

14. Radio Address, first draft, CPP.

15. *New York Times*, November 4, 1944.

16. C. W. Gray to Crowley, November 6, 1944, CPP, conveying the ailing Hull's congratulations; and W. J. Corry to Crowley, November 4, 1944, CPP, attaching a verbatim copy of speech from the *NYT*.

17. News Release of November 24, 1944, CPP.

18. Charles P. Taft to Stettinius, August 5, 1944, *Foreign Relations of the*

United States, 1944, (Washington, 1966) 3: 53, hereafter *FRUS*; and Harry L. Whitney to James M. McCamy, July 26, 1944, Box 772, RG 169.

19. Memorandum signed by Roosevelt and Churchill at Quebec, September 14, 1944, Confidential File, Papers of Harry S. Truman, Harry S. Truman Library, Independence, MO; also Senate Judiciary Committee, *Morgenthau Diary (Germany)* (Washington, 1967), 620; Hull to Winant, September 19, 1944, *FRUS, 1944,* 3: 58–61; and MD, September 20, 1944, 53–73.

20. MD, September 20, 1944, 53–73; and Notes on EPC Meeting, September 25, 1944, Box 772, RG 169.

21. Crowley to Byrnes, July 7, 1947, BP.

22. Stettinius's position, Hull's, and that of service chiefs, cited in Dobson, *Wartime Aid to Britain,* 200–201; also Hull to Roosevelt, September 8 and 30, and October 2, 1944, *FRUS, 1944,* 3: 53–56 and 61–66; for Hopkins and Leahy, MD, October 18, 1944, 23–25; and Crowley to Morgenthau, October 2, 1944, MD, 778, 32.

23. MD, October 6, 1944, 1–13; Notes on EPC Meetings October 2 and November 9, 1944, Box 772, RG 169.

24. Notes on Executive Policy Committee Meetings of November 15 and 16, 1944, Box 772, RG 169.

25. MD, November 15, 1944, 219 and 223; *FRUS, 1944,* 3: 75; William D. Leahy, *I Was There* (New York, 1950), 279–80; Dobson, *Wartime Aid,* 208; and Notes on Special Joint Meeting of the Executive Policy Committee and the Working Committee on Lend-Lease, Phase II, with Rough Outline of conclusions Reached at Joint EPC and Phase II Meeting, November 20, 1944, Box 772, RG 169.

26. Notes on Special FEA Staff Meeting on Phase II, November 22, 1944, Box 772, RG 169; and MD, November 22, 1944, 778, 24–49.

27. The modified terms appeared unofficially in Cox to Hopkins, November 27, 1944, Box 150, Cox Diary; officially in a FEA Press Release, November 30, 1944, *FRUS, 1944,* 3: 80–83; and *New York Times,* December 1, 1944.

28. U.S. Congress, House Committee on Foreign Affairs, *Hearings, Extension of Lend-Lease* (H.R. 2013), February 7–8, 1945, 1–44 and 48–55; Martel, *Lend-Lease, Loans, and the Coming of the Cold War,* 13; and *Hearings,* February 14, 1945.

29. Section 3-C, in *Hearings,* February 7, 1945, 2; *New York Times,* February 28 and March 1, 1945; and for background and detail, Daugherty, *The Politics of Wartime Aid,* 174–99.

30. *Hearings, Extension of Lend-Lease, March 5, 1945,* 55, 140–49, and 151–65.

31. Ibid.; Daugherty, *The Politics of Wartime Aid,* 174–83; *FRUS, 1944,* 3: 757–63; Ball, *The Past Has Another Pattern,* 38; and *Hearings, Extension of Lend-Lease,* March 5, 1945, 225–35 and 141–46.

32. *Hearings, Extension of Lend-Lease*, 225–35 141–46.

33. Martel, *Lend-Lease, Loans*, 15–20, *New York Times*, March 12, 1945; and Cox to Roosevelt, March 12, 1945, Cox Papers.

34. U.S. Senate, Committee on Foreign Relations, *Hearings, Extension of Lend-Lease*, March 28, 1945, 2–14.

35. Ibid., March 28, 1945, 15–20.

36. Ibid., pp. 22–24.

37. *FRUS, 1945*, (Washington, 1967), 97.

38. Senate. *Hearings, Extension of Lend-Lease*. April 4, 1945, 31–37.

39. Ibid.

40. *Congressional Record. Senate*, April 9, 1945, 3197–3202.

41. Crowley to Vandenberg, August 22, 1945, CPP; *Congressional Record*, April 9, 1945, 3198 and 3218–22.

42. *Congressional Record*, April 10, 1945, 3235–47; and Morgenthau and Stettinius to Roosevelt, March 15, 1945, Confidential File, HSTL.

43. *Morgenthau Diary (Germany)*, January 23, 1945, 905–10.

44. Notes on Executive Policy Committee Meetings, December 28, 1944, and February 5, 1945, Box 772, RG 169; as well as Crowley to Joseph C. Grew, February 9, 1945, BP.

45. Md, 812: 20–24, January 24, 1945.

46. Fowler to Crowley, January 10, 1945, Box 814, RG 169; and U.S. Senate, Subcommittee on War Mobilization of the Committee on Military Affairs, 79th Congress, 2nd Session, 4: 509.

47. Fowler to Crowley, February 3 and 15, 1945, Box 814; Crowley to Vannevar Bush, Harold Ickes, William J. Donovan, et al., February through April, 1945, Box 814, RG 169; Paul Y. Hammond, "Directives for Germany," 401, 405–6, 414.

48. Executive Order Establishing a Foreign Economic Policy Board, March 1, 1945, Confidential File, HSTL; and Crowley to Stettinius, Apri 9, 1945, BP. The President had signed the memo March 20, 1945, and informed Crowley March 23, 1945, CPP.

49. Crowley to Stettinius, April 10, 1945, Box 29, ASW 370.8—Germany, Control, National Archives.

50. As regards the waning influence of the FEA on Germany, see Sidney Sheuer to Crowley, April 12, 1945, Box 814, RG 169, reflecting on the president's directive of September 29, 1944: "If our authority for our extensive German activities is based solely on these memoranda it is very clear to me that we have worked up a a piece of business on a very thin basis," Crowley to Byrnes, April 4, 1945, BP; and Byrnes, *Speaking Frankly* (New York, 1947), 47. Byrnes submitted his resignation March 24, effective April 2.

14. The End of Lend-Lease

1. Cox Diary, April 17, 1945, FDRL; and Harry S. Truman, *Memoirs: Year of Decisions* (New York, 1955), 1: 8.

2. Truman, *Year of Decisions*, 227–29.

3. For a typical indictment of the Truman administration and Crowley, see Gar Alperovitz, *Atomic Diplomacy: Hiroshima and Potsdam* (New York, 1965). For more recent, relatively orthodox studies of American aid to Russia and of the collapse of the Grand Alliance, see Martel, *Lend-Lease, Loans;* George C. Herring, *Aid to Russia, 1941–1946* (New York, 1973), and Lewis Gaddis, *The United States and the Origins of the Cold War, 1941–1947* (New York, 1972).

4. Martel, *Lend-Lease;* Herring, *Aid to Russia;* and Gaddis, *The United States and the Origins of the Cold War.*

5. Martel, *Lend-Lease*, 25–35, and 131; Herring, *Aid to Russia,* 27–77. Acheson, the State Department's representative on the Soviet Protocol Committee, called the committee a group which "Harry Hopkins gathered together to hear orders from the White House about what must go to the Soviet Union."

6. Martel, *Lend-Lease*, 72–73.

7. Martel, *Lend-Lease*, 75.

8. Crowley to Roosevelt, January 20, 1945, BP.

9. Roosevelt to Crowley, et al., September 9, 1944, Box 773, RG 169; and September 29, 1944, CPP. Also, Roosevelt to Crowley, January 5, 1945, Cox Papers.

10. Crowley to Roosevelt, January 11, 1945, Cox Papers.

11. Notes on Executive Policy Committee, February 1, 1945, Box 1050, RG 169; Gaddis, *The United States and the Origins of the Cold War*, chapter 6; and Martel, *Lend-Lease*, 88–92.

12. File 40, Subject: "Mr. Crowley," October 1, 1950, to December 31, 1950, jumbled typewritten statement in CPP.

13. Crowley to Faber, CPP; and Martel, *Lend-Lease*, 93–94.

14. Eklund, *Adviser to Presidents.*

15. Ibid.

16. Herring, *Aid to Russia*, 191.

17. Truman, *Year of Decisions*, 79–82 and 88–89. Harold Smith Diary, April 26, 1945, 4–5, HSTL.

18. Crowley to Faber, October 4, 1955. Martel, *Lend-Lease*, 126, contends that there was no cabinet meeting that day, but admits that there was another meeting which Truman may have mischaracterized. It is likely, too, that Truman cited May 8 because it was V-E Day. As for Crowley, he apparently relied, as everyone then did, on the date Truman used in his *Year of Decisions.*

19. See Martel, *Lend-Lease;* Herring, *Aid to Russia,* and Gaddis, *The United States and the Origins of the Cold War,* for the most detailed narratives and

analyses; see Gaddis, 205, for Truman's "tough" talk and Davies' evaluation; and Truman's *Year of Decisions*, 82, for his characterization of his discussion with Molotov.

20. Herring, *Aid to Russia*, 204–53; Martel, *Lend-Lease*, 132; Crowley Memorandum, File 40, "Mr. Crowley, October 1, 1950 to December 31, 1950," CPP; and Vandenberg to Crowley, August 25, 1945, CPP, an ambiguous note which he could have meant to apply to either the cut-off of lend-lease after V-J Day or that of May 11–12.

21. Martel, *Lend-Lease*, 130–34, especially 133. Crowley's phone conversation with Grew, original in Grew Papers, "Conversations," 7, Harvard University Library; excerpt *FRUS, 1945*, 5: 999, fn.

22. Truman, *Year of Decisions*, 227–28, indicts Crowley and Grew for persuading him to sign the the the cut-off order and indicts Crowley alone for "literally" interpreting the order.

23. *FRUS, 1945*, 5: 999–1000; and Martel, *Lend-Lease*, 133–41.

24. Cox Diary, May 14, 1945, Cox Papers; and Truman to Crowley, June 6, 1945, "Hello Leo." Official File, HSTL.

25. Martel, *Lend-Lease*, 143; and E. S. Land to Truman, June 11, 1945, Confidential File, HSTL; Vorys et al. to Truman, May 31, 1945, Official File, HSTL; Truman to Crowley, June 6, 1945, and Crowley to Truman, Official File, HSTL.

26. Press Release, June 4, 1945, Official File, HSTL; and Crowley to Truman, July 6, 1945, CPP. After the publication of Truman's *Memoirs*, Eileen Downey, Crowley's secretary from 1935 to 1945, sent him her copy of the July 6 memo, pointing out in a jotted note that it "completely denies his [Truman's] statement re Mr. Crowley in his memoirs."

27. Crowley to Truman, July 6, 1945, CPP; and "Extracts from Testimony Relating to the Second Deficiency Appropriations Bill," CPP, revealing that Crowley was embarrassed in June when forced to admit to a House subcommittee that the FEA was providing relief as well as munitions.

28. On the Marshall Plan, see Crowley's testimony of January 29, 1948, in CPP.

29. House, Committee on Banking and Currency, *Hearings, Export-Import Bank of Washington*, July 11–12, 1945; and Senate, Committee on Banking and Currency, *Hearings* (H.R. 3771), July 17–18, 10–14; and see *Congressional Record* (July 18, 1945), 7663–64.

30. Senate, *Hearings*, 5; and *New York Times*, July 13 and 21, 1945.

31. *New York Times*, August 5, 1945, for the Export-Import Bank Act. Under it, the bank would become an independent agency when the FEA was dissolved.

32. Martel, *Lend-Lease*, 152–53; and Herring, *Aid to Russia*, 230.

33. *New York Times*, August 16, 1945; and Martel, *Lend-Lease*, 153, citing

Cox Diary of August 16, which recorded Truman's views as expressed to Harry Dexter White and Jean Monnet.

34. Martel, *Lend-Lease*, 158; and Herring, *Aid to Russia*, 231.

35. Martel, *Lend-Lease*, 155; Herring, *Aid to Russia*, 232–33; Byrnes, *All in One Lifetime*, 309; and Crowley to Faber, October 4, 1955, CPP.

36. Martel, *Lend-Lease*, 158–60; Herring, *Aid to Russia*, 232–33; *FRUS, 1945*, 5: 1031–51; and Julius Krug, insisting, "With the cut-back of lend-lease we find production going to hell."

37. Crowley to Truman, August 21, 1945, Official File, HSTL; and Hawthorne Arey, *History of operations and policies of Export-Import Bank*, (Washington, DC, 1953), 68, notes, "In September the Bank approved three loans which Mr. Crowley recommended to the Board of Trustees for the purpose of replacing Lend-Lease commitments that were being cancelled." The credits went to France, Belgium, and the Netherlands.

38. *Milwaukee Journal*, August 24, 1945; officially, Crowley to Vandenberg, August 22, 1945, Box 837, RG 169; and Vandenberg to Crowley, August 25, 1945, CPP.

39. *Milwaukee Journal*, August 25, 1945.

40. J. D. Ferguson to Crowley, August 27, 1945, CPP; *Milwaukee Journal*, August 24 and 25, 1945; and Crowley to Truman, July 6, 1945, Box 1050, RG 169.

41. Vinson to Truman, August 22, 1945, Official File, HSTL. Also, Truman, *Year of Decisions*, 476–77; Roger Tubby, Oral History, 8–9, HSTL; Martel, *Lend-Lease*, 162; and *Sheboygan Press*, September 1, 1945.

42. *Wisconsin State Journal*, September 19, 1945; *Milwaukee Journal*, September 26, 1945; *Chicago Sun*, November 8, 1945; and *Time*, October 8, 1945.

43. *Capital Times*, September 27, 1945.

44. Ibid., September 26, 1945.

45. *Milwaukee Journal*, September 26, 1945.

46. Article from *Labor*, reprinted in *Capital Times*, October 12, 1945; also, *Milwaukee Journal*, October 17, 1945; *Capital Times*, November 5, 1945; and *Chicago Sun*, November 5, 1945.

47. *Capital Times* and *Chicago Sun*, November 5, 1945.

48. Cabinet Meeting, Friday, September 7, 1945, CPP.

49. Crowley to Truman, "Compulsory Miltary Training," September 26, 1945, CPP.

15. Epilogue

1. Senate speeches, October 16, 1945; Virgil Jordan, president, Conference Board, to Crowley, October 16, 1945, inviting him to speak; Herbert

Hoover to Crowley, December 21, 1945, CPP; *Milwaukee Journal*, November 14, 1945, reported that Crowley was to be knighted again in a brilliant ceremony in January. The *Capital Times* reported November 27 and December 4, 1945, that Crowley was elected chairman of the Milwaukee Road; and for his success, clippings of October 18, 1963, October 21, 1966, and February 26, 1970, CPP; and for Crowley's loss in proxy fight at Standard Gas, see *New York Times* for 1946 and 1947, but especially November 25–27, 1947. Crowley obituaries in several newspapers from Madison to Milwaukee and from Chicago to New York, April 16, 1972.

    2. *Wisconsin State Journal*, April 18, 1972; and the *American Mercury*, June 18, 1944.

    3. Ball, *The Past Has Another Pattern*, 38.

Index

287

Stuart L. Weiss is professor emeritus of history at Southern Illinois University at Edwardsville. He received his Ph.D. degree from the University of Chicago and first taught at Purdue University Center in Fort Wayne and Northern Michigan University in Marquette. His writings while at SIUE include several articles on the New Deal period, including "Maury Maverick and the Liberal Bloc," in the *Journal of American History*, "Thomas Amlie and the New Deal," in *Mid-America*, "Kent Keller, the Liberal Bloc, and the New Deal," in the *Journal of the Illinois State Historical Society*, and "American Foreign Policy and Presidential Power: The Neutrality Act of 1935," in the *Journal of Politics*.